Qualitative Health Research

Qualitative Health Research

edited by
Janice M. Morse

SAGE Publications
International Educational and Professional Publisher
Newbury Park London New Delhi

For information:

SAGE Publications, Inc.
2455 Teller Road
Newbury Park, California 91320
E-mail: order@sagepub.com

SAGE Publications Ltd.
6 Bonhill Street
London EC2A 4PU
United Kingdom

SAGE Publications India Pvt. Ltd.
M-32 Market
Greater Kailash I
New Delhi 110 048 India

Printed in the United States of America

Library of Congress Cataloging-in-Publication Data

Qualitative health research / [edited by] Janice M. Morse
p. cm.
Includes bibliographical references and index.
ISBN 0-8039-4774-7 (cl).—ISBN 0-8039-4775-5 (pb)
1. Medicine—Research—Methodology. I. Morse, Janice M.
[DNLM: 1. Nursing Research—methods. WY 20.5 Q12]
R852.Q35 1992
610'.71—dc20
DNLM/DLC 92-20585
for Library of Congress CIP

97 98 99 00 01 02 10 9 8 7 6 5

Sage Production Editor: Tara S. Mead

Contents

Preface

This book is intended to be used to supplement courses on qualitative methods. I created it to save instructors time from having to scurry around to find examples of qualitative research of interest to health professionals and, at least, tangentially related to health. Although this book is not a methods book *per se,* I really had to struggle to stop those methodological notes from slipping in, and I apologize in advance for all the slips in purpose in the comments between the sections.

If this book is not a methods book *per se,* what is it? I developed this book out of my real concern that the *differences* in qualitative methods are poorly understood and not appreciated. Yet, when examples of several methods are placed together in this way, the differences are overwhelmingly apparent. Students will never again puzzle over the differences between phenomenology and ethnography; between grounded theory and ethnoscience. It becomes apparent that the magnitude of the differences goes beyond the style of the writing to the epistemological foundations, to the purpose of the study, to the methods of data collection and procedures for analysis. The "mix and match" school of generic qualitative methodologists, who do not concern themselves with the differences in methods, pales and fades away.

I also developed this book to meet the obvious need for examples of various types of qualitative methods. I have received many requests for a course bibliography over the years, and many courses in other institutions have been adopting these lists. Lists are to be shared; but it simplifies life for both my colleagues and for me if I can simply pass on a text.

Finally, I developed this book because my own copies of these articles were dying a slow death from being "borrowed" and mysteriously vanishing or being copied to death. I realized this must be a nice collection of readings when I noticed that students enjoyed them so much that they felt a need to acquire them by fair means or foul, lent them to their mothers as fun reading, mulled over them and laughed about them outside classroom hours. "We *loved* the readings!" they wrote on their evaluations, and I hope you do too.

I have many people to thank: Mary Haight, a wonderful meta editor, who puts both sentences and life into perspective; Julie Riden, whom no one can match on thc copy machine; and Anna Lombard who, when she was most needed, whisked into our lives with astonishing organizational and typing skills. And I wish to thank Christine Smedley, our nursing editor at Sage, who laughs and, overnight, moves mountains. Finally, I thank my colleagues, some of whom I know, and others whom I feel I know, whose work makes this book. Thank you.

JANICE M. MORSE

Introduction

To be immersed in qualitative research inquiry is fun and exciting. Although the process may be filled with many traps that trip the unwary researcher, the rewards are immense. Researchers get to know the participants in their studies as real people, become part of their lives and often make lifelong friends in the process. Researchers' lives are enriched as participants share their stories, their suffering, and their lives. Of most importance is the lack of predictability in qualitative research: The researcher cannot foresee what the results will look like, and though some researchers find this uncertainty disconcerting and the ambiguity frightening, it removes any sense of boredom and routine from the research process and makes the research life most exciting.

Because of this relative lack of structure, teaching qualitative research methods—and learning to be a qualitative researcher—are difficult tasks. Both the instructor and the student learn that the research *rules* are not really hard and fast but more like principles to follow. However, if these rules are not followed and are altered without care, reflection, or the full understanding of the ramifications, the results may be disastrous. For example, it may be easy for a researcher to be critical of the methods of sampling used in qualitative research and to yield to the pressure of quantitative research to use a random sample. But such a violation weakens qualitative inquiry and may impede the process. The research is weakened because the *best* informant (i.e., the most informed person who has the information needed) may never be selected in the random selection. Delay occurs as the researcher may be working with examples and knowledge that are not as clear or as *prototypical* as they should be. In fact, selecting informants randomly makes as much sense as seeking information in the library by randomly selecting a book from a randomly selected shelf.

But I promised you that this was not a *methods* book, so I will stop harping on methods. Part I of this book provides a brief explanation of the three characteristics of qualitative research and some examples illustrating various aspects of qualitative inquiry. Parts II through VI provide examples of five types of qualitative research: phenomenology, ethnography, ethnoscience, grounded theory, and semi-structured interviews. From these examples, one can see that qualitative research does contain different methods, and, although this book does not contain examples of *all* qualitative methods, the differences between each method presented should be instantly evident.

As I intend this book for classroom use, I have ended each section with a question to mull over and to argue. I have my opinion about the right answer to these questions, but only my opinion. Overall the jury is still out, and the *right* answer is still up for grabs. Keep working—that could be your contribution.

Meanwhile, the questions are fun to discuss, and they keep the class lively.

I

The Characteristics of Qualitative Research

Qualitative research is largely characterized by three features that distinguish it from quantitative research. These are the *emic perspective,* the *holistic perspective,* and an *inductive and interactive process of inquiry*. Although some may include other minor features of qualitative research (such as, its primary use of textual rather than numeral data and its purpose of describing rather than determining causality), such characteristics have so many exceptions that they frequently serve to confuse rather than assist the researcher in distinguishing between the two approaches. For this first section, I have selected five articles that discuss or illustrate the three characteristics I think are important.

First is the emic perspective—or eliciting meaning, experience, or perception from the participant's point of view, rather than from the researcher's perspective (the etic or the world view). Using the emic perspective involves identifying the informant's beliefs and values that underlie the phenomenon, and refraining from imposing the researcher's beliefs and theoretical perspectives on the data. Clearly such an approach is closely associated with inductive processes and is also the key to induction.

Differences in values and beliefs are easiest to identify when the investigator is not working in his or her own contemporary culture. In the first selection (Chapter 1)—a historical example—Engelhardt illustrates the relationship between the values associated with masturbation by the medical profession early in this century and shows how such beliefs may drive the deductive research process, with invalid results. Beliefs about disease causality from masturbation provided the theoretical basis for a treatment regime, and although wrong, the results from the treatment provided physicians with enough evidence for them to evaluate such a treatment as "successful." Although such false cause-and-effect linkages are clear in hindsight, the article provides a provocative example of the dangers of the scientific method.

The second selection, an article by Bohannan also related to the emic perspective, shows that meaning may differ drastically between the researcher and the informant. These differences cannot be anticipated, even for aspects that were previously thought to be cultural universals. Bohannan was instructed on the "true meaning" of Shakespeare's *Hamlet* by the *Tiv* in West Africa; her article is lighthearted, but important.

Second is the holistic perspective or an approach to the phenomena of interest by considering and including the underlying values and the context as a part of the phenomena. Quantitative research, on the other hand, relies on context stripping to remove contaminating variables.

In Chapter 3, Hinds and her colleagues describe the importance of considering context in qualitative research. They emphasize the significance of context as a multilayered concept so that the research topic may be targeted to focus on the aspects of context that the researcher considers most significant. In qualitative research, the inclusion of the context and the informant beliefs and values provide what Noblit and Engel have labeled the "holistic injunction" (Chapter 4).

The third characteristic is an inductive and interactive process of inquiry between the researcher and the data, with the researcher driving the analytic process as he or she gains comprehension and insight about the phenomena of interest. This is compared with the deductive approach, which has a predetermined conceptual framework and may include the testing of hypotheses where the results are not known until data collection is complete and the data are analyzed. Although this perspective should be clear in all the subsequent chapters in this book, one aspect of inquiry, the interactive search necessary for the process of building theory, may not be evident. In the type of qualitative research presented here, this process of questioning is most evident in the phenomenological examples. However, to clarify this process, I have included a short article "Euch, Those Are for Your Husband!" (Morse, Chapter 5) to illustrate the stance the researcher must assume when conducting qualitative inquiry. As some of the cultures' assumptions may be beyond the awareness of the informant, occasionally the informant or participant may be learning with, or in a process of self-discovery, as he or she informs the researcher. At other times the researcher is in the student role, asking questions and being instructed by the participant about the phenomena of interest.

1

The Disease of Masturbation: Values and the Concept of Disease

H. TRISTRAM ENGELHARDT, JR.

Masturbation in the 18th and especially in the 19th century was widely believed to produce a spectrum of serious signs and symptoms, and was held to be a dangerous disease entity. Explanation of this phenomenon entails a basic reexamination of the concept of disease. It presupposes that one think of disease neither as an objective entity in the world nor as a concept that admits of a single universal definition: there is not, nor need there be, one concept of disease.[1] Rather, one chooses concepts for certain purposes, depending on values and hopes concerning the world.[2] The disease of masturbation is an eloquent example of the value-laden nature of science in general and of medicine in particular. In explaining the world, one judges what is to be significant or insignificant. For example, mathematical formulae are chosen in terms of elegance and simplicity, though elegance and simplicity are not attributes to be found in the world as such. The problem is even more involved in the case of medicine which judges what the human organism should be (i.e., what counts as "health") and is thus involved in the entire range of human values. This chapter will sketch the nature of the model of the disease of masturbation in the 19th century, particularly in America, and indicate the scope of this "disease entity" and the

AUTHOR'S NOTE: I am grateful for the suggestions of Professor John Duffy, and the kind assistance of Louanna K. Bennett and Robert S. Baxter. This chapter originally appeared in Engelhardt, H. T., Jr. (1974). The disease of masturbation: Values and the concept of disease. *Bulletin of the History of Medicine, 48*, 234-248. Reprinted by permission of The Johns Hopkins University Press therapies it evoked. The goal will be to outline some of the interrelations between evaluation and explanation.

The moral offense of masturbation was transformed into a disease with somatic not just psychological dimensions. Though sexual overindulgence generally was considered debilitating since at least the time of Hippocrates,[3] masturbation was not widely accepted as a disease until a book by the title *Onania* appeared anonymously in Holland in 1700 and met with great success.[4] This success was reinforced by the appearance of S. A. Tissot's book on onanism.[5] Tissot held that all sexual activity was potentially debilitating and that the debilitation was merely more exaggerated in the case of masturbation. The primary basis for the debilitation was, according to Tissot, loss of seminal fluid, one ounce being equivalent to the loss of 40 ounces of blood.[6] When this loss of fluid took place in an other than recumbent position (which Tissot held often to be the case with masturbation), this exaggerated the ill effects.[7] In attempting to document his contention, Tissot provided a comprehensive monograph on masturbation, synthesizing and appropriating the views of classical authors who had been suspicious of the effects of sexual overindulgence. He focused these suspicions clearly on masturbation. In this he was very successful, for Tissot's book appears to have widely established the medical opinion that masturbation was associated with serious physical and mental maladies.[8]

There appears to have been some disagreement whether the effect of frequent intercourse was in any respect different from that of masturbation. The presupposition that masturbation was not in accordance with the dictates of nature suggested that it would tend to be more subversive of the constitution than excessive sexual intercourse. Accounts of this difference in terms of the differential effect of the excitation involved are for the most part obscure. It was, though, advanced that "during sexual intercourse the expenditure of nerve force is compensated by the magnetism of the partner."[9] Tissot suggested that a beautiful sexual partner was of particular benefit or was at least less exhausting.[10] In any event, masturbation was held to be potentially more deleterious since it was unnatural, and, therefore, less satisfying and more likely to lead to a disturbance or disordering of nerve tone.

At first, the wide range of illnesses attributed to masturbation is striking. Masturbation was held to be the cause of dyspepsia,[11] constrictions of the urethra,[12] epilepsy,[13] blindness,[14] vertigo, loss of hearing,[15] headache, impotency, loss of memory, "irregular action of the heart," general loss of health and strength,[16] rickets,[17] leucorrhea in women,[18] and chronic catarrhal conjunctivitis.[19] Nymphomania was found to arise from masturbation, occurring more commonly in blonds than in brunettes.[20] Further, changes in the external genitalia were attributed to masturbation: elongation of the clitoris, reddening and congestion of the labia majora, elongation of the labia minora,[21] and a thinning and decrease in size of the penis.[22] Chronic masturbation was held to lead to the development of a particular type, including enlargement of the superficial veins of the hands and feet, moist and clammy hands, stooped shoulders, pale sallow face with heavy dark circles around the eyes, a "draggy" gait, and acne.[23] Careful case studies were published establishing masturbation as a cause of insanity,[24] and evidence indicated that it was a cause of hereditary insanity as well.[25] Masturbation was held also to cause an hereditary predisposition to consumption.[26] Finally, masturbation was believed to lead to general debility. "From health and vigor, and intelligence and loveliness of character, they became thin and pale and cadaverous; their amiability and loveliness departed, and in their stead irritability, moroseness and anger were prominent characteristics. . . . The child loses its flesh and becomes pale and weak."[27] The natural history was one of progressive loss of vigor, both physical and mental.

In short, a broad and heterogeneous class of signs and symptoms were recognized in the 19th century as a part of what was tantamount to a syndrome, if not a disease: masturbation. If one thinks of a syndrome as the concurrence or running together of signs and symptoms into a recognizable pattern, surely masturbation was such a pattern. It was more, though, in that a cause was attributed to the syndrome providing an etiological framework for a disease entity. That is, if one views the development of disease concepts as the progression from the mere collection of signs and symptoms to their interrelation in terms of a recognized causal mechanism, the disease of masturbation was fairly well evolved. A strikingly heterogeneous set of signs and symptoms was unified and comprehended under one causal mechanism. One could thus move from mere observation and description to explanation.

Since the signs and symptoms brought within the concept of masturbation were of a serious order associated with marked debility, it is not unexpected that there would be occasional deaths. The annual reports of the Charity Hospital of Louisiana in New Orleans which show hospitalizations for masturbation over an 86-year period indicate that, indeed, two masturbators were recorded as having died in the hospital. In 1872, the reports show that there were two masturbators hospitalized, one of whom was discharged the other one having died.[28] The records of 1887 show that of the five masturbators hospitalized that year two improved, two were unimproved, and one died.[29] The records of the hospital give no evidence concerning the patient who died in 1872. The records for 1887, however, name the patient, showing him to have been hospitalized on Tuesday, January 6, 1887, for masturbation. A 45-year-old native of Indiana, a resident of New Orleans for the previous 35 years, single, and a laborer, he died in the hospital on April 8, 1887.[30] There is no indication of the course of the illness. It is interesting to note, though, that in 1888 there was a death from anemia associated with masturbation, the cause of death being recorded under anemia. The records indicate that the patient was hospitalized on August 17, 1887, and died on February 11, 1888, was a lifelong resident of New Orleans, and was likewise a laborer and single.[31] His case suggests something concerning the two deaths recorded under masturbation: that they, too, suffered from a debilitating disease whose signs and symptoms were referred to masturbation as the underlying cause. In short, the concept of masturbation as a disease probably acted as a schema for organizing various signs and symptoms which we would now gather under different nosological categories.

As with all diseases, there was a struggle to develop a workable nosology. This is reflected in the reports of the Charity Hospital of Louisiana (in New Orleans) where over the years the disease was placed under various categories and numerous nomenclatures were employed. In 1848, for example, the first entry was given as "masturbation," in 1853 "onanism" was substituted, and in 1857 this was changed to "onanysmus."[32] Later, as the records began to classify the diseases under general headings, a place had to be found for masturbation. Initially in 1874, the disease "masturbation" was placed under the heading "Male Diseases of Generative Organs." In 1877 this was changed to "Diseases of the Nervous System," and finally in 1884 the disease of "onanism" was classified as a "Cerebral-Spinal Disease." In 1890 it was reclassified under the heading "Diseases of the Nervous System," and remained classified as such until 1906 when it was placed as "masturbation" under the title of "Genito-Urinary System, Diseases of (Functional Disturbances of Male Sexual Organs.)" It remained classified as a functional disturbance until the last entry in 1933. The vacillation in the use of headings probably indicates hesitation on the part of the recorders as to the nature of the disease. On the one hand, it is understandable why a disease, which was held to have such grossly physical components, would itself be considered to have some variety of physical basis. On the other hand, the recorders appear to have been drawn by the obviously psychological aspects of the phenomenon of masturbation to classify it in the end as a functional disturbance.

As mentioned, the concept of the disease of masturbation developed on the basis of a general suspicion that sexual activity was debilitating.[33] This development is not really unexpected: if one examines the world with a tacit presupposition of a parallelism between what is good for one's soul and what is good for one's health, then one would expect to find disease correlates for immoral sexual behavior.[34] Also, this was influenced by a concurrent inclination to translate a moral issue into medical terms and relieve it of the associated moral opprobrium in a fashion similar to the translation of alcoholism from a moral into a medical problem.[35] Further, disease as a departure from a state of stability due to excess or under-excitation offered the skeleton of a psychosomatic theory of the somatic alterations attributed to the excitation associated with masturbation.[36] The categories of over- and under-excitation suggest cogent, basic categories of medical explanation: over- and under-excitation, each examples of excess, imply deleterious influences on the stability of the organism. Jonathan Hutchinson succinctly described the etiological mechanism in this fashion, holding that "the habit in question is very injurious to the nerve-tone, and that it frequently originates and keeps up maladies which but for it might have been avoided or cured."[37] This schema of causality presents the signs and symptoms attendant to masturbation as due to "the nerveshock attending the substitute for the venereal act, or the act itself, which, either in onanism or copulation frequently indulged, breaks men down."[38] "The excitement incident to the habitual and frequent indulgence of the unnatural practice of masturbation leads to the most serious constitutional effects. . . . "[39] The effects were held to be magnified during youth when such "shocks" undermined normal development.[40]

Similarly, Freud remarks in a draft of a paper to Wilhelm Fliess, dated February 8, 1893, that "Sexual exhaustion can by itself alone provoke neurasthenia. If it fails to achieve this by itself, it has such an effect on the disposition of the nervous system that physical illness, depressive affects and overwork (toxic influences) can no longer be tolerated without [leading to] neurasthenia. . . . *neurasthenia in males* is acquired at puberty and becomes manifest in the patient's twenties. Its source is masturbation, the frequency of which runs completely parallel with the frequency of male neurasthenia."[41] And Freud later stated, "It is the prolonged and intense action of this pernicious sexual satisfaction which is enough on its own account to provoke a neurasthenic neurosis. . . ."[42] Again, it is a model of excessive stimulation of a certain quality leading to specific disabilities. This position of the theoreticians of masturbation in the 19th century is not dissimilar to positions currently held concerning other diseases. For example, the first Diagnostic and Statistical Manual of the American Psychiatric Association says with regard to "psychophysiologic autonomic and visceral disorders" that "The symptoms are due to a chronic and exaggerated state of the normal physiological expression of emotion, with the feeling, or subjective part, repressed. Such long continued visceral states may eventually lead to structural changes."[43] This theoretical formulation is one that would have been compatible with theories concerning masturbation in the 19th century.

Other models of etiology were employed besides those based upon excess stimulation. They, for the most part, accounted for the signs and symptoms on the basis of the guilt associated with the act of masturbation. These more liberal positions developed during a time of reaction against the more drastic therapies such as Baker Brown's use of clitoridectomy.[44] These alternative models can be distinguished according to whether the guilt was held to be essential or adventitious. Those who held that masturbation was an unnatural act were likely to hold that the associated guilt feelings and anxiety were natural, unavoidable consequences of performing an unnatural act. Though not phrased in the more ethically neutral terms of excess stimulation, still the explanation was in terms of a pathophysiological state involving a departure from biological norms. "The masturbator feels that his act degrades his manhood, while the man who indulges in legitimate intercourse is satisfied that he has fulfilled one of his principal natural functions. There is a healthy instinctive expression of passion in one case, an illegitimate perversion of function in the other."[45] The operative assumption was that when sexual activity failed to produce an "exhilaration of spirits and clearness of intellect" and when associated with anxiety or guilt it would lead to deleterious effects.[46] This analysis suggested that it was guilt, not excitation, which led to the phenomena associated with masturbation. "Now it happens in a large number of cases that these young masturbators sooner or later become alarmed at their practices, in consequence of some information they receive. Often this latter is of a most mischievous character. Occasionally too, the religious element is predominant, and the mental condition of these young men becomes truly pitiable. . . . The facts are nearly these: Masturbation is not a crime nor a sin, but a vice."[47] Others appreciated the evil and guilty primarily in terms of the solitary and egoistic nature of the act.[48]

Such positions concerning etiology graded over into models in which masturbation's untoward signs and symptoms were viewed as merely the result of guilt and anxiety felt because of particular cultural norms, which norms had no essential basis in biology. "Whatever may be abnormal, there is nothing unnatural."[49] In short, there was also a model of interpretation which saw the phenomena associated with masturbation as mere adventitious, as due to a particular culture's condemnation of the act. This last interpretation implied that no more was required than to realize that there was nothing essentially wrong with masturbation. "Our wisest course is to recognize the inevitableness of the vice of masturbation under the perpetual restraints of civilized life, and, while avoiding any attitude of indifference, to avoid also an attitude of excessive horror, for that would only lead to the facts being effectually veiled from our sight, and serve to manufacture artificially a greater evil than that which we seek to combat."[50] This last point of view appears to have gained prominence in the development of thought concerning masturbation as reflected in the shift from the employment of mechanical and surgical therapy in the late 19th century to the use of more progressive means (i.e., including education that guilt and anxiety were merely relative to certain cultural norms) by the end of the century and the first half of the 20th century.[51]

To recapitulate, 19th-century reflection on the etiology of masturbation led to the development of an authentic disease of masturbation: excessive sexual stimulation was seen to produce particular and discrete pathophysiological changes.[52] First, there were strict approaches in terms of disordered nerve-tone due to excess and/or unnatural sexual excitation. Over-excitation was seen to lead to significant and serious physical alterations in the patient, and in this vein a somewhat refined causal model of the disease was developed. Second, there were those who saw the signs and symptoms as arising from the unavoidable guilt and anxiety associated with the performance of an unnatural act. Third, there were a few who appreciated masturbation's sequelae as merely the response of a person in a culture which condemned the activity.

Those who held the disease of masturbation to be more than a culturally dependent phenomenon often employed somewhat drastic therapies. Restraining devices were devised,[53] infibulation of placing a ring in the prepuce was used to make masturbation painful,[54] and no one less than Jonathan Hutchinson held that circumcision acted as a preventive.[55] Acid burns or thermoelectrocautery[56] were utilized to make masturbation painful and, therefore, to discourage it. The alleged seriousness of this disease in females led, as Professor John Duffy has shown, to the employment of the rather radical treatment of clitoridectomy.[57] The classic monograph recommending clitoridectomy, written by the British surgeon Baker Brown, advocated the procedure to terminate the "long continued peripheral excitement, causing frequent and increasing losses of nerve force, . . ."[58] Brown recommended that "the patient having been placed completely under the influence of chloroform, the clitoris [be] freely excised either by scissors or knive—I always prefer the scissors."[59] The supposed sequelae of female masturbation, such as sterility, paresis, hysteria, dysmenorrhea, idiocy, and insanity, were also held to be remedied by the operation.

Male masturbation was likewise treated by means of surgical procedures. Some recommended vasectomy[60] while others found this procedure ineffective and employed castration.[61] One illustrative case involved the castration of a physician who had been confined as insane for seven years and who subsequently was able to return to practice.[62] Another case involved the castration of a 22-year-old epileptic "at the request of the county judge, and with the consent of his father . . . the father saying he would be perfectly satisfied if the masturbation could be stopped, so that he could take him home, without having his family continually humiliated and disgusted by his loathsome habit."[63] The patient was described as facing the operation morosely, "like a coon in a hollow."[64] Following the operation, masturbation ceased and the frequency of fits decreased. An editor of the *Texas Medical Practitioner,* J. B. Shelmire, added a remark to the article: "Were this procedure oftener adopted for the cure of these desperate cases, many, who are sent to insane asylums, soon to succumb to the effects of this habit, would live to become useful citizens."[65] Though such approaches met with ridicule from some quarters,[66] still various novel treatments were devised in order to remedy the alleged sequelae of chronic masturbation such as spermatorrhea and impotency. These included acupuncture of the prostate in which "needles from two to three inches in length are passed through the perineum into the prostate gland and the neck of the bladder. . . . Some surgeons recommend the introduction of needles into the testicles and spermatic cord for the same purpose."[67] Insertion of electrodes into the bladder and rectum and cauterization of the prostatic urethra were also utilized.[68] Thus, a wide range of rather heroic methods were devised to treat masturbation and a near fascination developed on the part of some for the employment of mechanical and electrical means of restoring "health."

There were, though, more tolerant approaches, ranging from hard work and simple diet[69] to suggestions that "If the masturbator is totally continent, sexual intercourse is advisable."[70] This latter approach to therapy led some physicians to recommend that masturbators cure their disease by frequenting houses of prostitution,[71] or acquiring a mistress.[72] Though these treatments would appear ad hoc, more theoretically sound proposals were made by many physicians in terms of the model of excitability. They suggested that the disease and its sequelae could be adequately controlled by treating the excitation and debility consequent upon masturbation. Toward this end, "active tonics" and the use of cold baths at night just before bedtime were suggested.[73] Much more in a "Brownian" mode was the proposal that treatment with opium would be effective. An initial treatment with 1/12 of a grain of morphine sulfate daily by injection was followed after ten days by a dose of 1/16 of a grain. This dose was continued for three weeks and gradually diminished to 1/30 of a grain a day. At the end of a month the patient was dismissed from treatment "the picture of health, having fattened very much, and lost every trace of anaemia and mental imbecility."[74] The author, after his researches with opium and masturbation, concluded, "We may find in opium a new and important aid in the treatment of the victims of the habit of masturbation by means of which their moral and physical forces may be so increased that they may be enabled to enter the true physiological path."[75] This last example eloquently collects the elements of the concept of the disease of masturbation as a pathophysiological entity: excitation leads to physical debilitation requiring a physical remedy. Masturbation as a pathophysiological entity was thus incorporated within an acceptable medical model of diagnosis and therapy.

In summary, in the 19th century, biomedical scientists attempted to correlate a vast number of signs and symptoms with a disapproved activity found in many patients afflicted with various maladies. Given an inviting theoretical framework, it was very conducive to think of this range of signs and symptoms as having one cause. The theoretical framework, though, as has been indicated, was not value free but structured by the values and expectations of the times. In the 19th century, one was pleased to think that not "one bride in a hundred, of delicate, educated, sensitive women, accepts matrimony from any desire of sexual gratification: when she thinks of this at all, it is with shrinking, or even with horror, rather than with desire."[76] In contrast, in the 20th century, articles are published for the instruction of women in the use of masturbation to overcome the disease of frigidity or orgasmic dysfunction.[77] In both cases, expectations concerning what should be significant structure the appreciation of reality by medicine. The variations are not due to mere fallacies of scientific method,[78] but involve a basic dependence of the logic of scientific discovery and explanation upon prior evaluations of reality.[79] A sought-for coincidence of morality and nature gives goals to explanation and therapy.[80] Values influence the purpose and direction of investigations and treatment. Moreover, the disease of masturbation has other analogues. In the 19th century, there were such diseases in the South as "Drapetomania, the disease causing slaves to run away," and the disease "Dysaesthesia Aethiopis or hebetude of mind and obtuse sensibility of body—a disease peculiar to negroes—called by overseers 'rascality.'"[81] In Europe, there was the disease of *morbus democritus*.[82] Some would hold that current analogues exist in diseases such as alcoholism and drug abuse.[83] In short, the disease of masturbation indicates that evaluations play a role in the development of explanatory models and that this may not be an isolated phenomenon.

This analysis, then, suggests the following conclusion: although vice and virtue are not equivalent to disease and health, they bear a direct relation to these concepts. Insofar as a vice is taken to be a deviation from an ideal of human perfection, or "well-being," it can be translated into disease language. In shifting to disease language, one no longer speaks in moralistic terms (e.g., "You are evil"), but one speaks in terms of a deviation from a norm which implies a degree of imperfection (e.g., "You are a deviant"). The shift is from an explicitly ethical language to a language of natural teleology. To be ill is to fail to realize the perfection of an ideal type; to be sick is to be defective rather than to be evil. The concern is no longer with what is naturally, morally good, but what is naturally beautiful. Medicine turns to what has been judged to be naturally ugly or deviant, and then develops etiological accounts in order to explain and treat in a coherent fashion a manifold of displeasing signs and symptoms. The notion of the "deviant" structures the concept of disease providing a purpose and direction for explanation and for action, that is, for diagnosis and prognosis, and for therapy. A "disease entity" operates as a conceptual form organizing phenomena in a fashion deemed useful for certain goals. The goals, though, involve choice by man and are not objective facts, data "given" by nature. They are ideals imputed to nature. The disease of masturbation is an eloquent example of the role of evaluation in explanation and the structure values give to our picture of reality.

Notes

1. Alvan R. Feinstein, "Taxonomy and logic in classical data," *Ann. N.Y. Acad. Sci.*, 1969, *161:* 450-459.

2. Horacio Fabrega, Jr., "Concepts of disease: Logical features and social implications," *Perspect. Biol. & Med.*, 1972, *15:* 583-616.

3. For example, Hippocrates correlated gout with sexual intercourse, *Aphorisms*, VI, 30. Numerous passages in the *Corpus* recommend the avoidance of overindulgence especially during certain illnesses.

4. René A. Spitz, "Authority and masturbation. Some remarks on a bibliographical investigation," *Yearbook of Psychoanalysis*, 1953, *9:* 116. Also, Robert H. MacDonald, "The frightful consequences of onanism: Notes on the history of a delusion," *J. Hist. Ideas*, 1967, *28:* 423-431.

5. Simon-André Tissot, *Tentamen de Morbis ex Manustrupatione* (Lausanne: M. M. Bousquet, 1758). An anonymous American translation appeared in the early 19th century: *Onanism* (New York: Collins & Hannay, 1832). Interestingly, the copy of Tissot's book held by the New York Academy of Medicine was given by Austin Flint. Austin Flint in turn was quoted as an authority on the effects of masturbation: see Joseph W. Howe's *Excessive Venery, Masturbation and Continence* (New York: Bermingham, 1884), p. 97. Also the American edition of Tissot's book, to show its concurrence with an American authority, added in a footnote a reference to Benjamin Rush's opinion concerning the pernicious consequences of masturbation. See Tissot, *Onanism*, p. 19, and Benjamin Rush's *Medical Inquiries and Observations Upon the Diseases of the Mind* (Philadelphia: Kimber and Richardson, 1812), pp. 348-349; also Tissot, *Onanism*, p. 21.

6. Simon-André Tissot, *Onanism* (New York: Collins & Hannay, 1832), p. 5.

7. *Ibid.*, p. 50.

8. E. H. Hare, "Masturbatory insanity: The history of an idea," *J. Mental Sci.*, 1962, *108:* 2-3. It is worth noting that Tissot, as others, at times appears to have grouped together female masturbation and female homosexuality. See Vern L. Bullough and Martha Voght, "Homosexuality and its confusion with the 'secret sin' in pre-Freudian America," *J. Hist. Med.*, 1973, *28:* 143-155.

9. Howe, *Excessive Venery*, pp. 76-77.

10. Tissot, *Onanism*, p. 51.

11. J. A. Mayes, "Spermatorrhoea, treated by the lately invented rings," *Charleston Med. J. & Rev.*, 1854, *9:* 352.

12. Allen W. Hagenbach, "Masturbation as a cause of insanity," *J. Nerv. & Ment. Dis.*, 1879, *6:* 609.

13. Baker Brown, *On the Curability of Certain Forms of Insanity, Epilepsy, Catalepsy, and Hysteria in Females* (London: Hardwicke, 1866). Brown phrased the cause discreetly

in terms of "peripheral irritation, arising originally in some branches of the pudic nerve, more particularly the incident nerve supplying the clitoris. . . . " (p. 7)

14. F. A. Burdem, "Self pollution in children," *Mass. Med., J.*, 1896, *16:* 340.

15. Weber Liel, "The influence of sexual irritation upon the diseases of the ear," *New Orleans Med. & Surg. J.*, 1884, *11:* 786-788.

16. Joseph Jones, "Diseases of the nervous system," *Tr. La. St. Med. Soc.* (New Orleans: L. Graham & Son, 1889), p. 170.

17. Howe, *Excessive Venery,* p. 93.

18. J. Castellanos, "Influence of sewing machines upon the health and morality of the females using them," *Southern J. Med. Sci.*, 1866-1867, *1:* 495-496.

19. Comment, "Masturbation and ophthalmia," *New Orleans Med. & Surg. J.*, 1881-1882, *9:* 67.

20. Howe, *Excessive Venery,* pp. 108-111.

21. *Ibid.*, pp. 41, 72.

22. *Ibid.*, p. 68.

23. *Ibid.*, p. 73.

24. Hagenbach, "Masturbation as a cause of insanity," pp. 603-612.

25. Jones, "Diseases of the nervous system," p. 170.

26. Howe, *Excessive Venery,* p. 95.

27. Burdem, "Self pollution," pp. 339, 341.

28. *Report of the Board of Administrators of the Charity Hospital to the General Assembly of Louisiana* (for 1872) (New Orleans: The Republican Office, 1873), p. 30.

29. *Report of the Board of Administrators of the Charity Hospital to the General Assembly of Louisiana* (for 1887) (New Orleans: A. W. Hyatt, 1888), p. 53.

30. Record Archives of the Charity Hospital of Louisiana [in New Orleans] MS, "Admission Book #41 from December 1, 1885 to March 31, 1888 Charity Hospital," p. 198. I am indebted to Mrs. Eddie Cooksy for access to the record archives.

31. *Ibid.*, p. 287.

32. This and the following information concerning entries is taken from a review of the *Report of the Board of Administrators of the Charity Hospital,* New Orleans, Louisiana, from 1848 to 1933. The reports were not available for the years 1850-1851, 1854-1855, 1862-1863, and 1865.

33. Even Boerhaave remarked that "an excessive discharge of semen causes fatigue, weakness, decrease in activity, convulsions, emaciation, dehydration, heat and pains in the membranes of the brain, a loss in the acuity of the senses, particularly of vision, *tabes dorsalis,* simplemindedness, and various similar disorders." My translation of Hermanno Boerhaave's *Institutiones Medicae* (Vienna: J. T. Trattner, 1775), p. 315, paragraph 776.

34. "We have seen that masturbation is more pernicious than excessive intercourse with females. Those who believe in a special providence, account for it by a special ordinance of the Deity to punish this crime." Tissot, *Onanism,* p. 45.

35. ". . . the best remedy was not to tell the poor children that they were damning their souls, but to tell them that they might seriously hurt their bodies, and to explain to them the nature and purport of the functions they were abusing." Lawson Tait, "Masturbation. A clinical lecture," *Med. News, N.Y.*, 1888, *53:* 2.

36. Though it has not been possible to trace a direct influence by John Brown's system of medicine upon the development of accounts of the disease of masturbation, yet a connection is suggestive. Brown had left a mark on the minds of many in the 18th and 19th centuries, and given greater currency to the use of concepts of over and under

excitation in the explanation of the etiology of disease. Guenter B. Risse, "The quest for certainty in medicine: John Brown's system of medicine in France," *Bull. Hist. Med.*, 1971, *45:* 1-12.

37. Jonathan Hutchinson, "On circumcision as preventive of masturbation," *Arch. Surg.*, 1890-1891, *2:* 268.

38. Theophilus Parvin, "The hygiene of the sexual functions," *New Orleans Med. & Surg. J.*, 1884, *11:* 606.

39. Jones, "Diseases of the nervous system," p. 170. It is interesting to note that documentation for the constitutional effects of masturbation was sought even from postmorten examination. A report from Birmingham, England, concerning an autopsy on a dead masturbator, concluded that masturbation ". . . seems to have acted upon the cord in the same manner as repeated small haemorrhages affect the brain, slowly sapping its energies, until it succumbed soon after the last application of the exhausting influence, probably through the instrumentality of an atrophic process previously induced, as evidenced by the diseased state of the minute vessels" ([James] Russell, "Cases illustrating the influence of exhaustion of the spinal cord in inducing paraplegia," *Med. Times & Gaz., Lond.*, 1863, *2:* 456). The examination included microscopic inspection of material to demonstrate pathological changes. Again, the explanation of the phenomena turned on the supposed intense excitement attendant to masturbation. "In this fatal vice the venereal passion is carried at each indulgence to the state of highest tension by the aid of the mind, and on each occasion the cord is subjected to the strongest excitement which sensation and imagination in combination can produce, for we cannot regard the mere secretion of the seminal fluid as constituting the chief drain upon the energies of the cord, but rather as being the exponent of the nervous stimulation by which it has been ejaculated" (*ibid.*, p. 456). The model was one of mental tension and excitement "exhausting" the nervous system by "excessive functional activity" leading to consequent "weakening" of the nervous system. Baker Brown listed eight stages in the progress of the disease in females: hysteria, spinal irritation, hysterical epilepsy, cataleptic fits, epileptic fits, idiocy, mania and finally death; Brown, *Curability*, p. 7.

40. "Any shock to this growth and development, and especially that of masturbation, must for a time suspend the process of nutrition; and a succession of such shocks will blast both body and mind, and terminate in perpetual vacuity." Burdem, "Self pollution," p. 339. In this regard, not only adolescent but childhood masturbation was the concern of 19th-century practitioners; e.g., Russell, "Influence of exhaustion," p. 456.

41. Sigmund Freud, *The Standard Edition of the Complete Psychological Works of Sigmund Freud*, I (London: The Hogarth Press, 1971), 180.

42. *Ibid.*, III, "Heredity and the Aetiology of the Neuroses," p. 150.

43. *Diagnostic and Statistical Manual: Mental Disorders* (Washington, DC: American Psychiatric Association, 1952), p. 29.

44. "Mr. Baker Brown was not a very accurate observer, nor a logical reasoner. He found that a number of semi-demented epileptics were habitual masturbators, and that the masturbation was, in women, chiefly effected by excitement of the mucous membrane on and around the clitoris. Jumping over two grave omissions in the syllogism, and putting the cart altogether before the horse, he arrived at the conclusion that removal of the clitoris would stop the pernicious habit, and therefore cure the epilepsy." Tait, "Masturbation," p. 2.

45. Howe, *Excessive Venery*, p. 77.

46. *Ibid.*, p. 77.

47. James Nevins Hyde, "On the masturbation, spermatorrhoea and impotence of adolescence," *Chicago Med. J. & Exam.*, 1879, *38:* 451-452.

48. "There can be no doubt that the habit is, temporarily at least, morally degrading; but if we bear in mind the selfish, solitary nature of the act, the entire absence in it of aught akin to love or sympathy, the innate repulsiveness of intense selfishness or egoism of any kind, we may see how it may be morally degrading, while its effect on the physical and mental organism is practically nil." A. C. McClanahan, "An investigation into the effects of masturbation," *N.Y. Med. J.*, 1897, *66:* 502.

49. *Ibid.*, p. 500.

50. Augustin J. Himel, "Some minor studies in psychology, with special reference to masturbation," *New Orleans Med. & Surg. J.*, 1907, *60:* 452.

51. Spitz, "Authority and masturbation," esp. p. 119.

52. That is, masturbation as a disease was more than a mere collection of signs and symptoms usually "running together" in a syndrome. It became a legitimate disease entity, a casually related set of signs and symptoms.

53. C. D. W. Colby, "Mechanical restraint of masturbation in a young girl," *Med. Rec. in N.Y.*, 1897, *52:* 206.

54. Louis Bauer, "Infibulation as a remedy for epilepsy and seminal losses," *St. Louis Clin. Rec.*, 1879, *6:* 163-165. See also Gerhart S. Schwarz, "Infibulation, population control, and the medical profession," *Bull. N.Y. Acad. Med.*, 1970, *46:* 979, 990.

55. Hutchinson, "Circumcision," pp. 267-269.

56. William J. Robinson, "Masturbation and its treatment," *Am. J. Clin. Med.*, 1907, *14:* 349.

57. John Duffy, "Masturbation and clitoridectomy: A nineteenth-century view," *J.A.M.A.*, 1963, *186:* 246-248.

58. Brown, "Curability," p. 11.

59. *Ibid.*, p. 17.

60. Timothy Haynes, "Surgical treatment of hopeless cases of masturbation and nocturnal emissions," *Boston Med. & Surg. J.*, 1883, *109:* 130.

61. J. H. Marshall, "Insanity cured by castration," *Med. & Surg. Reptr.*, 1865, *13:* 363-364.

62. "The patient soon evinced marked evidences of being a changed man, becoming quiet, kind, and docile." *Ibid.*, p. 363.

63. R. D. Potts, "Castration for masturbation, with report of a case," *Texas Med. Practitioner*, 1898, *11:* 8.

64. *Ibid.*, p. 8.

65. *Ibid.*, p. 9.

66. Editorial, "Castration for the relief of epilepsy," *Boston Med. & Surg. J.*, 1859, *60:* 163.

67. Howe, *Excessive Venery*, p. 260.

68. *Ibid.*, pp. 254-255, 258-260.

69. Editorial, "Review of European legislation for the control of prostitution," *New Orleans Med. & Surg. J.*, 1854-1855, *11:* 704.

70. Robinson, "Masturbation and its treatment," p. 350.

71. Parvin, "Hygiene," p. 606.

72. Mayes, "Spermatorrhoea," p. 352.

73. Haynes, "Surgical treatment," p. 130.

74. B. A. Pope, "Opium as a tonic and alternative; with remarks upon the hypodermic use of the sulfate of morphia, and its use in the debility and amorosis consequent upon onanism," *New Orleans Med. & Surg. J.*, 1879, *6:* 725.

75. *Ibid.*, p. 727.

76. Parvin, "Hygiene," p. 607.

77. Joseph LoPiccolo and W. Charles Lobitz, "The role of masturbation in the treatment of orgasmic dysfunction," *Arch. Sexual Behavior,* 1972, *2:* 163-171.

78. E. Hare, "Masturbatory insanity," pp. 15-19.

79. Norwood Hanson, *Patterns of Discovery* (London: Cambridge Univ. Press, 1965).

80. Tissot, *Onanism,* p. 45. As Immanuel Kant, a contemporary of S.-A. Tissot remarked, "Also, in all probability, it was through this moral interest [in the moral law governing the world] that attentiveness to beauty and the needs of nature was first aroused." (*Kants Werke,* Vol. 5, *Kritik der Urtheilskraft* [Berlin: Walter de Gruyter & Co., 1968], p. 459, A 439. My translation.) That is, moral values influence the search for goals in nature, and direct attention to what will be considered natural, normal, and nondeviant. This would also imply a relationship between the aesthetic, especially what was judged to be naturally beautiful, and what was held to be the goals of nature.

81. Samuel A. Cartwright, "Report on the diseases and physical peculiarities of the negro race," *New Orleans Med. & Surg. J.*, 1850-1851, *7:* 707-709. An interesting examination of these diseases is given by Thomas S. Szasz, "The sane slave," *Am. J. Psychoth.*, 1971, *25:* 228-239.

82. Heinz Hartmann, "Towards a concept of mental health," *Brit. J. Med. Psychol.*, 1960, *33:* 248.

83. Thomas S. Szasz, "Bad habits are not diseases: a refutation of the claim that alcoholism is a disease," *Lancet,* 1972, *2:* 83-84; and Szasz, "The ethics of addiction," *Am. J. Psychiatry,* 1971, *128:* 541-546.

2

Shakespeare in the Bush

LAURA BOHANNAN

Just before I left Oxford for the Tiv in West Africa, conversation turned to the season at Stratford. "You Americans," said a friend, "often have difficulty with Shakespeare. He was, after all, a very English poet, and one can easily misinterpret the universal by misunderstanding the particular."

I protested that human nature is pretty much the same the whole world over; at least the general plot and motivation of the greater tragedies would always be clear—everywhere—although some details of custom might have to be explained and difficulties of translation might produce other slight changes. To end an argument we could not conclude, my friend gave me a copy of *Hamlet* to study in the African bush: It would, he hoped, lift my mind above its primitive surroundings, and possibly I might, by prolonged meditation, achieve the grace of correct interpretation.

It was my second field trip to that African tribe, and I thought myself ready to live in one of its remote sections—an area difficult to cross even on foot. I eventually settled on the hillock of a very knowledgeable old man, the head of a homestead of some 140 people, all of whom were either his close relatives or their wives and children. Like the other elders of the vicinity, the old man spent most of his time performing ceremonies seldom seen these days in the more accessible parts of the tribe. I was delighted. Soon there would be three months of enforced isolation and leisure, between the harvest that takes place just before the rising of the swamps and the clearing of new farms when the water

AUTHOR'S NOTE: This chapter originally appeared in Bohannan, L. (1956). Shakespeare in the bush. *Natural History, 75* (August-September 1966), 28-33. Reprinted with permission of the author.

goes down. Then, I thought, they would have even more time to perform ceremonies and explain them to me.

I was quite mistaken. Most of the ceremonies demanded the presence of elders from several homesteads. As the swamps rose, the old men found it too difficult to walk from one homestead to the next, and the ceremonies gradually ceased. As the swamps rose even higher, all activities but one came to an end. The women brewed beer from maize and millet. Men, women, and children sat on their hillocks and drank it.

People began to drink at dawn. By mid morning the whole homestead was singing, dancing, and drumming. When it rained, people had to sit inside their huts: there they drank and sang or they drank and told stories. In any case, by noon or before, I either had to join the party or retire to my own hut and my books. "One does not discuss serious matters when there is beer. Come, drink with us." Since I lacked their capacity for the thick native beer, I spent more and more time with Hamlet.

Before the end of the second month, grace descended on me. I was quite sure that *Hamlet* had only one possible interpretation, and that one universally obvious.

Early every morning, in the hope of having some serious talk before the beer party, I used to call on the old man at his reception hut—a circle of posts supporting a thatched roof above a low mud wall to keep out wind and rain. One day I crawled through the low doorway and found most of the men of the homestead sitting huddled in their ragged clothes on stools, low plank beds, and reclining chairs, warming themselves against the chill of the rain around a smoky fire. In the center were three pots of beer. The party had started.

The old man greeted me cordially. "Sit down and drink." I accepted a large calabash full of beer, poured some into a small drinking gourd and tossed it down. Then I poured some more into the same gourd for the man second in seniority to my host before I handed my calabash over to a young man for further distribution. Important people shouldn't ladle beer themselves.

"It is better like this," the old man said looking at me approvingly and plucking at the thatch that had caught in my hair. "You should sit and drink with us more often. Your servants tell me that when you are not with us, you sit inside your hut looking at a paper."

The old man was acquainted with four kinds of "papers": tax receipts, bride price receipts, court fee receipts, and letters. The messenger who brought him letters from the chief used them mainly as a badge of office, for he always knew what was in them and *told* the old man. Personal letters for the few who had relatives in the government or mission stations were kept until someone went to a large market where there was a letter writer and reader. Since my arrival, letters were brought to me to be read. A few men also brought me bride price receipts, privately, with requests to change the figures to a higher sum. I found moral arguments were of no avail, since in-laws are fair game, and the technical hazards of forgery difficult to explain to an illiterate people. I do not wish them to think me silly enough to look at any such papers for days on end, and I hastily explained that my "paper" was one of the "things of long ago" of my country.

"Ah," said the old man, "Tell us."

I protested that I was not a story teller. Story telling is a skilled art among them; their standards are high and the audiences critical—and vocal in their criticism. I protested in vain. This morning they wanted to hear a story while they drank. They threatened to tell me no more stories until I told them one of mine. Finally, the old man promised that no one would criticize my style, "for we know you are struggling with our language." "But," put in one of the elders, "you must explain what we do not understand, as we do when we tell you our stories." Realizing that here was my chance to prove *Hamlet* universally intelligible, I agreed.

The old man handed me some more beer to help me on with my story telling. Men filled their long wooden pipes and knocked coals from the fire to place in the pipe bowls; then, puffing contentedly, they sat back to listen. I began in the proper style, "Not yesterday, not yesterday, but long ago, a thing occurred. One night three men were keeping watch outside the homestead of the great chief, when suddenly they saw the former chief approach them."

"Why was he no longer their chief?"

"He was dead," I explained. "That is why they were troubled and afraid when they saw him."

"Impossible," began one of the elders, handing his pipe on to his neighbor, who interrupted, "Of course it wasn't the dead chief; it was an omen sent by a witch. Go on."

Slightly shaken, I continued. "One of these three was a man who knew things"—the closest translation for scholar, but unfortunately it also meant witch. The second elder looked triumphantly at the first. "So he spoke to the dead chief saying, 'Tell us what we must do so you may rest in your grave,' but the dead chief did not answer. He vanished, and they could see him no more. Then the man who knew things—his name was Horatio—said this event was the affair of the dead chief's son, Hamlet."

There was a general shaking of heads round the circle. "Had the dead chief no living brothers? Or was this son the chief?"

"No," I replied. "That is, he had one living brother who became the chief when the elder brother died."

The old men muttered: such omens were matters for chiefs and elders, not for youngsters; no good could come of going behind a chief's back: clearly Horatio was not a man who knew things.

"Yes, he was," I insisted, shooing a chicken away from my beer. "In our country the son is next to the father. The dead chief's younger brother had become the great chief. He had also married his elder brother's widow only about a month after the funeral."

"He did well," the old man beamed and announced to the others, "I told you that if we knew more about Europeans, we would find they really were very like us. In our country also," he added to me, "the younger brother marries the elder brother's widow and becomes the father of his children. Now, if your uncle, who married your widowed mother, is your father's full brother, then he will be a real father to you. Did Hamlet's father and uncle have one mother?"

His question barely penetrated my mind; I was too upset and thrown too far off balance by having one of the most important elements of *Hamlet* knocked straight out of the picture. Rather uncertainly I said that I thought they had the same mother, but I wasn't sure—the story didn't say. The old man told me severely that these genealogical details made all the difference and when I got home I must ask the elders about it. He shouted out the door to one of his younger wives to bring his goatskin bag.

Determined to save what I could of the mother motif, I took a deep breath and began again. "The son Hamlet was very sad because his mother had married again so quickly. There was no need for her to do so, and it is our custom for a widow not to go to her next husband until she has mourned for two years."

"Two years is too long," objected the wife who had appeared with the old man's battered goatskin bag. "Who will hoe your farms for you while you have no husband?"

"Hamlet," I retorted without thinking, "was old enough to hoe his mother's farms himself. There was no need for her to remarry." No one looked convinced. I gave up. "His mother and the great chief told Hamlet not to be sad, for the great chief himself would be a father to Hamlet. Furthermore, Hamlet would be the next chief; therefore he must stay to learn the things of a chief. Hamlet agreed to remain, and all the rest went off to drink beer."

While I paused, perplexed at how to render Hamlet's disgusted soliloquy to an audience convinced that Claudius and Gertrude had behaved in the best possible manner, one of the younger men asked me who had married the other wives of the dead chief.

"He had no other wives," I told him.

"But a chief must have many wives! How else can he brew beer and prepare food for all his guests?"

I said firmly that in our country even chiefs had only one wife, that they had servants to do their work and that they paid them from tax money.

It was better, they returned, for a chief to have many wives and sons who would help him hoe his farms and feed his people; then everyone loved the chief who gave much and took nothing—taxes were a bad thing.

I agreed with the last comment, but for the rest fell back on their favorite way of fobbing off my questions. "That is the way it is done, so that is how we do it."

I decided to skip the soliloquy. Even if Claudius was here thought quite right to marry his brother's widow, there remained the poison motif, and I knew they would disapprove of fratricide. More hopefully I resumed, "That night Hamlet kept watch with the three who had seen his dead father. The dead chief again appeared, and although the others were afraid, Hamlet followed his dead father off to one side. When they were alone, Hamlet's dead father spoke."

"Omens can't talk!" the old man was emphatic.

"Hamlet's dead father wasn't an omen; seeing him might have been an omen, but he was not." My audience looked as confused as I sounded. "It *was* Hamlet's dead father. It was a thing we call a 'ghost.' " I had to use the English word, for unlike many of the neighboring tribes, these people didn't believe in the survival after death of any individuating part of the personality.

"What is a 'ghost'? An omen?"

"No, a 'ghost' is someone who is dead but who walks around and can talk, and people can hear him and see him but not touch him."

They objected. "One can touch zombies."

"No, no! It was not a dead body the witches had animated to sacrifice and eat. No one else made Hamlet's dead father walk. He did it himself."

"Dead men can't walk," protested my audience as one man.

I was quite willing to compromise. "A 'ghost' is the dead man's shadow."

But again they objected. "Dead men cast no shadows."

"They do in my country," I snapped.

The old man quelled the babble of disbelief that arose immediately and told me with that insincere but courteous agreement one extends to the fancies of the young, ignorant, and superstitious, "No doubt in your country the dead can also walk without being zombies." From the depths of his bag he produced a withered fragment of kola nut, bit off one end to show it wasn't poisoned, and handed me the rest as a peace offering.

"Anyhow," I resumed, "Hamlet's dead father said that his own brother, the one who became chief, had poisoned him. He wanted Hamlet to avenge him. Hamlet believed this in his heart, for he did not like his father's brother."

I took another swallow of beer. "In the country of the great chief, living in the same homestead, for it was a very large one, was an important elder who was often with the chief to advise and help him. His name was Polonius. Hamlet was courting his daughter, but her father and her brother . . . [I cast hastily about for some tribal analogy] warned her not to let Hamlet visit her when she was alone on her farm, for he would be a great chief and so could not marry her."

"Why not?" asked the wife, who had settled down on the edge of the old man's chair. He frowned at her for asking stupid questions and growled, "They lived in the same homestead."

"That was not the reason," I informed them. "Polonius was a stranger who lived in the homestead because he helped the chief, not because he was a relative."

"Then why couldn't Hamlet marry her?"

"He could have," I explained, "but Polonius didn't think he would. After all, Hamlet was a man of great importance who ought to marry a chief's daughter, for in his country a man could have only one wife. Polonius was afraid that if Hamlet made love to his daughter, then no one else would give a high price for her."

"That might be true," remarked one of the shrewder elders, "but a chief's son would give his mistress's father enough presents and patronage to more than make up the difference. Polonius sounds like a fool to me."

"Many people think he was," I agreed. "Meanwhile Polonius sent his son Laertes off to Paris to learn the things of that country, for it was the homestead of a very great chief indeed. Because he was afraid that Laertes might waste a lot of money on beer and women and gambling, or get into trouble by fighting, he sent one of his servants to Paris secretly, to spy out what Laertes was doing.

"One day Hamlet came upon Polonius's daughter Ophelia. He behaved so oddly he frightened her. Indeed"—I was fumbling for words to express the dubious quality of Hamlet's madness—"the chief and many others had also noticed that when Hamlet talked one could understand the words but not what they meant. Many people thought that he had become mad." My audience suddenly became much more attentive. "The great chief wanted to know what was wrong with Hamlet, so he sent for two of Hamlet's age mates [school friends would have taken a long explanation] to talk to Hamlet and find out what troubled his heart. Hamlet, seeing that they had been bribed by the chief to betray him, told them nothing. Polonius, however, insisted that Hamlet was mad because he had been forbidden to see Ophelia, whom he loved."

"Why," inquired a bewildered voice, "should anyone bewitch Hamlet on that account?"

"Bewitch him?"

"Yes, only witchcraft can make anyone mad, unless, of course, one sees the beings that lurk in the forest."

I stopped being a story teller, took out my notebook and demanded to be told more about these two causes of madness. Even while they spoke and I jotted notes, I tried to calculate the effect of this new factor on the plot. Hamlet had not been exposed to the beings that lurked in the forests. Only his relatives in the male line could bewitch him. Barring relatives not mentioned by Shakespeare, it had to be Claudius who was attempting to harm him. And, of course, it was.

For the moment I staved off questions by saying that the great chief also refused to believe Hamlet was mad for love of Ophelia and nothing else. He was sure that something much more important was troubling Hamlet's heart.

"Now Hamlet's age mates," I continued, "had brought with them a famous story teller. Hamlet decided to have this man tell the chief and all his homestead a story about a man who had poisoned his brother because he desired his brother's wife and wished to be chief himself. Hamlet was sure the great chief could not hear the story without making a sign if he was indeed guilty, and then he would discover whether his dead father had told him the truth."

The old man interrupted, with deep cunning, "Why should a father lie to his son?" he asked.

I hedged: "Hamlet wasn't sure that it really was his dead father." It was impossible to say anything, in that language, about devil-inspired visions.

"You mean," he said, "it actually was an omen, and he knew witches sometimes send false ones. Hamlet was a fool not to go to one skilled in reading omens and divining the truth in the first place. A man-who-sees-the-truth could have told him how his father died, if he really had been poisoned, and if there was witchcraft in it; then Hamlet could have called the elders to settle the matter."

The shrewd elder ventured to disagree. "Because his father's brother was a great chief, one-who-sees-the-truth might therefore have been afraid to tell it. I think it was for that reason that a friend of Hamlet's father—a witch and an elder—sent an omen so his friend's son would know. Was the omen true?"

"Yes," I said, abandoning ghosts and the devil; a witch-sent omen it would have to be. "It was true, for when the story teller was telling his tale before all the homestead, the great chief rose in fear. Afraid that Hamlet knew his secret he planned to have him killed."

The stage set of the next bit presented some difficulties of translation. I began cautiously. "The great chief told Hamlet's mother to find out from her son what he knew. But because a woman's children are always first in her heart, he had the important elder Polonius hide behind a cloth that hung against the wall of Hamlet's mother's sleeping hut. Hamlet started to scold his mother for what she had done."

There was a shocked murmur from everyone; a man should never scold his mother.

"She called out in fear, and Polonius moved behind the cloth. Shouting, 'A rat!' Hamlet took his machete and slashed through the cloth." I paused for dramatic effect. "He had killed Polonius!"

The old men looked at each other in supreme disgust. "That Polonius truly was a fool and a man who knew nothing! What child would not know enough to shout, 'It's me!' " With a pang, I remembered that these people are ardent hunters, always armed with bow, arrow, and machete; at the first rustle in the grass, an arrow is aimed and ready, and the hunter shouts "Game!" If no human voice answers immediately the arrow speeds on its way. Like a good hunter Hamlet had shouted, "A rat!"

I rushed in to save Polonius' reputation. "Polonius did speak. Hamlet heard him. But he thought it was the chief and wished to kill him to avenge his father. He had meant to kill him earlier that evening . . ." I broke down, unable to describe to these pagans, who had no belief in individual afterlife, the difference between dying at one's prayers and dying "unhousell'd, disappointed, unaneled."

This time I had shocked my audience seriously. "For a man to raise his hand against his father's brother and the one who has become his father—that is a terrible thing. The elders ought to let such a man be bewitched."

I nibbled at my kola nut in some perplexity, then pointed out that after all the man had killed Hamlet's father.

"No," pronounced the old man, speaking less to me than to the young men sitting behind the elders. "If your father's brother has killed your father, you must appeal to your father's age mates; they may avenge him. No man may use violence against his senior relatives." Another thought struck him. "But if his father's brother had indeed been wicked enough to bewitch Hamlet and make him mad, that would be a good story indeed, for it would be his own fault that Hamlet, being mad, no longer had any sense and thus was ready to kill his father's brother."

There was a murmur of applause. *Hamlet* was again a good story to them, but it no longer seemed quite the same story to me. As I thought over the coming complications of plot and motive, I lost my courage and decided to skim over dangerous ground quickly.

"The great chief," I went on, "was not sorry that Hamlet had killed Polonius. It gave him a reason to send Hamlet away, with his two treacherous age mates, with letters to a chief of a far country, saying that Hamlet should be killed. But Hamlet changed the writing on their papers, so that the chief killed his age mates instead." I encountered a reproachful glare from one of the men whom I had told undetectable forgery was not merely immoral but beyond human skill. I looked the other way.

"Before Hamlet could return, Laertes came back for his father's funeral. The great chief told him Hamlet had killed Polonius. Laertes swore to kill Hamlet because of this, and because his sister Ophelia, hearing her father had been killed by the man she loved, went mad and drowned in the river."

"Have you already forgotten what we told you?" The old man was reproachful. "One cannot take vengeance on a madman; Hamlet killed Polonius in his madness. As for the girl, she not only went mad, she was drowned. Only witches can make people drown. Water itself can't hurt anything. It is merely something one drinks and bathes in."

I began to get cross. "If you don't like the story, I'll stop."

The old man made soothing noises and himself poured me some more beer. "You tell the story well, and we are listening. But it is clear that the elders of your country have never told you what the story really means. No, don't interrupt! We believe you when you say your marriage customs are different, or your clothes and weapons. But people are the same everywhere; therefore, there are always witches and it is we, the elders, who know how witches work. We told you it was the great chief who wished to kill Hamlet, and now your own words have proved us right. Who were Ophelia's male relatives?"

"There were only her father and her brother." *Hamlet* was clearly out of my hands.

"There must have been many more; this also you must ask of your elders when you get back to your country. From what you tell us, since Polonius was dead, it must have been Laertes who killed Ophelia, although I do not see the reason for it."

We had emptied one pot of beer, and the old men argued the point with slightly tipsy interest. Finally, one of them demanded of me, "What did the servant of Polonius say on his return?"

With difficulty I recollected Reynaldo and his mission. "I don't think he did return before Polonius was killed."

"Listen," said the elder, "and I will tell you how it was and how your story will go, then you may tell me if I am right. Polonius knew his son would get into trouble, and so he did. He had many fines to pay for fighting, and debts from gambling. But he had only two ways of getting money quickly. One was to marry off his sister at once, but it is difficult to find a man who will marry a woman desired by the son of a chief. For if the chief's heir commits adultery with your wife, what can you do? Only a fool calls a case against a man who will someday be his judge. Therefore Laertes had to take the second way: he killed his sister by witchcraft, drowning her so he could secretly sell her body to the witches."

I raised an objection. "They found her body and buried it. Indeed Laertes jumped into the grave to see his sister once more—so, you see, the body was truly there. Hamlet, who had just come back, jumped in after him."

"What did I tell you?" The elder appealed to the others. "Laertes was up to no good with his sister's body. Hamlet prevented him, because the chief's heir, like a chief, does not wish any other man to grow rich and powerful. Laertes would be angry, because he would have killed his sister without benefit to himself. In our country he would try to kill Hamlet for that reason. Is this not what happened?"

"More or less," I admitted. "When the great chief found Hamlet was still alive, he encouraged Laertes to try to kill Hamlet and arranged a fight with machetes between them. In the fight both the young men were wounded to death. Hamlet's mother drank the poisoned beer that the chief meant for Hamlet in case he won the fight. When he saw his mother die of poison, Hamlet, dying, managed to kill his father's brother with his machete."

"You see, I was right!" exclaimed the elder.

"That was a very good story," added the old man, "and you told it with very few mistakes. The poison Hamlet's mother drank was obviously meant for the survivor of the fight, whichever it was. If Laertes had won, the great chief would have poisoned him, for no one would know that he arranged Hamlet's death. Then, too, he need not fear Laertes's witchcraft; it takes a strong heart to kill one's only sister by witchcraft."

"Sometime," concluded the old man, gathering his ragged toga about him, "you must tell us some more stories of your country. We, who are elders, will instruct you in their true meaning, so that when you return to your own land your elders will see that you have not been sitting in the bush, but among those who know things and who have taught you wisdom."

3

Context as a Source of Meaning and Understanding[1]

PAMELA S. HINDS
DORIS E. CHAVES
SANDRA M. CYPESS

Abstract: The intent of health professions is to understand humans, their health, and other related phenomena and to use this understanding to promote meaningful life experiences. The ability to do this depends on knowledge of the multiple contexts in which these phenomena exist. The purposeful use of context is a central feature of thorough research and clinical assessments, and it allows for meaning to be shared and phenomena to be understood. This article offers a conceptual perspective on context, including a delineation of four nested contextual layers. Individual layers and combined layers of context have direct implications for research and practice.

The intent of health care professionals is to understand human beings and to help create conditions that promote health and meaningful life experiences. Whether asking a research question or assessing a clinical problem, the health care professional's goal is to understand the care situation and to use that understanding to promote the health of others. Understanding, regarded as the ultimate purpose of conducting research

---

AUTHORS' NOTE: Correspondence and requests for reprints should be addressed to Pamela S. Hinds, Coordinator of Nursing Research, St. Jude Children's Research Hospital, 322 N. Lauderdale, Memphis, TN 38101-0318. This work originally appeared in Hinds, P. S., Chaves, D. E., & Cypess, S. M. (1992). Context as a source of meaning and understanding. *Qualitative Health Research, 2*, 1, 61-74.

(Munhall & Oiler, 1986), occurs when what was previously unknown becomes known and meaningful (Spinelli, 1989). A researcher's efforts to understand are facilitated by the ability to attach meaning to and thus interpret observations, impressions, and experiences. Similarly, the clinician's efforts to understand are enhanced by his or her ability to interact with derived knowledge, extract meaning, and impart understanding to clients in a manner that helps them to experience this meaning in their lives.

The abilities to attach meaning to and to understand a phenomenon depend on the researcher's and clinician's knowledge of the multiple contexts in which that phenomenon occurs. Field and Morse (1985) stated that meaning exists when implicit knowledge is conveyed explicitly to others and that context must be addressed to do this adequately. Mishler (1979) emphasized that all human action and experience is context dependent and can only be understood within those contexts. A lack of context in research and practice becomes a threat to the accurate interpretation and application of findings. Our purpose in this article is to delineate a conceptual perspective of context and to describe the implications of this conceptualization for research and practice. We emphasize the purposeful use of context to determine the meaning of a studied situation and propose that a researcher's or clinician's intentional interaction with context increases the accuracy and completeness of interpretations, expands the explanatory value of findings, creates the conditions for understanding human life processes, and permits meaning and understanding to be shared.

Definitions and Use of Context

The use of the term *context* has varied, often markedly, in reports of qualitative and quantitative research. Hutchinson (1986) defined context as the environment or setting where behavior occurs, whereas Glaser (1978) viewed context as synonymous with ambience. Woods (1988) described context as the larger domain or larger picture of which a given phenomenon is a part. Miles and Huberman (1984) offered a more specific and narrower definition of context as the immediately relevant aspects of a situation, such as a person's physical location, the other people that are involved, and the recent history of their involvement, plus the relevant aspects of the social situation in which a person functions (a school, company, and so on). A more literary approach was taken by Kuhns and Martorana (1982), who referred to context as a "web of experience" that incorporates thoughts, acts, and the past. Welshimer and Earp (1989) equated context with a general frame of reference that directly influences current decision making about specific issues. Taking a more universal approach, Spradley (1979) suggested that context comprises a collection of symbols, with the meaning of any one symbol derived from its relationship with the other symbols in a particular culture.

These definitions and usages recognize the existence and importance of context in science but, with the exception of the definition proposed by Miles and Huberman (1984), are limited to a background or descriptive level. Our use differs by its inclusion of the health care professional's purposeful, systematic, and analytical interaction with a situation or event in order to discover meaning in totality and to understand the whole of that situation or event. Prediction, explanation, and understanding can result from this use of context. Excellent examples of nurses' purposeful, analytic interactions with context that resulted in positive changes for their clients are provided by Benner and her colleagues (Benner, 1984; Benner & Wrubel, 1989). Expert nurse clinicians reported how they proceeded from an awareness of vague uneasiness about a clinical situation to a definite gestalt of the situation that prompted their competent use of discretionary judgment. To achieve the gestalt, the nurses blended their knowledge of (a) immediately relevant aspects of the clinical situation, (b) the recent past of the individuals involved in the situation, and (c) the setting in which they were giving care.

Attention to context ranges from nonuse ("context stripping") to extensive use in the data collection or assessment processes and in the interpretation of findings. Context stripping exists in research when no information on the context of a study is provided or when the scientific quest is for universal context-free laws (Mishler, 1979). It exists in practice when only a client's presenting symptom or behavior is considered, regardless of the client's health history or current life situation. When this occurs, the implication is that the investigators or clinicians considered the context to be nonexistent or not relevant.

When context has been considered in previous studies, it has been operationally defined as a single characteristic, such as a setting, background, or a cause of positive or negative change (Ferris & Gilmore, 1984; Kahn, 1987; Mansfield, Yu, McCool, Vicary, & Packard, 1989; Murphy, 1985; Shoham-Yakubovich, Carmel, Zwanger, & Zaltcman,

1989), and as a source of historical meaning (Anderson, 1987; Curtis, 1982). When investigators merely describe the contextual aspects of a study, context is the background or backdrop. Often, such descriptions are not subsequently interwoven with the reported study methods, findings, or interpretation. Thus context is divorced from the study's process and outcomes. Readers are likely to find such descriptions interesting, but they may not consciously consider them when reviewing the outcomes and interpretations. If readers do attempt to incorporate the descriptions of context, the results are highly individualized. This process may be likened to readers' interactions with the text in literary studies to generate meaning (Fish, 1980; Holland, 1975).

The context of a study may also be considered a source of data. In such cases, the investigator describes and analyzes the contextual aspects, including how he or she was influenced by interacting with those aspects, and incorporates the resulting analyses of context into interpretations of study findings.

Conceptual Perspective on Context and Meaning

In this article, context is conceptualized as four nested, interactive layers that are distinguished from each other by (a) the extent to which meaning is shared (from totally individualized to almost universal meaning), (b) the dominant time focus (present to the future), and (c) the speed with which change within the layer can occur and be perceived (see Figure 3.1). Traditionally in science, the focus is primarily on the studied phenomenon, but in this conceptualization, the focus is the phenomenon *as it is embedded within its layers of context.* These layers and our descriptions of them follow.

IMMEDIATE CONTEXT

Immediacy is the major characteristic of this context layer. An example is observing an instant act of an individual. Because the focus is on the *present,* relevant aspects of the situation, such as space and other boundaries, are readily definable here, which facilitates predictions of behavioral patterns. An example of this would be the specific action of a nurse taking a client's blood pressure.

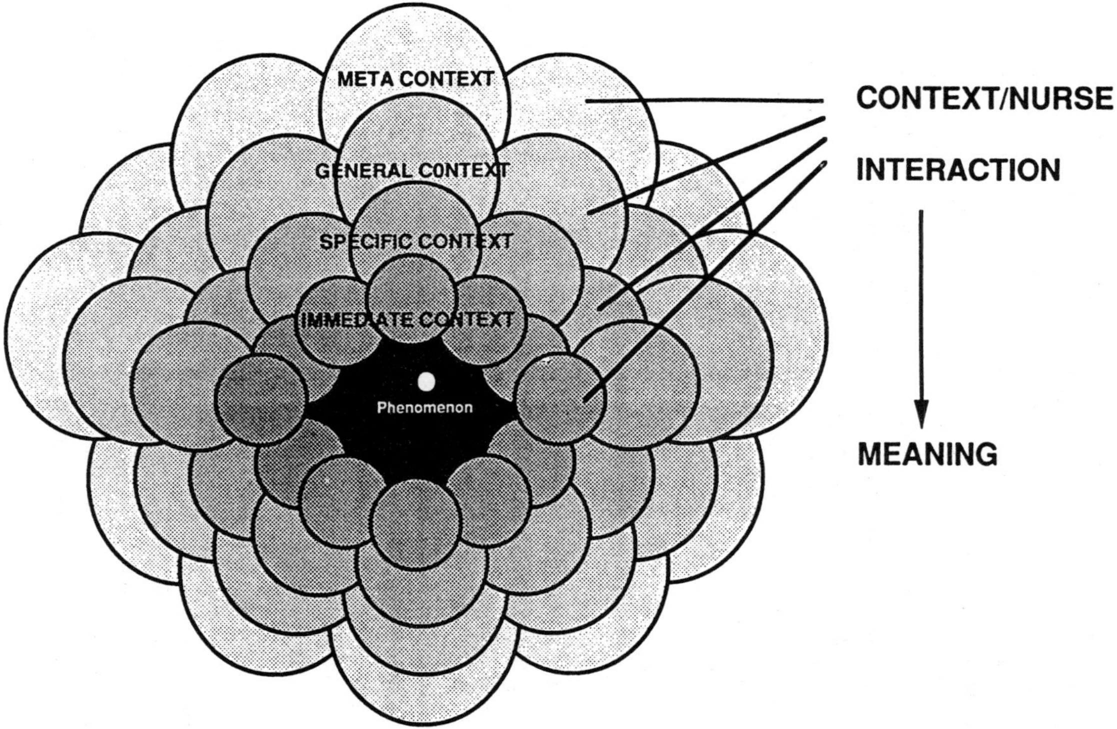

Figure 3.1. Depiction of the Four Nested, Interactive Layers of Context Surrounding a Phenomenon and the Meaning That Can Result From the Nurse's Purposeful Interaction With the Layers of Content.

SPECIFIC CONTEXT

An individualized, unique system of knowing that encompasses the *immediate past* plus relevant aspects of the present situation is the major characteristic of this context layer. The immediate past is influenced by circumstances such as the time of day, the mood, presence or absence of other persons, and other personal and environmental factors. Change in this layer can be rapid and easily detected and can reflect a series of related events. This context layer would be reflected in the observation of the influence on blood pressure readings of factors such as (a) the rapidity of position change, (b) the manner and mood of the nurse, (c) the volume or extent of unexplained background noise, (d) the presence or absence of a trusted family member or friend during the monitoring, and (e) the client's familiarity with the procedure and with the nurse doing the monitoring.

GENERAL CONTEXT

This layer of context is characterized by a general life frame of reference that has evolved from an individual's interpretations of past and current interactions. This layer is changeable but not usually to a dramatic extent because it constitutes a personal organization of events or behaviors and associated meanings developed over time. Current situations are interpreted in light of this layer; consequently, it can be a source of explanation and prediction. In the example of blood pressure monitoring, the general context would reflect the client's and nurse's personal and cultural beliefs about the relationship of blood pressure readings to general health status. These beliefs, used by the nurse and client to interpret the blood pressure readings and the process of being monitored, can influence the actual readings.

METACONTEXT

This layer is a socially constructed source of knowing that operates continuously and results in a generally shared social perspective. It is a source of explanation for and an indirect influence on behaviors and events. Because of its omnipresence, this layer of context often goes unrecognized unless it is intentionally sought. It is changeable but unlikely to show considerable sudden change. Although the metacontext reflects and incorporates the past and the present and sets conditions for and shapes the future, its predominant orientation is to the past. In the example of blood pressure monitoring, this context layer could reflect the client's and the nurse's shared view of health as involving responsibility to take action to prevent or control adverse health conditions.

Although they may not all be included in the focus of a study or a clinical assessment, all four layers are always present. When only one layer or interaction is the focus, an interpretation of the whole is possible, but there is a risk of distortion.

Meaning is derived from purposeful interactions with the layers. A new or altered configuration of meaning occurs with each interaction (see Figure 3.1). An example of a studied situation in which new configurations of meaning evolved from interactions with each layer of context is humorously reported by Punch (1986), who shared his experience of collecting data for his dissertation on an English private school known for its progressive, liberal educational philosophy. The phenomenon of the right to publish study data emerged when it became obvious that Punch's findings about the school were not favorable. The immediate context centered on the vituperative personal and legal proceedings undertaken by the school's administration to prevent his publication of the data. The meaning for the researcher at this layer was interference with the completion of his doctoral degree. The specific context included the setting (the private school) and the personalities of the current trustees and headmaster and Punch's dissertation chairman. When Punch interacted with this layer, he became aware that these people were not trying to prevent him from completing his doctoral work but were concerned with protecting their public roles and reputations. The general context included Punch's personal background and beliefs (a working-class Irish Catholic family background, a traditional English public education, and his view of the liberal, English upper class as a humorless and hypocritical lot) as well as the history of the private school. According to Punch, interaction at this layer revealed the differences in temperament, personalities, and cultural and social backgrounds between the researcher (Punch) and the researched and accounted for some of the study findings and their interpretations. The metacontext in this example was that of a society with pronounced social class distinctions, rather rigid adherence to civility in public and private interchanges, and strict deference for positions and roles. Meaning at this level helped to explain the impossibility of Punch being able to publish his unfavorable findings.

As exemplified in Punch's description, each of the four layers of context can serve as a source of both prediction and explanation and, as a result, understanding. However, the immediate and specific context layers are more predictive sources, and the general context and metacontext layers are more explanatory sources. For example, because of the easily definable relevant aspects in the immediate context, it would be possible, given certain information, to predict a behavior or an outcome. No theoretical frame of reference would be necessary to make the prediction; observed patterns could provide the basis. After interacting with the immediate context of his study, Punch (1986) could have predicted the school officials' continued refusal to allow him to publish his data, but he might not have been able to explain their opposition until he interacted with the phenomenon's other layers of context.

Implications for the Researcher and for Method

A researcher could describe a specific context by carefully, even painstakingly, noting all aspects that are obvious and therefore relevant to him or her. But without interacting with others in the context, the researcher may miss what is relevant to the others. Without the purposeful attempt to interact with the contexts of others, meaning will be more grounded in the researcher's contexts than in those of the phenomenon under study.

An example of interacting with the contexts of others is reported by Krysl (see Krysl & Watson, 1988), who described her experiences as an artist in residence for 9 months at the University of Colorado School of Nursing's Center for Human Caring, where she worked closely with nurses to understand how they made care-related decisions. Krysl accompanied nurses in their practice settings and observed that they saw things that she had not seen or had ignored. Her interactions with the nurses, through questioning, made their contexts more apparent to her. These contexts included attitudes, gut reactions, and cues that would not normally be visible to an outsider but that formed the basis for the care decisions. The once "invisible" factors were contextual influences on the phenomenon being studied, that of care decisions. Krysl experienced what Van Maanen (1988) described: Meaning comes from the interaction of self with the context and phenomena of others.

An example of a strategy used by one of us in a research methods course to convey the importance of context may illustrate the different outcomes from the use of single and then multiple layers of context. A video of a Bush tribe performing a ritual dance was played for the class.

It was first played without sound and without any introductory or background remarks. Class participants reported the patterns observed in the dance and predicted native behaviors that were subsequently confirmed in the video. However, participants described personal aversion to the dancing and emphasized its bizarre nature. At that point in the class exercise, participants were interacting from their own contexts with the immediate context of the tribe members. Then, the same portions of the video were replayed, but sound was added. The sound track included tribe members' descriptions of their reasons for participating in the ritual. Class participants all reported less aversion to the ritual, more interest, and beginning conceptualizations that could explain the ritualistic behavior. The class members were interacting from their contexts with the specific and general context of the tribal members, and a shared meaning was emerging. Finally, the same portions of the video were replayed after background information was provided on cultural values, historical events, and political and economic factors. Class participants then readily formulated a theoretical frame of reference based on their shared meaning to explain the observed tribal behaviors and commented (with relief) about their understanding of the importance and necessity of the ritual. Thus a rudimentary understanding resulted from the participants' consideration of all layers of context.

Implications for the Clinician

The importance of shared meaning between the health care professional and client has been emphasized as the foundation for care that fosters health. Our conceptualization indicates that the meaning cannot be identical for the health care professional and the client because their contexts are different. However, the meanings for both can be made explicit, which can result in an understanding of each other's context. As the health care professional interacts consciously with the context layers of clients and guides clients' interactions with contexts, the professional will become more aware of his or her own context and be better able to design and control the impact of health care. Others have advocated this approach to health care (Neuman, 1982; Orlando, 1961; Parse, Coyne, & Smith, 1985; Patterson & Zderad, 1988; Rogers, 1987, 1990; Watson, 1979).

A second implication is that health care interventions can be directed toward a specific context layer when certain outcomes are desired.

When a very specific behavior needs to be interrupted, created, or otherwise altered, the target layer is the client's immediate context. If, however, an aspect of a setting or situation needs to be altered or replaced, the intervention is focused on the client's specific context. If a client's belief or perspective is the focus of intervention, then the general context is the layer of concern. If a culturally based belief regarding health is the point of intervention, then the metacontext is the focus of the health care.

Conclusion

Our quest for universal laws to predict and explain the behavior of phenomena may be misdirected. Regularities or patterns that can contribute to prediction and explanation may be found not in the phenomenon itself but in its contexts. Gergen (1973) argued that the observed regularities noted in experimental and field research are bound to their historical contexts. This kind of thinking refocuses the researcher away from considering *only* the phenomenon to considering the *phenomenon as it exists within its multiple contexts.*

Our conceptualization implies the need for a researcher or a clinician to interact with the multiple contexts of a phenomenon to make explicit its context dependence and to yield explanatory statements. When first studying or assessing a phenomenon, it may not be possible or desirable to consider all of its contextual layers, as the researcher or clinician may become overwhelmed by the complexity of the phenomenon's existence. Careful, detailed observation of a single context may yield clearer direction for a subsequent multilayer approach. A single-layer approach, such as the purposeful study or assessment of a phenomenon in distinctly different specific contexts, could result in the identification of a predictive pattern of behavior that would uncover potential explanatory variables. Once these observations are completed, the researcher or clinician can plan a study or assessment that includes interaction through all the layers of context. It is also of critical importance that the researcher and clinician recognize that only limited or partial understanding may result if only a single layer of context is considered.

Context is a source of data, meaning, and understanding. Only through purposeful interactions with the layers of context will health care professionals be able to predict, explain, and control the effect of their care. Ignoring context, underusing it, or not recognizing one's own context-driven perspective will result in incomplete or missed meaning and a misunderstanding of human phenomena. The incorporation of context into a study can enrich and extend findings and conclusions and provide a basis for accurate clinical application of the findings.

Note

1. The authors acknowledge the helpful reviews of earlier drafts by Christy Wright and Tori Wentz at St. Jude Children's Research Hospital and Dean Michael Carter at the University of Tennessee, Memphis.

References

Anderson, J. (1987). The cultural context of caring. *Canadian Critical Care Nursing Journal, 4,* 7-13.

Benner, P. (1984). *From novice to expert: Excellence and power in clinical nursing practice.* Menlo Park, CA: Addison-Wesley.

Benner, P., & Wrubel, J. (1989). *The primacy of caring: Stress and coping in health and illness.* Menlo Park, CA: Addison-Wesley.

Curtis, M. (1982). History and qualitative methodology. In E. Kuhns & S. Martorana (Eds.), *Qualitative methods for institutional research* (pp. 55-61). San Francisco: Jossey-Bass.

Ferris, G., & Gilmore, D. (1984). The moderating role of work context in job design research: A test of competing models. *Academy of Management Journal, 27,* 885-892.

Field, P., & Morse, J. (1985). *Nursing research: The application of qualitative approaches.* Rockville, MD: Aspen Systems.

Fish, S. (1980). *Is there a text in this class? The authority of interpretive communities.* Cambridge, MA: Harvard University Press.

Gergen, K. (1973). Social psychology as history. *Journal of Personality and Social Psychology, 26,* 309-320.

Glaser, B. (1978). *Theoretical sensitivity.* Mill Valley, CA: Sociology Press.

Holland, N. (1975). *5 readers reading.* New Haven, CT: Yale University Press.

Hutchinson, S. (1986). Grounded theory: The method. In P. Munhall & C. Oliver (Eds.), *Nursing research: A qualitative perspective* (pp. 111-130). Norwalk, CT: Appleton-Century-Crofts.

Kahn, E. (1987). The choice of therapist self-disclosure in psychotherapy groups: Contextual considerations. *Archives of Psychiatric Nursing, 1*(1), 62-67.

Krysl, M., & Watson, J. (1988). Existential moments of caring: Facets of nursing and social support. *Advances in Nursing Science, 10*(2), 12-17.

Kuhns, E., & Martorana, S. (1982). *Qualitative methods for institutional research.* San Francisco: Jossey-Bass.

Mansfield, P., Yu, L., McCool, W., Vicary, J., & Packard, J. (1989). The Job Context Index. *Journal of Advanced Nursing, 14,* 501-508.

Miles, M., & Huberman, A. (1984). *Qualitative data analysis: A sourcebook of new methods.* Beverly Hills, CA: Sage.

Mishler, E. (1979). Meaning in context: Is there any other kind? *Harvard Educational Review, 49*(1), 1-19.

Munhall, P., & Oiler, C. (1986). *Nursing research: A qualitative perspective.* Norwalk, CT: Appleton-Century-Crofts.

Murphy, S. (1985). Contexts for scientific creativity: Applications to nursing. *Image, 17*(4), 103-107.

Neuman, B. (1982). *The Neuman systems model: Application to nursing education and practice.* Norwalk, CT: Appleton-Century-Crofts.

Orlando, I. (1961). *The dynamic nurse-patient relationship: Function, process and principles.* New York: Putnam.

Parse, R., Coyne, A., & Smith, M. (1985). *Nursing research: Qualitative methods.* Bowie, MD: Brady Communications.

Patterson, J., & Zderad, L. (1988). *Humanistic nursing.* New York: National League for Nursing.

Punch, M. (1986). *The politics and ethics of fieldwork.* Beverly Hills, CA: Sage.

Rogers, M. (1987). Rogers' science of unitary human beings. In R. R. Parse (Ed.), *Nursing science: Major paradigms, theories, and critiques* (pp. 139-146). Philadelphia: Saunders.

Rogers, M. (1990). Nursing: Science of unitary, irreducible, human beings. In E. Barrett (Ed.), *Visions of Rogers' science-based nursing* (pp. 67-81). New York: National League for Nursing.

Shoham-Yakubovich, I., Carmel, S., Zwanger, L., & Zaltcman, T. (1989). Autonomy, job satisfaction and professional self-image among nurses in the context of a physicians' strike. *Social Science and Medicine, 28,* 1315-1320.

Spinelli, E. (1989). *The interpreted world: An introduction to phenomenological psychology.* Newbury Park, CA: Sage.

Spradley, J. (1979). *The ethnographic interview.* New York: Holt, Rinehart & Winston.

Van Maanen, J. (1988). *Tales of the field: On writing ethnography.* Chicago: University of Chicago Press.

Watson, J. (1979). *Nursing: The philosophy and science of caring.* Boston: Little, Brown.

Welshimer, K., & Earp, J. (1989). Genetic counseling within the context of existing attitudes and beliefs. *Patient Education and Counseling, 13,* 237-255.

Woods, N. (1988). Designing prescription-testing studies. In N. Woods & M. Catanzaro (Eds.), *Nursing research: Theory and practice* (pp. 202-218). St. Louis: Mosby.

4

The Holistic Injunction: An Ideal and a Moral Imperative for Qualitative Research

GEORGE W. NOBLIT
JOHN D. ENGEL

Qualitative researchers are constantly involved in synthesis. We describe, we compare, and we demonstrate cases (Patton, 1980), all in the service of making something larger: an interpretation of what we have seen. All of this activity revolves around what may be called a *holistic injunction* in qualitative research. This injunction requires us to learn all, to take all into account, and to tell all. Holism is, of course, an *ideal*, for the world works against it on every level. It also carries a moral imperative for the research—it is what we ought to do!

Every project is constrained by practical issues—time, money, energy, commitments, and intellectual issues (e.g., ideologies and methodologies). Without the ideal (i.e., the holistic injunction), we could easily fall prey to analytic or systems thought (technical rationality), focusing solely on key pieces and their relations. We would miss the totality of relations, their significance to the participants, and their meaning in the wider human discourse. Further, without this injunction we would not need to be as concerned with how we synthesize our accounts and interpretations.

AUTHORS' NOTE: Correspondence or requests for reprints should be addressed to George W. Noblit, School of Education, CB 3500, Room 121 Peabody, University of North Carolina, Chapel Hill, NC 27599-3500. This chapter originally appeared in Noblit, G. W., & Engel, J. D. (1991). The holistic injunction: An ideal and a moral imperative for qualitative research. *Qualitative Health Research 1*, 1, 123-130.

In this article, we examine the holistic injunction, the problems that it creates for qualitative research, and how we normally go about moving toward holism. In the end, we believe that this requires understanding the nature of synthesis.

The Holistic Injunction

To be sure, qualitative research is about many things. Spicer (1976) and Marcus (1988), among others, noted that qualitative work is emic, comparative, historical, and holistic. In being emic, we must understand the multiple perspectives, the competing beliefs, the ways lives are lived, and their implications for social relations. In being comparative, we seek not only to contrast but to combine. We ask, what is the meaning of all perspectives taken together as well as in contrast to one another? In being historical, we not only put events and interpretations into sequence but try to discern how this history and other histories are implicated in present action and what this means for those involved. In all of these, we attend to the fourth criterion, holism. We are emic, comparative, and historical so that we may be holistic.

Holism, of course, is a difficult injunction. Marcus and Fischer (1986) saw it as "an unattainable idea . . . not to be taken literally" (p. 188). It purposely lacks some overall structure and may be understood in a variety of ways. Patton (1980) wrote:

> This holistic approach assumes that the whole is greater than the sum of the parts; it also assumes that a description and understanding of a program's context is essential for understanding the program. (p. 40)

In many ways, it is Patton's latter statement that gives meaning to his first. The key holism test is: Does the qualitative account allow the reader to understand the difference between "surface data and deep structure?" (Light, 1983, p. 57). Marcus and Fischer (1986) wrote:

> The essence of holistic representation in modern ethnography has not been to produce a catalog or an encyclopedia (although the classic assumption supporting the authority of the ethnographic writer is that he commands this sort of background knowledge), but to contextualize elements of culture and to make systematic connections among them. (p. 23)

Understanding holism as contextualization does not give more clarity, as Marcus and Fischer (1986) went on to explain:

> How to present rich views of the meaning systems of a delimited set of subjects and also to represent the broader system of political economy that links them to other subjects, who are also richly portrayed in their own world, is an experimental ideal. (p. 91)

The moral force of the holistic injunction admonishes us to be ambitious, to try to learn all, to take all into account, and to tell all.

LEARNING ALL

To learn all, we consciously search for all the variations in language, belief, social relations, events, and action. The holistic injunction is usually responded to by planning an early "mapping" phase in the research that involves searching for and documenting this variation. In mapping, we create the feature of a local terain—a social and cultural topography. In developing these local features, we observe and talk to those involved, using informants to validate what we think we know, and searching for disconfirming as well as confirming evidence. Learning all is an exhausting process of eagerly pursuing leads which all too often turn out to be false, then deciding which of all the possibilities to pursue next and always checking against yourself and your perceptions.

Qualitative researchers check themselves in many ways. In both fieldwork and analysis, multiple approaches are pursued. This strategy can operate at several levels. Denzin (1978) identified four:

> 1. *Data triangulation* has three subtypes: (a) time, (b) space, and (c) person. Person analysis, in turn, has three levels: (a) aggregate, (b) interactive, and (c) collectivity.
> 2. *Investigator triangulation* consists of using multiple rather than single observers of the same object.
> 3. *Theory triangulation* consists of using multiple rather than single perspectives in relation to the same set of objects.
> 4. *Methodological triangulation* can entail within-method triangulation and between-method triangulation. (p. 295)

When data from triangulation activities stop yielding new insights (a traditional sign that you have learned all), we begin to worry if it is us and not the evidence that is not yielding insights. We then try to take all into account as a way of checking our perspective.

TAKING ALL INTO ACCOUNT

Learning all is essentially naturalistic: You know what you have experienced, seen, been told, and sought out. Taking all into account is, in some sense, contextualizing the naturalistic understanding. Usually this begins in the later phases of fieldwork, where events are being compared and the scholar's understanding of the local terrain is being elaborated through strategic studies. As Asad (1986) and Turner (1980) suggested, taking all into account involves moving beyond point-by-point comparisons to translations.

Translations try to preserve the completeness and complexity of each event as they are compared. Turner (1980) saw translations as essentially creating analogies, the simplest form being *this is like that except* . . . . Of course, in practice, the analogies created by translating all of one scene into another are considerably more involved.

In fieldwork, taking all into account involves not just focusing on a few aspects of social and cultural relations but putting all the relations into their salient contexts. These contexts may involve larger belief systems and social trends or an established pattern of small group relations. To the qualitative researcher, the sense of things is often understood in terms of all the contexts to things taken together. We find the meaning of particular events in their myriad social and cultural contexts. We then translate the contexts and events into one another and develop an analogy that takes all into account.

The inexperienced field researcher often expresses concern over the perpetual motion possibility of infinite egress. There are so many contexts to be contextualized that taking all into account may never come to an end. The more experienced field researcher sees the process as iterative—working backward and forward until no new interpretations emerge (Glaser & Strauss, 1967).

TELLING ALL

The holistic injunction, finally, requires us to tell all.[1] In practice, we must "tell all" with some real constraints. We have come to think of these constraints collectively as "the audience" for our interpretation. Moreover, we think the audience is primary in that we always "tell all" to someone, real or imagined. This "someone" gives us a referent around which to organize our interpretation. Our interpretations are translations of what we understand into what we believe to be someone else's understanding.

For a translation to approximate holism, it must be "idiomatic," (Barnwell, 1980) in that the meaning of what is studied must be translated into the meaning system of the audience. Of course, some social and cultural scenes and meaning systems may not be directly intelligible to an audience. In this situation, the holistic injunction leaves us with three possibilities (Barnwell, 1980). First, we may use a broadly descriptive account so that the general meaning is conveyed. Second, we may use emic characterizations from the participant, while contextualizing as much as possible. This keeps the strange familiar. Third, we may use emic characterizations from the audience's meaning system, making the familiar strange. This obviously requires the qualitative researcher to be as much a student of human discourse as of the particular scene studied.

Clifford (1986) argued that in constructing this dialogue we are creating an "ethnographic fiction" (p. 6). The *fiction* must speak to how we make sense of anything, and we are keenly aware of the fact that the instrument affects the reading (Geertz, 1973). We use our own values as a template for this, often choosing to write our studies as journeys or quests, and may write in the first-person present tense to keep human authorship (Bowers, 1984) and the evolving nature of our understanding in the reader's mind.

Berger (1981) saw this issue as one of transposition. In telling all, we reorganize and reposition the elements of the fiction in the frame of the audience while discussing the problems of doing so. There are dual goals in this fiction making. The first is to "enlarge human discourse" (Geertz, 1973). The second is to defamiliarize so as to allow cultural critique (Marcus & Fischer, 1986) to take place. We will use what is taken to be conventional knowledge about the scene under study and reveal how incomplete and misguided this knowledge is to the comprehension of the scene. By giving the "sense" (Taylor, 1982) and "essence" (Merleau-Ponty, 1962), we defamiliarize our common understandings by comparing them with different conceptions of things. The holistic injunction engages the readers' critical conscience about the scene studied but, more important, about their own ways of being and thinking.

Conclusion

The holistic injunction in qualitative research leads to all kinds of trouble in everyday practice. Every time you create an interpretation, compare cases, or consider interpretations, you are driven by injunction to be more inclusive, more intelligible, and more complete. Without it, we could simply look at something and express our opinion about it. We could selectively seek and report evidence. We could favor one worldview over another. With it, the scholar must come forth, for it is the scholar who learns all, takes all into account, and tells all; it is the scholar who pursues a holistic description, an exhaustive interpretation, and takes the role of representing the particular to the universal and vice versa. The holistic injunction is not a technique or a standard but an ethic that is pursued by individual scholars in real-world contexts. Without the scholars, there is no ethic, no injunction. But without the holistic injunction, there is little value to qualitative research.

Note

1. Our discussion here is from the perspective or constructivist accounts of "telling all." We recognize the active debate regarding types of telling; however, space does not allow us to adequately explore this important issue. We suggest that the interested reader refer to Van Maanen (1988), Geertz (1988), and Clifford and Marcus (1986).

References

Asad, T. (1986). The concept of cultural translation in British social anthropology. In J. Clifford & G. Marcus (Eds.), *Writing culture*. Berkeley: University of California Press.

Barnwell, K. (1980). *Introduction to semantics and translation*. Horsleys Green, UK: Summer Institute of Linguistics.

Berger, P., with Kellner, H. (1981). *Sociology reinterpreted*. Garden City, NY: Doubleday.

Bowers, C. (1984). *The promise of theory*. New York: Longman.

Clifford, J. (1986). On ethnographic allegory. In J. Clifford & G. Marcus (Eds.), *Writing culture*. Berkeley: University of California Press.

Clifford, J., & Marcus, G. E. (1986). *Writing culture: The poetics and politics of ethnography*. Berkeley: University of California Press.

Denzin, N. (1978). *The research act: A theoretical introduction to sociological methods*. New York: McGraw-Hill.

Geertz, C. (1973). *The interpretation of cultures*. New York: Basic Books.

Geertz, C. (1988). *Works and lives: The anthropologist as author*. Stanford, CA: Stanford University Press.

Glaser, B., & Strauss, A. (1967). *The discovery of grounded theory*. New York: Aldine.

Light, D., Jr. (1983). Surface data and deep structure. In J. Van Maanen (Ed.), *Qualitative methodology* (pp. 57-69). Beverly Hills, CA: Sage.

Marcus, G. (1988). *Imagining the whole: Ethnography's contemporary efforts to situate itself.* Paper presented at the Ethnography in Education Forum, University of Pennsylvania.

Marcus, G., & Fischer, M. (1986). *Anthropology as cultural critique.* Chicago: University of Chicago Press.

Merleau-Ponty, M. (1962). *Phenomenology of perception* (C. Smith, Trans.). London: Routledge & Kegan Paul.

Patton, M. (1980). *Qualitative evaluation methods.* Beverly Hills, CA: Sage.

Spicer, E. (1976). Beyond analysis and explanation. *Human Organization, 35*, 335-343.

Taylor, C. (1982). Interpretation and the sciences of man. In E. Bredo & W. Feinberg (Eds.), *Knowledge and values in social and educational research.* Philadelphia: Temple University Press.

Turner, S. (1980). *Sociological explanation as translation.* New York: Cambridge University Press.

Van Maanen, J. (1988). *Tales of the field: On writing ethnography.* Chicago: University of Chicago Press.

5

"Euch,[1] Those Are for Your Husband!": Examination of Cultural Values and Assumptions Associated With Breast-Feeding

JANICE M. MORSE

Abstract: Examination of the assumptions underlying research and educational resources on breast-feeding reveals bias and a lack of data to substantiate perceived facts. In this paper four methods of examining research to assist in identifying assumptions and bias in breast-feeding research are presented. Four methods are (a) examining past research, (b) examining cross-cultural research, (c) asking anthropological questions, and (d) using inductive research techniques to reexamine the problem. Such techniques reveal new insights and permit the identification of new directions for breast-feeding research.

> Research is to see what everybody has seen and to think what nobody has thought.
>
> *Albert Szent-Gyorgy*

Cultural values and assumptions guide behavior. The failure of the "health culture" to influence breast-feeding behavior worldwide can be

AUTHOR'S NOTE: Support for this work was provided by a National Health and Development Research Program Scholar Award to the author. This chapter originally appeared in Morse, J. M. (1989). "Euch, those are for your husband!" Examination of cultural values and assumptions associated with breast-feeding. *Health Care for Women International, 11*, 223-232. Reprinted with permission of Hemisphere Publishing Corporation.

accounted for if one examines the biomedical bias of past research and the cavalier attitude of practitioners who attempt to impose their biases on their clients. Of equal importance is the breast-as-sex-object edict rampant in many cultures.

In the past two decades a vast amount of infant feeding research has focused on the benefits of breast-feeding. Most of this research has been conducted in the analysis of the biochemical constituents of breast milk and the nutritional and epidemiological aspects of breast- versus bottle-feeding. Evidence of the superiority of breast milk as an infant food resulted in an international policy to support breast-feeding (World Health Organization, 1981), and since that time an enormous amount of effort, energy, and funding has been spent on educational material and programs to encourage the rate and duration of breast-feeding.

As only a limited amount of this research has been conducted by social scientists, the view of researchers is that the reluctance of women to breast-feed is a physiological and/or medical concern rather than a behavioral problem. Further, they make a clear assumption that breast-feeding rates can be increased if breast-feeding is prescribed by a medical or nursing practitioner. The success of such an approach is limited, however, and increasing the rate and duration of breast-feeding remains a public health priority. Obviously it is time to reexamine the issue and to try new approaches to understanding the phenomenon.

The first step in the development of new directions in a research program is to examine the beliefs and values inherent in current research directions and educational practices. My purpose in writing this article is to illustrate several techniques for conducting such an analysis.

In science, most critics focus on methodological issues rather than beginning by examining the research question asked. Rarely do reviewers query "Why did the researcher ask *that* question?" Although research is culture bound, researchers seldom step back and examine the assumptions underlying the research question and do the necessary soul searching to identify paradigmatic, epistemological, or disciplinary bias that may be inherent in a research program. And, most embarrassing for nursing, this examination is rarely done when we examine questions that arise from clinical practice, where habits and dictum have not been closely scrutinized and are often accepted as a given fact.

Four techniques reveal the problems of mainline thinking with humbling clarity. The first technique is to examine past research. Tracing the development of a concept or trend over time, or simply delving into the distant past to explore research from a different time, fills one with awe at the earlier researcher's lack of vision. The second technique is to conduct cross-cultural research, when in the process of examining the beliefs and practices of others one's own beliefs and values are necessarily reexamined. The third technique is to ask anthropological questions about the context of breast-feeding, and the last technique is to begin again using inductive research methods designed to elucidate the values and assumptions in research and enable the researcher to reexamine the status quo. All of these exercises may be sufficiently shattering to challenge—and to change—one's own perspective and to force one's thinking away from the comfort of orthodox research plans to the discomfort of marginality. Illustrations of each of these techniques will be presented, using examples from a value-laden topic: breast-feeding.

Historical Research

Beginning with the historical method, the first example is an illustration of a "device for breast-feeding mothers" (Figure 5.1). A patent was awarded for this contraption in 1910, but it is not known if it was ever built. The purpose of the device was to permit mothers to breast-feed without shame when their infants were hungry—a purpose that we all agree is important. The inventor, however, achieved this goal by spatially separating the breast from the rubber feeding nipple. The important point is that this invention was one solution developed in response to the Victorian modesty norm (which was interfering with breast-feeding). The implicit values behind this inventor's work are that women should not show their breasts while nursing and that the infant must not be in close contact with the mother's breast. Everyone may want one—except, perhaps, women and children.

Clearly, the research and subsequent invention cited above were influenced by prevailing mores and values. We must ask ourselves what implicit values underlie our own research. Historical research can help illuminate this by helping us understand our own background.

Cross-Cultural Research

The second technique in evaluating research is to identify cultural values and beliefs, and this is simplified by working on other cultures.

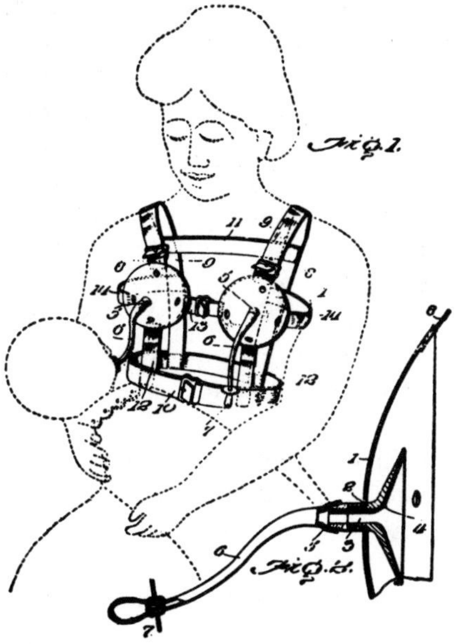

Figure 5.1. Breast-Feeding Device for Modest Mothers. (Nursing attachment, patented 15 February, 1910.) In A. E. Brown & H. A. Jeffcott, Jr., Eds. (1970). *Absolutely Mad Inventions.* New York: Dover, p. 94. Used by permission of Dover Publications, Inc.

For example, when Mead returned to the United States from fieldwork with the Mundugumor of New Guinea in 1933, she reported on the phenomenon of relactation (Mead, 1967). She wrote that she observed women who were past childbearing age or who had not been pregnant frequently stimulated lactation. When she reported that these adoptive mothers breast-fed by having the combination of the infant's suckling, forced fluids, and a definite intention, she was met with disbelief. "How do you know they produced milk?" she was challenged. And she could only reply that the "milk" was a "substance, white in color and emitted from the maternal breast, on which the infant lived and thrived." Similarly, a missionary from Fiji wrote in the 1940s that even childless Fijian women frequently suckled infants (Quain, 1948). (This missionary, incidentally, also wrote that Fijian women could not understand the stupidity of Europeans who did not know this fact [Quain, 1948, p. 353].)

As Margaret Mead noted, the skepticism with which her original observations were met "exemplifies the blindness induced by habituation within our own culture" (1967, p. 143). Not until 40 years later did relactation or the stimulation of lactation in adoptive mothers become an option for American women (Auerbach & Avery, 1981). Unfortunately, relactation is another example of reality unrecognized because the concept did not fit into the current paradigm.

Asking Questions

The next strategy of evaluation is to ask questions about our own beliefs and practices. The illustration shown in Figure 5.2 is from a book published in 1983, a book written to teach mothers how to manage breast-feeding, and this illustration is from the chapter on breast-feeding and work. As shown, this is a mother, perhaps in a nurse's uniform, sitting on a toilet expressing her breasts. At first glance this picture has a coping theme: the mother is trying to keep both her job and her milk supply. It is the only solution offered for a sticky problem.

I find it shocking! As a nurse, I bristle with horror at hygienic considerations. We do not take our coffee sitting on a toilet, yet we are *teaching* mothers to prepare their infant food in the room reserved for evacuating bodily wastes.

But let us look for a moment and ask anthropological questions about this illustration. Why is the mother in the bathroom? Is it because she has nowhere else to go to express her breasts? If so, why not? Does our culture *really* support breast-feeding? Someone (who?) has not provided mothers' rooms for nursing and, equally to blame, someone (who?) has not demanded them. Furthermore, our modesty norm has forced this mother to retreat to an undesirable place while she exposes her breasts.

Another aspect worth considering is that the mother may be in the bathroom because removing breast milk is considered an excretory function and breast milk is considered dirty and defiling. There is some evidence, though scant, for this notion. In 1983, Fallon and Rozin examined attitudes toward appropriate and inappropriate foodstuffs. On a multivariate scaling "fishing trip," they asked college students to rate many nonfoods (such as cockroaches, grass, and dirt), foods that some religions considered taboo (such as pork for Jews), and foods that often caused allergies. In this conglomerate, human milk loaded as "inappro-

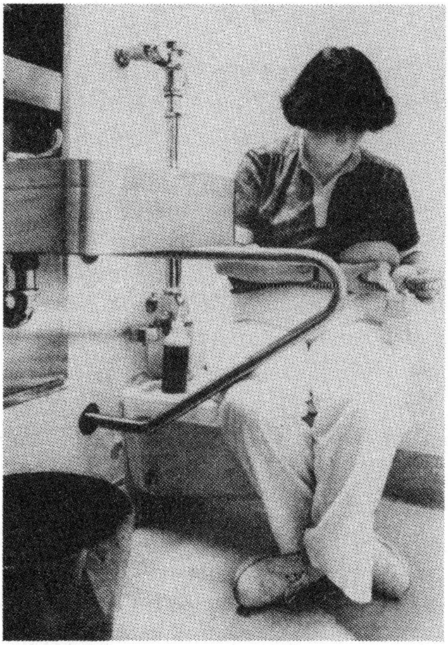

Figure 5.2. Expressing Breasts. From J. Presser, G. S. Brewer, & J. Freehand (1983). *Breastfeeding*. New York: Alfred A. Knopf, p. 105. Used by permission of Alfred A. Knopf, Inc.

priate" along with grass and dirt ($r > .8$). These, the authors suggest, are rejected because they are "not considered food." Human milk was correlated ($r = .77$) with "mild disgust" (and loaded in this category in an earlier study [Rozin & Fallon, 1980]). This category contained foods that were rejected on the *idea* of what the substance is. These foods are offensive. The thought of eating these substances causes nausea, and foods are rejected even when they are contaminated with undetectable amounts of these substances.

Why is breast milk considered a disgusting food? A graduate student tells a wonderful story that a mother reported when she asked her if she had ever tasted breast milk (Williams, personal communication, 1986). "Well," the mother replied, "one evening I wanted to make Kraft® dinner for supper, but we were out of milk. So I took one of my frozen baggies [of breast milk]. . . . Dinner was delicious! But if my husband ever found out . . . !"

I mulled over this extraordinary fact. Then, in order to prevent embarrassment, I told a class of undergraduate anthropology students to close their eyes and asked: "How many of you have ever seen breast milk?" Of more than 100 students, 6 hands went up. I asked how many could *remember* tasting breast milk, and only 3 hands remained. Isn't that strange for such a common, and essential, food? Several studies have reported that mothers may wean their infants because they believe their milk is weak.[2] *If* mothers don't know what normal breast milk looks like, the blueish watery appearance may be misconstrued as weak. Clearly, a description of breast milk must be incorporated into our teaching.

One of the priorities of infant feeding in the United States is to increase the duration of breast-feeding (Smith, 1984). Yet if mothers do not consider breast milk to be food, have not tasted it, and have not seen it, then I am not surprised that breast milk is not commonly fed to infants.

This is only conjecture. Despite the hundreds of articles written on breast-feeding annually, researchers have not scratched the surface of understanding this complex phenomenon.

In addition to examining the cultural meanings of breast milk, examinations of the beliefs, values, and norms of womens' breasts in our culture have rarely been considered in the research. The modesty norm is still a significant factor in our culture, and occasionally one reads of a woman harassed by authorities (or even arrested) for breast-feeding in a public place (Landsberg, 1983). Mothers tell us that it is the sexual connotation of *breasts* that is an important factor inhibiting breast-feeding, yet the sexual significance of the breast has been virtually ignored in breast-feeding research. We recognize that a mother's libido may decrease during nursing (Kayner & Zagar, 1983). Do husbands, noticing this, fear that a mother may prefer the stimulation received from the suckling rather than the stimulation received from sex?

When the infant becomes aware, are others afraid that the child will become sexually excited (at least subliminally) and, in future years, have an unusual attachment for his or her mother? During interviews, mothers reported:

"My mother-in-law is afraid that her grandson is turning into a sexual pervert!" (infant 10 months).

"What *is* a big boy like that doing *there*!" (husband; infant 12 months)

And one mother reported her own feelings about breast-feeding, as:

"I thought: 'Euch, those are for your husband!' "

The sexual stimulation arising from breast-feeding is rarely addressed in books on infant feeding. Yet it is possible that the worldview of fear of incest is embedded in this aspect of infant feeding. (And it is also worth considering that this is the value underlying the advice given to mothers *not* to share their bed with the infant.)

We know that infants are weaned when developmental milestones are reached (Brazelton, 1974; Clarke & Harmon, 1983; Williams, 1986). Is it possible that breast milk is sanctioned for the newborn, but when the infant acquires characteristics such as speech, the ability to walk, or teeth to eat—in short, becomes an aware *person*—then breast-feeding is no longer considered an appropriate food, and the infant is weaned? Again, these notions are conjecture. Researchers have a lot of work to do in this area.

Inductive Research

The last approach to identifying the biases and assumptions in a research program is to begin again to set aside the research of others and what is known about breast-feeding and to take a new look at what breast-feeding mothers actually do, think, and feel about breast-feeding.

An excellent example is our challenge to research that was accepted as statistically significant but that we suggest may be theoretically invalid. Although the theory of social coercion for weaning (Morse & Harrison, 1987) is yet untested, it challenges the great volume of research correlating variables in the perinatal period (such as nipple preparation, nurses' attitudes, opportunity to nurse immediately after delivery, and so forth) with the duration of breast-feeding. This theory suggests an alternative explanation: breast-feeding is a dynamic relationship involving significant others beyond the "nursing couple," and the attitudes of these "others" change toward the breast-feeding mother over the course of lactation. Initially, these significant others support the mother in her breast-feeding. But when the infant is considered "old enough to wean," these others also facilitate weaning. The *doula,* in addition to facilitating the establishment of lactation, also has a role in facilitating weaning and assists with severing the mother-infant breast-feeding relationship.

Another example concerns infant feeding patterns. Until the 1980s research examining patterns of breast-feeding had only two categories for comparison: breast-feeding and bottle-feeding. Not until the late 1970s was it noted that some mothers were using both breast-feeding and formula and that a third variable existed (i.e., mixed feeding), despite the fact that for many years clinicians supplied complementary and supplementary bottles for infants in hospitals. In our present research, using participant observation and unstructured and semistructured interview methods, we are now examining the ways that mothers combine breast-feeding and formula, known as mixed feeding (Morse & Harrison, 1988).

The implications for teaching these patterns of mixed feeding are important. Clearly, not all mothers desire or are able to totally breast-feed their infants for 6 months, as pediatricians recommend. This medical dictum demands that mothers fit their lives to the breast-feeding schedule, which is unrealistic for mothers returning to work, places the onus for successful breast-feeding on the mother and ignores the receptivity and response of the infant in the nursing relationship, and assumes that if the mother is to leave her infant's side for even a single feed, she will be able to express and leave breast milk for her infant. Given that some breast milk is better than none, mixed feeding is preferable to weaning. Identifying alternative styles of mixed feeding, such as minimal breast-feeding (Morse & Harrison, 1986; 1988), and partial and flexible breast-feeding (Morse & Harrison, 1988), and incorporating these into our teaching repertoire gives mothers the option of allowing breast-feeding to fit their lives and the option for maintaining lactation.

It is difficult to lay aside a professional facade and to learn from our clients, from expert mothers and their *doulas*. Yet by using the qualitative techniques of phenomenology, participant observation, ethnography, and grounded theory, the researcher may examine breast-feeding from the mother's perspective. Furthermore, the "training" in nursing, the learned patterns of interaction from our education, and the norms of the workplace destroy the opportunity and advantages for open and honest interaction with our patients. We are too busy to listen to what we are being told by patients, and our ethnocentric and structured methods of health assessment do not permit the flexibility to examine the situation or ourselves. We are immersed in our own culture, and it takes a special sensitivity, analysis (rather than acceptance) of published materials, and self-reflection to develop a perspective of "detached immersion" (Glaser, 1978) that allows us to link the theoretical rationale between theory and practice. And it takes guts to challenge the status quo. To challenge, not only the physicians or our fellow nurses, but the norms of our very own practice and ask: "Why did I do [or say] *that*?"

Notes

1. "Euch," a Scottish word that expresses a disgust beyond the North American "yuk." First published in Stern, P. N. (Ed.). (1989). *Pregnancy and Parenting* (pp. 185-194). Washington, DC: Hemisphere.

2. Since the publication of Gussler and Briesemeister's (1980) study on insufficient milk syndrome, researchers have focused on mother's perception of the *quantity* of breast milk, and have forgotten to examine emic categorizations of the *quality* of breast milk (for example, see Tully & Dewey, 1985). In a recent study, Williams (1986) observed that mothers delayed dieting prior to weaning, fearing that the dieting would affect infant nutrition by reducing the quality of the milk supply.

References

Auerbach, K. G., & Avery, J. L. (1981). Induced lactation: A study of adoptive nursing by 240 women. *American Journal of Diseases of Children, 135*, 340-343.

Brazelton, T. (1974). *Toddlers and parents: A declaration of independence.* New York: Delacorte.

Brown, A. E., & Jeffcott, H. A., Jr. (1970). *Absolutely mad inventions.* New York: Dover.

Clarke, S., & Harmon, R. (1983). Infant-initiated weaning from the breast in the first year. *Early Human Development, 8*, 151-156.

Fallon, A. E., & Rozin, P. (1983). The psychological bases of food rejections by humans. *Ecology of Food and Nutrition, 13*, 15-26.

Glaser, B. G. (1978). *Theoretical sensitivity.* Mill Valley, CA: The Sociology Press.

Gussler, J., & Briesemeister, L. (1980). The insufficient milk syndrome: A biocultural explanation. *Medical Anthropology 4*(2), 145-174.

Kayner, C. E., & Zagar, J. A. (1983). Breast-feeding and sexual response. *Journal of Family Practice, 17*(1), 69-73.

Landsberg, M. (1983). *Women and children first.* Markham, Ont.: Penguin.

Mead, M. (1967). Cultural patterning of perinatal behavior. In S. H. Richardson & A. F. Guttmacher (Eds.), *Childbearing: Its social and psychological implications* (pp. 142-147). Baltimore: Williams & Wilkins.

Morse, J. M., & Harrison, M. (1986). Minimal breastfeeding. *Journal of Obstetrical, Gynecological, and Neonatal Nursing, 15*(4), 333-338.

Morse, J. M., & Harrison, M. (1987). Social coercion for weaning. *Journal of Nurse Midwifery, 32*(4), 205-210.

Morse, J. M., & Harrison, M. (1988). Patterns of mixed feeding. *Midwifery, 4*, 1-5.

Presser, J., Brewer, G. S., & FreeHand, J. (1983). *Breastfeeding.* New York: Alfred A. Knopf.

Quain, B. (1948). *Fijian village.* Chicago: University of Chicago Press.

Rozin, P., & Fallon, A. E. (1980). The psychological categorization of foods and non-foods: A preliminary taxonomy of food rejections. *Appetite, 1,* 193-201.

Smith, S. J. (1984, June 13). Surgeon General urges more moms to breastfeed babies. *Times-Union,* Rochester, NY.

Tully, J., & Dewey, K. G. (1985). Private fears, global loss: A cross-cultural study of the insufficient milk syndrome. *Medical Anthropology,* 9(3), 225-243.

Williams, K. M. (1986). *Weaning patterns of primiparous mothers.* Unpublished masters thesis, University of Alberta, Edmonton.

World Health Organization. (1981). *International code of marketing of breast-milk substitutes.* Geneva: Author.

II

The Qualitative Synthesis of Research

For many years, there has been somewhat of a debate in the qualitative methodological literature about the amount of library research a researcher must do before beginning data collection. Some researchers consider the knowledge of others to be a possible contaminant, a possible source of bias, and a threat to validity. As such, seeking information beyond that required to identify the research problem or question in the first place is considered a possible risk to the inductive and creative processes inherent in qualitative research. Therefore, these researchers go into the field "untarnished," prepared to learn everything from their informants.

On the other hand, some researchers are not comfortable with such dependency on informants. They spend an inordinate amount of time in the library, intending to set out as "well prepared" as possible for their fieldwork. What is the right approach?

I can only present my opinion. That is, do what your advisor advises—unless, of course, she or he is as inattentive as "The Young Man's" teacher in Arnold van Gennep's story (see Chapter 6). It seems to me that library research must be thorough and complete enough to give the researcher the confidence and knowledge to discuss the major theoretical perspectives and to recognize whether or not data obtained are congruous or anomalous and interesting. If one stays in the library too long, the search for the elusive fact may become futile; if one avoids the library work or makes only skimpy attempts at preparation, one runs the risk of having to reinvent the wheel. This means that efforts in the field will be less fruitful than one would wish (even perhaps a waste of time), and the results are less likely to be publishable.

How much library work is required to gain an adequate knowledge base, and how does one prevent "theoretical contamination"? As good qualitative researchers *ask* only one question at a time, I shall answer the first, first.

The hardest lesson I learned as a student was that the answers to my questions were not always in the library. And more alarming—even if the answers were in the library, there was no guarantee that the answers would be complete, accurate, or even sensible. Once you realize this hard lesson, you take one step closer to acknowledging that if these respected researchers don't really know all the answers—and that theories are someone's perception of reality, or merely someone's best guess—you, as a student or as a researcher, have the same privilege of guessing, creating, or building the most plausible explanation, model, or theory about how facts fit together. In short, theory construction is anyone's game.

Once you realize that theories, by definition, are not fact, are modifiable, and are just ways of organizing reality, then the answer to the second question on "preventing contamination" becomes less threatening. It is helpful as a researcher to know and to understand so-and-so's conception of this-and-that, *if* at the same time you realize you do not have to *believe* in the theory and do not have to *accept* the formulation as fact. Rather than becoming a learning task, theories become an interesting alternative framework, as someone else's point of view. Such a detached attitude is important in qualitative research, for it enables the researcher to objectively compare and contrast various published formulations with the theory emerging from his or her own research without feeling an iota of betrayal if the "best" theory doesn't fit, or without feeling obliged to formally embrace the original theorists if the work appears reasonably correct. Such an attitude is the essence of the "bracketing" described by phenomenologists. Moreover, it goes without saying, if you have not been to the library and are unfamiliar with the work of others, your own research will move more slowly. The possible significance of every gem, every important clue in the data, will be missed by the researcher who is not both *informed* and *skeptical* of established social science theory.

Research is a conceptual process, and unless the results are pushed to some level of abstraction, the research results are less than they otherwise could be. They are less exciting, less generalizable, less interesting, less broad and more parochial. So, take a deep breath and do it. And read and remember the demise of van Gennep's eternal student.

Now for Chapter 7: Literature reviews should not simply be listings of previous work. A review should be an in-depth discussion; in short, the review itself should be a theoretical analysis and provide an interesting and possibly new perspective on the problem. Occasionally, something important is derived from assimilating literature and reflecting on the underlying assumptions of the authors. Qualitative researchers recognize that the process of synthesizing the literature and sorting piles of articles is not very different from analyzing research data. The results may be as interesting and almost as much fun as doing the real thing. And often the results are publishable.

In Chapter 7, my coauthors and I analyze the different perspectives of caring. Doing this was not a quick task nor an easy task. But we had a research team, and that made the process fun and the discussions lively. Sorting the various perspectives of caring had not been done previously in a comprehensive manner. Such a task could be accomplished, for example, by a doctoral seminar in a semester. The intellectual gains were significant when, following the analysis, the process of synthesis allowed us to feel we had control over a very large body of literature. We were critical, and, as is evident, retained the necessary skepticism.

6

The Research Topic: Or, Folklore Without End

ARNOLD VAN GENNEP

I

The Young Man, pale and earnest, at 16 read *The Future of Science,* at 17 the complete works of Nietzsche in Henri Albert's translation, and at 18 resolved to be a great scholar, all this in a continual effort to improve himself. When he had passed his matriculation examination, The Young Man left his province, registered at the Sorbonne, got his degree, and then went to his teacher and said:

"I believe I have it in me to be a great scholar. Would you please give me a research topic?"

"But of course, willingly! A research topic, you say? Very well: prepare a doctoral thesis on the Evil Eye. You know the scientific method: first you compile a complete bibliography, then you go through the literature, and eventually you make an advance in the subject. When you have done that, come back and see me. I shall then instruct you how to prepare your monograph."

II

The Young Man thanked him effusively. He was an orphan, and had an annual income of 2,400 francs. The next day, as soon as the doors

AUTHOR'S NOTE: This chapter originally appeared in van Gennep, A. (1967). *The semi-scholars* (pp. 32-36). London: Routledge & Kegan Paul. Reprinted with permission of Routledge.

opened, he went into the *Bibliothèque Nationale*, sat down in seat No. III, and started to work.

In those days neither the *Revue des Traditions Populaires* nor *Mélusine* yet existed. The Young Man therefore had to compile his bibliography volume by volume, journal by journal, title by title. After several years of uninterrupted labour, and taking advantage of the periods when the library was closed to classify his notes, The Young Man had extracted from the French literature everything that had to do with the Evil Eye.

The French facts, however, were directly connected with the facts of classical antiquity. A new effort, and all the Latin and Greek authors were reduced to notes.

The interpretation of ancient texts is often difficult. The least of them has been the object of innumerable commentaries, which a conscientious scholar could not ignore. The Young Man therefore made a bibliography of commentators, limiting himself, though, to copying the titles in Hungarian, Finnish, Basque, Albanian, and other hirsute languages, scarcely understanding what exactly they meant.

He then perceived that the Evil Eye occupied a preponderant place in the preoccupations of savages; so all the collections of voyages, all the missionary accounts, and all the ethnographical journals took their places also in his pigeon-holes. All the same, towards his thirty-fifth birthday, The Young Man concluded that his bibligraphy was "quite complete."

III

He then proceeded to the second part of his programme: going through the literature. He took out his bibliographical notes one by one, and set himself, pen in hand, to read all the French, Greek, Latin, Italian, Spanish, and German authors on whom he had made out references. This took him about twelve years.

Then he realized the necessity to learn the Scandinavian and Slavonic languages, and Finnish and Hungarian. He launched himself at this task with enthusiasm and drove the librarians mad at the *Bibliothèque Nationale*, the School of Oriental Languages, the Sorbonne, the Museum of Natural History, the *Musée Guimet*, and the International Ethnographical Institute with his pursuit of untraceable works.

This methodical life had led him to make economies; for he spent money wildly in procuring pamphlets, extracts from journals, and clippings from newspapers which, on the strength of their titles, he thought were of decisive importance.

His researches aroused interest at the School of Oriental Languages, and he was most kindly supplied with references to Armenian and Georgian publications, Chinese encylopaedias, and Turkish, Persian and Arabic manuscripts. It would have been ridiculous, shameful, and unscholarly to neglect these valuable sources of information.

The Young Man learned Arabic, Persian, Turkish, Chinese, Armenian, and Georgian; then at one go he devoured Japanese, Tibetan, Sanskrit, twenty or so languages of India, Malay, Javanese, Samoan, Maori, and Tasmanian, a dead language; finally, he assimilated the languages of the three Americas, from Eskimo to Fuegian.

By the age of fifty-four, he knew 843 languages and dialects, his bibliographical references numbered 27,000, and as for his notes he did not know exactly how many there were; at any rate, he had 22,312 cartons, each containing on the average from four to five hundred slips of paper. Some years later, he estimated roughly that there were about 12,000,000 notes in his collection.

IV

At this point he decided that the time had come to pass on to the third part of his programme: the investigation of his topic. He was afflicted, however, by a preliminary scruple. He went to unbosom himself to his teacher.

The teacher had long since retired. He lived near Paris in a tiny house with a large garden. In his house he had neither books, nor paper, nor ink. He received his visitor courteously.

"I am The Young Man," said the latter, "to whom you suggested, some years ago, a magnificent research topic."

"Oh, really? A research topic? Do tell me, what topic was that? My memory has deteriorated, and you must excuse me if I do not place you at once."

"There is nothing to be surprised at in that, sir. You told me not to come back and see you until I had reached that stage of scientific research which consists in examining the subject-matter and writing it up. Not without trouble, I am now at that point. I think I may say that I now know more than anyone else in the world about the Evil Eye."

"Ah, the Evil Eye!"

"Yes, the Evil Eye. But before writing my monograph, sir, I should like your advice on two serious questions. First, ought I to give my evidence *in extenso,* accompanying it with a commentary in note form, or ought I rather to write the commentary in a discursive style and content myself with summing up my evidence?

"Second, should I publish such evidence, either in whole or in part, in the original—Algonkin, Pali, Icelandic, Savoyard, and so on—or should I instead translate it into French, or perhaps into Latin on account of the obscene passages?"

"The grave questions that you have put to me, my dear pupil, cannot be answered without mature reflection," said the teacher. "Come back and see me one of these days, and I shall give you my opinion. It is now for me to ask you a question, though. While you have been investigating your topic, have you thought about keeping your bibliography up to date?"

V

The Young Man made a despairing gesture. Without saying a word, he went away, rushed into the main room of the *Bibliothéque Nationale*, dropped into seat No. III, which by a semisecular tradition was regarded as his quasi-property, and feverishly attempted to make up for lost time.

Death came to him in this very seat, breaking a cervical vertebra. In his will, he left his fortune and his notes to his excellent teacher. The latter accepted the money, but as for the eighteen million notes—no one knows what became of them.

7

Comparative Analysis of Conceptualizations and Theories of Caring

JANICE M. MORSE
JOAN L. BOTTORFF
WENDY NEANDER
SHIRLEY SOLBERG

Abstract: We delineated and compared various definitions of caring according to the five major conceptualizations of caring: *caring as a human trait; caring as a moral imperative; caring as an affect; caring as an interpersonal interaction; and caring as an intervention.* The implications of these diverse conceptualizations of caring for nursing practice are identified, and the commonalities, strengths and weaknesses discussed. It is concluded that caring is relatively undeveloped as a concept, has not been clearly explicated and often lacks relevance for nursing practice.

Caring is emerging as a significant concept for the nursing profession, and it is rapidly influencing nursing theory, nursing research, nursing practice and nursing education. Caring is even described as the "essence of nursing and the central, dominant and unifying feature of nursing" (Leininger, 1988, p. 152). Although caring has met with almost universal acceptance, it has received little critical comment. Perhaps this

AUTHORS' NOTE: This work originally appeared in Morse, J. M., Bottorff, J. L., Neander, W., & Solberg, S. (1991). Comparative analysis of conceptualizations and theories of caring. *Image, Journal of Nursing Scholarship, 23,* 2, 119-126. Reprinted with permission of the publisher.

acceptance is due to the fact that the concept of caring is central to nursing, and reflection in the form of a critique is not necessary. On the other hand, perhaps this acceptance is because caring is considered a "motherhood" issue and, therefore, sacrosanct, and as a result, *not* to believe in caring appears almost incomprehensible.

The few critiques that have appeared relate to the uniqueness of caring to nursing as a profession and the relevance of caring to nursing practice. Some theorists argue that caring is not unique to nursing because it is embedded in the work that women in Western society do, both inside the home and in the paid labor force. Therefore, as caring defines the activities and identities of all women, there is no justification for using caring as the basis for an "exclusive body of knowledge for a particular profession" (Lundh, Söder, & Waerness, 1988, p. 40). Dunlop (1986) questioned the claim that nursing is *the* form of caring because of the way the concept of caring is emerging in contemporary nursing theories (e.g., see Watson, 1988a) in that there is a tendency to "ignore the body and its associated physical care" (Dunlop, 1986, p. 664). It becomes difficult, if not impossible, to distinguish nursing from other "caring" professions and to see caring as a framework for guiding nursing practice. A related issue, reflected in critical examination of the research approaches advocated for the development of caring knowledge, is the identification of the most appropriate ways to develop knowledge that is applicable to nursing practice. Lundh et al. (1988) characterize nursing caring theories as "airy and consensus-oriented" (p. 40). If this is the case, the question can be raised as to whether these theories can provide the theoretical foundations for research designed to solve nursing practice problems. Ben-Sira (1990) raises a more serious issue about nursing research on caring, suggesting that if nursing continues "stressing subjectivity and rejecting the empirical approach" it might lose its standing as "an academic profession" (p. 519). She notes that Benner and Wrubel (1989) "seem to be content with a basically warm-hearted common-sense approach" rather than developing "accountable professional practices and a systematic accumulation of an experienced-based effective body of knowledge" (p. 519).

If caring is really the "essence of nursing" then it must be demonstrated and not simply proclaimed. If caring is the "central, dominant, and unifying feature of nursing," then it must be relevant to practice and to the patient and not merely an internalized feeling on the part of the nurse. Ben-Sira (1990) is correct in implying that we lose legitimacy as a profession and as a discipline if caring has no behavioral outcomes.

Finally, if caring is a theoretical basis that can facilitate nursing research and nursing practice, then the utility of caring for nursing must be evident as it is nonsensical to use a concept so vague that it threatens the scholarly base of the profession.

Examination of the caring literature reveals that the concept is diffuse, yet, to date, there has been no examination of the various perspectives that address the diversity in meaning, scope and implications for practice. Diversity may be necessary in this early stage of concept development in order for the concept to be explored and developed as fully and as richly as possible. It is important that these varying assumptions and conceptualizations of caring be explicated and that the implications of these various conceptualizations for practice be compared and analyzed. Furthermore, such criticism and analysis may shed light on any problems associated with the concept and aid in rebutting criticisms that would facilitate the development of the concept. Hence, the purpose of this article is to review critically the nursing literature pertaining to caring and to explore the implications various conceptualizations of caring have for the discipline of nursing.

When conducting this review, nursing articles describing the concept of care or caring or articles that used caring as the focus of a research project were analyzed and grouped into one of five conceptualizations of caring. The five conceptualizations originated from an analysis of the assumptions underlying or implied in authors' perspectives of caring (Morse, Solberg, Neander, Bottorff, & Johnson, 1990). In this present review, articles were categorized using these same five conceptualizations, but here the analysis was based on the author's *explicit* definitions and foci of caring and, when specified, included the processes and outcomes of caring. During this process of analysis and sorting, no new categories or conceptualizations of caring were identified; however, it is important to note that the five conceptualizations are not intended to be rigid or inflexible categories, no value judgment is intended as to the appropriateness or inappropriateness of the conceptualizations and no causal relations are implied. Whenever the author's definition of caring was broad and clearly explicated, the process of caring could be traced (often through other categories) to patient outcomes. In Table 7.1, direct linkages are indicated with a black arrow and implied or indirect linkages with an outlined arrow. If the author explored caring within a category and the definitions of caring did not extend into other categories, then this is indicated with inverted arrows.

Text continued on page 77.

TABLE 7.1 Comparative Analysis of Conceptualizations and Theories of Caring

Author(s)	*Definition*	*Linkages*	*Purposes*	*Outcome/Goal*
Caring as a Human Trait				
Griffin (1983)	• "... primary mode of being in the world, which is natural to us, and of significance in our relationships with others ..."	⇨Moral Imperative ⇨Interpersonal Interaction Therapeutic Intervention Affect	• protect the humanity of the patient • "... understand that person's emotional life; his wants, desires and priorities" (p. 291)	• restore the patient's humanity • personal growth • "... provide quality care ... that is congruent, satisfying, and beneficial ..." (1988, p. 155)
Leininger (1981, 1988)	• "...powerful means to help..."(1988, p. 152) "...actions directed toward assisting, supporting, or enabling ..."(1989, p. 156)	➡Therapeutic Intervention ⇨Affect ⇨Interpersonal Interaction ➡Patient's Subjective Experience ➡Patient's Physical Response	• "... ameliorate or improve a human condition or lifeway" (1988, p. 156)	• "... care constructs influence the health or well-being ..." (1988, p. 158)
Ray (1989)	• context dependent concept modified by "... its structures (ethical, religious/spiritual, social, educational, political, economic, legal and technological/physiological)" of the bureaucracy as a "vital part of the whole structure of humankind" (1989, p. 40)	➡Moral Imperative ⇨Interpersonal Interaction		• "... the professional ... become(s) authentically human through the human act of caring" (p. 132) • "... to improve health care to people" (1981, p. 12)
Roach (1987)	• "... the human mode of being" (p. 2) • "... synonymous with being-in-the-world" (p. 3) • "... those rare, precious moments of unique encounter when the participants recognize their common base of humanity" (p. 19)	⇨Moral Imperative ⇨Affect ⇨Therapeutic Intervention		

Caring as a Moral Imperative				
Brody (1988)	• "... a basic nursing virtue ..." (p. 88)	⇨Therapeutic Intervention ⇨Affect	• "... perform the tasks for which they are responsible because of the role they have assumed" (p. 94) • "... do what is morally right or praiseworthy" (p. 92)	• "... determine what action best demonstrates the virtues valued by ... the nursing profession" (p. 95)
Fry (1989)	• "... a fundamental value" derived from the nurse-patient relationship (p. 9)	⇨Human State	• develop a theory of nursing ethics with caring as fundamental value.	• ethical nursing behavior
Gadow (1985)	• "... attending to the 'objectness' of persons without reducing them to the moral status of objects" (p. 33)	➡Therapeutic Intervention ➡Interpersonal Interaction ...Patient's Subjective Experience	• "... overcomes objectivity by touching the self of the patient ..." (p. 41)	• "... protection and enhancement of human dignity" (1985, p. 32)
Watson (1988)	• "... involves values, a will and commitment to care, knowledge, caring actions and consequences" (p. 29)	➡Interpersonal Interaction ...Therapeutic Intervention ➡Patient's Subjective Experience	• enhance development of "a higher sense of self and harmony with his or her mind, body, and soul" (p. 70)	• "... the protection, enhancement, and preservation of the person's humanity, which helps to restore inner harmony and potential healing" (p. 58)

continued

TABLE 7.1 Continued

Author(s)	*Definition*	*Linkages*	*Purposes*	*Outcome/Goal*
Caring as an Affect				
Bevis (1981)	• " . . . a feeling of dedication to another to the extent that it motivates and energizes action to influence life constructively and positively by increasing intimacy and mutual self actualization" (p. 50)	➡Interpersonal Interaction ➡Patient's Subjective Experience	• "facilitate mutual self-actualization." • "facilitate an improvement in the cared one's state, condition, experiences, and being." • "further the caring relationship." • express feeling about the relationship" (p. 51)	• nurse and client personal growth and self-actualization. • reaching full human potential.
Fanslow (1987)	• "extension of self beyond one's job description in the patient's behalf" (p. 37)		• provides nursing care based on facts and feelings . . . " (p. 37)	
Forrest (1989)	• " . . . a mental and emotional presence that evolves from deep feelings for the patient's experience" (p. 818)		• "Being able to put oneself into the patient's position is the source for the depth of feeling which allows the nurse to 'put the patient first' in both mind and action" (p. 818)	• provides compassionate care • needs of nurse and patient are met following the compassion process.
Gendron (1988)	• "feeling that has a sensory pattern or form" (p. 5) • " . . . occurs in interaction" (p. 7). • " . . . behaviors which indicates therapeutic interest and concern" (p. 3)	⇨Therapeutic Intervention ⇨Interpersonal Interaction	• promotes growth	• personal growth
McFarlane (1976)	• "feeling of concern, of interest, of oversight, with a view for protection" (p. 189)	⇨Therapeutic Intervention	• helping, assisting with ADLs	

Caring as an Interpersonal Interaction				
Benner & Wrubel (1989)	• "... being connected ... it fuses thought, feeling and action-knowing and being" (p. 1) • "... basic way of being in the world" (p. 398)	⇨Affect ➡Therapeutic Intervention ➡Patient's Subjective Experience	• "... essential requisite for all coping" (p. 2) • enables one to be connected and concerned • "... sets up possibility of giving help and receiving help" (p. 4)	• "the one caring is enriched in the process" (p. 398)
Horner (1988)	• "... a complex interpersonal interaction between a nurse and a client, in which each perceives the other as a unique responsive individual, and which incorporates both feeling and behavioral, or commitment responses which are directed toward humanistic goals" (p. 169)		• increasing attainability of humanistic goals	• "... client identified goals, the support development, and health" (p. 171)
Knowlden (1988)	• "... an interpersonal communication between nurses and patients in which the content and the relationship aspect of the communication are integrated in the nurses' action" (p. 321)	⇨Therapeutic Intervention		
Weiss (1986)	• "... as a process that exists when the nurse harmoniously demonstrates ... verbal caring, nonverbal caring, and technically competent behavior" (p. 140)	⇨Therapeutic Intervention		• holistic caring

continued

TABLE 7.1 Continued

Author(s)	*Definition*	*Linkages*	*Purposes*	*Outcome/Goal*
Caring as Therapeutic Intervention				
Brown (1986)	• ". . . is a process occurring between patient and nurse focused on the attainment and maintenance of health or a peaceful death" (p. 58)	⇨Patient's Physical Response ➡Patient's Subjective Experience	• choose and implement an action based on knowledge, tobring about positive change	• patient perceives that he or she has been cared for, about; i.e., experiences caring
Gaut (1986)	• ". . . as an ordered series of actions beginning with goal setting and ending with implementation" (p. 79)			• changed condition judged on the basis of nursing competencies
Larson (1984)	• ". . . the acts, conduct and mannerisms enacted by professional nurses that convey to the patient concern, safety and attention" (p. 47)			• "feeling cared for, the sensation of well-being and safety that is the result of enacted behaviors of others" (p. 47)
Orem (1985)	• ". . . attention, service, and protection provided by persons in a society who are in a position that requires them to be 'in charge of' or 'take care of others." • ". . . signifies a state of mind of an individual characterized by concern for, interest in, and solicitude for another" (p. 9)	⇨Human Trait ➡Patient's Subjective Experience ➡Patient's Physical Response	• promotion of normalcy • develops self-care capacity • prevent hazards to well-being • maintain a realistic self-concept • human development • integrity of one's human structure and functioning	• achievement of optimal self-care so patient can achieve and maintain optimal health
Swanson-Kauffman (1988)	• ". . . behaviors that were perceived as caring: knowing, being with, doing for, enabling and maintaining belief" (p. 58)	⇨Interpersonal Interaction	• promote recovery • sensitive to on-going fears • supportive of patient decision. • improved patient welfare	
Wolf (1986)	• ". . . actions and attitudes" ranked highly by surveyed nurses as important to the caring process" (p. 92)			

Conceptualizations of Caring

Five conceptualizations of caring have been identified: *Caring as a Human Trait, Caring as a Moral Imperative, Caring as an Affect, Caring as an Interpersonal Interaction* and *Caring as a Therapeutic Intervention* (Morse et al., 1990). Outcomes of caring are categorized as the *Patient's Subjective Experience,* the *Patient's Physical Response* and the *Nurse's Subjective Experience,* although authors occasionally combined these categories or used more than one to describe the perceived outcomes of caring.

CARING AS A HUMAN TRAIT

Theorists in this category claim that caring is a part of human nature; that it is common to and inherent in all people (see Table 7.1). As a universal characteristic, caring is generally perceived to be a basic constant characteristic that forms the foundation of human society. Caring is considered necessary for human survival—an essential component of being human.

Although caring is considered a part of being human, these theorists use different levels of analysis to describe caring; for example, caring characteristics of groups or caring between individuals. Two theorists, Leininger (1988) and Ray (1989) allow for differences in caring expressions or emphasis between human *groups.* Leininger (1988) uses cultural variation to explain that different caring expressions or emphases form different and unique caring modalities and cultural patterns of care in different cultural groups. By suggesting that the provision of culturally congruent care is the responsibility of nursing (and that violating the client's norm is ethnocentric and non-therapeutic), Leininger (1988) considers caring the motivator of nursing action and the basis for providing culturally congruent nursing interventions. Although the outcome of Leininger's Theory of Cultural Care Diversity and Universality is cited as "health" (and thus classified for purposes of this review as extending into the *Patient's Subjective* and *Physical Response* categories), this has not been demonstrated clearly.

On the other hand, Ray (1989) uses the organizational structure in which caring occurs to define caring. She offers a broad conceptualization of caring in her theory, placing caring within the larger framework of the bureaucratic or organizational context in which it occurs. Beginning with a substantive theory, Differential Caring, she developed a formal theory, Bureaucratic Caring. Caring seems not only to be differentiated according to the roles and positions of people within the organization, but also within specific clinical units. Although Ray (1989) studied non-nurses as well as nurses, the implications are that nurses working on oncology units would use different descriptors to identify caring than nurses working in the emergency department because different structural components (i.e., legal, social, political, ethical, spiritual) are more important to one area than to another area. At this stage, the theory of Bureaucratic Caring raises important issues that are related to patient care; for example, how decisions are made in a bureaucracy and what types of policies are needed to enhance the human perspective in the corporation (Ray, 1989).

A second group of theorists in this category, Griffin (1980, 1983) and Roach (1987), describe caring as "an essential way of being." Griffin (1983) considers caring a part of the essence of humanness; the major aspects of caring in nursing are complementary "activities and attitudes and feelings mediated through the nurse-patient relationship" (p. 291). Thus, nurse activities may be called *caring* because they are "performed in a certain way; as the expression of particular emotions" (p. 192). Similarly, Roach (1987) recognizes that caring is "the most common, authentic criterion of humanness" (p. 2) and, in addition, emphasizes the knowledge, skills and experience (manifest as the "five C's": "Compassion, Competence, Confidence, Conscience and Commitment" [p. 58]) that make caring unique *in* nursing.

For the outcome of the caring interaction, both Griffin (1983) and Roach (1987) focus on the experience of the nurse. Although Griffin (1983) alludes to the patient as the "receiver of care," the nurse, as the "giver of care," is the primary beneficiary, accruing such benefits as "increased powers of perception" (p. 293) and an "increased sense of personal worth" (p. 294). As an educator, Roach (1987) emphasizes the need for educational programs to professionalize the human capacity to care. To the degree that this is achieved, "what is done for others will be authentic service; and what the professional does for him- or herself is to become authentically human through the human act of caring" (p. 132).

CARING AS A MORAL IMPERATIVE

Theorists in this category consider caring to be a "moral virtue," and they are concerned about patient good and maintaining the dignity and respect of patients as *people*. Brody (1988), Gadow (1985), and Watson

(1988a) consider caring as a foundation for nursing practice whereas, Fry (1989) believes caring is basic to humanity in general. According to Brody (1988), the value of caring for the nurse is that caring enables the nurse to identify appropriate actions. Gadow (1985) and Watson (1988a) are more patient-focused, suggesting that the ultimate purpose of caring is to "preserve the *dignity* of the patient" (Gadow, 1985) or to preserve the "individual's humanity, inner harmony and potential healing" (Watson, 1988a). Gadow (1985) is pragmatic and brings caring theory directly to the practice setting: "In the caring relationship, the body is regarded-and-touched-by the nurse as the immediate, lived reality of the patient" (p. 40). On the other hand, Watson (1988a) views caring as a moral ideal and she considers "caring actions themselves and the various ways caring is revealed are not so much instances of caring *per se* as approximations of caring" (p. 34). This view places "true caring" on a pedestal and renders it unattainable.

Watson's (1988a) Theory of Human Care emphasizes mutual, reciprocal and interactive experiences directed toward the preservation of humanity. A caring factor or intervention "affirms the subjectivity of persons and leads to positive change for the welfare of others" (p. 74-75). This change is simultaneously reflected in the mental and spiritual growth of the nurse which she describes as "finding meaning in one's own existence and experiences, discovering inner power and control and potentiating instances of transcendence and self-healing" (p. 74).

Brody (1988) considers caring as a central virtue in nursing and focuses on the nurse as the "moral agent" (p. 88). She uses caring to demonstrate how "virtue ethics" (defined as a personal attribute, actions reflective of the nurse's personal nature and actions that meet the nurse's role obligations) can be applied to nursing practice. From a similar ethical perspective, Fry (1989) conceptualizes caring as a common value for the nursing profession with the goal of "enhancing human dignity." She argues that foundation values in nursing, rather than being a derivative value of some *obligation* in nursing (similar to the physician's "obligation to do good" [p. 16]), should be derived from "the nature of the nurse-patient relationship instead of from models of patient good" (p. 9) (as in medicine). She also suggests that caring is a foundation and central value from which a theory of nursing ethics must evolve. Although she stresses that caring "seems to be more than a mere behavior between nurse and patient" (p. 18), this theory is undeveloped.

The refinement of such a theory has the potential to guide nursing decision making and actions.

CARING AS AN AFFECT

From this perspective, theorists argue that caring *is* an affect. They describe caring as an emotion, as a feeling of compassion or empathy for the patient which motivates the nurse to provide care for the patient. They suggest that these feelings must be present in order for the nurse to care. Whether the patient's condition improves or a peaceful death occurs, the nurse benefits from *caring* for the patient, and alternatively, the nurse may experience the "emotional burden that arises as a result of caring" (Forrest, 1989, p. 822). Although they do not emphasize or encompass *therapeutic interventions* in their conceptualizations of caring, the "forms" of caring described by Fanslow (1987), Gendron (1988), Forrest (1989), and to a lesser extent McFarlane (1976), remain nurse-centered.

Gendron's (1988) central thesis is that the expressive form of the caring emotion or feeling must be sincere and expressed in an appropriate form and is congruent with the underlying emotion. Therefore, a part of the art of nursing is the "ability of the nurse to become skilled in creating the forms which express caring" (p. 6). The means by which nurses acquire this depth of feeling are described by Forrest (1989) as "being able to put oneself into the patient's position," which "allows the nurse to 'put the patient first' both in mind and action" (p. 818).

One of the earliest caring theorists, McFarlane (1976), argues that nursing is "virtually synonymous with caring" (p. 187). Although agreeing that caring is a feeling of "concern, of interest and oversight with a view to protection" (p. 189), she differs from the other theorists in this category in that she clearly states that caring consists of acts of "helping and assisting with daily living activities which may be simple or complex" (p. 187).

CARING AS AN INTERPERSONAL INTERACTION

From this perspective, caring is a mutual endeavor between the nurse and the patient. When caring occurs, both parties must be communicative, trusting, respectful and committed to each other. The reciprocal interaction means that as the patient is enriched, so is the nurse. Three theorists, Horner (1988), Knowlden (1988), and Weiss (1988), consider caring to be an interpersonal interaction with the patient. They emphasize the integration of feelings and actions in the caring encounter so that the nursing intervention that is administered *caringly* is qualitatively different than a noncaring encounter. However, Horner (1988) and Knowlden (1988) view the process as occurring between the nurse and client, whereas Weiss (1988), in her study using manipulated role playing of nurse-patient interactions, focuses entirely on the nurse. In her analysis, Weiss examined the integration of verbal caring, nonverbal caring and technically competent behaviors.

Benner and Wrubel (1989) define caring as thoughts, feelings and actions—being "connected and concerned" with the client so that caring "sets up the possibility of giving and receiving help" (p. 4). Further, they suggest that caring helps the client cope and enables them to successfully deal with whatever they find stressful and find meaning in the situation. The reciprocal nature of caring is evident as the nurse "is enriched in the process" (p. 398).

CARING AS A THERAPEUTIC INTERVENTION

Theorists who view caring as a therapeutic intervention are patient centered: the patient must demonstrate needs that the nurse can meet, and generally, the nursing occurs (and the patient improves) regardless of *how the nurse feels.* The patient's goals are paramount and the nursing care is aimed at meeting those goals. Thus, these theorists also emphasize nursing competencies and skill related to caring. For example, Gaut (1986) considers caring to be an "intentional human enterprise" and explicitly states that "any action may be described as caring if and only if the carer (S) has identified a need for care and knows what to do for X (the one cared for); S chooses and implements an action intended to serve as a means for positive change in X; and the welfare of X or what is generally considered good for X is used to justify the choice and implementation of the activities identified as caring" (p. 78).

Theorists in this category are task oriented; their descriptions of caring are discrete actions that could be identified as caring. For example, Brown (1986) describes caring as "recognition of individual qualities and needs" the nurse uses to modify her nursing actions—the patterns and process of care—to "fit the unique needs of the individual" (p. 58). Specific caring actions have been identified and include some of the following tasks and activities; being present in a reassuring manner, providing information, assisting with pain, spending time with the patient, promoting autonomy and observing the patient (Larson, 1984; Swanson-Kauffman, 1988; Wolf, 1986).

The most highly developed theory in this category is Orem's (1985) theory of self-care. She argues that self-care is necessary for the maintenance of life (p. 84), linking the outcome of "deliberate action" nurses provide a "helping service" (Orem, 1985, p. 38), which is aimed at regulating the individuals' capacities to engage in self-care. She views the achievement of optimal self-care as essential for the maintenance of health.

As summarized in Table 7.2, an examination of these five conceptualizations of caring reveals that each type of caring has distinct characteristics. To some extent, the complexity of the concept of caring is captured by the diversity of these conceptualizations. Comparisons across the five conceptualizations indicate differences related to the focus, purpose and variability of each of these.

Issues

As a result of the preceding analysis, additional characteristics emerged and raised questions that further illustrated the diversity of conceptualizations of caring among theorists. These characteristics included the uniqueness of caring in nursing, the constant or varying nature of the caring capacity of nurses, whether caring may be reduced to behavioral tasks and whether the outcome of caring influences or affects the nurse, the patient, or both (See Table 7.3).

Is caring unique in nursing? This question is critical *if* caring is to attain and/or retain a central position in the development of nursing theory. Surprisingly, there is disagreement among nurse theorists regarding the uniqueness of caring in nursing. Although some agree that caring is unique *in* nursing, several theorists (Benner & Wrubel, 1989; Bevis, 1981; Fry, 1989; Horner, 1988) do not consider caring to be unique in nursing. For example, Benner and Wrubel (1989) state, "Caring practices are lived out in this culture primarily in parenting, child care, nursing, education, counseling and various forms of community life" (p. 408). Others, Bevis (1981), Fry (1989), and Horner (1988), emphasize the universality of caring as opposed to attempting to identify the unique characteristics of caring in nursing.

TABLE 7.2 The Major Components of Five Perspectives on Caring

Human Trait	*Moral Imperative*	*Affect Interaction*	*Interpersonal Intervention*	*Therapeutic*
Essential for being human	Foundational basis—Nurse virtue	Empathy, feeling and concern for another	An exchange characterized by respect and trust	Nursing actions that meet patient's needs
Universal	Nurse-centered	Nurse-centered	Mutual involvement	Patient-centered
Necessary for survival	Maintain dignity of patients	Nurse must feel compassion to be able to nurse	Develop a type of intimate relationship	Implementation meets patient's goals
Essential way of being	Guides decision making, provides the "oughts" behind the "shoulds"	Feeling motivates the nurse; Nurse feels better when able to nurse	Process that can enhance growth of both patient and nurse	If actions are appropriate, the patient improves regardless of how nurse feels
Constant, long-lasting	Constant concern for patient	Nursing is defined in relation to affect. However, affect may vary with kind of patient, stage of relationship, and/or situational demands	Is likely to vary with ability or desire of patient to be involved with nurse and situational demands	Varies with situational demands and in relation to knowledge and skill of nurse

TABLE 7.3 Author's Perceptions of Selected Characteristics of Caring

Is caring unique in nursing?

Yes		*No*	
Brody	Roach	Benner & Wrubel	Horner
Knowlden	Watson	Bevis	Ray
Leininger		Fry	
McFarlane		Griffin	

Does the caring intent of nursing vary between patients?

Yes	*No*	
Griffin	Brody	Gendron
Horner	Fanslow	Leininger
Ray	Fry	Watson

Can caring be reduced to behavioral tasks?

Yes	*No*	
Brown	Benner & Wrubel	Gadow
Gaut	Bexis	Griffin
Larson	Brody	Horner
Leininger	Fanslow	Knowlden
Orem	Forrest	Roach
Swanson-Kauffman	Fry	Watson
Weiss		
Wolf		

Does the outcome of the caring affect:

The patient?	*The nurse?*	*Both the patient and the nurse?*
Brown	Brody	Benner & Wrubel
Gaut	Fanslow	Bevis
Gendron	Forrest	Gadow
Larson	Fry	Griffin
Leininger	Roach	Horner
Orem		Watson
Swanson-Kauffman		
Wolf		

Does the caring intent of nursing vary? This question considers whether caring is a constant and unchanging motivator within the nurse regardless of characteristics of the patient. Again, several theorists agree that the intent to care changes according to the patient's characteristics or other variables. This position has received some support from Kahn and Steeves's (1988) study of the meaning of the caring relationship for nurses. While the majority of the informants (who were nurses) believed that caring should be an unconditional aspect of nursing, they provided many examples that indicated that caring depended upon "having enough time, getting along with each other and not having too many other demands" (p. 213). Examples in this study show that nurses found it easier to care for patients that they liked. The authors state that "nurses indicated that those patients who made it easier for them to do the caring activities, to engage in praxis, more readily illicited caring" (p. 214). Nurses have also reported that patients use strategies, including giving manipulative gifts and using behaviors, such as making themselves "no trouble," so that nurses will be more willing to care for them during their illness (Morse, 1991). Watson (1988b) advocates that while caring at the "surface level" may vary in relation to situational factors, caring in nursing at the moral and philosophical level "is underpinned by a moral stance that goes beyond the like or dislike of a patient . . . to touch the human center of the person" (p. 218). Thus, from this perspective, *if* caring is held as a moral ideal in nursing, *then* the forms of caring may vary due to external constraints, such as the amount of time the nurse and patient have together, while the caring intent remains constant.

Can caring be reduced to behavioral tasks? If caring is to be considered measurable and intervention studies and evaluation research developed, this question is critical. Theorists who view caring as a moral ideal unanimously agree that caring is not reflected in a set of techniques but provides the stance from which one intervenes as a nurse, thereby influencing judgments, decision making and action. Brody (1988) states, "It is not just the competent performance of technical skills that evokes the image of caring, but the compassionate attitudes and feelings of the nurses toward the patient as they perform their tasks that is the essence of caring" (p. 92). With the exception of McFarlane (1976), theorists who view caring as an affect do not consider the behavioral tasks of nurses as characteristic of caring: "Caring involvement and interaction incorporates on the part of the nurse a preference for 'being with' rather than 'doing to' a patient" (Forrest, 1989, p. 818).

Not surprisingly, all the theorists who were included in the therapeutic intervention category considered caring as specific nursing actions. These actions were both indicators of caring and evidence that caring had taken place. Some of these theorists were quite specific in the delineation of caring tasks (Brown, 1986; Orem, 1985), while others used a more global approach (Leininger, 1981, 1988; Swanson-Kauffman, 1988).

Does the outcome of the caring affect the patient, the nurse, or both? With the exception of the theorists who view caring as a therapeutic intervention, there was no clear pattern in the caring outcomes for either the nurse or the patient. Nurse outcomes that were identified included personal enrichment (Benner & Wrubel, 1989), increased understanding, emotional capacity, sense of personal worth (Griffin, 1983) and increased emotional burdens (Forrest, 1989). When mutual outcomes are discussed these theorists indicate that both the nurse and patient experience self-actualization (Bevis, 1981), enhanced subjectivity (Gadow, 1985) or increased spirituality (as reflected by Watson, 1988a). Watson (1988a) states: "In a transpersonal caring relationship a spiritual union occurs between the two persons where both are capable of transcending self, time, space and the life history of each other" (p. 66). On the other hand, theorists who describe the outcomes of caring in terms of patient responses include enhanced health, well being, comfort, self-integration and patient satisfaction. For these theorists, the goal of caring would be to affect a desirable outcome in the patient. That outcome could be in terms of a subjective experience on the part of the patient or some actual physical response that could be measured. For example, Gaut (1986) operationalizes her conceptualization of caring with an example; that is, ensuring a patient recovering from surgery is adequately hydrated.

The different qualities of power associated with caring are emphasized by Benner (1984). Some qualities—the transformative, integrative, advocacy and healing qualities of the power of caring—have a direct bearing on patient outcomes. For instance, nurses who cared for patients with prolonged and permanent disabilities have been instrumental in "assessing the importance of helping the patient to continue with normal activities to minimize the isolation, loss of meaning and inactivity . . . [and nurses have] offered the option of reintegration by providing the patients and families with new possibilities in the midst of deprivation and loss" (p. 211). On the other hand, the power of creative problem solving associated with caring provides effective care and, indirectly influence patient outcomes. The power of caring has not been recognized fully by nurses who see their caring role as a source of their powerlessness; yet, as argued by Benner (1984), any definition of power for nursing must include the power that resides in caring.

Discussion

If caring is the "essence of nursing," then the issue of which theoretical perspective of caring is most descriptive of this essence is vital. Given the present diversity in the conceptualizations of caring, all of the attempts to delineate caring may have some application to the central paradigm of nursing. Presently, the concept is poorly developed, and as a result it may not be comprehensive enough to encompass *all* the components of caring that are necessary to guide clinical practice. There remains a loose link between many definitions of caring and patient outcomes. In particular, the previously unspoken controversy concerning whether caring may be reduced to behavioral tasks and the underdeveloped links to specific patient outcomes form the Achilles' heel of caring theory. If the relevance of caring to practice and to the patient cannot be clearly explicated, or *if* it is claimed that caring cannot be reduced to behavioral tasks, *and* if caring is the essence of nursing, then nursing no longer will be a practice discipline. Either the central core of nursing will need to be reformulated or the gap between theory and practice will be widened to insurmountable proportions.

This analysis of caring literature was exceedingly difficult, due in part to the paucity of definitions of caring and a lack of clarity in describing caring. Further, some of the difficulty was due to the way the ideas about caring were presented. For example, "we offer descriptions of how nurses help patients to recover caring, to appropriate meaning, and to maintain or reestablish connection" (Benner & Wrubel, 1989, pp. 2-3). Gendron (1988) overuses metaphor in her descriptions. She writes: "In caring behaviors, the characteristic quality of polarity is positive, and that of temperature is warmth" (p. 10). And Watson (1988a) writes: "The art of transpersonal caring in nursing as a moral ideal is a means of communication and release of human feelings through *coparticipation of one's entire self in nursing*" (p. 70, emphasis added). Such obfuscation increases confusion. There is a need for theoretical preciseness, clarity and parsimony, especially when describing such complex concepts as *care* and *caring*.

Does caring take place with individuals or groups? This may not be an either/or question. Perhaps the question to ask is: *If caring occurs at the group or population level, how do these caring strategies differ from the individual level?* For instance, caring is well described between individuals, with most of the caring theorists focusing on the interaction at this level. Leininger (1988) and Ray (1989) write on caring at the societal and institutional levels respectively, but, theorists have not described caring at the family or the community level. These aspects need further development. It is interesting that despite the volume of literature on support systems and family nursing, caring theorists have not addressed directly caring for families and have not delineated small group caring strategies.

There is room for further enrichment of the conceptualizations of caring. For the researcher, the various conceptualizations of caring appear to be inextricably linked with research method. It is with concern that a new trend is evolving in the role of nurse theorists and theory *testing*. Earlier, nurse-theorists were content with theory construction and critique, leaving theory testing to an independent cadre of nurse-researchers. With the emergence of qualitative methods and the extraordinarily large number of caring theorists skilled in qualitative research methods, the roles of theorist and researcher are merging. One would expect, therefore, that caring theories would be developed inductively from qualitative data. However, with the exception of Benner and Wrubel (1989), Ray (1987), and, in part, Leininger (1988), this is not occurring. Some caring theorists find themselves in a conflicting position. While supporting the strength of inductive theory development, they are developing theory deductively and violating standard procedure by using qualitative methods to test their own theories (Watson, 1988a). They advocate this position on the basis that the underlying assumptions of qualitative research are more compatible with the phenomena of caring. Perhaps the problem that is contributing to the lack of progress in the development of knowledge related to caring is the premature development of deductive theory and/or the use of qualitative methods to test or explicate caring theory.

These criticisms are germane for the scientific development of the concept of caring. It goes without saying that those who are studying caring using philosophical (including ethical) and historical approaches are also making a substantial contribution to the development of caring knowledge. It is imperative that dialogue continue among all caring researchers, but for progress to be made, this dialogue must also include debate.

References

Benner, P. (1984). *From novice to expert.* Menlo Park, CA: Addison Wesley.

Benner, P., & Wrubel, J. (1989). *The primacy of caring: Stress and coping in health and illness.* Menlo Park, CA: Addison Wesley

Ben-Sira, Z. (1990). Book review [Review of *The primacy of caring: Stress and coping in health and illness*]. *Social Science and Medicine, 30,* 517-519.

Bevis, E. O. (1981). Caring: A life force. In M. M. Leininger (Ed.), *Caring: An essential human need. Proceedings of Three National Caring Conferences* (pp. 49-59). Thorofare, NJ: Charles B. Slack.

Brody, J. K. (1988). Virtue ethics, caring and nursing. *Scholarly Inquiry for Nursing Practice: An International Journal, 2,* 87-101.

Brown, L. (1986). The experiences of care: Patient perspectives. *Topics in Clinical Nursing, 8,* 56-62.

Dunlop, M. J. (1986). Is a science of caring possible? *Journal of Advanced Nursing, 11,* 661-670.

Fanslow, J. (1987). Compassionate nursing care: Is it a lost art? *Journal of Practical Nursing, 37*(2), 40-43.

Forrest, D. (1989). The experience of caring. *Journal of Advanced Nursing, 14,* 815-823.

Fry, F. T. (1989). Toward a theory of nursing ethics. *Advances in Nursing Science, 11*(4), 9-22.

Gadow, S. A. (1985). Nurse and patient: The caring relationships. In A. H. Bishop & J. R. Scudder (Eds.), *Caring, curing, coping* (pp. 31-43). Birmingham: University of Alabama Press.

Gaut, D. A. (1986). Evaluating caring competencies on nursing. *Topics in Clinical Nursing, 8,* 77-83.

Gendron, D. (1988). *The expressive form of caring.* Toronto: University of Toronto Press.

Griffin, A. P. (1980). Philosophy and nursing. *Journal of Advanced Nursing, 5,* 261-272.

Griffin, A. P. (1983). A philosophical analysis of caring in nursing. *Journal of Advanced Nursing, 8,* 289-295.

Horner, S. (1988). Intersubjective co-presence in a caring model. In *Caring and nursing explorations in the feminist perspective* (pp. 166-180). Denver: Center for Human Caring, University of Colorado Health Sciences Centre.

Kahn, D. L., & Steeves, R. H. (1988). Caring and practice: Construction of the nurse's world. *Scholarly Inquiry For Nursing Practice, 2,* 201-216.

Knowlden, V. (1988). Nurse caring as constructed knowledge. In *Caring and nursing explorations in the feminist perspective* (pp. 318-339). Denver: Center for Human Caring, University of Colorado Health Sciences Centre.

Larson, P. J. (1984). Important nurse caring behaviors perceived by patients with cancer. *Oncology Nursing Forum, 11*(6), 46-50.

Leininger, M. M. (1981). The phenomenon of caring: Importance, research questions and theoretical considerations. In M. M. Leininger (Ed.), *Caring: An essential human need* (pp. 3-16). Thorofare, NJ: Charles B. Slack.

Leininger, M. M. (1988). Leininger's theory of nursing: Cultural care diversity and universality. *Nursing Science Quarterly, 1,* 152-160.

Lundh, U., Söder, M., & Waerness, K. (1988). Nursing theories: A critical view. *IMAGE: Journal of Nursing Scholarship, 20,* 36-40.

McFarlane, J. (1976). A charter for caring. *Journal of Advanced Nursing, 1,* 187-196.

Morse, J. M. (1991). Commitment and involvement in the patient-nurse relationship. *Journal of Advanced Nursing, 16,* 455-468.

Morse, J. M., Solberg, S. M., Neander, W. L., Bottorff, J. L., & Johnson, J. L. (1990). Concepts of caring and caring as a concept. *Advances in Nursing Science, 13* (1), 1-14.

Orem, D. E. (1985). *Nursing: Concepts of practice.* Chevy Chase, MD: McGraw-Hill.

Ray, M. A. (1989). The theory of bureaucratic caring for nursing practice in the organizational culture. *Nursing Administration Quarterly, 13*(2), 31-42.

Roach, M. S. (1987). *The human act of caring: A blueprint for health professions.* Toronto: Canadian Hospital Association.

Swanson-Kauffman, K. (1988). Caring needs of women who miscarried. In M. Leininger (Ed.), *Care discovery and uses in clinical and community nursing* (pp. 55-70). Detroit: Wayne State University Press.

Watson, J. (1988a). *Nursing: Human science and human care. A theory of nursing.* New York: National League for Nursing.

Watson, J. (1988b). Response to "Caring and practice: Construction of the nurse's world." *Scholarly Inquiry for Nursing Practice: An International Journal, 2,* 217-221.

Weiss, C. J. (1988). Model to discover, validate, and use care in nursing. In M. M. Leininger (Ed.), *Care: Discovery and uses in clinical and community nursing* (pp. 139-149). Detroit: Wayne State University Press.

Wolf, Z. R. (1986). The caring concept and nurse identified caring behaviors. *Topics in Clinical Nursing, 8,* 84-93.

III

Phenomenology

I cannot imagine doing a phenomenological study without "knowing something" personally about the phenomenon I was interested in pursuing. The phenomenological method is one of direct inquiry in which constant questioning provides further insights into the lived experience. This forces the researcher to delve deeper into the essence of the topic by pursuing every aspect. The process of inquiry is moved along by writing and rewriting during the process of reflection. The writings of other phenomenologists stimulate thought and these contributions are incorporated as data into the text.

What does the result look like? What is special about phenomenology, which we glibly describe as "getting to the essence" of the meaning?

Excellent phenomenology touches us; it reaches our own souls, beneath the part of us that superficially declares, "that's it!" so important to the validation process in grounded theory or ethnoscience. We may never have had birthing pains, been up at night with an asthmatic child, or watched over a child going through the excruciating jeopardy of cardiac surgery. The power of phenomenology is in the sharing, not because the experience is shared, but because the glimpses of pain, indecision, and uncertainty revealed by the writer during his or her own exploration are imprinted on our souls. It is the uniqueness of living that is vital, that makes our life ours, and that is sought in phenomenological expression. It is that task of exploration, reflection, and expression that permits our understanding, our insight. Yet, because of this, phenomenology is the antithesis of ethnography. Phenomenologists do not seek the human common differences, but seek the differences that make us common, that make us human.

Look for the person, the "I," in these three examples. By reading phenomenology we share and at some level identify with the experience. Is that sharing a kind of generalizability? What other ways do phenomenologists ensure that their writings are generalizable?

8

Birthing Pain

VANGIE KELPIN

Birth is the art and mystery of women. We regard birth with awe; we are breathless, silent as we await the first breath of the baby. As women we birth, we become mothers, mothers like our own mothers, like other women who have carried and birthed a child, and like our daughters who someday will carry and birth our grandchildren. As we come face to face with birthing, we come face to face with pain. The pangs of childbirth accompany the opening of our bodies to allow the passage of the baby into life in the world. Looking at the experience of birthing pain may give us more clues to understanding our nature as women, our relationship to ourselves and others, our attachment to our children, and our place in the cycle of human life: birth, death, and rebirth.

"The pains of labour," says Rich (1976), "have a peculiar centrality for women, and for women's relationship—both as mothers and simply as female beings—to other kinds of painful experience" (p. 15). What do the pains of birth tell us about ourselves, about our sufferings and our joys? Is there something in the pangs of childbirth which holds true for all women: those who pleasure and ride above the pain? those who endure it? and those who suffer? Some birthings are short and intense, some are long and exhausting, and some need medical intervention and treatment with forceps, medication, or Caesarean delivery. Is it possible that viewing pain-as-lived may reveal the sublimity and joy as well as the agony, the hurtfulness of the pain of childbirth? Our immediate

AUTHOR'S NOTE: This chapter originally appeared in Kelpin, V. (1984). Birthing pain. *Phenomenology + Pedagogy: A Human Science Journal, 2*, 2, 178-187. Reprinted with permission of Vangie Bergum.

appraisal of pain-as-experienced may bring to light inner meanings that go beyond theoretical and practical approaches. By coming to an understanding of the pain as experienced by women, we may be able to come to grips with the significance or essence of the pain.

In order to let the meaning of birthing pain show itself as it presents itself in lived experience, we must let go, for a moment at least, of some of our assumptions. For pain to show itself as it presents itself directly and primordially, we must be set free from held notions in order to attune ourselves to hear what the experience itself tells us. These assumptions, theories, and explanations about pain in childbirth may include:

1. The idea that pain should be denied. As childbirth educators we have thought that by removing the word "pain" from the language of birthing, we will prepare women to take a more positive posture and therefore experience more readily the challenge and joy of the birth. Some of us talk of "contractions"; others refer to "rushes" or to "discomfort" to mean the experienced pain. While a woman's positive attitude is important, denial of pain may create expectations not borne out in reality. What is being denied in the denial of birthing pain?

2. The idea that pain must be relieved. The belief that pain must be relieved pervades our society: from the advertisement of "over-the-counter" drugs to the medical need to "give something for the pain." Although we agree that human suffering must be reduced, let us stand back from our expectation that avoidance of pain is a primary and valuable goal. Rich (1976) suggests that this notion "is a dangerous mechanism, which can cause us to lose touch not just with our painful sensations but with ourselves" (p. 152). What do we take away in relieving the woman from birthing pain?

3. The assumption that pain is only negative. Childbirth pain is a normal accompaniment of birthing and may arise from dilation of the cervix, the contraction and distension of the uterus, distension of the outlet, vulva, and perineum, and other factors such as pressure on the bladder, rectum, and other pain sensitive structures in the pelvis (Bonica, 1975). The fact that birthing is now a medical event, occurring in an atmosphere associated with sickness and death, supports our underlying belief that pain is associated with disease. As the experience of birthing pain is normal and is associated with life, one questions the value or, indeed, the possibility of comparing birthing pain to the pain of cancer, or arthritis (Melzack, Taenzer, Feldman, & Kinch, 1980). Can pain be shown to be a positive experience?

4. The assumption that pain can be explained. There are theories that explain pain physically, psychologically, sociologically, and culturally. These theories and explanations contribute to our understanding of pain, but they also fragment our sense of wholeness of the pain experience. Exploring the essence of birthing pain is an attempt to grasp that primordial wholeness of the experienced pain. What is the nature of this experiential wholeness?

By freeing ourselves from these and other assumptions, we may again bring to awareness what the painful experience itself shows us about the nature of its painfulness. What then is the pain of birthing? How can we interpret the seeming senselessness of the pain? Can we find meaning in the pain for ourselves as women, for ourselves as mothers, and further, but not discussed here, for the new beings born out of the pain? To find the essence, we must turn to the immediate, original experience of the phenomenon of birthing pain.

Birthing Pain

> Let the vexed rejoice in the house of the one in travail!
> As the Bearing one gives birth,
> May the mother of the child bring forth by herself!
>
> (Meltzer, 1981, p. 19)

Women[1] say that the pain of childbirth is powerful, intense, overwhelming, cramp-like, stretching, burning, pressuring, tiring, and exhausting. They say,

> I withdrew into myself, had few thoughts.
>
> I was immersed in a physical sensation, with lack of awareness of time, or what was going on around me.
>
> I tried to find a comfortable position, was impatient, angry, and shaking.
>
> I feared that I wouldn't be able to stand the pain, which would be to lose myself and maybe even die. I screamed, or wanted to scream, to bite on something, I cried because it hurt so much.
>
> I didn't know what to do and needed someone to help me.
>
> I was brought to the core of myself, pitted against myself.

In exploring these descriptions, it must continually be remembered that, as Buytendijk (1961) reminds us, birth pangs, however violent, are connected to the birth of a child and are experienced in relation to this objective event: As one woman recalled, "I reached down and took him out . . . put him on my belly . . . I couldn't take my eyes off him."

We will explore the experiential structure of the birthing pain by listening to the original (etymological) speaking of language and to the language of the voices of women as they attempt to re-achieve a direct contact with their own experience.

Bearing

The origin[2] of the word "birth," from the Old Norse *burdhr* or *bher,* means to carry, to bear children. The carrying, the holding of the child, the woman-body-vessel (Neumann, 1955) is the nature of life. The nature of life for woman, as the carrying vessel, is the source of distress and pain and also the source of joy. As a woman, I *am* this body, I *am* this pain, I *am* this joy. This symbol is vividly understood in the birthing experience. Is it possible that non-acceptance of the pain or the fear of pain comes as a result of alienation from our own bodies, fear of our helplessness, fear of our dependence, and fear of our own behavior? One woman said:

> The pain is powerful, overwhelming. I feared that I couldn't handle it. My anxieties related to how I would perform.

The fear and anxiety of this truly female experience stand in the way of drawing on the fundamental source of life and spirit we have. Fear of the pain may be a result of tales, anecdotes, literature, and medical approaches to childbirth. Until recently, the written texts about birth were from the hands and minds of men who had observed and described but had not experienced. The knowledge and support that was originally available to women, from mother to daughter, from midwife to laboring woman, from older to younger, is once more becoming available. The reclaiming of the childbirth experience has done much to dispel untruths and has reaffirmed the "reproducers" themselves as the center of the action. The mind and body are one, and as we accept our bodies, our bigness, our appetites, and our feelings as well as our intellect, we will regain our sense of power. Rich (1976) says, "we need to imagine a world in which every woman is the presiding genius of her own body. . . . Then women will truly create new life" (p. 292).

The word pain, from the Greek *poine* meaning "penalty," is suggestive of the notion that we women are being punished for the "crime" of our pregnancy, our sexuality: that is, for our tasting of the fruit of knowledge. Rather than accepting that notion, indeed, as we acknowledge our physicality, our passion, our sexuality, the whole femaleness of our existence, we will regain our lost and alienated powers. To change our fear, the pain of childbirth must be recognized, acknowledged, and understood. It must not be ignored, denied, or passively accepted.

Enduring: Standing

Birth, *bher,* also refers to bearing in the sense of enduring. To bear, to carry on, to endure the pain is a part of the birth experience. Bearing pertains broadly to the capacity to carry oneself in a specific way; endurance specifies a continuing capacity to face the pain; suffering suggests resignation.

The way we bear the pain (to carry or ride above; to endure; to suffer) depends on our relationship to the experience of pain itself and to the reason for the pain—the birth of a child. Our relationship to the pain is intentional; that is, our pain is experienced by our stance in the world—as a woman of power and knowledge or as a woman at the mercy of the doctor, alienated from her body and subject to fearful thoughts and imaginings. As we accept and take hold of our power, to literally and figuratively "stand up" and actively birth our own children rather than be delivered of our children (such as in the vulnerable "lying on one's back" position which is mainly for the convenience of the doctor), we will not deny the pain but carry it. One woman, accepting rather than pushing the pain away, said:

> The breathing doesn't make the pain any less. The breathing was to stay relaxed while you feel the pain.

We see, then, that our pain-as-experienced is empowered by our way of standing in relationship to it: our riding with it, our enduring it, or our being overwhelmed by it.

As we explore further the etymology of the word "birth," we find that "to bear children" is tied to the root *bára* (Old Norse), meaning wave, billow, or bore. "Bore" is defined as "a high and often dangerous wave caused by the surge of a flood tide upstream in a narrowing estuary or by colliding tidal currents." The wave metaphor has often been used to describe the contractions (the pains) of childbirth (Kitzinger, 1979). Like each wave flowing in with the tide, the baby is carried by the contraction wave to the mother's arms. But the wave analogy goes even further. As with ocean waves, we can have the pain wave of birthing, the sense of being carried by the pain as we ride with it, by being caught by the pain and thus enduring it, or by being overwhelmed by the power of the pain that "throws us upon the beach only to pull us out again to the sea." The contractions of birthing, like the colliding of the tidal currents, are most painful at the point in the process when the baby moves down the "narrow estuary" of the birth canal. The metamorphic wave tells us about the coming and going of the pain, the developing intensity, the climax, the release, and the moment of gathering resources for the next coming of the pain wave.

Knowing where to stand in relationship to the coming and going of the pain wave gives us a chance to choose our experience of it. As our perspectives change, so does our experience of what is pain and what is joy. Factors that may affect our perspective are hunger, tiredness, fear, anger or our own self-concepts. It makes a difference where we stand.

Doing: The Cry of Pain

Labor, the work of birthing, is seen in the cry of pain. The regular, intense, continuous contractions take their toll of energy and resources. Tired, exhausted, overwhelmed with the pain of fatigue, the feeling is one of "I just cannot go on." As Chesler (1979) said:

> Too tired to say anything, I push with all my might.
> I'm the Lilliputian. I may not be able to do it.
> It's beyond me to give birth to you. (p. 115)

The work, exertion, effort, is not just the physical power of the uterus, nor is it just the intellectual power of the mind, but the unity of self which calls us to use all our resources. One woman said, "George said he had seen many sides of me but had not known the determination, the work, the pure effort!" In spite of this overwhelming exhaustion and fatigue, we carry on especially as we are aware that progress is occurring and the baby is soon to be born.

Of course, there is no other option.

Work means doing something. The pain of labor demands action; it forces us to ask what is to be done. Grunting, screaming, walking, finding a comfortable position, active relaxation, breathing patterns, focusing free us from the state of passively suffering. The cry of birthing pain is commented in Isaiah 42:14 (*The Holy Bible*, 1953) where it reads, "For a long time I have held my peace, I have kept still and restrained myself. Now I will cry out like a woman in travail, I will gasp and pant." The Australian myth of Eingana (referred to as the great earth mother, fertility herself, the source of all life, all forms of being) gives a clue to this cry. It says,

> Eingana's travail to give birth is also the explanation of the sound made by the "bull-roarer" in the Kunapappi ritual. . . . Eingana was rolling about, every way, on the ground. She was groaning and calling out . . . making a big noise. (Meltzer, 1981, p. 11)

Following the home birth of her third child one woman said:

> The "noise" came from where? . . . my depths for sure. It amazed me. The bull's roar . . . it is a perfect description for what it felt like and sounded to me.

Comments like "perhaps you need a sedative" cause personal doubt and loss of confidence. Is it possible that the offer of medication to obliterate pain is accepted by women as it is the only support that is offered in the face of an experience of overwhelming helplessness and suffering? The offer of medication confirms the fear that, yes indeed, we will not be able to stand it. There is nothing else to do but suffer or be medicated and thus relieved of our primordial task. This is not to say that we do not ever need the help of medication to complete this work.

Support must be there without the asking. "I needed support . . . I needed to know I was doing okay." Support may take the form of back rubs, direct suggestions, sips of water, a soothing touch, the words of encouragement, the presence of a caring person, and an understanding of what is happening. All of these actions help us to "do whatever it takes to get the baby out."

Knowing

It's time. The baby is coming! The pains are our knowing. The pains begin; women feel excitement and apprehension. This is what we've been waiting for; this is it! The pains are our knowing that the time has come, but what do we "know?" We may know the stages of labor, know the procedures to expect, know the things to do, and yet we ask, "How will I handle it? What will it *really* be like?" Each time we birth, we know more about what to expect and do, but the mystery of "this" time is still present. Each time is its own time.

Yet, our bodies have wisdom to deliver the baby without our intellectual knowing. Odent (1981) recognizing this body wisdom, says:

> These last years, we understand better and better what to do to help the mother become more instinctive, to forget what is cultural, to reduce the control of the neocortex, to change her level of consciousness so that the labour seems to be easier. For example, assistance by a female is always beneficial. . . . Women must engage themselves effectively to bring love, and at the same time to bring experience, as a mother would. (p. 9)

The knowing that women share with other women has been lost in the replacement of midwives by doctors (who are primarily male) as birth attendants. The challenge by women to regain control of the childbirth process is a recognition of this knowledge and of the importance of women sharing our knowing with women.

Being in Pain

> It was as if the pain was all there was . . . it would never end . . . there would be no result . . . I would live it forever. . . . (and later) . . . After the pain I almost had the feeling that perhaps I imagined the pain. Was it really as hard as I thought it was?

When asked to describe the pain of birthing, we sometimes find it hard to remember. We know we experienced something deep and powerful, but we find that the words elude us:

> It's different than I've ever experienced; an internal rather than a surface pain; low back pain; deep pubic pain.

There is the localized, more surface pain, such as the burning and stinging as the tissue stretches to release the baby's head, but there is also that deep inner pain which expresses itself as "being in pain." This inwardness is also experienced by the feeling of unreality, of being in a fog, a sense that time has stopped or is irrelevant, with little awareness of the people around. "I don't remember what was talked about. I was totally inward." And yet in this inwardness there is an attentiveness to the deep significance of the momentous quality of the pain. One woman said, "I was annoyed when someone was making light conversation with my husband; I felt it was disturbing and irrelevant to what was happening to me." Another said, "I couldn't talk, didn't want to, in fact, I wanted to be alone at this point." And another:

> It was an incredible sensation being totally into myself. I didn't have thoughts. I was really in tune with my body. I think it must be something in you that just happens. In meditation you can go so far but this was much, much different. In those last few hours there was no straying of the mind. I couldn't talk because I was on one plane and he was on another. Mine was an inward focus.

This deeply felt experience reaches to the core and, as Buytendijk (1961) says, "throws us back on ourselves," demands us to muster up even more strength to survive, to live through it. We need to help each other through it. As Harrison (1982) described:

> I look at Marie and I see the terror of childbirth in her eyes. I feel it. I remember it. I know it can be survived. I tell her that. (p. 105)

As we are surrounded by the deep senses of inwardness, we are forced to recognize our independence, our loneliness, our selfhood, to be conscious of our own existence. This actual self-consciousness exposes to us our wholeness, our strengths and our endurance. As was stated so beautifully by one woman, "I feel great for the process to have happened through my body, proud of realizing such stamina, strength, and determination."

And the Birth! The Child

> I couldn't take my eyes off him. I cut the cord, that was *really* cutting the cord, really making the break from the baby. It's one relationship, and then when he is born that relationship dies and another relationship begins.

Deliver, deliverance, the act of transferring to another. The pains are a literal expression of the narrow gateway leading to release in the expanse of life. The involvement changes from the self-as-world to the baby-as-world. The bearing, the enduring, the doing, the knowing of the pain releases to allow the birth of a new life, a new being:

> Something in me was released. I turned away from my somewhat egotistic involvement in my labour towards my child, and since that moment my love has grown so that . . . it actually hurts sometimes. (Kitzinger, 1977, p. 161)

The pain is released, with possibility of a new and different pain tied to the incredible and awesome awareness of a separate being. Relief, disbelief, joy, and incredible exhilaration surround the excitement of the baby's presence. The focus is now the child.

Becoming: The Mother

Phyllis Chesler (1979) wrote, "Being born with motherhood is the sharpest pain I've ever known" (p. 281). With the pain of childbirth we become mothers. Can pain be transformed into something "usable," as Rich (1976) said, "something which takes us beyond the limits of our experience itself into a further grasp of the essentials of life and the possibilities within us" (p. 151). What is it that can be learned? One woman remarked:

> I think I have a right to feel good about myself. In a way, this birth is helping me to accept myself . . . both the limitations and capabilities. Accepting myself is the other side of the coin of accepting the pain of birthing. I need

to think further about it but have a sense that, for me, *this* has considerable significance.

To have experienced birthing pain offers the possibilities of self knowledge, knowledge of our limitations and capabilities, knowledge of new life, as mother, and of our place in the mysterious cycle of human life: birth, death, and rebirth. As we birth our children, we, in a sense, birth ourselves. We are mothers, like other mothers, and our daughters after us. Frans said:

> Rose, the only other mother there . . . I had something in common with her. I started to cry when she hugged me.

Notes

1. Twelve women were initially interviewed and nine of these reviewed and commented on early drafts. All quotations not referenced are from conversations with these women.
2. The origins of the words were explored through both *Klein's Comprehensive Etymological Dictionary of the English Language* (1971, New York: Elseview Publishing Company) and *The American Heritage Dictionary of the English Language* (1969, Boston: Houghton-Mifflin Company).

References

Bonica, J. J. (1975). The nature of pain in parturition. *Clinics in Obstetrics and Gynaecology, 3*(2), 449-517.

Buytendijk, F. J. (1961). *Pain*. London: Hutchinson.

Chesler, P. (1979). *With child, A diary of motherhood*. New York: Thomas Y. Crowell.

Harrison, M. (1982). *A woman in residence*. New York: Random.

The Holy Bible. (1953). Revised standard version. Toronto: Thomas Nelson.

Kitzinger, S. (1977). *Giving birth, The parents' emotions in change*. New York: Schocken.

Kitzinger,S. (1979). *Education and counseling for childbirth*. New York: Schocken.

Meltzer, D. (Ed.). (1981). *Birth. An anthology of ancient tents, songs, players, and stories*. San Francisco: North Point.

Melzack, R., Taenzer, P., Feldman, P., & Kinch, R. (1980). Labour is still painful after prepared childbirth training. *CMA Journal, 125*, 357-363.

Morris, W. (Ed.). (1969). *The American heritage dictionary of the English language*. Boston: Houghton-Mifflin.

Neumann, E. (1955). *The great mother: An analysis of the archetype* (Trans. Ralph Manheim). Princeton, NJ: Princeton University Press.

Odent, M. (1981, Spring). The evolution of obstetrics at Pithivers. *Birth and the Family Journal, 1*(8), 7-15.

Rich, A. (1976). *Of woman born*. New York: Bantam.

9

Operating on a Child's Heart: A Pedagogical View of Hospitalization

STEPHEN J. SMITH

There are many occasions during a child's hospitalization when tensions run high. But none seem as tense as when the child's needs appear to be ignored by the surrounding medical personnel. I recall, for instance, my child being brought into the children's ward from the Intensive Care Unit (ICU) where, for the past 24 hours, he has been recovering from heart surgery. My child, after being monitored so closely, is left in a room with only a parent watching over him—watching as he sleeps, watching as he stirs, and listening as he begins to complain of the soreness in his chest and arm. The last of the morphine is wearing off, so I ring for the nurse to come and give him some more medication. "I'm sorry," says the nurse, "but I can only give him Demerol every six hours, and it is only four hours since he came out of the ICU. All I can give him now is Tylenol. I'll come back in a few minutes with it." He falls asleep waiting for her to return, sleeping for over an hour. It is now close to two hours since he first indicated his discomfort. As he wakes it is clear that the discomfort has turned to pain. I go the nurses' station to seek some assistance for my child and am told that someone will be there shortly. Again we are left waiting as the pain grows steadily worse. I wonder why there can be so much paperwork to be done when my child is in such distress just down the

AUTHOR'S NOTE: This chapter originally appeared in Smith, S. J. (1989). Operating on a child's heart: A pedagogical view of hospitalization. *Phenomenology + Pedagogy: A Human Sciences Journal, 7,* 145-162. Reprinted with permission.

corridor. Why does it take so long for someone to attend to my child? The system is askew—the priorities and procedures seem so removed from the care of my child. Strong words are said and they have a beneficial effect. From then on there are more visits to his room. Nurses check on him regularly; the residents inquire after him; and the woman who cleans his room stays a while to talk with him. My child is on their minds. He is being looked after.

I guess it pays to complain; however, this is not the main lesson to be drawn from this situation. There are times during a child's hospitalization when he must be spoken for, when those closest to him must speak up to ensure that medical attention is responsive to his needs. At issue here is the matter of responsibility for the care of the child, the issue of who is ultimately responsible for the child and who is best placed to know what is best for the child. At issue is a view of the child's hospitalization which is more expansive yet inclusive of a medical view, indeed, a view of hospitalization which may provide a corrective to the excesses and neglects of a predominantly medical view.

The purpose of this article is to describe phenomenologically what such a view of hospitalization might entail. By writing about a particular child who undergoes a heart operation, my aim is to show that the health of the child is not solely determined by the medical intervention that takes place. In fact, through a critique of the medical view of the child and by attending to the child's experience of hospitalization, I want to show how an orientation to the good of the child can make sense of what we may think is good for the child. I wish, in other words, to describe a broadening of the medical view of hospitalization and the formulation of what I shall call a pedagogical view of hospitalization.

The Medical View

In the CBC program *Heroic Measures: Dilemmas in the Care of Sick Children* (1987), attention is drawn to the possibility of a one-sided medical view. The chief of pediatrics at Toronto's Hospital for Sick Children says:

> I have to look through the eyes of a physician who looked at a child and said, "I think that we have a treatment for that child that I think could benefit that child." And whether the outcome for success, however we are going to define that, was 40% or 16%, I think that those are the sorts of decisions that we have to make every day. I think my role is to try and ask

> what any reasonable person would try and do for that child who's in the situation that he or she can't make up their mind for themselves. I think we have to divest ourselves from what's in the best interests of everybody else and focus on that child. What would the child, given the ability to make this decision, prefer?

The interviewer on the program then asks:

> Do you think it's possible to do that? Do you think it's possible for you to in effect separate the child from what he is not actually separate from, that is his parents, and say what is in the best interests of the child as opposed to what is in the best interests of the family?

The interviewer does not simply ask a question of whose interests are being served—the parents' or the child's? But rather, he asks, how can a medical decision be made in presumably the best interests of the child by ignoring those of us who have been responsible until now for the welfare of the child? If we, the parents of a particular child, want to remain close to our child, what might we be up against when a crucial medical decision is made as to what should be done for our child? What sort of logic would deny the fundamental responsibility we feel for our child?

A PATH OF LOGIC

"So, how long has your son had a heart murmur?" asks the GP during what we think is merely a routine checkup. From this point on we must face the fact of having a defective child. "But he has always seemed so healthy. Why wasn't the murmur detected before? Why weren't there any signs of a problem earlier on?" Tests are carried out: blood tests, ECG, X-ray, 2-D Color Echogram. The child is physically and comprehensively examined. A diagnosis is made—Patent Ductus Arteriosus, PDA for short. "You can be thankful. It could have been a lot worse," says the physician. "At least this is one thing we can operate on where you'll end up having a 100% healthy child. You want a perfect child, don't you?"

Is there no way out of this child having a heart operation? "Well there is no need to rush," says the pediatric cardiologist. "He's had this condition for four years already, so a month or two won't make a great deal of difference. You can discuss with the surgeon a convenient time for the operation." The operation is a fait accompli. The physicians seem so sure of its necessity; they seem to know thoroughly the condition of this child and the conditions under which we will continue to have him. Their diagnosis of a congenital heart defect is an utterly distinguishing, discerning, determining, inescapable decision about the nature of this child. And yet, do they really know *this* child, or do they only know what type of child this child should be? What view of the order of things is at stake here in this diagnosis of our child?

Foucault (1973) says:

> Up to the end of the eighteenth century medicine related much more to health than to normality; it did not begin by analysing a "regular" functioning organism and go on to seek where it had deviated, what it was disturbed by, and how it could be brought back into normal working order; it referred, rather, to qualities of vigour, suppleness, and fluidity, which were lost in illness and which it was the task of medicine to restore. To this extent, medical practice could accord an important place to regimen and diet, in short, to a whole rule of life and nutrition which the subject imposed upon himself. This privileged relation between medicine and health involved the possibility of being one's own physician.

Nineteenth-century medicine, on the other hand, was regulated more in accordance with normality than with health; it formed its concepts and prescribed its interventions in relation to a standard of functioning and organic structure, and physiological knowledge—once marginal and purely theoretical knowledge for the doctor—was to be established . . . at the very centre of all medical reflexion. (p. 35)

With this "birth of the clinic" came a profound change in the way we look at individuals and especially children. The medical gaze superimposes the "body" of knowledge about disease on the body of the child (Foucault, 1973, p. 3), which is to say it is based on a way of thinking about the course of a disease which likely overlooks the circumstances of particular children. The medical view of the child constitutes a pathology, a path of logic, which so easily leaves the child behind.

Logically speaking, there is not a great deal of risk to this operation. "It's the appendectomy of heart operations," they tell us. "Of course there is always risk in any major surgery; but at this hospital we have one of the best surgeons in the field. Really, there is no need to worry. Besides, the risks of the operation are less than the risks of leaving the child's heart condition untreated." These words of reassurance do not offer much comfort. To contemplate not operating implies dooming the child to a shortened life span and having him face the prospect of congestive heart disease, frequent pulmonary infections, and restricted physical capacity; on the other hand, thinking about the operation means thinking about the procedure that will literally open this child up, the surgery this child is yet too young to understand, the operation that risks taking away the innocence of this child. As parents, we are fearful for our child. "Look, don't worry," chides the physician, "he'll be in good hands. We have a very good record in treating this problem." But can our fears be so unfounded? It seems that within this technologic of medicine there is no body of knowledge that addresses any real difference between having a child and having an operation on a child. Nobody speaks for the child, for preserving not only the biology that is important for being a child, but also the experiences that make a good childhood possible. Inevitably the condition of the child, his childhood, comes down to the problem of his medical condition. The question of this child's existence is reduced to the risks of a surgically operable problem.

We accept that this heart operation must go ahead. Having come this far, there is no turning back. Sure, we request a second opinion just to see if the condition has improved, but this willfulness on our part only confirms the direction in which we are headed. Nothing has changed medically; the murmur is as loud as ever. Our task now is to face the scheduled operation and to prepare the child; in other words, to put the best possible face on the situation. "By the way, the boy must be free of dental caries," the surgeon's office warns us. "His teeth will have to be checked before he is admitted. The surgeon will not operate if there is any risk of infection. And a cavity is as bad as an infection." His front teeth—there are cavities in many of them. His dentist said they could be left because the second ones would soon come in to replace them. Now it seems imperative to have them attended to. But what should be done? His dentist advises extracting all the suspect teeth. He says: "My position is a conservative one. Extract the teeth and do away with any risk of infection at all. If it was my child, that's what I would do. Still, if you're worried, I'll refer you to a pediatric specialist who may know some whiz-bang way of saving the teeth." The pediatric specialist is more conciliatory. He agrees that extracting the teeth is rather drastic and that restoration is quite possible; nevertheless, he says: "Keeping the teeth is really for aesthetics." Tell this to the child who cries on being told he will lose his teeth, the child who wonders how he will be able to talk, the child who becomes distraught at the thought of his friends all laughing at him. For this dentist it may be largely a matter of preserving the look of the child, but for the child it is a matter of self-preservation. So we see other dentists who each give different advice. What do we do? To whom do we listen? The pediatric cardiologist comes to the rescue with some good advice. He says: "Just do what you would normally do for your child in repairing his teeth. After all, it is your responsibility that they are the way they are." The decision of what to do is now ours to make. In preparing the child for his operation, it is we who must take ultimate responsibility. We must do what we think is best for the child; we must preserve the integrity of the child's smile in the face of the inevitable operation.

CRACKS IN THE LOGIC

"The medical establishment has become a major threat to health," writes Illich (1976, p. 3); and yet to attempt to dismiss the medical view of one's own child exposes us to charges of gross neglect and almost criminal irresponsibility. Such critical posturing as that of Illich's *Limits to Medicine* fails to acknowledge the power of the medical view in situations of real existential conflict, such as having to respond to a child with an operable heart condition while knowing the medical diagnosis of his preoperational life expectancy. Nevertheless, it *is* possible to still be critical in those situations where it appears that the body of the child, his corporeality, and his physically-constituted relations to the world are being denied altogether. Here, where we find blind spots in the medical perception, we also find ways of seeing what is actually being done to the child. Here, within these cracks in the logic of medicine, we can reflect on what might be best for the child.

What is required is a way of seeing that reconciles two things: the image of a child in his or her generality as an organism with a medically-defined problem, that is diagnosed within the context of professionally-defined relations, and that is resolvable by means of technologically-defined solutions, with the reality of a child in his or her uniqueness, as someone who lives first and foremost within the context of particular family and community relationships. Thus, when a child is being spoken about medically, we should know that this child has already been spoken for existentially. and it is this authorship (this authority) that takes precedence when considering what can be done for his or her sake, especially when medical intervention is being considered.

Perhaps one of the most routine procedures is that of admission to the hospital. There are a number of forms to sign—registration forms, health insurance forms, hospital indemnity forms—before our child is admitted. Then, once admitted to the wards, there are more forms. On one it asks: "Has your child been in hospital before? How does your child react to strangers? How does your child react to pain?" Soon there are frequent visits by hospital personnel. Nurses, doctors, nurses' aides look in, take measurements, give instructions. Meal orders are taken. For a while there is even a stream of medical students, each one saying that he or she will only take a minute or two as he or she starts prodding and poking the child, listening to his chest, taking his blood pressure, and generally keeping the child from doing the things he would rather do. "Is all this necessary?" we wonder. The child has been admitted to the hospital. We have admitted him, and in so doing we have admitted our compliance to the rule of the hospital. And yet I do not think that this admission takes away our obligations to stand up for the child, especially when the logic of things done to him seems unclear.

Cousins (1983) in his book *The Healing Heart* admits:

> There are qualities beyond medical competence that patients need and look for in their doctors. They want reassurance. They want to be looked after and not just looked over. They want to be listened to. They want to feel that it makes a difference to the physician, a very big difference, whether they live or die. They want to feel that they are in the doctor's thoughts. In short, patients are a vast collection of emotional needs. Yes, psychological counselors are very helpful in this connection—and so are the family and clergy. But the patient turns most of all and first of all to the physician. It is the physician who has the most to offer in terms of emotional needs. It is the person of the doctor and the presence of the doctor—just as much as, and frequently more than, what the doctor does—that create an environment for healing. The physician represents healing. The physician holds the lifeline. (p. 136)

On the other hand, although these sentiments may stand up to some scrutiny in certain cases of adult hospitalization, such a relation does not seem possible in cases of children's hospitalization. In fact, Petrillo and Sanger (1972) state:

> Physicians who may spend considerably less time with the children [than nurses do], are correspondingly less involved, though their decisions can have momentous effects. Lacking the satisfactions to be enjoyed from

> intensely developed interactions with young people, they may not be stimulated toward gaining knowledge of the child's world. (p. 62)

What Cousins (1983) says about the quality of the physician-patient relation does not really apply to children, not just because physicians spend little time with children, nor because they don't enjoy interacting with them, nor even because their world is separate from the world of children, but simply because they are not the parents of the children they operate on, they are not part of their family, and they are not part of the communities from which the children come. Except for a child who is chronically hospitalized, any relation a physician has with a child is at best a mediated one.

A better approximation of the physician-patient relation which Cousins holds up would seem to be the parent-child relation. In fact, there are clear indications in the literature on child hospitalization and in changing hospital regulations that the adult-child relation has come to be recognized as crucial to the welfare of the child (Hardgrove & Dawson, 1972; Robinson & Clarke, 1980; Thompson & Stanford, 1981). For example, Anderson (1985) recounts:

> The most significant step ever taken toward reducing patient fear at Children's was the lifting of all restrictions on parental visiting. Today the benefits seem obvious. Yet historically parents were not welcome in pediatric hospitals or wards. Their presence, it was thought, would contribute to the spread of infection and to the demoralization, according to someone writing in 1907, of "the discipline of the hospital and the other children." Mothers who insisted on remaining at their sick children's bedsides were sometimes viewed with irritation. Hospital staff of the period, noting that patients shed tears when their parents left, concluded that visits from parents made children unhappy. . . . Open visiting became a fact of life on general floors at Children's in the mid-1960s and in the intensive care units in 1975, though parents are still asked to check with a nurse before entering ICU. By lifting the restrictions, hospital administrators in essence acknowledged that children even as patients belong first and foremost to their mothers and fathers. (pp. 48-50)

Still, the significance of the adult's presence has yet to be recognized medically. Parents, family, community are still regarded as, at best, supportive of the medical processes of child hospitalization. I would argue that in order to make sense of what is being done to a child, especially when he or she faces an operation, it is necessary to move beyond such a spatially- and temporally-limited medical view and to consider the health of the child in the context of how he or she lives with others beyond the hospital. After all, the child's medical treatment only makes sense when it is consistent with his or her treatment by those with whom he or she lives. And the success of the medical treatment is dependent on an acknowledgment that a meaningful adult-child relation needs to be made the focus of the child's hospitalization.

BEYOND THE MEDICAL VIEW

I look to Cousins (1983) for ways in which this relation can be understood. At the level of methodology, he says:

> Few words in the medical vocabulary carry more connotations of scorn and even contempt than the term "anecdotal." Not to the writer. The writer makes his living by anecdotes. He searches them out and craves them as the raw material of his profession. No hunter stalking his prey is more alert to the presence of his quarry than the writer looking for small incidents that cast a strong light on human behavior. If nothing is valid to the physician except as it proceeds from masses of data, very little has meaning to the writer except as it is tied to the reality of a single person, and except as that reality can illustrate a larger lesson or principle.

A single case may be suspect to the medical scientist. To the writer, the universe begins with a single case, a single emotion, a single encounter—in short, a single person. (p. 140)

The methodology suggested here involves accenting a single case of a child being operated on and working out where we stand as concerned adults in situations that arise where a medical logic is transcended. It involves interpreting this stance in a way that allows for a public discourse on the hospitalization of children.

The task of writing such an account is to keep in mind the flesh and blood child—my child, your child, the child we know, and the child for whom a heart operation makes us feel personally responsible. The anecdotes on which this writing is based should enable us to draw closer to the child, to see things as the child might see them, to open up the cracks in a medical view that would deny the child's sense of what is happening to him or her. Writing about a particular hospitalization would constitute, therefore, a child-oriented view—a perspective that acknowledges the child's experiences. In Petrillo and Sanger (1972) when the child says

> Some people think they know it all. I tried to tell the doctor that I couldn't hold still in that position but she said I was being silly. I said it was cold; she said it was just right. O.K. for her, she was dressed up to her ears in a gown, cap and mask and there I was cold and practically naked. She said I wouldn't feel any pain; I said I did. She said she'd get it (the specimen) the first time; I know she didn't. So who the hell would know better? (p. 106)

We should acknowledge what the child knows and speak with him against the procedure to which he has been subjected.

A Child-Oriented View

How does the child understand his hospitalization? What things stand out in his mind? Perhaps they are the little things that would otherwise go unnoticed unless one is attentive to the fact that the medical account is not the only story that can be told. The seemingly trite incidents that stand out in the child's mind may in fact constitute a narrative of greater significance than the medical record alone. Let us consider, therefore, some anecdotes of a child's experience of hospitalization, some little things like having to wear the hospital gown, seeing the scar from the operation, and taking things home from the hospital.

WEARING THE GOWN

While flipping through the television channels I come across a medical program. It features a heart operation, a documentary of a coronary bypass procedure. A timely feature, I think, as I call my son over to watch it with me so that he can see what having an operation means. And yet as he sits beside me I wonder if this might not be too much for him. He may see things for which both he and I are ill prepared. But even before I think I must shield him from certain sights, he begins to cry. "Do I have to wear that?" he asks in reference to the surgical gowns worn by the surgeons appearing on the program. "Only girls wear dresses. My friends will all laugh at me." Can this be his concern? It seems so minor in comparison to that which I thought might bother him as he watches the program. "Well, when your friends come to visit you they will have to wear a gown as well," I tell him. His good humor returns. He smiles at the suggestion of Dorian and Diego getting dressed up to see him. Soon he forgets his concern over the gown and leaves me to go back to what he was doing before I called him over.

Nothing more is said of the hospital gown until the day of the operation when the time comes for him to be wheeled over to surgery. The nurse in attendance asks me to help him put on his gown. For the past day and a half he has lived in the clothes he brought from home; now he must change into the costume set aside for him. But he refuses. He cries, he kicks, he screams as we force the gown on him. He cries inconsolably for all the ward to hear. So we strike an agreement: He can wear his shorts underneath the gown until we get to the operating theater.

On the way to the theater various people pass by. They smile as people are wont to smile at a young child who is obviously going for an operation or to have some technical procedure performed. But the child thinks they are laughing at him, staring at him, seeing his nakedness. He pulls the gown down over his knees and does not stop crying until we move out of the main corridors and reach the surgical preparation room. Here we distract him with talk of presents and gifts that might come after his operation. Here we play "I spy" while waiting for him to be taken from us. He appears happy for the moment. Then he remembers the gown, "that dumb old gown" he calls it. He cries again. "Why do I have to have this operation?" he asks pleadingly. Is this what the gown is about? Is this the reality which the gown can only partially hide? "Look, we have gowns on too," I say, not really knowing what to say. We, too, are trying to disguise the operation, this rupture, this separation, and all the risks that go with it. We, too, are party to the way medical procedures are disguised and dressed up so that we lose sight of the stark reality of exposing the flesh of the child.

This incident suggests that the child already understands the magnitude of what is happening to him, and that our task is to deal with his fearfulness in a language that recognizes and mollifies his fears. Of course, it may have been better to prepare the child for hospitalization through some less traumatic means—through one of the "many existing methods of preparation which have been devised to help children and their parents cope with hospital admission or a medical procedure" (Rodin, 1983, pp. 21, 22; see also Chapter 2). But, at a more practical level, the incident makes us wonder if hospital staff might not attend more closely to the child's words and to the situations where they are most suggestive. Why, for instance, when so many professionals have visited the child, is the task of taking the child to surgery left to the hospital orderly? Why is the preparation for surgery reduced to a scrubbing of the hands—a washing off of the dirt and grime of everyday life? Perhaps the preparation of a child for a heart operation may be enhanced if the child's concerns are not dismissed so readily.

SEEING THE SCAR

Five days after the operation, when my child is able to move with much greater ease, he goes to clean his teeth before settling down for the night. I hear him calling to me in the adjoining room, and by the sound of his voice all is not well. I rush into the bathroom to find him standing on the stool in front of the washbasin with his back turned toward the mirror above it and his neck craned in order to get a good look at the sutured incision from the operation. Suddenly I realize this is the first time he has seen it. What with the medications he has been taking, coupled with his immobility, all he knew of the incision was what he could feel of the three stitches lower down where a tube had been inserted to drain fluids from his chest. The real incision had been hidden from view and out of touch. Now, however, he can see it for the first time. He can see it extend from his back all the way around under his arm.

"How did they do that?" he asks nervously. "Did they do it with a scalpel?" I am reminded as he asks these questions of the day he and Michael found a scalpel in the garbage and of how Michael sliced his finger before we could get it away from him. I suspect he also remembers this occasion and the pain Michael felt. I recall this being the first time he saw a scalpel and how he found it so hard to understand that this particular sort of knife is used to open up the body. So when he asks "How did they do that?" his question seems more a statement of incredulity at the thought of being intentionally cut than a question of procedure. His question brings Michael to mind, along with the anxiety he felt about this implement. Now, seeing his body disfigured, he cannot fathom how it is that someone would treat him in his manner.

I try to calm him down by telling him that it will soon disappear, even showing him my own operation scar. Still he remains tense. "When did they do it to me?" he asks. Such a strange question. I would have thought the timing of the operation was now perfectly clear to him, but apparently he does not see his stitched incision as I do. "When did they do it to me?" In an objective sense, they did it five days ago, but according to the child's sense of things, they have done it only now that he can see their handiwork.

That evening he does not sleep well. He moans and groans and tosses in his bed. Half-asleep, he calls for us. "What's up? Does your chest feel sore? Is anything wrong?" "No, nothing," he replies to our ministrations. But something is wrong. He is cut, mutilated, mutated, changed. In his eyes something looks strange, something looks foreign. There is something the matter. But when asked what the matter is, there is nothing, nothing, to be said.

When he sees the scar, it is not so much the medical procedure that matters to him as it is his awareness of how the procedure affects his relation to those around him. Throughout his hospitalization, the child is having things done to him, and yet he strives to maintain an identity in the face of such intrusions of his body. For instance, we speak to the surgeon immediately after the operation. She tells us that "the child has a small to medium ductus that was ligated and a metal clip was used between the ties." A metal clip! She left a metal clip inside! What effect will this metal clip have? Will it cut into his tissue? Will it affect his magnetism? For the child, however, there are different concerns for normalcy. While we are concerned about the metal clip, his first concern in the Intensive Care Unit is that we should bring his pyjamas. He wants to wear his pyjamas. Even as we leave the ICU with the morphine taking its toll, he protests at having to wear the hospital outfit. And by the second day back in the ward room, no more is to be seen of the green-striped pyjamas. By this time he is looking fairly normal. The ECG monitor is all that he has attached, and yet he protests at having to carry the monitor in a bag slung around his neck. He wants to carry it. "I'm sorry," says the nurse, "but you have to put this around your neck if you want to go to the playroom." He complies, but as soon as he reaches the playroom he takes the bag from around his neck and hides it under the table where he sits down. Later on the nurse brings a wheelchair to take him to the X-ray clinic, but he wants to walk by himself. "You can sit back and enjoy the ride," she tells him in an attempt to entice him onto the chair. Still he insists on walking even though she warns him, "it is such a very long way." In each of these situations the child chooses the path of normalcy, of familiarity. Wearing pyjamas brought from home, holding the ECG monitor under the table, and walking to the X-ray clinic—each action defies the strangeness of the hospital. Each preference allows him to feel himself in this foreign place. Consequently we can appreciate how seeing his scar for the first time can be so traumatic. It cuts through the attempts he is making to act normally and to be the child he thinks he is. It makes him a stranger to himself and to those around him.

TAKING THINGS HOME

The child comes home with a new lease on life. Through the operation he has been given the chance of a normal life span. For him, however, there are more immediate things to be concerned with. There are the souvenirs of the hospital to be remembered. He must take home the identification band he wore on his wrist and the gauze hair covering which came from the operating room. These mementos of hospital life take precedence over the expensive gifts from well-wishing friends, the get-well balloons that filled the room for the past few days, even the toys, crayons, and books which he brought from home to occupy himself during his stay in the hospital.

The usual things of childhood are attended to after he has been home for a while. Here they have their place. But at the hospital their place is uncertain, or at least it is for him. A plastic tube decorated with cartoon characters is not meant to be played with, but to serve a particular medical purpose as a spirometer for clearing the mucus from his lungs. What appears to be a toy is actually a device that causes the child some distress. I ask him, as we make ready to leave the hospital, if he wants to take the spirometer home. His indifference to my question takes me back a few days to the second day after the operation when the intravenous tubes have been disconnected and all that remains attached is a telemetric electrocardiogram monitor. The child is now disconnected from machines for the most part, from home, and perhaps even from us. I see him lying on his bed in the ward room when only a day ago he was in the Intensive Care Unit, monitors attached, and a nurse constantly monitoring his vital signs. Now he is alone, resentful of the pain those around him have caused. "Listen, Dad," says the nurse who has just entered the room, "we've got to clear that mucus from his chest. You've got to get him to blow into the tube at least five times every hour. Otherwise I have to use the suction. And he certainly won't like that. Here, you hold his chest and we'll get him to cough it up." I do as I am told, although I am apprehensive at the thought of being co-opted in a seeming conspiracy against him. I touch his wound, but not in the way I would like. I hold his chest firm in what seems to be an act of betrayal. "I can't do it," he tells the nurse, sobbing at the suggestion of a few more tries. "It hurts. I can't do it." "Of course you can," she says. "Did you ever hear about the little red engine who says, 'I think I can, I think I can'?" "But I can't," he says, turning in my direction and perhaps hoping I will intervene for him. "Sure you can do it," the nurse chides him. "Just five more coughs." She turns to me and says. "See if you can get him to cough a bit, and make sure he blows into his tube." I look at the tube again—the cylinder with its cartoon characters indicating the varying pressure levels, and I think that for the child even Disneyland conspires against him. Maybe it would be less confusing if he had his chest suctioned and be done with it.

The things around him bring little comfort. They fail to acknowledge the pain of his recuperation. Even the playroom, this supposed sanctuary of childhood within the hospital, has a look of sickness to it. The children hobbling around with their IV drip machines in tow, the hospital toys so carefully selected, the children who disappear and then reappear from their required therapies—this place is not like the rumpus room or the backyard where the child plays at home. So when it is time for the child to leave the hospital, he takes home the only things that make sense to him—the wrist band and the gauze hair covering.

His taking home these seemingly inconsequential things has us wonder what we should give him to hang onto. What should we give a child to help him through the difficult times of hospitalization? We begin to wonder if perhaps the thinking about the hospitalization of children has more to do with accoutrements of childhood than it does with ensuring that the conditions necessary for children to accept medical intervention are met. Here amid toys, a playroom, and equipment designed with children in mind the child finds his own attachments—his wrist band and the gauze hair covering. These become the props of his childhood. Although there is a need to fashion a childlike landscape—a ward designed for children with things children normally like—there must be an awareness that what are more important are the things and the experiences they evoke which the child takes home with him. By attending to such things perhaps we may even see that the child's experience is much closer to our own than our designs would have us believe.

A CHILD'S STORY

Some weeks later I ask my son to tell me a story about going to the hospital. He uses his felt pens to draw a series of four pictures and then he tells me the words that go with them. His story is called "Peter is Going to Hospital."

> Peter is going to the hospital room now to have his operation. And someone is pushing him, too.
>
> Peter is lying in his bed, and there is a door behind him. There is a window on the door. A nurse is coming in.
>
> There is a shelf underneath Peter's bed and there is a suitcase on it. There are clothes in the suitcase. A pillow is behind Peter's head. Peter feels good.
>
> The nurse feels Peter's chest. She has tools in her pocket, and she is going to look into his ear. Peter has a sore arm.
>
> Peter and his Mom are walking home. Peter has grown up. But he still has a sore arm.

This story, which resonates with the discussion of some critical incidents of the child's hospitalization, serves to keep us in touch with the child's experience of hospitalization. It brings us back to the life world of the child and helps us see what is at stake. For the child, the correction of a medical defect is much less comprehensible than the wearing of a hospital gown, seeing the scar of an operation, and taking things home. And yet the child understands through these experiences of hospitalization that his life has been profoundly altered. As he says in his story: "Peter has grown up. But he still has a sore arm." For him, just as for Peter, there seems to be little difference medically, although there has been a profound change experientially. His story reminds us that it is his maturity which is fundamentally at issue, and that it is our concern for the direction of his maturity which authorizes our actions on his behalf, including our acceptance of those medical interventions which we see as being necessary.

A Pedagogical View

The question remains: To what extent does this child-oriented understanding of medical procedure carry its share of responsibility for the child's life? It would seem to me that we must not only hear what the child has to say about the things happening to him or her, but we must also gain from our attunement to the child's experiences in the here and now an awareness, which medicine claims to have, of the child's future. The task of writing about a child's experiences of hospitalization is thus to explicate a pedagogical view that recognizes the child's future as contingent on the quality of his or her treatment (his or her care) in the here and now. For example, a nurse comes in first thing in the morning to take some blood from the child. "Can you come back in an hour or so?" his mother asks the nurse. "He has only just woken up." The nurse does not seem too put out by this request and agrees to return later on. But a few minutes later a second nurse enters the room and asks if the child has had a blood sample taken. An explanation is given of what has only just transpired; however, this nurse is not happy with this flagrant change in procedure. She insists on doing the job herself, at once.

Now there may very well be good reasons for taking blood first thing in the morning, and if so, then these reasons could be explained to the mother. On the other hand, there are also very good reasons for waiting until a child has woken up and had time to himself before a needle is inserted into his arm. Which reasons ought to prevail will depend on whose interests are being served, the child's or someone else's. Of course, this does not mean that the child's comfort is being placed above his medical care; on the contrary, the health of the child is profoundly affected by the atmosphere of his hospitalization. To be woken up by a needle in the arm is not only discomforting, but it also denies the child the opportunity to wake up feeling somewhat invigorated for the recuperation that lies ahead. And even if there is little chance of the child's awakening in what Bollnow (Vandenberg, 1975) calls a mood of "morningness," of cheerful expectancy for the coming day, the responsibility of the adult in attendance is to at least ensure that the possibility is not denied him.

This remembering of the child's experience, and on this basis, advocating what is thought to be best for the child in light of a medical knowledge which purports to make the child better, is what a pedagogical view of hospitalization entails. Accordingly, when wearing the gown, seeing the scar, and taking things home stand out as critical incidents in this child's hospitalization, they are occasions for trying to understand the child's predicament and for coming to terms with the nature of a caring relation to the child during and beyond his hospitalization. These situations matter to us both; moreover, it is through a reflective participation in the type of situations I have described that a pedagogical view of child hospitalization can be taken. Our task is to see how maturity is gained through hospitalization and how it is that we can help the child when medical procedures make the child grow up too quickly. In particular, we need to question those procedures of hospitalization that undermine our pedagogic relatedness to the child.

We might ask: How is it that such procedures can be so removed from a knowledge of the particular child? For instance, the surgeon comes into the ward on the afternoon prior to the operation. She has not seen the child before; this was the responsibility of the cardiologist. "Is this Peter's room?" she asks no one in particular. There are two beds in the room, each with a boy in it. She walks past the first bed and looks at the child in the second bed. "This is Peter, is it? I thought he was going to be smaller." It seems, from these words, that a personal knowledge of the child has no real bearing on the conduct of the operation. All the tests have been done; the only surprise is that the child is a little bigger than expected. But this is of no consequence because the body to be operated on need not be any particular child's body.

And yet the consequences of this anonymity soon become apparent. After the operation, the surgeon visits the child on her daily rounds. Yes, she admits, the boy is doing well. "But he has got to start using his left arm more. We don't want the muscles that were cut to knit too tightly." "Can you lift your arm over your head?" she asks him. He holds his arm close to his chest and tries to lift it up with the other hand. "No, see if you can touch the top of your head." He tries, leaning his head to one side, and manages to touch his ear. But the surgeon is not happy. "You want to go home, don't you?" she says sternly. "You can't go home until you can raise your hand up in the air. You might have to stay here over Christmas. You don't want that, do you? Tomorrow I'm coming back and I want to see how high you can raise your arm." The surgeon leaves the room and continues her rounds of the children's ward. He looks at me through moist eyes. I reassure him: "Yes, you will be out of here very soon." But first he must raise his arm. He must still make the gesture that will let him out of this place. He must excuse himself from the presence of the one he barely knows.

What is required in such situations is a mindfulness of the child, a sensitivity to the child's experience of being hospitalized, and an understanding of how the child is placed when medical procedures seem necessary. Perhaps by acknowledging a relation to the child we might also see how his hospital care can be most beneficial. We might see how certain episodes of a child's hospitalization, such as wearing the gown, seeing the scar, and taking things home, show a more complete perspective than the narrowly medical one, each episode suggesting a view of medical intervention which balances what is thought to be good for the child against the more fundamental question of what is the good of this particular child. Even when we give the child over to the medical specialists for the operation itself, even when our part in the child's hospitalization is diminished, still we must ensure that "the child is in good hands"—that he is in the hands of one who is both technically proficient and caring of the good of this particular child. Perhaps for the most part no dramatic changes need occur in hospital settings for such a pedagogical view to be adopted, merely a greater sensitivity to the child's experience. The important thing is that we attend to the child's experience and that we who are reflectively engaged in his daily life learn how to speak up for the child during his hospitalization.

References

Anderson, P. (1985). *Children's hospital.* New York: Harper & Row.

Canadian Broadcasting Corporation. (1987). *Heroic measures: Dilemmas in the care of sick children.* Written and presented to David Cayley, June 16, 17.

Cousins, N. (1983). *The healing heart: Antidotes to panic and helplessness.* New York: Norton.

Foucault, M. (1973). *The birth of the clinic: An archaeology of medical perception.* London: Tavistock.

Hardgrove, C. B., & Dawson, R. B. (1972). *Parents and children in the hospital: The family's role in pediatrics.* Boston: Little, Brown.

Illich, I. (1976). *Limits to medicine.* Toronto: McClelland and Stewart.

Petrillo, M., & Sanger, S. (1972). *Emotional care of hospitalized children: An environmental approach.* Philadelphia: Lippincott.

Robinson, G. C., & Clarke, H. F. (1980). Family centred care in hospital. *The hospital care of children: A review of contemporary issues* (pp. 68-89). Oxford: Oxford University Press.

Rodin, J. (1983). *Will this hurt? Preparing children for hospital and medical procedures.* London: Royal College of Nursing of the United Kingdom.

Thompson, R. H., & Stanford, G. (1981). *Child life in hospitals: Theory and practice.* Springfield, IL: Charles C Thomas.

Vandenberg, D. (1975). Openness: The pedagogic atmosphere: In D. Nyberg (Ed.), *The philosophy of open education* (pp. 35-37). London: Routledge & Kegan Paul.

10

Memories of Breathing: A Phenomenological Dialogue: Asthma as a Way of Becoming

MONICA CLARKE

Bronchial asthma is a common disease characterized by spasmodic attacks of wheezing and shortness of breath.

Cole, 1971, p. 113

We were bound on the wheel for an endless conversation.
Inside this shell, a tide waiting for someone to enter.
A monologue waiting for you to interrupt it.
A man wading into the surf. The dialogue of the rock with the breaker.
The wave changed instantly by the rock; the rock changed by the wave
returning over and over.
The dialogue that lasts all night or a whole lifetime.
A conversation of sounds melting constantly into rhythms.
A shell waiting for you to listen.
A tide that ebbs and flows against a deserted continent.
A cycle whose rhythm begins to change the meanings of words.

Rich, 1971, p. 53

In the fall of 1988, my 15-year-old daughter won the Munro book prize for an essay that she called "Memories of Breathing." I remember our

AUTHOR'S NOTE: This chapter originally appeared in Clarke, M. (1990). Memories of breathing: A phenomenological diaglogue: Asthma as a way of becoming. *Phenomenology + Pedagogy: A Human Sciences Journal, 8,* 208-223. Reprinted with permission.

exchange as she cast around in frustration searching for a topic that could be special. I offered my usual array of maternal teacher-type advice. Write about something you know well, a happening, a feeling that is yours. And so she did, and afterward I will speak to this.

There are other voices embedded in our dialogue, those written in italics. They are the voices of poets, as illustrators, and whisperers, destined to give what Merleau-Ponty (1962, p. 179) calls a "gestural meaning," which lives in the emotional content of the word, and fill the frame of Heidegger's (1971, p. 140) description as "the sayers who more sayingly say."

Memories of Breathing

SASHA'S STORY

Most people don't think about breathing. They breathe 20 times a minute; they breathe faster or slower; they take great gulps of morning air; but still, they don't think about breathing.

I remember sitting in the waiting rooms of hospitals over the years with my mother when I was between seven and 11 years old and trying desperately not to stare at the other people sitting, waiting. I would watch them waiting, wondering what on earth they were doing there. They just sat and waited.

Some of them never looked the least bit sick to me, but maybe I always imagine sick as dying, or maybe it was because they looked like ordinary people you might see in a parking lot or the supermarket. They wore ordinary clothes, but one thing was that most of them seemed to have all these three-to-five-year-olds who would jump all over the chairs and make too much noise so that their parents were always asking them to sit down or shut up. I always wished that they would too because they reminded me that I could hardly walk.

I can't decide what I hated more, the waiting or the idea that everyone was watching me be sick, not throw-up sick. Just sitting there fighting for air and the pain of the ache in my chest. Sometimes I would get so scared I was gonna die. I sometimes even used to make my will out sitting there, waiting, and wondered if anyone would miss me. I always thought my Mum would cry and my sister would get all my stuff, but I decided that I would tell my Mum (if things looked really bad) that my sister was under no circumstances allowed to have my things and that would she please give them to Laurie Lunden, my best friend.

We used to wait for such a long time. I can remember. Sometimes it gets a little hazy and things always come in the wrong order, but I still remember. I always felt like I was running out of time for some reason. I think maybe it was that I thought I couldn't last a second longer. It was as though my chest was going to cave in on me and I just wasn't going to be able to take enough breaths so that I would last until they could fix me.

I always told my Mum that this was the worst one ever but she always said that it was just the same as last time. I never believed her. I used to think she wouldn't say that if she could crawl inside my body right now, but I learned later that she was right. I think it was just because I was so scared. Sometimes I used to cry and that only made it worse, so I stopped. I remember when we were checking in, it always reminded me of checking into a hotel, but for sick people, I guess.

The only thing that made it sometimes okay was that I got to ride in a wheelchair. I loved that. I would try and get people to wheel me all over the place. If I got admitted I would ride up and down the hallway outside my room as fast as I could, dragging my IV with me.

Once I met another girl, older than me. She was there because she had been hit by a car. I remember she had a broken leg and a black eye and I was really sad because she had the prettiest long brown hair. I thought it was so sad because she was so pretty and people with hair like that, well . . . things like that just shouldn't happen to them. My Mum brought me a game of checkers one time and we played so many games of it. Thinking back, I think my Mother must have been going bananas by the time I left.

I didn't always check in though. It would get better and they said I could go home, but sometimes I wanted to stay just in case I got sick again. Lots of times I just went into Emergency and sat on a bed that always reminded me of my bed because it was so springy. They used to make me get changed into one of those nighties with only ties in the back. They were always a grey color that reminded me of a misty, rainy morning. I used to get so embarrassed, because I thought people could see. The doctor would come in and listen to me breathe. What he heard I don't know. I used to get less scared by this time because I knew I was gonna get better. I would lay back on this springy bed and they put an oxygen mask over my face. I always found this incredibly farcical when I lay down and my nose started to run. I couldn't imagine why I had been so scared. It was also that my Mum used to start saying breathe in, breathe out whenever I sniffed. I can remember how cold the railings on the bed used to feel, just like popsicles in summer.

Now looking back and trying to find a way to make myself more descriptive, I find I can't change a word because to me the words are trapped in the time and to change the words is to change the time. Some people say they hate hospitals but I could never understand why because to me it was the place I went to get fixed. It was safe. They can make me breathe again.

***

So Sasha tells her story of what she knows well, a happening, a feeling that is hers. I am there in her story but it seems that I really lived mostly in the preface.

I hold her in my arms again, another night, like other nights. It is two o'clock in the morning. She is five years old and I am ageless, ancient with fatigue.

Throughout the day I have watched and listened, feeling the gradual escalation of the asthma attack. This path is well known to us. A few nights ago saw the beginnings of a small cough that joined and smudged with the night sounds. The days were fine, almost surface normal, except for the wheezing noises after the somersaults on the carpet, or the bubbly cough that was with her in the warm steamy bathroom.

I knew our steps were quickening when I saw her shoulders held tight and high and her nostrils flare on inspiration. Despite this I made no plans, no preparation for contingencies, no decisions. I kept thinking about the side effects of the course of steroids only just finished again, and I could see that the theophylline for her breathing was making her restless, irritable, and anorexic.

Her pulse is very fast from the side effects. She is so small.

I was asleep when I heard the asthma find a new tempo of assault. Closed doors, but I knew and I was up, the dark house sliding past me. She sits Buddhawise in the middle of her bed, hands on knees, shoulders high and wide, mouthing speechless words. I help her with the inhaler and there is some relief for the words come—"Mummy, Mummy"—a small breathless chant.

I pick her up, her arms around my neck. She grips but holds herself away, straining upward and leaning back with the need to have space all around her chest. We go into the kitchen, all blue shadows in the night light. I put her on a high stool, her arms up on a pillow on the kitchen counter. We try the inhaler again. This is wrong, I know. She has already had too much and it is not working.

Dark curls matted stuck to her forehead, all of her sweaty under my hands. Little shoulders, ribs. Her lips are dark blackish in the dim kitchen light. I have to decide what to do, but I am empty and stupid. My thoughts fly high above the moment, not touching us, not present. I am outside myself watching the scene that unfolds like a bad movie.

We wait in the darkened kitchen for nothing. Time is gone. There are only the two of us in this other world where moments are measured by the flailing labored breathing.

She starts a barking cough so demanding that there is no space for breaths. Her eyes fill to cry and I am there living in my anger and my fear. "Stop that, don't cry, just breathe damn you, breathe." I have my car keys, a coat, a blanket. I throw words to the others in the sleeping house. "We are going to the hospital."

***

"I remember," said Sasha "I was shouting so loud mummy, mummy, mummy, but I knew it wasn't loud enough. I knew you couldn't hear me."

***

"I remember," Sasha said, "you always seemed pissed off at me when my asthma started. It just always made you mad. I would ignore it for as long as I could and then suddenly it was always too late. I knew it was a real hassle for you and messed everything up, but it was a hassle for me too because I couldn't do it without you. If I forgot my Ventolin you would get so mad, even if we had not made it out of the driveway you would be beserk. I had to ask you to go back though because I had to have it. Now I never forget it, it is just a part of my stuff. Alex my friend used to say to me, 'Sasha, have you got your Ventolin?' and I would say to him, 'Hey, what is this, are you my mother or something?' "

***

> My voice goes after what my eyes cannot reach,
> With the twirl of my tongue I encompass worlds and volumes of worlds.
>
> Whitman, 1891-1892, p. 47

Two minutes from the house hears my unconscious litany of daily checks. "Have you got your Ventolin?" The small voice is defenseless, and the flattened tone is my answer. It is only a forgetting: an accident that begets a twisted pileup of tangled emotion. My anger collides with my body and slams me back against the car seat and my driverless tongue becomes a whiplash of frustration. I am a scourge.

Anger. Anger. It spreads like orgasmic heat through my belly and my chest. White fists on the wheel. Ugly hands that match the wild harridan.

My throat is thick with some unnamed feeling and my breathing as ragged as hers will be later when the asthma comes and the Ventolin is not there.

We turn around and go back to the house.

> And our two souls so left
> Achieve no unity:
> We are each one bereft
> And weeping inwardly.
>
> Livesay, 1986, p. 79

Do you remember Sasha, when you learned to use the inhaler? You were really small when I taught you. Once, we went to see the allergist and after the tests he asked to watch you so that he could assess if you did it correctly. He said he had never seen a small child use an inhaler so effectively. But I already knew because I had taught you. Do you remember? You would sit in the curve of my lap like a spoon, upright, chest to chest, with my face next to your face over your shoulder. And my lungs next to yours felt the bellows hiss and my chest burned from the weight of weightless air.

I would shake the inhaler and then you would shake it. Now, "Ready, blow right out as far as you can blow, blow and then blow some more. Now . . . PUFF . . . PUFF . . . the Ventolin into your mouth, all hands together, and slowly . . . slowly . . . pull the air in through your teeth and over your tongue and then deeper . . . and deeper . . . NOW HOLD IT, HOLD IT! start to count. Oh, so good, you are so good" . . . big bug eyes rolling around. "Pretty funny eh!" and all the extra air wanting to come out pushing out your cheeks like a trombone player, pretty funny, mine too, "Look Look!"

"Oh, yes, my mother, I remember that! It was always such fun. I would try and count and see if I could get to 20. Sometimes I could only get to eight or 10 but the second time I could get to 14 usually."

***

"When I take my Ventolin now, I can pull everything that is me into this tiny little space. My vision gets unfocused and goes completely black. Then when I let go, I go back out again."

> to kneel; and hold with choking breath one's own
> contracted contours, trying to expand,
> tight in one's heart like horses in one's hand.
>
> Rilke, 1964, p. 34

***

"I remember," Sasha said, "I remember when I first started hiding my asthma. It was in grade 8 and there were boys and we would always be fooling around. Well, I would palm my inhaler and then shake it under my arm . . . like this. . . . Then I would kind of twirl around and then when I was facing the other way I would have a puff and hold my breath in my twirl and then they didn't notice. That is the worst thing. How people notice. Some people ask lots of questions and then I have to answer even if I don't want to; some people just look at the inhaler and then just look away quickly. But whatever they do, they always notice. The guys seem more accepting than the girls. Except for Becky—it always frightens other people, but I'm glad it frightens them, it has frightened me for years. I want it to matter to them and to be important so that I don't seem to be neurotic, because a lot of people think that asthma is nothing. I don't resent them because I have asthma but I can never be perfect and sometimes I feel like I am physically handicapped or something. I want to start where everyone else started. I want to be on equal terms."

> If there are guardians around you
> they do not reveal
> how ably you'll take hold of pain

> and shake it off
> and twist the corkscrew in your heart
> and turn and laugh again.
>
> Livesay, 1986, p. 47

Oh my Sasha, I remember when you went to high school. So anonymous. You with your A's. A for French, English, and Math. A for asthma. The PE teacher was a big blonde woman with affronting muscles. So aggressively living what she was that she wore her fitness like a uniform, never knowing how her great shoulders and gesticulations intimidated us. And in her goal oriented gradedom she assigned you meaningless reports and the dust laden duty of putting away the mats.

I had to get you a medical release from Phys Ed, knowing as I did so that you would no longer value your small athletic achievements like riding your bike to school. The signatures on that piece of paper were reminiscent of the era when the frail and failing adolescent schoolchild had feathers burned under his nose.

> and to divine the whelming desolation,
> the inexorable impersonality,
> of all that childhood needed to withstand:
> And even then depart, hand out of hand,
> as though you tore a wound that had been healing,
> and to depart: whither?
>
> Rilke, 1964, p. 30

"I remember," Sasha said, "It was only a few months ago. You guys were out. It was a Saturday night and you had gone to a barbecue at four. I felt it coming and I just started sitting in a chair because I would need Ventolin without doing anything. Then it just seemed to pick up momentum from there.

"I was watching TV but I don't know what was on. There was the digital clock on the VCR above the TV and I was watching that. I saw every minute go by like 8:30, then 8:35, and 8:40, and then it would be 9:30 and I would not know how the time came, I was just there. I was wishing that you would come home, I had decided to spend the night in the chair. There was no way that I could lie down. There was nothing I could decide to do till you came home. I knew that you would give me prednisone. I suppose I could have gone to the hospital or taken the prednisone myself. I knew how many pills and where it was. I sat up till you got home. I wasn't scared, it was all too familiar, I knew every stage. I was frustrated. I waited for you."

***

You gasp "Hi! It's bad," and your hands extend and smile. You can only speak in phrases that are guillotined. Your body lines mirror the planes of the chair: drafted mathematically. Your back and head upright and your forearms flat on the chair arms. Your eyes show gladness that I am here, as I would be glad if the plumber came for a recalcitrant drain. You are waiting for me and I am wine warm and soporific.

You are waiting for me and I did not think to leave a number.

You were waiting and the dead hours that were your breathless limbo are lost to you forever.

We are both calm. I give you a loading dose of prednisone, not liking to make medical type decisions, but knowing it is the only decision against the mad flutter of xanthines. I leave the bedroom doors open so that I can hear if you are in trouble. But I know that you will manage now till morning.

***

Sasha said, "It is good to talk about all this and stop pretending that it hasn't made any difference to me, that it hasn't made me what I am. Of course (joke, joke), you realize that I can never leave home because I couldn't afford to support my habit."

The Fabric of Asthma

Merleau-Ponty (1962) reminds us that communication between consciousness is not based on the common meaning of our respective experience, for it is equally the basis of that experience. Rich (1981) writes about our essential separateness and our urge to reach for one another when she says:

> I can't know what you know
> unless you tell me
> there are gashes in our understandings
> of this world

> We came together in a common
> fury of direction
>
> Rich, 1981, p. 21

For Sasha and me this is just a beginning. Our stories bring meaning into existence, essences that are for us not only embodied in the text but part of our Being, of our history. Merleau-Ponty (1962) writes that, "the end of the text will be the lifting of a spell. It is at this stage that thoughts on the speech or text will be able to arise" (p. 180). The stories we have written are the fabric of our Being in the world. We are, Sasha and I, the warp and weft of our own weaving. But before we laid the warp or cast across the weft, the essential fibers of our separateness were already spun by genetics, in the world, and with others to make us what we are.

For the Child

Sasha: Et Spiritu

The word *air* in the old French form of *aire* is related to a sense of place; it is also related to song as in *aria*; and again in *eyrie* as the wild hawk's high place in the air.

The verb "to breathe" is rooted in spirare; esprit; spiritus, collectively as inspiration; breathing; breath; air; life; soul; pride; courage. What is it like, then, for a child with asthma to have difficulty with all such essential elements, and does a difficulty with one transpose to a difficulty with all? Whitman (1891-1892) in *The Body Electric* paints the full dimension with words

> and if the body does not do fully as much as the soul?
> and if the body were not the soul, what is the soul?
>
> Whitman, 1891-1892, p. 75

Sasha describes "fighting for air," "so scared I was going to die." When her fear was with her we never spoke of death, and now I wonder what was her sense as a young child of body and soul. What would death have meant to her, and would the meaning be similar for any child? From where did she draw her courage?

ASTHMA AS AMBIGUITY

A child with asthma must dwell in conflicting realities; after all, until events are out of hand there is no classic look of sickness. The episodic nature of asthma and the triggering mechanisms of everyday occurrences feed the constant doubt that any difficulty will be perceived "to be neurotic . . . because a lot of people think that asthma is nothing." Heidegger (1977) speaks of "dwelling" as the manner in which mortals are on earth. How does a child, then, dwell in sickness and in wellness? There are rules and expectations for being "sick," and we learn quite early on how to behave in this role. One should be seen to take care of oneself, eat well, rest, be compliant and concerned. The asthmatic child is given a different set of rules known only to those experienced with asthma. Asthma isn't sickness, behave normally, do as much as you can. In other words, act well until you get sick, but don't act too well, such as pushing against your limits and making yourself sick. If the child dwells in the world of sickness he or she will be considered neurotic. If the child dwells in the world of health, then the existing rules and mores will soon find him or her "wimpy" and deficient in stamina.

LIMITED TIME

Running out of air is experienced as "running out of time" that the child cannot "last a second longer." Is this because she is not in space or time as we measure it, or rather that the child belongs to space and time together? As her space recedes and closes and the capacity for air diminishes, time becomes measured by every gasping breath. Time becomes breathing. Breathing is time.

We constitute ourselves in the historical present. For a small child in the throes of a severe asthma attack, "every time is the worst one ever." Could it be as Merleau-Ponty (1962, p. 140) thinks, "that the body necessarily exists now; it can never become past; and we cannot retain in health the living memory of sickness" . . . these "gaps in memory" merely express the temporal structure of our body? This is possible, or perhaps the experience of running out of air and time is the ultimate crisis and threat to self. The sudden acceleration of time as a diminishing resource gives an asthma attack a sense of immediacy and urgency. The experience of crisis must be experienced as crisis: a turning point in life.

THE COMFORT OF TEARS

Comfort is rooted in *confortare* to strengthen. To gain comfort is to be "with strength" but the release of tears as a way of regaining strength is rarely an option in an asthma attack. In any other situation the catharsis of tears is an allowable refuge; in asthma, it becomes a catch 22. The throat-swollen thickness that crying brings is no panacea. "Don't cry, damn you. Breathe, don't cry." The cry of the parent shackles the child in emotional bondage. The fear of the parent that crying will only make things worse becomes evident to the child. As Sasha said, "the crying made it worse, so I stopped," but the burden of fear remained.

THE HOSPITAL AS LIBERATION

The hospital can become a haven, a place of diversion, a place of safety. For a child in the throes of recurrent phases of asthma the hospital can begin to represent a place of liberation from fear. Often treatment routines follow a predictable pattern and as expectations are met, such as access to the nebulizer and the oxygen mask, fear starts to ebb away and be replaced by other feelings. The sense of liberation that Sasha describes is evocative of the paradoxical whimsy of Kundera (1984, p. 314) when he says, "happiness fills the space that sadness owned." Things can become "incredibly farcical" and the child cannot imagine "why I had been so scared." Yet when Sasha reflected to write her story she remembered all her fear collectively. Is this how fear is remembered over time? It seems that in the immediate situation when fear is relieved, experience of the crisis becomes more temporal. This was the time when Sasha remembered deciding who would get her belongings if "things looked really bad." In an arena of safety, of knowing that "I was gonna get better," fear gave way to play: "riding in the wheelchair" and pleasure: "I loved that."

ASTHMA AS CONCEALMENT

A child who cannot breathe effectively at both predictable and unpredictable occasions quickly senses the disadvantages that a disability can bring. What is it like to feel that you can "never be on equal terms" in a world that cries equality for all; never to be "perfect" in a world that reifies perfection? What is it like to feel "physically handicapped" in a world of sleek athleticism?

Hiding asthma becomes a ritual, a personal behavior, a way of life, and like all hiding it eventually becomes a secret: a personal burden. What is it like for the child to share the experience of the man looking through the keyhole that Sartre (1966) wrote about. Should she abandon her asthmatic body and try to join the scene on the other side of the keyhole, then to be observed and feel shamed and defenseless? For the child asthma is often a hidden affliction trivialized before the world. And the abnegation does not end here. Real achievements are diminished. The child's grand efforts with their faint rewards are made to seem small and insignificant when judged by the harsh criteria of the healthy-lunged world. What is it like to keep trying in the face of this? Where is such a child's place in the curriculum for physical education? What does she come to know about the hidden curricular values?

Van den Berg (1972, p. 110) examines aspects of self-concealment in relations with others: one can hide, keep something secret, disguise. In her story Sasha did all of these at one time or another. The experience of the child when the hidden trappings of asthma are observed and noted are, as Sartre (1966) observed, that "his body clots under the other person's stare" (p. 112). Sasha is very aware that "it frightens people" and that "they always notice." It is on being discovered that the child experiences being seen as different and the aggregate of these experiences becomes a stigma, internalized and worn as a psychic tattoo.

SILENCE AS ABSENCE

Absence is by definition the nonexistence of essence. There was in Sasha's story a sense of isolation when she was calling for her mother or when she was waiting for a parent to come home. It seems for a child in distress that there is no innate certainty that the parent will immediately come to help, and they must wait the slow wait. In absence there was silence, and in silence, absence. For Sasha these were abstractions and her concrete, lived experience was wanting her mother to come and calling "Mummy, mummy, mummy," and "I was just wishing you would come." Compressed years of calling shifted this experience into an accepting patience: "I just waited." The parent remains essential to the experience.

WAITING AND FREEDOM

For the child on the threshold of adulthood there is a sudden surge of independence that is frustrated and held back by the asthma. The child still needs the comfort of the parent to be "with strength." At bad times even when the child knows what action the parent will take to help, there is a reluctance to assume an autonomy. Self-administration of drugs is an unwanted responsibility for the adolescent to assume, and difficult for the parent to abrogate now that there is also the beginning realization of the drug costs involved. Within the warp and weft of the relationship, the dialogue of a thousand nights, the parent and child develop a kind of symbiosis with the asthma: the child says, "I was waiting (for you)"; the mother says, "you were waiting (for me)." With such ties still in place, it is as Merleau-Ponty (1962, p. 456) says, that "freedom flounders in the contradiction of commitment."

ASTHMA AS A WAY OF BEING IN THE WORLD

Asthma can become the child's way of being in the world. It is the esprit, the spiritu. It is, as Sasha says, "what I have become," "What I am." In this statement she moves closer to Heidegger's (1977) concept of "understanding," so closely bound to unconcealment and disclosure. For Sasha, as for Whitman, if the asthmatic body is not the soul, what is the soul of Sasha?

For the Mother

THE FACE OF THE NIGHT

Any particular night of being up with a sick child can disappear into the memory of a thousand other nights. It is "another night, like other nights" when there is

> The dialogue of the rock with the breaker
> The wave changed instantly by the rock; the rock changed by the wave
> returning over and over.
> The dialogue that lasts all night or a whole lifetime.
>
> Rich, 1971, p. 53

The experience returns over and over. No one night is really the same as another, but the variations in events were minimal, leaving an essential theme of what it is for a parent to experience a child's night with asthma. Always the fatigue, the ageless ancient quality, the inexorable press of circadian rhythm which left my body cold and slow. There was a sameness to the nights. It is only on reflection that I can perceive how the small changes in existence altered the experience from the early years to recent nights.

The house is different at night. The sense of space, color, and sounds cause me to relate to it differently. The limits of the room slide away into shadows, moving the immediate space closer to my body. The light has a quality that only darkness can bring. The house sounds different. It is sensitive to my unusual presence, and echoes back my movements. It is the world of being-up-in-the-night-with-a-sick-child.

THE SENTIENCE OF ASTHMA

The parent watches the escalation of the asthma in the child. She is the silent reader of the voice, the gestures, the movements; she is the interpreter of the language of asthma, the receiver of the gestalt.

The image of the sick child waiting for the parent becomes like an icon imprinted into visual memory. It is like a frame frozen in time, stripped of movement.

> a tide waiting for someone to enter.
> a monologue waiting for you to interrupt it.
>
> Rich, 1971, p. 53

There is a sense of suspension. In a way it is like watching the media coverage of some catastrophe to which our eyes and brain have become immured, but it is more subtle than that. The experience is intuitive and incremental. There is the same sonar essence that is present when the parent hears the child through the curtains of sleep. The parent can feel the asthma. The waiting is helpless and devoid of anticipation.

Waiting for the illness to recede is like waiting for nothing. Like a "tide that ebbs and flows against a deserted continent" (Rich, 1971, p. 53).

Normal breathing is an unconscious action. Asthma is a conscious struggle, it is something, so it is in polarity that waiting for normal breathing is waiting for nothing. There is a sense of disconnection, of "being outside," of "watching a scene unfold," of "being in another world."

ANGER AS ANGUISH

The parent feels powerless in the deep desire to help the child who suffers. The parent feels bodily the "weight of weightless air" and shares the "ragged breathing" even in anticipation of something that may not happen. There is an anger born of helplessness for the anonymity and the trivializations the child has to cope with.

Anger shares the roots of grief. *Anger* is rooted in *angere* which is anguish, *anguisse* is narrowness, *agkhein* to strangle.

There is a physical quality to the feeling of powerless anger. It is a collision, heat, and an unnamed thickness; I am anguished and I become anger. On reflection I feel my shame again, I see myself, "the wild harridan" in her defenseless tone of voice. I remember clearly the clenching stranglehold, the *agkhein,* the anger on my body. My experiences of anger have had many faces, but those angry responses for forgetting the Ventolin were significant in their predictability, almost a culmination. In part, I anticipated her helplessness if she became breathless and had nothing to help her. There was also a feeling of helplessness for myself, of responsibility, of weight, of a burden of trust. This could be, I think, the other side of freedom. The price of being-for-the-other.

COMFORT AND RITUAL

The response to a chronic illness like asthma becomes ritualized. There is relief and goodness in the ritual because they become rites of faith. Creating the rituals together gives parent and child a physical bond and a close tactile sensing of breathing. The rituals were akin at times to prayer or some form of meditation, and at other times there was a sense of "fun" and of togetherness. Rituals have a presence and an order, and I know that Sasha still counts and breathes in the same learned way.

Relief is sought in the embrace as well as in the medicine. In this poem "On the beach at night" Whitman (1891-1892, p. 189) writes

> Weep not, child,
> Weep not, my darling,
> With these kisses let me remove your tears

and in these lines we live the urge to give strength in an embrace, to make up for the denial of tears. Within the embrace the Ventolin can be administered, and anguish lessened for both parent and child.

BEING THERE

The parent can hear the distress of a child through closed doors and through the curtains of sleep. What bonds there are here can never be just temporal. Whether nonhuman or human, we respond to the sonar call of distress as if the very words were screamed inside our sleeping brain.

> A conversation of sounds melting constantly into rhythms.
> A shell waiting for you to listen.
>
> Rich, 1971, p. 53

Who is the shell? The parent or the child? When we place an ear to the shell, when we are aware of a child's distress, do we also listen for the echo of ourselves? Is this experience of heightened awareness also the child inside us, remembering the need for presence and comfort, or just that in the nighttime quietness of our minds we are more open to each other? We are the ear and the shell: a paradox.

ASTHMA AS A WAY OF BEING-IN-THE-WORLD

Asthma cannot be healed. However in writing our stories and searching for a thematic consciousness within them, Sasha and I have healed some "gashes in our understandings." Over the last few weeks we have mused, laughed, and sometimes cried at "our common fury of direction." The experience of asthma is Sasha's experience. Mine is the experience of loving a child living with asthma. The stories themselves are a reflection. We have learned from the stories, from the themes and from each other.

References

Cole, R. B. (1971). *Essentials of respiratory disease.* Toronto: Pitman.

Heidegger, M. (1971). *Poetry language thought.* New York: Harper & Row.

Heidegger, M. (1977). *Basic writings.* New York: Harper & Row.

Kundera, M. (1984). *The unbearable lightness of being.* New York: Harper & Row.

Livesay, D. (1986). *The self-completing tree.* Victoria, BC: Press Porcepic.

Merleau-Ponty, M. (1962). *Phenomenology of perception.* London: Routledge & Kegan Paul.

Rich, A. (1971). *The will to change; poems 1968-1970.* New York: Norton.

Rich, A. (1981). *A wild patience has taken me this far; poems 1978-1981.* New York: Norton.

Rilke, R. M. (1964). *Rilke: Selected poems*. London: Penguin.
Sartre, J.-P. (1966). *Being and nothingness*. New York: Washington Square.
Whitman, W. (1891-1892). *Leaves of grass*. Mount Vernon, NY: Peter Pauper.
Van den Berg, J. H. (1972). *A different existence*. Pittsburgh, PA: Duquesne University Press.

IV

Ethnography

Ethnography is a method used to describe a cultural group or to describe a phenomenon associated with a cultural group. The method is based on the assumption that culture is learned and shared among members of a group and, as such, may be described and understood. The ethnographic method relies primarily on the techniques of participant observation and unstructured interviews, but invariably both of these techniques are supplemented with other data, according to the needs of the study. For example, a researcher may use minutes from a meeting, medical records, photographs, or anything that has been produced by or reports on the culture or cultural group that will assist in getting at what Stein (1991) calls "the story behind the story." In addition, investigators may use standardized questionnaires to supplement information about a culture. Davis's ethnography of the Newfoundland fishing village (Chapter 11) is such an example.

Traditionally, ethnography was conducted in a clearly delineated setting, such as a village or a small settlement. However, in health care research, an institution may be considered a cultural group, as is the nursing home in Golander's article, "Under the Guise of Passivity" [Chapter 13], or a professional group may be treated as a cultural group, as are the surgeons in Cassell's article (Chapter 12). Occasionally, ethnography is conducted in such settings as a patient care unit where the members of the group are brought together for a relatively short time yet are socialized enough to learn the cultural rules of the setting (see Rosenhan's description [Chapter 14]). Other researchers have used ethnography with individuals who are separated geographically but have some aspect of their lives in common, such as being a diabetic or experiencing a mastectomy. In such cases, participants may be identified in the community and interviewed in their own homes, and the experience of the particular illness provides the basis that allows for the synthesis of data. The foundations of ethnography lie in anthropology where the essence of good ethnography is understanding cultural rules, norms, and values. Some of these rules may be clear and diverse and well described by the participants in the study; others may be implicit, more difficult to elicit, and not immediately obvious to the members of the group. However, when the findings of the study are presented to the group, they should be immediately recognizable and should intuitively make sense.

There are various types of ethnography ranging from a basic description of the cultural group to interpretive ethnography, which seeks to understand the less obvious nuances of the behavior of the group. As with all qualitative research, the onus is on the researcher to focus the ethnography according to the topic, to describe aspects of behavior clearly, and to illustrate using quotations from dialogue or interviews or descriptions of the setting. As Hinds and her colleagues pointed out in the introductory article (Chapter 3), context is important and is included in ethnography as a part of the data, rather than stripped or excluded from the phenomenon as it is in quantitative research. Although standardized tests may be incorporated into ethnography, this is usually done cautiously for the use of questionnaire data does not permit the investigator to present the "symbolic context" or emic perspective of the concept being studied. In addition, as is clearly illustrated in the chapter by Davis, the use of the questionnaire data may not be particularly valid or reliable in all settings, in all contexts.

I have selected four articles to illustrate the ethnographic method. The first is "The Meaning of Menopause in a Newfoundland Fishing Village" by Dona Lee Davis (Chapter 11). In this chapter, Davis illustrates the analysis of menopause by examining the semantics of menopause or the folk or lay terms that the harbor women use to refer to the "change," and the symbolic meaning that menopause has in their lives. She uses the women's concepts of "nerves" and "blood" to link the biological aspects of menopause with the symbolic and affective dimensions. Finally, she places these data in the context of the "social and symbolic organization of life" in the fishing village (Davis, 1983).

In contrast, in the chapter "On Control, Certitude, and the 'Paranoia' of Surgeons" (Chapter 12), Joan Cassell describes the use of ethnography for understanding a cultural group that is a subculture of both medicine and of the medical institution (the hospital). Cassell's chapter is an excellent example of the ways that the underlying values of a cultural group may be identified. These values are reflected in the members' attitude to work, and they provide and maintain group solidarity and form an underlying matrix of beliefs and attitudes that are reflected in their behavior. This chapter is unusual in its point of view. Cassell, as a researcher, is not outside but is a part of the setting and has included herself in the setting by writing the ethnography in the first person.

The third ethnography I selected is "Under the Guise of Passivity" by Hava Golander (Chapter 13). Golander uses a greater proportion of participant observation than interviews. Even so, she provides the reader with a vivid description of the ways that elderly residents in a nursing home cope with physical discomfort; balance their relationships with staff members, with other residents, and with family members; maintain their independence in a dependent state; and help time pass in an environment in which little happens. From her careful observations of the behavior of the residents, Golander is able to describe the hidden or less obvious meanings behind behaviors that could easily be misinterpreted. For example, she notes that a resident who appears to be doing nothing may be planning his time or protecting his legs from being injured or planning a strategy to get to the bathroom. This interpretive approach provides invaluable information for clinicians.

The final ethnography selected, "On Being Sane in Insane Places" by D. L. Rosenhan, is an example of covert participant observation. It includes almost no interview data, and data obtained from the records concerns the researchers themselves as pseudo patients. This research caused much concern when it was conducted in 1973 for the research was done covertly without the knowledge and consent of the staff or the institution. Ethical issues aside, the chapter is important because it clearly demonstrates the role of perception in the diagnosis of mental illness. It is not a very large leap to move one stage further to recognize the risk that perception may also play with ethnographic research results. Verification of the findings is an essential and ongoing process in ethnographic research.

An important and frequently asked question is, Is an ethnographic report, derived from one setting or a relatively small sample, generalizable? Compare and contrast the reports of Davis, Cassell, Golander, and Rosenham and decide what, if any, aspects are generalizable and why.

References

Davis, D. L. (1983). *Blood and nerves: An ethnographic focus on menopause*. St. John's, Newfoundland: Institute of Social and Economic Research.

Stein, H. F. (1991). The role of some non-biomedical parameters in clinical decision making: An ethnographic approach. *Qualitative Health Research, 1*, 6-26.

11

The Meaning of Menopause in a Newfoundland Fishing Village

DONA LEE DAVIS

Abstract. A comparison of etic and emic options for climacteric research shows that the emic option is best suited to the study of the meaning of menopause in the Southwest coast Newfoundland outport fishing village of Grey Rock Harbour. Standard menopause survey instruments, as the Neugarten Attitudes Toward Menopause checklist (1963) and the Datan et al. Sociocultural Patterns and the Involutional Crisis interview schedule (1981) were administered to 38 women and found to be of limited utility because they assume the following: (1) that respondents can rank stimuli along linearly constructed continuums, (2) that the questionnaire items contain sufficient contextual information for Harbour women to make psychosocial judgments such as agree and disagree, and (3) that respondents are capable of and experience no difficulty in making public pronouncements based on insightful self-evaluations. More qualitative ethnographic description and emic analysis address, yet go beyond, the popular semantics of menopause to explore the meaning of middle-aging in the symbolic, moral and institutional spheres of Harbour life. For more suitable context for understanding the role that sociocultural factors can play in shaping women's experience of middle-aging, in depth analyses of the following are offered: (1) the continued importance of the fishery and the idealized social image of outport Newfoundlanders as a "tough race"; (2) the expectation that women should endure hardship and solve problems rather than create them; and (3) the strict enforcement of an egalitarian ethic throughout the community.

AUTHOR'S NOTE: This chapter originally appeared in Davis, D. L. (1986). The meaning of menopause in a Newfoundland fishing village. *Culture, Medicine, and Psychiatry, 10,* 73-94. Reprinted by permission of Kluwer Academic Publishers.

Introduction

This chapter compares and contrasts the utility and validity of questionnaire and participant observation methods in climacteric research. Presentation and discussion of data is directed at what is commonly called the etic-emic "issue" (Jahoda 1977; Trimble et al. 1981) or "option" (Harris 1969). Although the etic-emic distinction has become increasingly recognized as an important issue in crosscultural research, climacteric research has tended to overlook the emic dimension of middle aging.

As an explanatory model of health states the etic option entails the systematic and scientific knowledge of the scholarly community of social science and biomedical observers. Methods of etic research include biomedical models of disease and the development and use of standardized means of assessing climacteric symptomatics and attitudes. The emic option studies behavior as it actually functions (Harris 1969), and rests on the explication of idiosyncratic and folk views of health systems or the nature, purpose and meaning of menopause or equivalent phenomenon in the local, native context. Emic methods include ethnography or prolonged periods of participant observation of the daily life of members of the population under study. The ethnographer is concerned with semantic and communication phenomen
a and the intentions, purposes, motives, goals, attitudes, thoughts and feelings of those whose culture is studied.

The conclusions as to the relative merits of the etic and emic options are based on my own experience in attempting to use both research options in a study of women's experience of menopause in a Newfoundland fishing village.

THE ETIC DIMENSION OF CLIMACTERIC RESEARCH

Scientific models of the climacteric and menopause tend to be characterized by biomedical reductionism, of what Engel (1984) terms the simplified concept of disease as a deviation from a norm of some measurable biological or somatic variable. Although commonly referred to as "ovarian failure" (Greene 1984), in the extreme, menopause may be defined as "a sex-linked, female dominant, endocrine deficiency disease" (Wren 1984) to be alleviated through medical intervention.

The major emphasis of climacteric research has been etic—the identification and measurement of specific symptoms held to originate in the biology of aging. What was once simply known as "the menopause" has been elaborated into "the climacteric." The climacteric can span up to thirty years and is subdivided into pre-, peri-, and post-menopausal stages. Each stage is supposedly characterized by identifiable symptomatics.

Symptoms themselves are grouped into categories based upon etiology, such as vasomotor, somatic and psychological. The primary symptoms—those related to ovarian failure, including the flash or fluid and atrophic vaginitis—are major subjects of biomedical research. Mood shifts or psychic problems, often relegated to the domain of "secondary symptoms," are of particular interest to the social sciences. Sociocultural analysis appears to be concerned with how psychosociocultural factors may effect variability in the experience of the climacteric in different sociocultural settings (Davis 1983c).

A central aim of etic, sociocultural research is to develop standardized instruments designed to assess climacteric symptomatics and attitudes towards menopause, which can be correlated with additional data on psychic history, employment status, socioeconomic group, social change or any number of measurable sociocultural variables.[1] The great advantage of these studies is that they involve minimal expense, allow for random sampling of large populations and are amenable to quantitative analysis. Such studies have provided numerous data with which to evaluate biomedical models and supplement clinical data with findings from "normal populations." Their great contribution has been to question the disease model of menopause and to point to potential roles (identified through statistical correlations) which social and cultural factors may play in women's experience of menopause (e.g., Goodman 1980; Kaufert 1980, 1984; McKinlay 1984).

Measurement is common to all sciences, "without measurement there can be no data and without data there can be no science" (Trimble, Lonner, and Boucher 1981: 260, 268). Yet to what extent can computerized information compensate for lack of acquaintance with sample individuals? Does a research emphasis on a precoded questionnaire format result in the recording of relevant information (Wilbush 1984:767)? To what extent does the statistical study of individuals detract from an examination of shared cultural categories of thought and action? To what extent are such data torn from their cultural context, providing at best a fragmented picture of the social and cultural matrix in which menopause related phenomena occur? Are the created significances of the expert's etic perspectives in the form of quantitative analysis of climacteric symptom and attitude data the same as or similar to the subjective meanings and purposes that characterize the lay, local, folk or emic perspective?

THE PROBLEM OF THE EMIC

Humans experience themselves through the mediation of language, culture, symbols and networks of meaning (Good and Good 1981:187-189). An alternative way of understanding the meaning of menopause is to view it in terms of everyday folk (emic), rather than empirical, medical or scientific (etic) discourse. The experience of middle-aging is embedded in tradition, folk culture, societal values and the social construction of knowledge. One of the most important cognitive features of the lay health system is that it cannot be understood apart from every day reality and every day common sense and knowledge (Blumhagen 1980).

Etic techniques of measurement and assessment in the form of paper and pencil scales are held to be more scientific than emic techniques which are said to "defy capture." The emic approach is dismissed as exotic, irregular, ephemeral and not conforming to standardization (Jahoda 1977). A less critical view of the etic-emic issue recognizes the research process as a compromise between the "theoretically desirable and the operationally practical" (Trimble et al. 1981:264). Yet, while the etic option of information gathering and measurement—the use of standardized tests—is seen as a pragmatic although complex methodological issue, the emic is seen as the very essence of methodological simplicity. Trimble et al. (1981:264) flippantly comment that, "One can always 'find' the emic if one has time enough to soak up an adequate amount of the culture one is investigating."

In a recent review of climacteric research, Greene (1984:163, 167) states that, "much of the content of cultural attitudes to, and behavior during, the climacteric may be peculiar to a particular cultural group and defy generalization." Primacy of reality of the menopausal experience is seen by Greene as best assessed by standardized indices. According to Greene the major methodological issues in climacteric research are (1) obtaining an adequate random sample, (2) operationally defining menopause and climacteric status, and (3) adequately measuring symptomatology. This certainly seems to preclude the emic. Indeed Greene (1984:156) has little truck with "complicated cultural accounts of how women . . . conceptualize the menopausal experience."

Should the emic be relegated to the domain of "unscientific" because it is difficult to measure or defies generalization? Is it to be considered irrelevant precisely because it recognizes the complex nature of culture? In my own research, I have found that there is very little that is systematic about menopause. The remainder of this chapter demonstrates how women's experience of menopause in a Southwest Coast, Newfoundland fishing village,[2] is not readily amenable to etic assessment with standardized measures for a number of reasons. First, the use of disease models in menopause research is problematic, since women's experience of menopause exists on a continuum from normal, for the vast majority of women, to abnormal, for a minority. Second, etic analysis obfuscates the idiosyncratic nature of menopause, where each woman's experience may generate new ideas that can be incorporated into the cultural domain. Third, women's experience of menopause cannot be understood apart from the local psychological and sociological implications of middle-aging, sickness and health. Understanding the folk, popular or lay dimensions of menopause cannot take place apart from understanding the role of the local community in the process of negotiating meaning of aging in the social and symbolic contexts of village life.

The Ethnographic Background

The term, output, commonly refers to the necklace of small, rural comparatively isolated fishing villages that surround the shores of the island Province of Newfoundland. Located on the Southwest coast of Newfoundland, the outport fishing village of Grey Rock Harbour is populated by approximately 800 inhabitants of English descent. The major source of employment is a year round, inshore fishery. Most villagers (74% of the work force) gain their livelihood by fishing or working at the Harbour fish plant.

Settled less than 200 years ago, Grey Rock Harbour is a comparatively new village by Newfoundland standards. As in other outports, the history of Grey Rock Harbour is for the large part a chronicle of dismal poverty, isolation and the struggle of survival in a harsh environment. However, since confederation with Canada in 1949, material conditions have steadily improved. In the mid 1960s, a dirt road was built connecting the village to larger population centers where health service facilities and consumer products are readily available. Today, Harbour life is characterized by all the modern conveniences and welfare and unemployment benefits that typify other rural areas of Canada. Yet Grey

Rock Harbour continues to be a small-scale, bounded and homogeneous community. The social and symbolic organization which characterized the community in the past continues to provide a common fund for the articulation of private and public concerns. The distinctive flavor of local life continues to rest on the fishery. Locals continue to take a great deal of pride in the tradition of the fishery. Their stoic endurance of hard times past and preservation of the valued traditions are seen as intrinsic elements in the Newfoundland character.

Because status is a multifaceted and complex phenomenon, the evaluation of women's status in Grey Rock Harbour is problematic (see Davis 1983c, for a detailed discussion). However, factors indicative of a high status for Harbour women can be briefly summarized. In Grey Rock Harbour, male and female spheres of activity are sharply divided and have different systems of evaluation. Status conferring roles of good mother, good housekeeper and hardworker are well-defined, highly valued and easily attainable. Women's labor at the fishplant, ownership and clerking of local stores and selling of crafts are recognized as important components in the family's standard of living. A history of village endogamy has been conducive to the formation of strong and continuing female kinship bonds. Women more than men represent the community. They are instrumental in planning community wide ceremonial events and are active in female voluntary associations.

The household and the family are the major multi-purpose groups in Harbour life. Who heads the household is determined by personality rather than sex. It is misleading to attempt an analysis of the roles of women in terms of power or authority since men and women, alike, lack culturally legitimated leadership roles. An egalitarian ethic pervades the community and effects the behavior of men and women of all ages.

In this study emphasis is placed on the ideological rather than formal, structural dimensions of status. According to Ortner and Whitehead (1981) each society has multiple, integrated prestige structures. Prestige for both men and women in Grey Rock Harbour stems from their affiliation with the fishery and the outport tradition. Outporters view themselves as a fortuitous distillation, a tough race who have been bred for endurance. The Newfoundland humorist Ray Guy (1975) states that for every death among the Lower Canadians, the Newfoundlander "can claim a thousand sacrifices through starvation, overwork, disease, forced exile, and persecution" that went into the making of them. Today's middle-aged women are the contemporary heroines of the shore-side of fishing. As young women, they worked under conditions of extreme poverty and husband's absence to rear and keep their family together.

The Meaning of Menopause

In the analysis that follows, the emic consists of what Good and Good (1981:178) refer to as "shared intersubjective meanings that are drawn upon by individuals to construct, interpret and reinterpret their experience." Women's experience of menopause in Grey Rock Harbour must be viewed as a collective, as well as an individual, phenomenon. The meaning of middle-aging in Harbour life is shaped by, and inseparable from, key symbols that dominate the village ethos and reflect the local social and symbolic organization. Just as friendship groups develop an in-group knowledge, argot, and shared orientation, many of the idioms of Harbour life and shaped by a long heritage of common experience, such as shared Anglican faith, occupation, concerns of life and a strong realization that survival of the community in a rapidly changing world rests on everyone remaining the same or equal (Davis 1983a).

The following analysis of the meaning of menopause among the women of Grey Rock Harbour takes into account both the collective and idiosyncratic elements of village life which help to explicate the emic perspective of menopause. These include (1) the semantics of menopause, (2) lay symptomatics and (3) local institutions and the moral order.[3]

THE SEMANTICS OF MENOPAUSE

The vocabulary of menopause shapes women's experience in a meaningful and convincing way. The significance of menopause in terms of objective, biological realities—such as ovarian failure, cessation of menses or onset of infertility—are of minor importance to Harbour women. Local women are unfamiliar with the terms "menopause" or "climacteric." In folk usage, the term "the change" would be somewhat equivalent. "The change" entails the processes which may accompany the cessation of menses and any coincident disturbances or benefits. "The change" may also be referred to as "the change of life," "[being] on your changes," "the change from woman to child," "the turn of life," "the final clearing out," or simply "clear" [I'm clear].

The term "the change" is also used in U.S. mainstream culture but the local outport meaning of the terms are more complex. Among

Harbour folk "the change" can refer to any number of female, age-graded complaints, including the following: (1) menarche or the onset of puberty; (2) any stage of the menstrual cycle; (3) menstrual cycle irregularities; (4) menstrual cycle complaints, such as cramps, mood changes, etc.; (5) vaginal secretions or discharge; (6) time of ovulation or "the time when it [sex] can take;" (7) any stage of pregnancy including labor and birth; (8) post-partum bleeding, mood change or general health; (9) menopause; and (10) post-menopausal mood changes or problems ascribed to aging reproductive organs. Conversing about "the change," one must specify to which "change" one refers. The identity of the person being referred to usually provides sufficient context.[4]

In a closed folk community such as Grey Rock Harbour every person has intimate knowledge about everyone else, their daily activities, their life histories, their families and their family histories. All interactions take place on a face-to-face level. Talk about health and illness is characterized by parsimony. A few key words such as "blood" and "nerves" are used to describe widely varying states of health and illness. Locally, it is the individual who defines the illness or complaint rather than the complaint that defines the person. Individual variation in somatic state is tolerated and of special interest in the community. Variation in psychic states, although characterized by more strict standards of tolerance and individual responsibility, is also recognized. Simple reference to "the change" lacks meaning in local life, rather it is "Cassie on the change," "Victoria's changes" or "when Betty took to the change" that place climacteric comments into a meaningful context.

In local lore, the lifespan is characterized by a series of seven-year cycles. The seven cycles are poorly articulated, but it is generally agreed that during the seven years marking menarche onwards, it is difficult to become pregnant. Then one should expect to have a child every seven years. Midlife involves two seven-year cycles. The first cycle of the midlife change consists of seven years of irregular or changing menstrual patterns; the onset of the second seven-year cycle of the change can only be known retrospectively since it is marked by the last menses. This is followed by a period of seven years, in which the potential for pregnancy remains. Then there is seven years of old age remaining, followed by death. In this view "the change" can take up to fourteen years. Within these broad parameters most women between the ages of 40-60 would identify themselves as on their "changes".

In actuality, age more than menstrual patterning is used by Harbour women to define themselves as "on the change." For example, a 35-year-old woman who had her ovaries removed was considered too young to be on "the mid change" and a 43 year old pregnant woman was defined as having a "change of life baby." The discrepancy between actual experience and lay lore does not bother or confuse women. This can better be understood with a closer look at popular symptomatics.

SYMPTOMATICS: NERVES AND BLOOD

Popular concepts of "nerves" and "blood" serve to link symbol, affect, and biology and to provide the basic structure of menopausal discourse. "The change" is considered to be a normal, natural part of the aging process. The natural history of menopause is shaped by the fact that somatic, psychological and sociocultural processes or phenomena are not compartmentalized. Symptom semantics, for women of all ages, cannot be understood apart from the local language of nerves and blood. As a general rule women do not refer to "the change", instead they are more likely to refer to what happens "to your nerves on the change." The most frequent symptom reported by middle-aged women and all women ages 35-60 was nerves (80%).[5] Women complain of "bad nerves", "good nerves", "strong nerves", "more nerves", "thin nerves", "tight nerves", "weak nerves" and "nerves are gone" or "come unstrung". Understanding the semantics of nerves is intrinsic to understanding how women conceptualize and experience the menopause. Nerves may be caused by stress, biology, heredity or trauma. Physically, nerves are seen as "the little strings that run through your body and hold you together." Stressful or traumatic events can "pull on the nerves," "thin the nerves," "grate on the nerves," or "fray the nerves." Nerves were commonly referred to as "like rubber bands". The etiology of nerves is conveniently teleological, e.g., nerves can cause stress and stress can cause nerves.

Nerves may be directly or indirectly related to women's experience of menopause. Some women believe that the biochemical changes of menopause "all those 'ormones' [juices or germs] running through the body," can physically effect the nerves.[6] More often problems with nerves at midlife are related to the fact that, like female reproductive organs, nerves age at a greater rate than other body structures.

The term "blood" also acts as a multipurpose complaint engendering diverse levels of meaning which can only be understood in the context of discourse. "Blood" problems may effect males and females. However, many of the characteristics of blood complaints in females relate to perceptions of menstrual blood as an indicator of health. Menopause is seen as the final purge—the final cleaning out. Viscosity and color of menstrual blood are said to indicate states of health. "Black blood" is said to be "good blood" and "red blood" indicates poor health, or vice versa depending on the informant. There is little agreement as to how the character of blood relates to states of health. Instead one refers to "Laurie's thin blood" or "Effie's thick blood". In the local view, regular, copious menses are good for one. They represent the body purging or cleaning itself out. On "the change" it is healthy to bleed profusely and in a prolonged fashion (if one sees this as the final phase of the menstrual cycle). The final cleaning out must last for the rest of life and should be thorough.

Characteristics of blood are used to explain many of the symptoms of menopause. Flashes and flushes are caused by "too much or bad blood" and welcomed as purifiers. Although emotional states are usually referred to in terms of nerves, being "low-lifed" may be the result of having too thin or not enough blood.

Menopause is an experience that is subject to a high level of individual variation. Women do not experience the same symptoms or difficulties on "the change." Some women report having no complaints or problems. Yet the change is a process that all women go through. Women freely discuss and analyze the variation in their experiences. States of both gynecological and general health are popular topics of conversation for women at all stages of the reproductive process.

The nature of behavior on "the change" and the semantics of blood and nerves cannot be understood apart from the purposes, motives, goals, attitudes, thoughts and feelings of Harbour women as products of their village culture. In lay life there is no mind/body dualism nor is there any marked self/society dualism. In Harbour culture the meaning of menopause cannot be reduced to symptomatics, folk or otherwise. Through continued participation in village life, I began to see how "the change" functioned as conversation capital in both institutional settings and the moral order.

INSTITUTIONAL SETTINGS AND THE MORAL ORDER

The primary concerns of village women of all ages are inseparable from the social and symbolic organization of life in this small, isolated and homogeneous fishing community. The family and the fishery are the two major institutions in Harbour life, each intrinsically bound to the valued traditions of outport life. Even with modernization and improved material well-being, the values of traditional outport culture—when fishing was even more dangerous, unpredictable and overcrowded households were characterized by mind numbing poverty—continue to govern the behavior and world view of contemporary middle-aged women.

Grey Rock Harbour is an egalitarian community. There is a strongly felt sentiment that "We all come up together or we don't come up at all." This type of perspective has been labeled by Foster (1965) as "the image of limited good" and is said to characterize peasant societies. Limited good refers to the view that all good things are finite and in short supply; therefore, an individual or family can improve their position only at the expense of others. The concept of limited good and consequent leveling have characterized Grey Rock Harbour's economic and social adaptation for as long as elders can remember. Leveling in Grey Rock Harbour exists in both the economic and the moral orders. Thematically, all men are fishermen and all women are fishermen's wives. Grey Rock Harbour has been in the past and continues to be a single occupation community. It is the drama of the fishery which shapes the local ethos. A good woman is synonymous with good fisherman's wife; she is a quiet hardworking woman, who will sacrifice personal gain to keep her family together and well cared for. She stoically endures life's lot as victim of marriage into a dangerous, unpredictable and, at times, unremunerative occupational household. Her role is to endure hardships and to solve problems, not to create them.

Nerves illustrate the role that language may play in linking social experience to disease; they are related to the role of women and the moral order of outport society. Nerves stem from and manifest themselves in worry, and women are justified in their worry. Worry has a symbolic role in Harbour life and women have a moral duty to worry, especially about their husbands who are at sea. Symbolically, a woman's worry, it is thought, keeps her husband's boat afloat. Women's worry, their responsibility for the family, and an ability to carry on if something should happen to the husband, frees the husband to get on with the business of fishing. Worry ties women into and gives them an active and valued role in the fishery. The "grass widow" overlooking the harbor, waiting for her husband or men folk to come home, is a romantic and powerful image in Harbour life (Davis 1988). A lifetime of worry causes nerves and conversely, nerves can cause worry in a neatly circular system of reasoning which allows all women to put symptom complaints into a valued context. It also allows wide-ranging expression, communication, and sympathetic support from others.

Hardship and suffering are said to wear out the nerves. Consequently, the middle-aged woman (or for that matter the old woman) who suffers from nerves can claim that her present day problems stem from a lifetime of self-sacrifice, hard labor and stoic endurance. If the community of women accept this claim, then nerves, although still a minor malady, is also a claim to the status and prestige of the good woman. However, the body of village women, as local judges of character, are extremely intolerant of self-centeredness, selfishness, or any departure from tradition of the wife/mother/fisherman's helpmate roles. Those who err from the moral pathway of the "good woman" will be forced to leave the community, shunned, have their property vandalized, or shamed into proper behavior by vicious gossip. Thus, there is a strategic dimension to the use of health and illness language in Grey Rock Harbour, which is shaped by the social and political stance of the leveling. Illness in Grey Rock Harbour means not being able to perform one's daily tasks. Labeling an individual as ill without proper justification is a means of negative reinforcement for inappropriate behaviors.

Although "the change" is a collective trait, in that every woman goes through it, it is recognized to be individualized for everyone. The personal relevance of this common fund of symbols may differ for individual women. Each woman charts her own itinerary through the midlife change. Yet each woman is also subject to collective assessment of her behavior by others. One's behavior is acceptable or unacceptable as the result of personal impression management. Politics does not rest in the judgment of whether or not one is ill, but whether or not one deserves to be ill. If a woman can successfully present herself as having earned enough life status to adopt the sick role, she will not compromise the respect accorded to her by the community. Loss of status does not come to those who are considered to be genuinely ill, but only to those who are seen as "empty" or chronic complainers. Lack of agreement over the legitimacy of illness does not arise over whether or not a woman is ill but over whether a woman has maintained her good character, kept up the fight.

Against this background "giving in" to sickness or "being a problem" are not valued female traits. Yet women do have license to complain, be sick, or impose themselves on others for support if they can maintain a culturally appropriate impression of the "good woman". Behavior unacceptable in its very essence can be acceptable if placed in proper context. One gets high status from stoically enduring life's lot. Suffering is stoic. It is intrinsic to the danger and drama of fishing. It is good, a test for the moral fiber of a "tough race". Those who can face and fight their problems receive the admiration of their peers. However, silent suffering brings limited social rewards. Suffering must be communicated.

With less objective suffering in a modernized fishery, menopause and getting through it has provided a substitute moral battlefield for middle-aged women caught up in rapid social change (Davis 1983c). One can have difficulties and express them, impressing upon others that it is a "tough fight" but you are not "giving in to it". Most women encounter no difficulty with image management. Only one village woman had the reputation of being weak or giving in to the change. It is not the experience or nature of incapacitating symptoms that determines the acceptability of complaints. It is impression management of the "good woman" image—an image that is inextricable from the major institutions of fishery and family—an image that shapes social reaction and gives meaning to menopause.

THE FOLK PERSPECTIVE

The meaning that Grey Rock Harbour attributes to menopause makes it a non-event, a normal, prolonged part of the aging process. It is a biological, psychological and social phenomenon. Cultural beliefs about "the change" are not so much grounded in experience of symptoms as they are rooted in the symbolic order of Harbour life. Menopause is viewed as a series of gains and losses. The vocabulary of menopause makes it an experience open to a wide age-range of women and an experience that can be identified with by all. Sympathy and support are available in the community along with specified roles to play and means of personal expression of self importance and community identity. Even women who do not have nerves complain of them.[7]

Since the change is not seen as a disease there is no recovery. It is simply a life stage, albeit a potentially difficult one, to be lived through by drawing on the same coping skills and tough nature that have been forced onto women by negative circumstances (poverty, etc.) earlier in their lives. Although attitudes toward menopause may be negative, menopause has meaning as a status enhancing developmental task—yet another challenge to be faced and overcome by a long suffering and exceedingly durable race. Nerves and blood may be problematic at menopause but they are not distinctive to menopause. One is not cured of "the change", one simply gets through this prolonged period of life as best one can.

Assessment and Measurement

Now that the emic view of the complexity of the meaning of "the change" in the context of the symbolic and organizational realms of Harbour life has been presented, attention may be focused on the etic option and the critical evaluation of the extent to which Harbour women's experience of the climacteric can be adequately evaluated using scientific assessment measures designed for the statistical study of individuals. Or as Trimble et al. (1981:267) more caustically ask, "Can human behavior in all its variability ultimately be placed into tidy little boxes?"

Although they are not part of mainstream middle America, outporters are English-speaking folk whose cultural heritage is similar to that of most U.S. and Canadian populations. One would expect minimal problems in cultural appropriateness with a Newfoundland sample. Yet, my own experience in attempting to administer scientifically standardized assessment instruments with this population has led me to question the extent to which these women are "testwise" or the extent to which they possess sets of skills and values such as the ability to read and understand instructions, and the desire to do well (Trimble et al. 1981).

The need for reliability, validity, sensitivity, comparability and utility dominate almost all approaches to social science measurement. The need for scientific objectivity, however, can be grounded in a very rigidly conceptualized approach and can create measurement problems when introduced to culturally diverse populations. Three questionable assumptions of measurement theory have been identified by Trimble et al. (1981: 260-264). First is the notion that psychometric categories exist that are grounded in linearly-conceptualized mathematical frameworks. Is it appropriate to assume that subjects can order or rank stimuli along a linearly constructed continuum? A second questionable notion is that individuals are able to generate psychosocial judgments about social and psychological stimuli by resorting to comparative and contrasting cognitive mechanisms. Do questionnaire items always supply enough context for the elicitation of the judgments they request? And, third, is the notion that individuals are capable of self-assessment by using evaluative and reflective cognitive processes. Is public acknowledgment of a self-statement or a request for a self-assessment always an appropriate question for an individual?

Questionnaire data on this Newfoundland menopause study came from oral administration of the Sociocultural Patterns and Involutional Crisis [SPIC] interview schedule developed and used by the Datan consortium (1981) and the Neugarten (1963) Attitudes Towards Menopause (ATM) checklist. Given the importance of: (1) the duties of worry, the nature of impression management and the role of the good wife; (2) the nature of Grey Rock Harbour as a small, bounded fishing community; and (3) the local view of the nature of menopausal phenomena as expressed in the language of change, blood, nerves, and seven year cycles, one may ask if the putative psychological states supposedly measured by the ATM and SPIC are anything more than a redundancy or repetition of the central themes of public life? With these emic themes in mind I will now use examples from my own study to address the three questions raised by Trimble et al. (1981).[8]

First, I had a great deal of difficulty obtaining questionnaire information (Davis 1986). Questionnaires were administered during my last three months in the field. Although the sample is small, 38 women between the ages of 35-60, it represents an almost total sampling of village women in that age group. All check-box answers were supplemented with open-ended questions. Interviews lasted several hours and, while both interviewer and interviewee enjoyed the "visit", the process of getting the informant to commit herself to a single check-box answer was sometimes extremely painful for both parties. The interviews were orally administered, since many women could not read at a proficiency level sufficient for the surveys and since the surveys, themselves, were initially designed for oral administration.

Personalized, intimate questions are never asked in such a straightforward direct fashion in polite outport society. Even such innocuous questions as how many children do you have, are fraught with difficulty, as women with illegitimate children see this as some sort of indirect assessment of their morality. Women tolerated this infringement on their privacy out of personal friendship to me, rather than out of any motive to make a contribution to science or improved health care.

The most common responses to my questions were, "My dear, you know all about that sort of thing. You fill in (the questionnaire) as you sees fit;" and "My dear, who told you to ask such a thing?" Ironically many women could not accept the questions at face value and thought that I was conducting some sort of projective test of their intelligence or personal morality. Every time that I have returned to the village since the fieldwork was completed in 1978, woman warily ask me if I am "going to do any more of those questions."

ORDERING STIMULI

Although developed specifically for a cross-cultural sample, the Datan et al. (1981) SPIC interview schedule contains many items which assume the informant is capable of ordering social stimuli. Newfoundland informants often had difficulty with these ranking tasks. A case example illustrates the problem that Harbour women tended to have with psychometric measures. There is a section on the Datan questionnaire, which is used to assess topics (e.g., husband's health, your own health, finances, growing old, etc.) and degrees of worry (1. especially worried, 2. quite worried, 3. not so worried, 4. almost not at all worried, or 0. not relevant). Although this woman represents an extreme case, the verbal exchange generated by this supposedly straightforward question illustrates the problem she had with ranking categories. In this and following examples "A" refers to myself and "B" to the Harbour woman.[9]

A: To what extent do you have worries and problems about your work about the house? Are you 1. especially worried, 2. quite worried, 3. not so worried, 4. almost not at all worried, or 0. not relevant?

B: Which do you mean dear? Worry or problems? You can have one with out the other you know. Mabel over in Crow Cove. . . .

A: This is about you. (Repeat question and answer items 1-4, 0.)

B: Well my dear, why you ask that is beyond me, but I do tells you, I do worry some awful. To tell the truth, I worry more than most, always have . . . [I] got it from my own mother, her nerves you see . . .

A: What about worry over your work in the house?

B: Tell me again what I'm supposed to say?

A: (Repeat question and answer items 1-4, 0.)

B: I used to find it worrisome when my mother-in-law was living with us. She wouldn't let me alone . . . [she] said I never knew how to do anything right. Is that what you mean?

A: Is it a worry for you now—at your present age?

B: What does that 1 mean, again?

A: Especially worried.

B: And the others?

A: (Repeat question and answer items 1-4, 0.)

B: What's the difference between "quite" and "not so" worried?

A: The "quite" means you're more worried than the "almost not at all" does.

B: That's not how we mean it, my dear. I'd say "quite" was the four, not the "almost not at all."

A: That's not the question. Here "quite" means more "than not at all." Do you worry about housework, now?

B: No, I shan't be so silly as to get all worked up over that. Give me a naught. That's how we say zero.

A: That means it's not relevant.

B: What does relevant mean?

A: Here, it would mean that you don't do housework, like if I asked you about your husband and you didn't have one.

B: This test is some stunned [dumb], I have a husband.

A: I know, but do you worry about your work in the house?

B: I find doing the dishes four times a day [to be] a bother.

A: I think worry here is supposed to mean stress, or anxiety.

B: What?

A: Like does it get on your nerves?

B: Well then dear, you understand it better than I, you check what you sees fit.

A: You tell me what you think first?

B: Either you worry or you don't. Some days. It grates on my nerves. Some days it doesn't.

A: Housework?

B: No that'd be foolish, unless mother's trying to help and its spring cleaning time. I worries that she's too old but you can't hold her back. Poor dear's had one hard life.

A: (Repeat the question and answer items 1-4, 0.)

B: What did Betty tell you on this one?

A: This one's for you. I need your answer.

B: It's hard to say, I want to do well on this test but I must be some stunned because I'd never thought about it like this.

A: It's not a test. In this case you're the expert, you have all the right answers. I'm just here to learn from you.

B: Well, my dear, if that's how you see it I'll take the five.

A: There's no five. (Repeat answers for items 1-4, 0.)

B: O.K. It's probably a lie but I'll take the four.

A: Thanks, ready for the next question?

Although this is an extreme case it does reflect the dilemma and confusion that women can experience answering such questions. One may say that I was not assertive enough about the questioning or it might appear that this woman was giving me "the run-around". However, I believe, based on our friendship established over the last twelve months, that she seriously wanted to help as best she could.

The Datan (1981) worry section was especially problematic. Women tended to feel very comfortable with this part of the questionnaire as it is a topic on which they consider themselves to be experts. Yet, relying solely on the questionnaire, one would overlook the symbolic context, or local meaning of worry in the occupational and historical context of village life.

This was not the only ranking problem that I encountered. In trying to interview one area of the village at a time, I discovered a "patch" of women who came out "almost not at all worried" about everything. I thought this unusual because the role of women is to worry. It was only much later that my landlady's mother informed me that my informants had gotten together and decided that the best strategy was to pick the high numbers, because I was adding them up and, like their children at school, it was best to have a high score. The highest scores won. In this case the questionnaire was seen as an intelligence test for "those who think big."

This was not what Trimble et al. (1981) would call a testwise sample. Nominal ordering is difficult for women who have not had a basic math education. Two additional problems arose from the method in which I administered the questionnaire. They both stem from the relationship between the researcher and the subject. Although local women did not understand what anthropology was, they did realize that I was a very educated person. According to local rumor I had graduated from the 22nd grade. Before I started to ask questions, I tried to reassure my informant of the value of her contribution and the importance of her own knowledge, experience and perspectives. I also tried to communicate what the study would be used for, telling them that we (social scientists) wanted to know more about women, and how different life experiences and social factors can influence the middle-aging process.

I wanted to compare the Newfoundland women with women who had already been studied in the United States. Unfortunately, many women did not want any researcher to take action on anything they might say. Hence, they were extremely unwilling to make any responses. In addition, I tried to show my appreciation for their taking the time to answer my questions, assuring that our sessions were not interrupted by husbands or children, and providing a tea afterwards by presenting a small present I had made especially for this purpose. Some women saw this as a prize they earned for doing well on "the test." Thus inadvertently I gave credence to the intelligence test rumor.

THE NECESSITY FOR CONTEXT

The problem of eliciting judgments is a second issue in measurement research, which assumes that individual are able to generate psychological judgments about social and psychological stimuli by resorting to comparative and contrasting cognitive mechanisms. Here it is assumed that subjects can produce judgments that are representative of the way judgments are made by typical members of a cultural group—that there are universal cognitive approaches to generalizing judgments (Trimble et al. 1981).

The process of forming an opinion in Grey Rock Harbour entails the consideration of three relatively undifferentiated phenomena, the idiosyncratic, the situational and the social (community ethos). In light of the complexity of these interrelated factors, it is difficult for women to come to the concise and assertive judgments demanded by the ATM, subjects had difficulty accepting the notion that all the relevant information was contained in the question. The following example illustrates how the informant kept seeking additional contextual information.

A: Agree or disagree. Going through the menopause [the change] really does not change a woman in any important way.

B: You mean does "the change" change a woman?

A: Yes.

B: Why do you think its called "the change?" We say "change from women into child." That means there's no more babies.

A: Is that important?

B: Depends, T'was'nt for me. I was glad to see the end of it.

A: Agree or disagree. (Repeat question.)

B: Well it was important for Emmie she was always hoping for a little boy.

A: Do you think this is generally true for women in the Harbour? (Repeat question.)

B: Well, there's Victoria who took to nerves on the change, and Annie uses the vaseline, you know.

A: Yes, but is it important for women in general?

B: My dear, I can only speak for myself. T'would not be fair of me to speak for others.

A: (Repeat question.)

B: This is some silly. You don't know and you don't care till it happens to you. But then you're too young to know that, my dear.

A: Yes, but when you talk about the change with your friends you must come to some kind of conclusion.

B: Well my dear, you talk to my friends, I can only speak for myself.

A: Well, answer the best you can, I've got to check something. (Repeat question.)

B: O.K., the first one . . . agree is it?

Based on this discussion, I would conclude that there certainly is a lore of changing "on the change". The informant has raised the issues of termination of fertility, problems with nerves, and problems with sex ("the vaseline" refers to treatment of vaginal dryness). Yet, the ATM statement does not ask what the changes are, it asks if they are important. My informant obviously thought that some changes were more important than others and that what was important could vary in the case of each individual woman. The discourse generated by the ATM statement shows an attempt by my informant to clarify its meaning. She did not feel that there was sufficient information contained in the statement which would allow her to relate it to local life. Although she knew about these changes she was unwilling to judge whether or not they were important changes for women in general. She was unwilling to generalize beyond the context of her own personal experience.

PERSONAL ASSESSMENT

The third dimension of measurement requires self-reflection and assumes individuals are capable of self-assessment by using evaluative and reflective cognitive processes (Trimble et al. 1981). Yet impression management among the women of Grey Rock Harbour operates to deflect personal assessment into a wide number of emically relevant factors including past life history, situational circumstances and image of the good woman. In local parlance one does not "Toot your own horn". The strategies by which an individual presents herself for collective assessment are complex and indirect. The less familiar one was with the interviewer (me) the more one evoked platitudes such as "I does the best I can," and stolidly refused to allow me to commit her to a check box answer.

Given the intimate nature of Harbour life, women's knowledge of each other is thorough and articulated through conversational levels of revelation depending on the nature of the relationship between those conversing. To use the analogy of an onion, women reveal themselves in layers. The outside self is revealed in casual conversation on the level of a platitudinous statement such as "My nerves are some bad." In contrast a more specific statement such as "I have a pain in my side and can hardly make it through the day" is made only to intimates as it is considered a request for help. Detailing a complaint in this way demands a commitment from the other party to provide aid if needed. Such requests may engender complex reciprocal obligations that are not entered into lightly. How does this relate to the interview situation? If a woman gave me specific information about her health rather than a more general statement she would feel that she had obligated me to help her in some way (Davis 1984).

The rhetoric of social self-assessment in Grey Rock Harbour is a rhetoric of self-effacement. The forces of leveling keep individuals from making statements which may be taken to indicate conceit. Therefore when asked questions normally used to measure self-esteem, such as questions about pride in appearance or sexual attractiveness, women check the most modest answer, despite the fact that they take great pride in their appearance.

Women are not asked to evaluate themselves in local life. Positive self-presentation is seen as "being above yourself," and is a major infraction of village norms. However, women are much more open to the open-ended questions, on the SPIC interview schedule, because they are allowed to maneuver within the realms of impression management. Women do not want to be reported as above themselves in such a leveling society. Women would often avoid evaluating themselves through escape to joking or humor.

A final point related to impression management concerns the negative affect that women attribute to menopause on the ATM. This negative attitude toward the menopause is not based upon symptoms or actual experience of menopause as much as it is rooted in strategies of impression management. The rhetoric of ethnic survival values the trait of being able to endure adversity. The greater the life challenge, the more one suffers, the more prestige one may derive from "being on the changes."

Conclusion

The etic option in climacteric research is based on a biomedical model and the development of standardized instruments designed to collect objectively measurable data. Issues in etic research are specific and pragmatic and concerned with sampling methods, the determination of climacteric status, and symptomatics. Cross-cultural studies of the climacteric which employ the etic orientation are concerned with gathering limited amounts of data on sociocultural variables which are generalizable across cultures and have import for health policy planning. The emic option of climacteric research is primarily concerned with semantics and communication as elements of culture and how these reflect inner psychological states and feelings. It addresses broad ranging issues such as how culture may shape the motives, goals, attitudes, and thoughts of its carriers.

In this article I have contrasted the utility of these two research options in a study of women's experience of menopause in a Newfoundland outport fishing village. The village study is a traditional ethnographic method of anthropology (Mead 1980) and the very nature of Grey Rock Harbour as a marginal, isolated, single occupational, and homogeneous village makes it especially amenable to emic analysis.

Despite the existence of a rich and diverse body of emically oriented research, critics of the emic option continue to label its exotic, simplistic, not generalizable, too creative, or too culture-specific. The emic approach has also been criticized for its potential for dumping even more data into the already overburdened Human Relations Area Files (Trimble et al. 1981).

Although more amenable to measurement, overemphasis on an etic analysis assumes that we have nothing to learn from other cultures or that complex behaviors are reducible to simple hypotheses or mathematical formulas. Although I collected questionnaire data in as conscientious and responsible a fashion as I felt was possible I have little reason to expect that my quantifiable data is either reliable or valid. The outport women in my sample were not testwise,[10] they had problems ranking response data, found questions to lack sufficient context, and were personally offended by directed questions involving self-assessment.

Only through ethnographic observation and daily participation in all spheres of everyday life could I have become sensitive to the semantics of nerves, blood, and seven-year cycles; the symbolic importance of the image of the good woman and her moral duty to worry; and the insular, egalitarian nature of Harbour life, as they affect women's collective and individual experience of the meaning of menopause.

Notes

1. See Greene (1984) for an up-to-date and comprehensive review of the climacteric literature.

2. Fieldwork was conducted from October 1977 to December 1978. Research was funded through a two-year traineeship from the U.S. National Institute of Child Health and Development administered by the University of North Carolina Population Center. Grey Rock Harbour is a fictional name.

3. This analysis is loosely based on the model for understanding and explaining illness theory developed by Good and Good (1981), which includes explanation of (1) the pathways linking the affective and psychologic with the symbolic, (2) the role of language in linking social experience to disease and (3) the strategic use of illness language.

4. For matters of clarity, unless otherwise specified, further use of "the change" in this chapter refers to the midlife change.

5. Other symptoms frequently reported by women ages 45-56 included hot flashes (60%), cold sweats (27%) and irritability (26%).

6. Women were familiar with the term "hormone" because some were taking post-hysterectomy "hormone pills". When I asked what hormones were, I was told that they were juices or germs in your body. One may speculate that juices were seen as good or benign hormones and germs were bad ones. I did not pursue this question. The term "germ(s)" may also refer to sperm and is used in reference to contraceptive technology (see Davis 1983a).

7. Nerves are such a conversational convention that women will often complain of them when they are actually feeling fine. At breakfast one morning my landlady, who often suffered from nerves in the form of headaches, told me that a miracle must have happened because she got up with no nerves (head pain) at all. Soon after her daughter called to ask how she was, the woman replied "My dear my nerves are some bad today". After the call I questioned the woman about her nerves and she reassured me that they had gone away and could not remember telling her daughter that her nerves were bad today. (For further explanation of this and other cases of no nerve nerves see Davis 1984).

8. Since I have dealt with the issues of reliability, validity and cultural appropriateness elsewhere (Davis 1983b), I will focus attention here on the three issues raised by Trimble et al. (1981).

9. The reconstruction of this and the following conversation is based on notes taken in the margins of my questionnaire.

10. It might be argued that the sample was testwise but the problematic wording of the questions made them invalid. However, I do not feel that rewording questions or answer options would avert the problems I have attributed to lack of context or local strategies of self-revelation or impression management.

References

Blumhagen, D. 1980. Hyper-tension: A folk illness with a medical name. *Cultural Medicine and Psychiatry 4*: 197-227.

Datan, N. et al. 1981. *A Time to Reap*. Baltimore: Johns Hopkins University Press.

Davis, D. 1983a. The family and social change in a Newfoundland outport. *Culture 3*(1): 19-32.

———. 1983b. Women the worrier: Confronting feminist and biomedical archetypes of stress. *Women's Studies 10*(2): 135-146.

———. 1983c. *Blood and Nerves: An Ethnographic Focus on Menopause*. St. John's: Memorial University of Newfoundland Institute of Social and Economic Research.

———. 1984. Medical misinformation: Communication difficulties between Newfoundland women and their physicians. *Social Science and Medicine 18*(3): 273-278.

———. 1986. Changing self-image: Studying menopausal women in a Newfoundland fishing village. In *Sex and Gender Role Boundaries in Cross-Cultural Encounter*. T. Whitehead and M. Conaway (eds.). Urbana: University of Illinois Press.

———. 1988. "Shore skippers" and "grass widows": Active and passive women's roles in Newfoundland fishery. In *To Work and to Weep: Women in Fishing Economies*. St. John's, Newfoundland: Institute of Social and Economic Research, Memorial University of Newfoundland.

Engel, G. L. 1984. The need for a new medical model: A challenge for biomedicine. In *Culture and Psychopathology*. E. D. Mezzich and C. E. Berganza (eds.). New York: Columbia University Press.

Fostér, G. 1965. Peasant society and the image of limited good. *American Anthropologist 67*(2): 293-315.

Good, R. J. and Good, M.J.D.V. 1981. The semantics of medical discourse. In *Sciences and Cultures: Anthropology and Historical Studies of the Sciences*. E. Mendelsohn and Y. Elkana (eds.). Dordrecht, Holland: D. Reidel.

Goodman, M. 1980. Toward a biology of menopause. *Signs 5*(4): 739-53.

Greene, J. G. 1984. *The Social and Psychological Origins of the Climacteric Syndrome*. Hampshire, UK: Gower.

Guy, R. 1975. *You May Know Them as Sea Urchins, Ma'am*. Portugal Cove, Newfoundland: Breakwater.

Harris, M. 1969. *The Rise of Anthropology Theory*. London: Routledge and Kegan Paul.

Jahoda, G. 1977. In pursuit of the emic-etic distinction: Can we ever capture it? In *Basic Problems in Cross-Cultural Psychology*. Y. H. Poortinga (eds.). Amsterdam: Swets and Zeitlinger.

Kaufert, P. 1980. The perimenopausal woman and her use of health services. *Maturitas 2*: 191-205.

Kaufert, P. 1984. Women and their health in the middle years: A Manitoba project. *Social Science in Medicine 18*: 279-281.

McKinlay, S. 1984. Sociocultural aspects of the climacteric. Paper presented at the 4th International Congress on the Menopause, Orlando, Florida.

Mead, M. 1980. On the viability of villages. In *Village Viability in Contemporary Society.* P. Reining and B. Lenkerd (eds.). Boulder, CO: American Association for the Advancement of Science Selected Symposium 34.

Neugarten, B. et al. 1963. Women's attitudes toward menopause. *Vita Humanica 6*: 140.

Ortner, S. and H. Whitehead. 1981. Introduction: Accounting for sexual meanings. In *Sexual Meanings: The Cultural Construction of Gender and Sexuality.* S. Ortner and H. Whitehead (eds.). Cambridge, UK: Cambridge University Press.

Trimble, J. E., Lonner, W. J. and Boucher, J. D. 1981. Stalking the wily emic: Alternatives to cross cultural measurement. In *Human Assessment and Cultural Factors.* S. H. Irvine and J. W. Berry (eds.). Dordrecht, Holland: D. Reidel.

Wilbush, J. 1984. Clinical information—signs, semions and symptoms: Discussion paper. *Journal of the Royal Society of Medicine 77*: 766-773.

Wren, B. 1984. The health care needs of climacteric women. Paper presented at the 4th International Congress on the Menopause, Orlando, Florida.

12

On Control, Certitude, and the "Paranoia" of Surgeons

JOAN CASSELL

Since the emergence of distinct occupational specialties, people have observed that each seemed to engender its own ethos and its own set of personality traits. In stable societies with unchanging techniques and technologies, the patterns were evident, and often were associated with ethnic groups, which were themselves often thought to exhibit the specific virtues, or vices, and the personality types. In contemporary times, the effects are not so conspicuous, and our reluctance to typify ethnic and racial groupings—or indeed the members of any social category—contribute to a diminution of scientific interest in the question. Publicly, we decry any such labeling, and brand it as "stereotyping."

Compounding the problem is the bias inherent in our vocabulary for classifying personality. Stemming from psychiatric literature, we have a plangent set of terms which serve to evoke types and traits, but frequently at the cost of implying mental pathology.

In the project with which I am currently engaged, the issue must nevertheless be faced. For more than two years I have been observing surgeons, and it has become clear that they and their colleagues recognize an ethos, a "standardized system of emotional attitudes" (Bateson 1958: 119), and a set of traits distinctive of that profession. In this essay, I propose to examine the relationship between the work of surgery and the ethos and personality traits of those who practice this specialty.[1] I

AUTHOR'S NOTE: This chapter originally appeared in Cassell, J. (1987). On control, certitude, and the "paranoia" of surgeons. *Culture, Medicine and Psychiatry, 11*, 229-249. Reprinted by permission of Kluwer Academic Publishers.

will then explore some of the dynamics, and personal costs and benefits, of maintaining the ethos and set of traits.[2]

Process, Event, and the Work of Surgery

Recent literature has emphasized a processual understanding of medical care (e.g., E. J. Cassell 1977). Consideration is not limited to a specific event or events; instead, care is presented as a *process,* with the passage of time perceived as an integral part of the interaction between doctor, patient, and disease.

Surgery, however, unlike specialties such as internal medicine, is based primarily upon *event,* rather than process. Although processes, such as preoperative and postoperative care, affect outcome, the *act of surgery* occurs in a measurable and sharply delimited period of time. During this event, the surgeon does something that alters the patient's body irrevocably and, on occasion, radically. Surgeons are rarely allowed the luxury of second thoughts; they cannot try a treatment, see if it works, augment or alter it, and then, if their first attempt is unsuccessful, try another approach. At the operating table, the surgeon must manifest decisiveness, certitude, control; emergencies must be resolved, unexpected findings anticipated, small advantages exploited. Although every medical specialist enacts the metaphor of the "war on disease," for the surgeon, the encounter is more likely to be a battle than an extended war. Tactics, not strategy, are paramount,[3] as the surgeon strives to extirpate disease, rather than attempting to outthink and outmaneuver it to slow its ravages.

The Surgical Temperament[4]

Surgeons manifest a recognizable temperament, which fits in well with the requirements of a specialty focused primarily on event, rather than process. Not all surgeons exhibit every characteristic, but almost every surgeon encountered during two years of research has exhibited many.[5] This temperament, or set of traits, is selected for when Chiefs of Surgery interview house officers; self-selection is involved, as well.[6] Those who lack this temperament are unlikely to be attracted by surgery; if they enter a training program, are likely to leave, voluntarily or involuntarily; and, if they remain, to be ill-suited to the practice of surgery. I am going to describe this temperament, in the words of the surgeons I have been observing at work, and indicate how this set of traits is related to the occupational requirements of surgery. I will then discuss what surgeons have described as the "paranoia"[7] of surgeons and explore its relationship to the temperament and ethos of surgeons.

"Surgeons are very different from medical doctors" explained the Chief of Surgery, my first day at the community hospital where I first studied surgeons. By "medical doctors," he meant internists; the competition between the two is longstanding.[8] The relations between the two specialties resembles those in segmentary societies (Evans-Prichard 1971: 142-143): surgeons and internists may oppose one another (e.g., Bosk 1979:105) but, as doctors, they unite against the non-medical world.[9]

"We all sit together," explained the Chief, as we walked into the cafeteria and he looked for the patch of green that marked the surgical table, where several young men sat, wearing green surgical scrub suits covered by white coats, the "diacritical signs" (Nadel 1957: 30) that identify them as surgeons.[10] Three house officers sat at another table; this was due to the presence of a female outsider said the Chief, who indicated that it would take six months for the surgical house officers to accept a woman, and even longer for the senior attending surgeons.

I learned that the camaraderie and exclusion (or, at least, distrust) of women were characteristic of surgeons.[11] "There's a kind of comradeship," said the Chief, describing the relationship between surgeons, "almost the comradeship of someone you've faced death with—even though it's not your own death."

The right stuff. The masculine society of surgeons admires cars, sports, speed, competence. The two non-surgical subjects most frequently discussed at the surgeons' table in the cafeteria were cars and sports. The sports discussed were team sports: football, baseball, basketball, occasionally, soccer. Many of the young surgeons talked about previous prowess in sports, regretting they lacked the time to continue these activities. The Chief, too, occasionally mentioned his career in semiprofessional football; after interviewing prospective house officers, he mentioned sports ability in tones of interest and approval. Of one candidate, he remarked dismissively, "he looks frail." "Frail" was not the term that occurred to me but upon reflection, this particular medical student did seem to lack the confident, athletic, outgoing air exhibited by more preferred candidates.

I noticed that a number of the surgeons, including the Chief, wore no overcoats—even in freezing temperatures; a (coatless) senior surgeon explained, only half-jokingly: "Surgeons are macho, cold doesn't bother us!" (Wondering which came first, the choice of surgery or avoidance of overcoats, I asked an intern, wearing only a white cotton lab coat in below-zero weather, when he stopped wearing winter coats: "Since I was old enough to do it without my mother yelling at me," he responded.) A house officer described how, when he moonlights at another hospital, he likes to see how hard he can drive himself; he discovered his best friend does the same thing; it's almost an addiction, he reported, they work nights when they don't really have to; after discovering he can function adequately without sleep, he finds himself looking down on people who complain or look tired when they've been up all night. I have observed a senior surgeon operate for seven hours without taking a break; a number have described occasions where they operated as long as thirteen hours without a break.

The archetypal surgeon is invulnerable, untiring, unafraid of death or disaster. Of thirty-two general surgeons surveyed, eleven never wore automobile seatbelts, while five reported that they reluctantly began to use them when a law mandating seatbelts went into effect. Said one: "I resent them trying to force me to use them . . . it doesn't hurt anyone but myself . . . "

When, in 1980, I interviewed ten senior surgeons on the training of surgical house staff (Cassell 1981), three compared themselves with the test pilots trained as the first cadre of astronauts (Wolfe 1979). The more I studied surgeons, the more similarities became apparent between the macho, death-defying, almost exclusively masculine world of general surgeons and that of test pilots and astronauts: not only occupational similarities—in the lengthy training, high level of technical skill, pyramidal system of advancement, and scarcity of women in anything but supporting roles—but similarities in ethos and temperament, as well. The legendary Chuck Yaeger, who walked away from demolished planes to become the first man to fly faster than the speed of sound, might well be the surgeon's heroic ideal. Like Yaeger, the successful surgeon takes risks, defies death, comes close to the edge, and carries it off.

Like the test pilot, the surgeon must have nerve. "Why does a surgeon need nerve?" a young urologist was asked. "Because we have to make snap decisions," he responded. He explained that a surgeon is constantly faced with the unexpected: something unexpected is found during an operation or something unexpected occurs and the surgeon must decide instantly what to do and then take action. There's one surgeon at our hospital who lacks nerve, he said: he has technical skills but cannot make snap decisions, consequently, he's slow, so slow that it's dangerous for his patients. (Although the man was not named, I had heard jokes about this man's slowness; the disastrous consequences of that slowness, however, were not yet apparent to me.)

A group of house officers were asked: "Why does a surgeon need nerve?" "What do you mean, nerve?" inquired one. "What Doctor Vespi calls 'balls!' " responded another. "You need nerve to cut," he explained, eloquently describing the tension and excitement he feels when operating; his pulse, he said, goes from 70 to 135.

"You have to approach an operation like a battle," said an orthopedist, "you have to know ahead what may go wrong and have three solutions planned for every problem. When something goes wrong, you have to be able to try the first solution, then the second, then the third. I had a house officer," he continued, "who used to get on dead center, then he couldn't move, he couldn't make decisions; he would get onto a single point. In surgery, you have to keep moving, it's sort of like riding a bicycle, if you stop moving you're finished; you have to be able to shift and move about and make decisions."

"Manly Courage . . . ".[12] When the almost exclusively masculine cast of the senior surgeon's world was described to an anthropological colleague, he expressed surprise. "You'd think women would be particularly good at surgery," he said: "they have manual dexterity, they're used to sewing, and they're traditionally empathetic and good with people." The manual dexterity of surgeons is associated with a sophisticated technology, however: curved surgical needles are manipulated by specialized implements; a complex array of instruments are used to cut, probe, hold, staple, and stem bleeding; none resemble the simple homely technology associated with traditional female tasks. As for sympathy, empathy, and an aptitude for human relations, these traditionally female traits seem somewhat peripheral to the most obvious and easily observed characteristics of a good surgeon, many of which are exhibited when the patient is unconscious. It is *cutting,* not sewing, that is central to surgery, and cutting into a human body is (to a non-surgical observer, at least) terrifying. To take a knife and cut into human flesh takes courage, nerve: one has to have an invincible belief in oneself—traditionally a masculine trait.

Said John Woodall, a sixteenth century surgeon: "It is no small presumption to dismember the image of God." Perhaps only a confident, indeed arrogant person can so presume.

Arrogance. "We all believe we can do anything better than anyone else," explained a house officer, "better than the attending, better than any other surgeon, better even than the person sitting next to us, even if he's a friend. Better than you!" he said, turning to his close friend, who said, smilingly, at almost the same moment, "Better than *you*!"

"I wouldn't be doing this, if I didn't think I could help him," proclaimed a young orthopedist, carrying out a new and complex procedure; the nurse whispered that an old-time orthopedist had once announced, "All surgeons think they're the best; they wouldn't be here, otherwise!" And, after a long and difficult operation, a Chief Resident announced, only half-jokingly, "another miracle!"

Certitude. "Surgeons are involved in important things," said a Chief of Surgery, "they're decisive. The surgical motto is 'Sometimes in error, never in doubt.' . . . A guy who becomes a surgeon rather than an internist is a guy who needs a lot of positive ongoing feedback; every day the moment of truth occurs in the operating room and that confirms he is right, right about the diagnosis, right about the timing, right about the procedure . . . A surgeon can't stand a chronic patient, he likes to be able to define the patient's problem, do something definitive about it, and see that resolve the problem. The results are clear then, to the patient and to the surgeon."

Positive feedback. Said one young surgeon, describing the choice of specialty:[13]

> . . . as soon as I got to surgery, it didn't take me one day to figure out this was where I belonged. Just the whole aura. I mean the surgeons are the macho people, of all the specialties. And the immediate gratification—every surgeon knows about that. Just making a sick person better and having them sit up and say, 'Gee thanks, doc, you saved my life!'

Activism. "They're more intelligent," said an orthopedist, who reported that his brother-in-law was an internist; when I indicated that the surgeons I had met were extremely bright, he responded: "Well *they* have it here," pointing to his head, "while we have our intelligence here," pointing to his hands.

"A surgeon just can't walk away when he sees stones!" said one, justifying a decision to pursue a risky course of action; while at a Mortality and Morbidity conference, where deaths and complications are discussed, several men admitted they were unable to stand by and let a patient bleed to death when there was an emergency procedure they could perform—even when they knew they had virtually no statistical chance of success! And, as a team prepared for an emergency operation on a young man who had swallowed lye for his second, possibly third, suicide attempt, a Chief Resident was asked what he thought about operating on someone who might well go out and try again if the operation succeeded: "I think he's twenty-six years old and he's dying!" he rejoined.

Their activism may be reinforced by surgeons' fondness for surgery. "A surgeon is never so happy as when he's operating," said a Chief, singing tunelessly as he scrubbed for an operation, while a senior resident remarked, after operating, "I was in such a bad mood and now I feel good. I love to operate, it always makes me feel good!" When surgeons discuss operating, they sound like men describing why they love war: said a Vietnam veteran about war,[14] "The intensity, the intensity . . . everything goes on tilt!" I suspect that operating too, is terrifying—and addicting—and that the everyday world seems drained and dull after the highly-colored confrontation with death.

Leadership. "Surgery is a body-contact sport," and a surgeon to Charles Bosk (1979: 13). It is also a *team* sport. The "surgical team" is hierarchical, with an all-powerful captain, who calls the plays and accepts responsibility for success or failure. It includes the anesthesiologist, two or more nurses and a First, and on occasion, Second Assistant. In a "teaching hospital," the Assistants are likely to be house officers, who frequently perform the operation, guided by the senior surgeon.[15] The attending surgeon, whose patient is on the operating table, directs: he decides how much the senior house officer scheduled on his case will do, how it will be done, and what to do if the resident gets into difficulties. The attending shows where to make the incision, what kind of incision, what instrument to use for each procedure; much of this is done nonverbally, with the attending holding instruments, helping, and indicating what should be done next. At the same time, junior house officers are taught how to insert and hold retractors and perform simple procedures. The attending sets the mood in the operating room: he quizzes house officers, testing their surgical knowledge; commends or chastises the operating room nurses; is serious, or decides it is time for joking (usually, when the patient is being "closed" after a successful procedure [see P. Katz 1981]). Not surprisingly, one of the qualities a Chief of Surgery told me he looks for in house officers is "leadership ability." With hierarchy goes responsibility: a second year house officer teaches and directs a first year intern; the third year resident teaches both; the Chief Resident teaches and directs all the house officers, and is, in turn, taught and directed by the attending surgeons. A non-team player would make a poor surgeon: it is not a one-on-one sport.

Being a team player is essential, but the game is brutal and, as the legendary football coach once said, winning isn't everything, it is the *only* thing. "Yes, he's good," said a senior surgeon of a house officer, "but I wish he were more *aggressive*." "Mark would have made a good general surgeon," said a Chief Resident, of an intern going into plastic surgery, "he's smart, aggressive, and a little bit of a son-of-a-bitch." When asked, "Why son-of-a-bitch?," he explained, "Because you have to stand up for yourself sometimes and insist on doing things your own way."

Technical mastery. Control in the operating room is based on more than absence of doubt: a first-rate surgeon must have technical sureness, or "good hands." An orthopedist, who was described as a superb technical surgeon with "great hands," said: "I tell my patients 'you're not using me because of my personality or because of my bedside manner, you're using me because of these five fingers,' " holding up one hand, " 'and these!' " holding up the second. When one observes a surgeon with "good hands" operate, everything looks easy, almost inevitable; the performance has a kind of rhythm, speed, and flow; even emergencies, such as an unexpected hemorrhage, appear to be under control. A house officer reported that a particularly successful surgeon had "golden hands"; indeed he did! Lack of technical competence is recognized, covertly discussed when it is a senior surgeon whose abilities are in question, 0and made the subject of pointed "jokes" when it is a house officer; a senior surgeon at one hospital gave yearly awards to house staff for "Hands of Wood," "Marble Mitts," and (to a resident whose patients had an unacceptably high level of hemorrhaging) "Captain Blood."

The wrong stuff. The medical student, whom the Chief of Surgery dismissed as "frail," had good recommendations and was accepted into that hospital's surgical training program. Although he displayed no interest in sports or cars and lacked the macho swashbuckling air affected by the other surgical house officers, he was intelligent, conscientious, hardworking, and beloved by patients.[16] "He's fantastic, one of the three best interns in the country," said his Chief Resident: "he knows everything, absolutely everything about his patients!" The Chief admitted he was "very good," but still expressed misgivings: "I don't know how he's going to be able to direct everything, he's so retiring." In the middle of his second year, this house officer decided to change specialties: "he's very good," said his [new] Chief Resident, "but he has a terrible time making decisions; he can do all the preparation, but he hates to make the actual decision; he'll come to me and ask, and be very grateful if it's made for him."

The resident who used to "get on dead center, then . . . couldn't move . . . couldn't make decisions," was another with wrong temperament for surgery, as was the senior surgeon who lacked nerve and, consequently, operated too slowly.[17]

The "Paranoia" of Surgeons

I have used surgeons' own words and observed behavior to illustrate their emphasis on control and certitude. The difference between event and process, battle and war, tactics and strategy helps explain why the arrogant martial macho characteristics displayed by surgeons are adaptive to their task. A surgeon must act boldly, resolutely, confidently in the limited time available to him at the operating table; his thinking is done, at least partially, with his hands; hesitation or doubt can be deadly. He must be certain, as he performs, that what he is doing will help the patient, and that he is the best possible person to be doing it. He must be physically sure, as well: his touch must be certain, delicate, yet firm; he must seize each advantage, altering technique and touch with every unexpected finding and happening. Sureness of temperament and technique enable the surgeon to cut into the human body—an awesome thing to do—and alter it forever. As one young surgeon said of what he does for and to his patients: "It's a scar on their bodies, it's a scar on their lives."

The fit between these temperamental characteristics and the requirements of the specialty, however, does not explain why two unusually thoughtful and intelligent surgeons would tell me that surgeons, as a group, were "paranoid." What do they mean by "paranoid"? Why should surgeons be so described? And, how is this "paranoia" related to the surgical temperament?

When asked to explain his use of the term, one man said that surgeons feel everyone conspires against them, to take patients away and find fault with their work. This "paranoia" is not a result of today's hostile climate, he contended, surgeons have always been like this. "Surgeons feel everyone's against them, even disease," explained the second. It gets worse as you get older, he continued; young surgeons, especially house officers, don't feel like this, because someone else is taking responsibility for the patient. You feel that way even when you don't get a patient, when a referring doctor sends a patient to someone else; his older partner is like that: when an internist who refers a large number of patients to their group gives a patient to another surgeon, his partner goes *crazy,* he'll look at the chart and wonder what he did wrong.

Both surgeons spoke as though this "paranoia" was related to surgeons' belief in themselves. "Surgeons have tremendous egos," said the first, "they attribute every challenge to their judgment as a personal assault," while the second explained: "You've got to believe you're the greatest to do what you do, you've got to feel you're gonna lick disease . . . and when it doesn't work, you ask what you or somebody else did to make things go wrong."

Let us examine this "paranoia" in action in the operating room to learn more about it:

> "This is a really big operation, and yet they give me the smallest room in the place," remarked a surgeon in a complaining tone, as he scrubbed hands and arms with an antiseptic solution before entering the operating room, where the anesthetized patient was on the table. It *was* a big operation, and the family had replaced the young surgeon prepared to carry out the complex and time-consuming procedure with an older man, who divided his practice between this suburban community hospital and a celebrated hospital in the neighboring city. The patient's family had telephoned him on Sunday, said the surgeon, to inquire about the result of tests carried out two days before; "Aren't you on call seven days a week?" they asked, when he wanted to know why they were calling on Sunday. A difficult family and a tricky case, he said, walking into the adjoining operating room.
>
> "Jones, you know when to give a case away!" he said sourly to the young surgeon who had been supplanted, who observed and assisted during the first half of the operation. Later, another young surgeon, who came into the operating room to inquire how the case was going, commented: "This is a case where we used to say, 'call the big boys!' " "Even the big boys are having trouble," responded the older surgeon, frowning. When he jerked his left hand from deep within the patient, saying: "Ow, goddam, I cut

myself!," it was the younger man who asked the nurses for an antiseptic and a new glove, saying "He did it to himself, surrounded by enemies!" (Later, when asked why his colleague had joked about his being surrounded by enemies, the operating surgeon explained, "that's what I always say.")

As the surgeon carried out a particularly difficult maneuvèr, the younger man groaned, "Oooh, that tweaks your testicles, that one," commenting admiringly when the maneuver was completed, "that was a bold move!" "That's because I had an audience," replied the older man. Although he snapped once or twice at the Chief Resident who was assisting him ("Easy, Chuck, either you do the case or I do the case!"), and got angry at one of the nurses who was talking loudly to another nurse about something that had nothing to do with the operation in hand ("I'm a temperamental surgeon," he said) he talked and joked with his younger colleague and, later, described the course of events to another young surgeon, who dropped in to observe for a few minutes, and then with a colleague his own age, who strolled in to observe and comment.

He directed the Chief Resident and Dr. Jones, who was originally supposed to perform the operation, to feel a mass in the patient's abdomen: "Wow," said Jones, "that might be severe benign disease!" "Well is it, or isn't it?" inquired the surgeon's contemporary, who had entered the Operating Room a second time. That was the question: was the mass "malignant" or "benign"? A sample of tissue had been sent to the pathology laboratory for analysis, but the pathologist wanted to examine more specimens before committing himself. "We're going to have to close him, whether it's benign or not," announced the surgeon, explaining that the tumor was connected to too many internal organs to be removed. The pathologist's feelings had been hurt: he thought he heard laughter on the intercom from the pathology lab to the operating room; the surgeon had to reassure him by telephone that no one had been laughing at him before the pathologist would announce that he had found cancer cells in the specimens.

The surgeon called for a radiologist to pass a catheter to drain the patient's gallbladder (which could not be excised) and thus relieve the jaundice the patient was suffering from. The radiology resident, however, adamantly refused to insert the catheter until the next day. "When I get in my next case, I'll take it too [the celebrated hospital in the city] said the surgeon, "I don't have to take all this abuse!"

He discussed draining the gallbladder with his contemporary, who returned with the younger surgeon to check on developments. "I would have put it [the catheter] in yesterday," he said, "but the damn family's so difficult!" "There *is* no such thing as an easy family any more," responded his colleague.

> As he helped the Chief Resident sew the successive layers of tissues to close the incision, the surgeon complained, "The whole damn world's against me!"

First, let me note that although one might use the term "paranoid" to describe aspects of this surgeon's verbal (and perhaps cognitive) style, he is in fact an exceedingly sane, confident, successful man, highly respected by peers, admired and loved by patients.[18] His remarks about the world being against him, exaggerated to the point of caricature, are presented as "jokes" and treated as such by the young surgeon who teased him about nicking his own finger. "Beleaguered" is another term we might use to describe his attitude of being surrounded by hostile forces.

What are the hostile forces against which the surgeon contends?

The most important are disease, and by extension, death. The surgeon's job is (in the words of my informant) to "lick disease," and in this case, disease won. The patient's tumor was diagnosed as malignant and the surgeon was unable to stem its course by removing it. The term "malignant" assigns intention to cancer and, in fact, surgeons often behave (with cancer and other diseases, as well) as though locked in personal combat with a tricky, strong, and deceitful enemy.

Why is the surgeon's relationship with disease so personal? Two factors come to mind. The surgeon's victory is *attributable,* both doctor and patient know who was responsible; it is also *visible,* it occurs before an audience.

Unlike other specialties, such as internal medicine, where the course of illness is likely to be longer, results more ambiguous, and attribution more difficult, in surgery, victory is rapid, definitive, and ascribable. When a patient effects a dramatic recovery after surgery, it is incontrovertably the surgeon's art that has made that patient better.

Moreover, unlike the work of other specialists, surgery is a *public* act. It takes place before a limited and specialized "public" (from which the public is rigorously excluded—unless cast in the role of patient, which involves being naked, horizontal, and anesthetized), composed of other professionals, who admire victory and note defeat. The surgeon performs in an operating theater,[19] under spotlights, in front of an audience that judges every move. The public glory of victory is balanced by the fear—and shame—of public defeat. In addition to the anthropologist, the following people observed all or part of this operation: (1) the anesthesiologist; (2) the Chief Resident; (3) an intern; (4,5) two nurses; (6) a third nurse who successively relieved the others, so they could have lunch; (7) Dr. Jones, the original surgeon on the case; (8) a radiology resident, who came to discuss placing a catheter in the patient's gallbladder; (9) a younger surgeon, who observed for a few minutes; (10) another younger surgeon, who (11) with his older partner, each came in three times to observe and comment.

Surgeons are often characterized, by themselves and others, as prima donnas. This "temperament" may be related, in part, to the public performative aspects of their work. The act of surgery is, among other things, a "cultural performance" (Turner 1984), a healing ritual enacted in a liminal area, barred to nonadepts (see P. Katz 1981). I will not discuss the performative and ritual aspects of surgery here; what I wish to emphasize is that the surgeon knows his performance is being observed and evaluated by a knowledgeable and critical audience. If not "surrounded by enemies," he is surely surrounded by observers, watching and judging. Moreover, each member of the audience may discuss the performance with others; "bold moves" are described; errors in technique or judgment recounted: wins and losses calculated.

Four senior surgeons watched some part of the operation. Dr. Jones, who had lost the case to an older, more experienced man,[20] and three others. Everyone in the Operating Room Suite that day knew this was going to be a complex and challenging case; there had been talk of undertaking a particularly difficult and time-consuming procedure that was rarely performed at this community hospital. The bystanders may have been motivated by curiosity, friendship, collegiality. Also, perhaps by a certain competitive interest. Surgeons are competitive animals[21]—perhaps the onlookers wanted to see how well this particular surgeon met this particular challenge. They wanted to savor his victory or, perhaps, his defeat. The internist's victory is rarely as complete or attributable as the surgeon's, but it occurs in private, with no colleagues keeping score.

The surgeon has other elements to contend with. The people who schedule rooms, times, and assistants can help or hinder his work, and he often perceives them as hindering it. He wants an adequate operating room (not the smallest room in the place, where the staff and equipment necessary for a long and complex operation will be jammed together), proper scheduling (an operation that is likely to take a long time is best scheduled for the first thing in the morning, when everyone is fresh, not noon, or mid-afternoon, when nurses change shifts), a skilled anesthesiologist, good assistants (a capable and highly-trained First Assistant, and for a complex procedure, a Second Assistant, as well), experienced nurses, who keep their attention on the work (giving him what he asks for, and having it ready even before he asks). In this case, the surgeon had to contend with the pathologist, whose hurt feelings had to be soothed before he would analyze the specimens. The radiology resident was also recalcitrant, refusing to insert a catheter while the patient was on the operating table. Had the surgeon been able to remove the tumor and arrest the patient, he might have overlooked these difficulties. Instead, he was defeated by disease, "abused" by pathologists, radiologists, and the Head Operating Room Nurse (who scheduled operating rooms and times), and overlooked by nurses, who conversed with each other rather than anticipating his needs.

Another potentially hostile force was the patient's family. The surgeon perceived them as difficult and demanding. They had bypassed the young surgeon, who had been following the patient and was prepared to operate, telephoning a famous hospital in the neighboring city for names, and then asking this man, whose name they had obtained, to perform the surgery. They called him on Sunday to inquire about the results of a test performed on Friday (about which they had been informed the day it took place). After the operation, he would have to talk with them, tell them that he was unable to remove the tumor and that "this tumor will kill him."[22] Difficult families, tricky cases, and operations that do not result in a cure add up to trouble. And in the stories surgeons tell one another in the operating suite lounge, "trouble" consists of six million dollar lawsuits against men with "only" one million dollars of malpractice insurance, whose fault was to lose the battle against disease and death.

Among the forces against which the surgeon must contend, then, are disease, which the surgeon battles in a very personal, even personified form; the possibility of defeat, where instead of his "licking" disease, disease may lick him; the public character of his battle, and consequently, defeat, with his "public" composed of those who are qualified, and perhaps eager to pass judgment upon his performance; his dependence upon others, who may hinder his efforts (anesthesiologists, pathologists, radiologists, house officers, nurses); and the patient's family, who may love a winner but sue a loser. All these may be described, in psychiatric terms, as "reality factors." At least one is culture-specific: American patients and their families are far more litigious today, than, for example, their British counterparts (Schwartz and Grubb 1985); as a result, contemporary American doctors may perceive families, in part, as potential enemies, poised to sue if they do not get a good result ("There *is* no such thing as an easy family, any more").

But there is more to it.

The surgeons who identified this "paranoia," in the first place, spoke as though it were related, in some way, to surgeons' certitude, to their intense belief in themselves. How can this be?

In a celebrated essay, based on more than four years of participant observation, sociologist Renée Fox (1957: 208-209) describes how medical students are trained to deal with three basic kinds of uncertainty in medicine:

> The first results from incomplete or imperfect mastery of available knowledge. No one can have at his command all skills and all knowledge of the lore of medicine. The second depends upon limitations in current medical knowledge. There are innumerable questions to which no physician, however well trained, can as yet provide answers. A third source of uncertainty derives from the first two. This consists of difficulty in distinguishing between personal ignorance or ineptitude and the limitations of present medical knowledge.

Discussing the mechanisms students used to cope with uncertainty, Fox observes, in a later paper (1980: 7), that:

> Students gradually evolved what they referred to as a more "affirmative attitude" toward medical uncertainty. . . . In clinical situations, they were more prone to feel and display sufficient "certitude" to make decisions and reassure patients.

Jay Katz (1984: 184-206) interprets Fox's data differently.[23] He notes that the students described by Fox exhibited increasing certainty as their schooling proceeded, and he observes that such certainty is encouraged by instructors, who criticize students when they display too much unsureness, indicating that doubt will impair their effectiveness with patients. Katz suggests that medical socialization involves *training for certainty,* not uncertainty. This training begins in medical school, continues in post-graduate training, and is reinforced by specialization

(1984: 188), "which tends to narrow diagnostic vision and to foster beliefs in the superior effectiveness of treatments prescribed by one's own specialty." Katz contends (1984: 198) that true training for uncertainty would teach doctors how to remove the "mask of infallibility," and alter the "traditional authoritarian relationship that governs interactions between physicians and patients." Perhaps it is not entirely fortuitous that, in his discussion, the examples of (what he considers dogmatic) "certitude" offered by Katz, are surgical.

I have argued that surgeons value decisiveness, control, and certitude, that these characteristics are selected for in surgical training programs and reinforced during that training. I have also argued that these characteristics are adaptive, that a person who is insufficiently decisive, certain, and in control is likely to make a poor surgeon.

Yet, in surgery, as in the other medical specialties, uncertainty remains. No one can command all the surgical skills and knowledge; knowledge, itself, falls short, there are questions no surgeon today can answer; and, surgeons may have difficulty distinguishing between their own lack of skills and knowledge, and the limitations of present knowledge. Moreover, all medicine is a probabilistic enterprise, and the application of the laws of probability to specific cases is always filled with uncertainty.

It is conceivable that this tension, between certainty and uncertainty, is stronger and more stressful among surgeons. The more certitude surgeons exhibit, the more troubling their inevitable feelings of uncertainty must be.

Hence the "paranoia." A classic description of "paranoid style" (Shapiro 1965: 54-107) discusses the "suspicious thinking" and "projection" characteristic of this mode of functioning.[24] Shapiro points out (1965: 68) that the mechanism of *projection—"the attribution to external figures of motivations, drives, or other tensions that are repudiated and intolerable in oneself"*—is so central to the understanding of paranoid style, pathology, and symptoms, that it has almost come to define the term "paranoid" in psychiatry.[25]

What I am suggesting is that surgeons, who must display control and certitude to presume to "dismember the image of God," may project their feelings of uncertainty to others, who are perceived as conspiring against them. The certainty can then be perceived as an inner state, related to the surgeon's confidence and competence, while the uncertainty is attributed to outside forces, to those who impede and find fault with his work.

We can then understand why this "paranoia" might increase as a surgeon grows older. The greater the surgeon's reputation and responsibility, the greater the demands on him to exhibit certainty; the greater the doubts he must defend himself against, the more strongly the surgeon may project them outwards, perceiving them as engendered by the behavior of others. If "you've got to believe you're the greatest to do what you do, you've got to feel you're gonna lick disease," then when disease wins, you retain certitude by inquiring what *somebody else* did to make things go wrong.

(Let me note that I do not attribute this "paranoia" exclusively to socialization or to self-selection. Instead, this behavioral style is the result of a dialectic between socialization into a tertiary role and self-selection of certain personality types. It is not one or the other, but both interacting together.[26])

The "paranoia," like the ethos and temperament of surgeons, may go (at least in part) with the territory. It may be a concomitant of the control and certitude necessary to dismember and permanently alter the image of God in the surgeon's battle against disease and death.

Implications

If I am correct in contending that the temperament and ethos of surgeons are adaptive and that those who lack these traits and attitudes make poor surgeons, these findings should affect our expectations and critique of surgeons. If indeed a good surgeon has a very special temperament, being activist, egocentric, decisive, and confident to the point of arrogance, then when we criticize the surgeon's work and the way he relates to patients, we must be careful to criticize him as a *surgeon,* rather than expecting him to behave like a member of a more reflective and less activist specialty. Lord Hamlet, whose flaw was "thinking too precisely on the event," would have made an abysmal surgeon; it is the martial and decisive Fortinbras, who goes to war "to gain a little patch of ground that hath in it no profit but the name," who exhibits the surgical temperament. What I am saying is that it is unrealistic to expect a surgeon to display the intellectual and personal virtues of a Hamlet; although some surgeons may be extraordinarily reflective, if they have the traits that make them good surgeons, they are likely to behave at times in ways that, today in particular, we may find difficult to accept. For example, some of the behaviors that Katz (1984) and other medical critics call for from doctors, including acknowledging uncertainty and giving patients a greater voice in decision making, may be particularly difficult for many, perhaps even most, surgeons to manifest.

Evans-Prichard (1965) criticized early anthropologists of religion for attributing their own temperament and values to the people they described. Their reasoning, he contended, went as follows: "If I were a horse, I would feel and do thus and so"; therefore, when studying horses, these scholars expected them to behave as they would have (were they horses), and criticized them for doing otherwise. "If I were a horse" reasoning is still widespread, possibly even among such sophisticated and highly educated critics as Katz (1984). A psychiatrist, or almost any other academic-based critic, is a very different person than a surgeon, and expecting a surgeon to exhibit the temperament and ethos of a psychiatrist, medical anthropologist, bioethicist, or sociologist, is a variety of "if I were a horse" reasoning.

Does this mean that we should expect little or nothing from surgeons, save for technical facility, that we should countenance every variety of arrogance, lack of consideration, and unfeelingness from the profession? I do not believe so. I do think, however, that we must be aware of who and what surgeons are, why they are that way, and that their particular temperament and ethos may be to our advantage in the operating room, when they are dealing with event rather than process. We must, in short, criticize surgeons, at least partially, on their own terms. This approach is not rare in anthropology. We tend, however, to exhibit such consideration only when we study down: contemporary anthropologists do not apply "if I were a horse" reasoning to disadvantaged peoples or groups. It is important, from a very practical point of view, that we show the same consideration when we study up. If we want to truly understand powerful groups, in order to meliorate or alter aspects of their behavior, we must understand who they are, why they are that way and (on occasion) how it is to our benefit that they are that way. If we do not achieve such understanding, our critiques will be useless and our abilities to achieve change, short-circuited.

Notes

1. Robert Hahn's exploration (1985) of the correspondence between a practicing internist's premises, attitudes, and values and the work of internal medicine touches on some of these issues.

2. I am grateful to the Chiefs of Surgery, who allowed me to study their Departments, and who were unfailingly generous with their time and assistance; I wish to thank the surgeons, as well, who put up with my presence and questions and who, on occasion, answered questions that I did not yet know enough to ask. I wish to thank Eric J. Cassell and Arthur Kleinman for their helpful comments on earlier drafts of this paper. I also wish to gratefully acknowledge the critical comments and editorial assistance of Murray L. Wax.

3. Carl von Clausewitz defined tactics as "the formation and conduct of single combats in themselves," and strategy, as "the combination of single combats with each other" (*Encyclopedia Britannica* 1974:572)

4. In the following sections, I do not follow the more traditional ethnographic procedure of omitting the anthropologist, as though she were an invisible all-observing eye. As Hahn notes (1985: 50), ethnographers' presence in their ethnographies is not invisible but manifest. The epistemological problems of observing and knowing cannot be solved by a false verbal "objectivity," where the anthropologist writes herself out of the picture; using "scientific" language that obscures these issues is scientism, not science. Following Victor Turner (personal communication), Bateson (1958), Geertz (1973), Myerhoff (1978), I have included myself in my ethnography. When presenting data based on the intensely personal method of fieldwork, one way to confront problems of objectivity and bias is for ethnographers to include themselves; in this way, readers learn where the anthropologist was, physically and personally, when particular data were collected; this can help them discount for researcher bias. In this particular research, where I, as a lower status female outsider, spent more than two years studying the hierarchical and closely guarded world of surgeons, I believe it is particularly important for me to present myself, in the act of studying, so that informed readers can decide, on occasion, that the surgeons (who had total control over access and self-presentation) were actively or inadvertently misleading me.

5. My study of self-regulation among surgeons was funded by the National Endowment for the Humanities (RH-2051484). Data for this paper come primarily, but not entirely, from participant observation at two medium-sized community hospitals in the New York City area. After my study was approved by each hospital Institutional Review Board, I was allowed to circulate freely within the hospitals: I observed people (Chiefs of Surgery, senior surgeons, Chief Residents, operating room and intensive care unit nurses, and anesthesiologists); and settings (operating rooms, operating room lounges, charge desks, surgical wards, intensive care units, surgical clinics, emergency rooms, cafeterias, women's dressing rooms). In addition, I followed fourteen surgeons throughout an entire day, and administered an open-ended questionnaire on attitudes and practices to thirty-two surgeons. Although I observed members of surgical subspecialties, many of whom share the ethos and traits I describe, my study concentrates on general surgeons, and consequently, the ethnographic data, unless otherwise specified, come from this group.

6. For example, a Director of General Surgery, explaining why he chose to go into surgery, said: "I liked [internal] medicine, but I didn't like the people in it. They were all . . . well, when I was a kid they were the kind of kids I would have beaten up!"

7. I have used quotations around "paranoid" and "paranoia" to emphasize (1) that it is not my term, and (2) that I am referring to a tendency or style of behavior (Shapiro 1965), not an abnormal condition. Although many of the surgeons I observed displayed behavior that might merit such a description, not all did so.

8. The distinction between surgery and medicine has a long history: surgeons, who descend from the medieval barber-surgeon, who pulled teeth and lanced abscesses

(Robinson 1984), were looked down upon by the more highly educated physicians (Garrison 1929: 393-394). Colonial America followed the pattern of 18th century England, where physicians, as members of a learned profession, distinguished themselves from the lower orders of surgeons, who practiced a craft (Starr 1982:37).

9. Within surgery, and internal medicine, the resemblance to segmentary societies continues: academic (or "full time" salaried) surgeons, who work at hospitals connected to medical schools are differentiated from practitioners; practitioners affiliated with elite hospitals are differentiated from those affiliated with uncelebrated institutions; practitioners in uncelebrated institutions who are board-certified are differentiated from those who have not passed their specialty board examinations; among practitioners who are not board-certified, graduates of American medical schools are differentiated from FMGs (foreign medical graduates). In each case, the smaller segments unite against a larger opposing segment.

10. As the emblems that distinguish the role of surgeon, the scrub suits, or "greens," are highly valued. Some hospitals prohibit the wearing of greens outside the operating room suite; such regulations are greeted by indignation. I observed one hospital where the sole female surgical house officer wore nothing but greens; she claimed, with some justice, that they were more comfortable and easier to launder than traditional female garb. Also, of course, greens covered by a white lab coat instantly identified her as a surgeon rather than a nurse.

11. In two years of research at three hospitals (two where I carried out participant observation and a third, where I observed one surgeon for several weeks) I encountered only one senior female general surgeon. And, although more women are being accepted into training programs, there is some question whether they are completing the programs: a recent survey (Greco et al., n.d.) found that of Chief Residents in general surgery in the United States, only 8.3% were women. Consequently, when I refer to the surgeon as "he," the ascription of gender is descriptive.

12. "Manly courage in the face of physical danger" is one of Wolfe's (1979: 165) descriptions of "the right stuff," which is clearly related to the "heroic ideal of grace under pressure, into which surgeons are socialized" (Bosk 1979: 144). Let me emphasize that although this ethos is stereotypically "masculine," it is not necessarily gender-specific. Many men do not exhibit the right stuff, some women do. Culturally, however, these values and the behavior which exemplifies them are perceived as masculine.

13. This quotation comes from a tape-recorded interview, in response to the question: "How did it happen that you became a surgeon?"

14. The remark was made by a veteran during a televised discussion of why men love war; the discussion was initiated by an article on the subject in *Esquire* (Broyles 1984).

15. In some hospitals, Operating Room Technicians or Physicians' Assistants supplement or replace house officers as First and Second Assistants.

16. Before being anesthetized, one patient asked to talk to "the tall doctor." She said, to this intern: "Thank you so much, you've been *wonderful*!" This is the only conversation of this sort, between a patient and a house officer, I heard while observing more than 150 operations.

17. I have heard a number of jokes and anecdotes about such surgeons; their behavior is presented as amusing, pathetic, dangerous, but the surgeons, themselves, do not describe these men as having the wrong temperament for surgery; this is my interpretation. Several of the men who were so described reported that they wore seatbelts and drove less sporty cars than their more swashbuckling colleagues. As Wolfe (1979: 166) points out, the right

stuff is exhibited in all areas of life; those who lack it are unlikely to be attracted by the danger and ego gratification of surgery or test flying.

18. When I observed this man's office hours, conversation indicated that he attended patients' weddings, birthday parties, bar mitzvahs, and that he possessed a great deal of personal information about patients and their families. Of 12 surgeons whose office hours I observed, only this man and one other exhibited this kind of intensely personal relationship with their patients.

19. One of my informants told me that he has not heard the term "operating theatre" for the last ten years; he assured me that the term is known, however, and is still used in Great Britain.

20. Before the operation commenced, Jones told me, in a disconsolate tone, that the patient's family wanted him to operate, but wanted "the name" of the more celebrated surgeon.

21. The measurability and attributability, as well as the "public" or their work, facilitates comparisons.

22. I was present during this conversation.

23. Katz is a psychiatrist as well as a lawyer, and consequently went through the socialization process described by Fox (1957).

24. Those who exhibit this style (Shapiro 1965: 59), "are not merely capable of remarkably active, intense, and searching attention; they seem essentially incapable of anything else. They are always sharp-eyed and searching, always intensely concentrating"; such people (Shapiro 1965: 62) manifest a quality which can be described as "hyperalertness"—they are ready for anything unexpected and immediately become aware of it. These are useful characteristics for a surgeon. (I am indebted to Arthur Kleinman for bringing Shapiro's work to my attention.)

Let me again emphasize that the discussion concerns *paranoid style* or *mode of functioning,* rather than "delusional paranoia" or "paranoid schizophrenia"; I am talking about a tendency, not a psychotic state.

25. Shapiro is but one of the authorities (e.g., Noyes and Kolb, 1959: 436; American Psychiatric Association 1969: 72; Fleischer 1951: 295) who stress the projection involved in "paranoid" feelings of persecution, where a person's own hostile or destructive impulses are ascribed to others, who are then suspected of conspiring against that person.

26. My thanks to Arthur Kleinman who helped clarify my argument.

References

American Psychiatric Association. 1969. *A Psychiatry Glossary.* Third Edition. Washington, DC: American Psychiatric Association.

Bateson, Gregory. 1958. *Naven: A Survey of the Problems Suggested by a Composite Picture of the Culture of a New Guinea Tribe Drawn From Three Points of View.* Stanford, CA: Stanford University Press (originally published in 1936).

Bosk, Charles. 1979. *Forgive and Remember: Managing Medical Failure.* Chicago: University of Chicago Press.

Broyles, William. 1984. Why Men Love War. *Esquire.* November.

Cassell, Eric J. 1977. Error in Medicine. In *The Foundations of Ethics and Its Relationship to Science, Volume II: Knowledge Value and Belief.* H. Tristram Engelhardt, Jr., and Daniel Callahan, eds. pp. 295-309. Hastings-on-the-Hudson, NY: The Hastings Center.

Cassell, Joan. 1981. Technical and Moral Error in Medicine and in Fieldwork. *Human Organization 40*: 160-168.

Encyclopedia Britannica, 15th Edition, 1974, volume 19, "Warfare, Conduct of": 558-597.

Evans-Prichard, E. E. 1965. *Theories of Primitive Religion*. London: Oxford University Press.

———. 1971. *The Nuer: A Description of the Modes of Livelihood and Political Institutions of a Nilotic People*. New York and Oxford: Oxford University Press (originally published in 1940).

Fox, Renée. 1957. Training for Uncertainty. In *The Student Physician*. Robert Merton, George Reader, and Patricia Kendall, eds. pp. 217-241. Cambridge, MA: Harvard University Press.

———. 1980. The Evolution of Medical Uncertainty. *Milbank Memorial Fund Quarterly 1*: 1-49.

Fleischer, Joachim. 1951. *Mental Health and the Prevention of Neurosis*. New York: Liveright.

Garrison, Fielding H. 1929. *An Introduction to the History of Medicine*. Philadelphia: W. B. Saunders.

Geertz, Clifford. 1973. Deep Play: Notes on the Balinese Cockfight. In *The Interpretation of Cultures*. New York: Basic Books.

Greco, Ralph, Anthony Donetz, Robert Brolin, and Stanley Trooskin. n.d. Career Development of Residents in University and Individual Training Programs. *Surgery*.

Hahn, Robert A. 1985. Portrait of an Internist. In *Physicians of Western Medicine: Anthropological Approaches to Theory and Practice*. Robert A. Hahn and Atwood D. Gaines, eds. pp. 51-111. Dordrecht, Holland: D. Reidel.

Katz, Jay. 1984. *The Silent World of Doctor and Patient*. New York: Free Press.

Katz, Pearl. 1981. Ritual in the Operating Room. *Ethnology, XX*(4): 335-350.

Myerhoff, Barbara. 1978. *Number Our Days*. New York: E. P. Dutton.

Nadel, S. F. 1957. *The Theory of Social Structure*. London: Cohen and West.

Noyes, Arthur P. and Lawrence C. Kolb. 1959. *Modern Clinical Psychiatry*. Fifth Edition. Philadelphia: W. B. Saunders.

Robinson, James O. 1984. The Barber-Surgeons of London. *Archives of Surgery 119*: 1171-1175.

Schwartz, Robert and Andrew Grubb. 1985. Why Britain Can't Afford Informed Consent. *Hastings Center Report 15*(4): 19-25.

Shapiro, David. 1965. *Neurotic Styles*. New York: Basic Books.

Starr, Paul. 1982. *The Social Transformation of American Medicine: The Rise of a Sovereign Profession and the Making of a Vast Industry*. New York: Basic Books.

Turner, Victor. 1984. Liminality and the Performative Genres. In *Rite, Drama, Festival, Spectacle: Rehearsals Toward a Theory of Cultural Performances*. John J. MacAloon, ed. pp. 19-41. Philadelphia: ISHI.

Wolfe, Tom. 1979. *The Right Stuff*. New York: Random House.

13

Under the Guise of Passivity

HAVA GOLANDER

Institutionalization of the aged is a topic that evokes intense emotional reaction and great controversy, yet it is an increasing phenomenon among developed countries.[1,2,3] It is true that only 4% to 5% of the aged are in institutions, but it is also true that one out of five persons will stay in an institution, if he or she lives long enough to reach the age of 80 and over.[4,5]

Nurses, among others, are very concerned about the quality of care provided in nursing homes, yet we know so little about the residents' perception of their quality of life in those settings. Many vital questions are still unanswered.

- What does it mean for a person to live in a nursing home?
- Can a person actively shape his or her life in a nursing home despite limitations and dependencies?
- How do old people actually cope in institutions?
- What are the personal attributes or the environmental factors that might influence modes of coping and adaptation?

AUTHOR'S NOTE: Research for this chapter was supported by grants from the Brookdale Institute of Gerontology in Jerusalem and the Tel Aviv University Recanati Fund. This chapter originally appeared in Golander, H. (1987). Under the guise of passivity: We can communicate warmth, caring, and respect. *Journal of Gerontological Nursing, 13*, 2, 26-31. Reprinted by permission of Slack, Inc.

Nurses have for too long tended to focus on weaknesses, problems, losses, or unmet needs of the aged, and therefore have forgotten that old people are old survivors. The aged succeed in reaching old age because of their strengths and their ability to cope with stressors and changes throughout their long lives.

The purpose of this chapter is to reveal the active role that even disabled residents were able to demonstrate in shaping their everyday lives in a nursing home reality. The data that are presented were collected by the author during a two-year period, using the anthropological fieldwork approach. In studying the aged, the inductive qualitative approach offers several advantages over the deductive quantitative approach, which employs questionnaires or structured interviews:

1. It enables the researcher to study the actual behavior in its natural context and not merely the declared action, stated perception, or knowledge.
2. It enables the researcher to include individuals who are usually "sampling drop outs,"[6,7,8] but nevertheless are an integral part of the studied reality; e.g., the confused, the blind, the deaf, and people who do not have a good grasp of the language.
3. It is the course of events that dictates the research topic and not the researcher who can only find what he or she had planned a priori.[9]
4. It enables the researcher, who becomes a native in the situation, to understand the members' worlds of meaning.[10]

Review of Literature

Review of the extensive literature on long-term institutionalization of the aged reveals that findings reflect the negative effects institutionalization has on the aged residents. The relocation process itself is often perceived as a stressor as well as the quality of care provided inside institutions. Institutionalization is often associated with, if not accused of, high mortality and morbidity rates of aged residents.[11,12] Institutionalization is also associated with the residents' increased disorientation, helplessness, disengagement, depression, and depersonalization.[13,14,15]

A different picture has been described by Kayser-Jones,[16] who compared two long-term care institutions for the aged. Using the anthropological fieldwork method, she concluded that institutionalization by itself does not necessarily bring despair, low morale, or depersonalization. In one of the facilities she found residents who were happy and fulfilled in spite of their disability and institutionalization, in the other she found the exact opposite.

Gubrium,[17] in his enlightening book *Living and Dying at Murray Manor,* unveiled the existence of a social world among residents of a geriatric center; a complex world of which the care providers knew very little. Tobin and Lieberman[18] added the dimensions of personality traits and timing to the complexity of adjustment to nursing home environments. Following the latter's approach, this research was directed at understanding the complexity of adjusting to nursing home reality by the physically and cognitively disabled aged.

Study Method

This part of the chapter presents a preliminary report of a more extensive, ongoing study using the participant observation techniques.

Setting. Data collection took place in one of the long-stay wards for disabled aged in a large geriatric center in Israel. The facility has a multilevel program for 1,000 elderly residents, which is adapted to the ambulant independent aged, the frail aged, the geropsychiatric cases, and the very disabled aged. The latter are the subjects of this research.

Out of the nine long-stay wards for disabled aged, one ward was randomly selected to become the central base for data collection. Observations were also conducted in other wards, but mainly to verify selected phenomena. Each ward is located in a separate building and houses 30 to 33 residents. Care is provided by nursing aides under the supervision of a nurse and a physician. It should be noted that once a resident enters the disabled ward, it is usually his or her last home.

Procedure. The fieldwork lasted a full year, from November 1983 to November 1984. The 500 hours of observation were planned to cover all 24 hours of the day, weekdays, and weekends. Observations were also scheduled during holidays, special events such as national election day, birthday parties, or periods of ill health. Most of the time was spent among the residents, observing their actions, listening to their thoughts and beliefs, and learning about their feelings, ideas, values, and morals. Observations were also conducted during joint activities such as personal care hours, family visits, and during meal times. I joined them through solitary times and during the endless hours of "Waiting for

Godot"; that endless waiting for something to happen, so vividly described by Beckett.[19]

Communication presented some difficulties and dictated the necessity to converse in different languages. Although many residents were multilingual, their Hebrew was limited because they emigrated from 12 different countries to Israel late in life. Conversation, however, was restricted to Hebrew, English, and Yiddish.

The other two main information sources were the family members and the nursing staff. The nursing staff not only knew the residents well, since they had worked in the same ward for many years, but were also familiar with many of them or their families before admission to the facility. Many of the staff lived in the same area. Very little of the staff's information was recorded anywhere.

Study population. The target population included the total number of residents who stayed in the ward during the year in which the study was conducted. The population consisted of 43 aged, all Jewish, of whom 27 were women and 16 were men. Their ages ranged from 65 to 95, with an average age of 80. About one third of the residents had a living spouse, but only two resided in the facility, none of them in the same ward. Eight (18.6%) of the residents had neither a spouse nor a living child. The majority of the aged (81.4%) however had at least one child who lived in the area.

As Israel is a young country populated by immigrants, the majority of its aged were born abroad. About one fifth of the residents were born in Israel, the majority immigrated to Israel, some in their youth (28%) and others in their advanced age (46.2%). Of the non-Israeli born, 29 (82.6%) came from European countries and North America, the others emigrated from Islamic countries in Asia and Africa. All the residents are limited in their ability of self-care. Eighty-eight percent (38) were confined to wheelchairs, the remainder used walking accessories. The length of stay in the facility ranged from a few months to 20 years, with a median and average of 4 years.

Of the original group of residents who lived in the ward at the beginning of the study in November 1983, 27 residents (81.8%) were alive at the end of the first year and 19 residents (57.5%) by the end of the second year. In comparing the characteristics of the deceased to those of the survivors, there was a higher incidence of cancer among the deceased, more were men, and more were married. Both groups were similar in age, length of stay in the institution, country, and date of immigration.

Data Analysis and Findings

Close acquaintance with the residents revealed a unique and dynamic world that an outsider on a short visit could neither notice nor appreciate. This world has its norms, sanctions, and taboos; its own social hierarchy, coalition formations, cliques, rivalries and competitions. It has its social order as well as its chaos. There is a great deal of activity under the mantle of passivity. What seems to the outsider as aimless behavior or daydreaming is merely a cover for a rich, alive world. I would like to shed light on another layer of this hidden world of nursing home inmates, a world that consists of their reality and the wide array of survival strategies they use to cope.

THE CORE DILEMMAS

The ethnographic material revealed that the disabled residents had four major concerns they had to overcome. Not only did each concern contain a paradoxical element within itself, but often contradictions arose among the interrelated concerns. The four major concerns identified were:

1. How to achieve fast relief from physical discomfort in a situation of continual discomfort.
2. How to maintain a balanced relationship with staff, fellow residents, and family members in an unbalanced reality.
3. How to retain a sense of independence and self-uniqueness in a state of dependence and collectiveness.
4. How to make time pass in a meaningful way, while acknowledging their own finitude.

Physical discomfort is a common occurrence among the residents during the day and night. Many experience persistent pain, sensations of numbness or itching, burning, pressure, physical fullness, or shortness of breath. Relief of physical discomfort becomes, therefore, their main concern. The major resources to fulfill these urgent needs are the residents themselves, the staff, and occasional visitors. A great deal of the residents' time, energy, and effort is invested in searching for modes to avoid discomfort, or minimize its effect.

In the course of this chapter, I will illustrate several of the many strategies residents use to fulfill their basic needs. To achieve this goal without jeopardizing the relationship with the staff or affecting the self-image of residents is a complicated task. As we will see it demands that the beholder be a scholar as well as an implementor of the decision-making process, to have the change agent's skills and the negotiator's expertise. All names are, of course, fictitious.

COPING STRATEGIES

The first survival strategy residents use is to study their own bodies carefully and serve them patiently and skillfully by acknowledging posture, functions and limitations, body time, and body signals.

For Shmuel, a 65-year-old hemiplegic male, the "exact and right" position of his paralyzed leg could make the difference between unbearable pain combined with trembling of his whole body or rest and comfort. It is only natural for him to spend most of his time planning, calculating, and guarding his legs from fellow table partners or a nurse's careless movement. An outsider might judge this behavior as "doing nothing" or "daydreaming"; whereas, in fact, he is very busy doing what is crucial and meaningful to him.

Rebecca, an 87-year-old-woman in a progressive state of rheumatoid arthritis, has the same dilemma every day after lunch. "What will be better for me? Should I take a nap now and rest my back or maybe it will be better to have a good night's sleep for a change?" Building a daily schedule and changing it constantly according to unexpected occurrences is another active survival technique.

Another example is Rosa, an 82-year-old hemiplegic woman who recently emigrated from Russia. She is one of the few "fortunate people" in the ward because she is able to use the toilet without help, except for a walker. She has learned that it takes her more time to get to the bathroom in the afternoons when she is tired and on days she gets "water pills," then she really has to rush to stay dry. Rosa is well aware of her body functions and adapts her activities accordingly.

Sometimes studying one's body signs and symptoms can be a difficult and ambiguous task, as it is for Veronica. Veronica is severely restricted by rheumatoid arthritis, osteoporosis, and duodenal ulcers caused by years of steroid treatments. "This pressure I feel," she once told me, "I really don't know what it means. If I ask to be taken to the toilet again and again with no results, I will bother the workers, but I also hate to think what might happen if I am mistaken and it turns out to be not just a pressure."

Studying their own bodies as opponents as well as friends is a vital necessity for the disabled residents. They become prisoners of their own bodies, which have to be served constantly. They memorize the "right" postures and positions that agree with their bodies. They learn the body's signs and signals, its limitations, and its possibilities. They plan their daily, hourly, or momentary schedule according to their bodies' demands. New and imaginative strategies have to be discovered to please their bodies, disabled as they are.

Planning one's actions carefully is another widespread and useful survival technique. Careful decision making involves attending to environmental assessment: weighing help requests, including amount, manner, timing, and person; and regulating resources. The residents use attentive listening and observation techniques. All information might have relevance for them. If a nursing aide calls in sick, they might not get the appropriate attention. Listening and observing also provide some interest and good topics for conversation. Attentive listening is often misinterpreted as passivity or endless waiting, whereas it is, in fact, a vital survival skill.

The residents need to ask for help for many of their daily activities. Careful planning is practiced to decide when to ask, for which kind of service to ask and from whom, and what is the right manner of asking for help. Residents must also weigh whether it is not wiser at times to rely on their own limited capabilities or just to give up. This process takes present and future costs and rewards into consideration.

Careful planning is also needed in regulating one's scarce resources concerning material goods. "What are they serving for dinner tonight? Should I open my last can of sardines?" Benjamin, who is 82 years old and a heavy smoker, counts his remaining cigarettes again and again with his shaking parkinsonian hand. He has to be certain that his daily rate of cigarette consumption does not exceed the rate of cigarette supply.

The new supply is expected to arrive only with his son's next visit. Although his son visits every week, the exact day of the visit always remains a puzzle for Benjamin. The uncertain variable poses a great difficulty and often makes the careful rationing of cigarettes useless.

For the disabled residents, these decisions are important and deserve systematic assessment and planning. Careful appraisal is needed to evaluate choices and regulate resources for decision-making processes.

Avoiding unnecessary dependence is an important survival strategy among residents. The residents know from their own long experience that dependency demands its own dues. Being in a dependent role, they try to maximize their potential and rely first of all on themselves. Veronica has a specially designed glass that enables her to drink her morning coffee by herself. A friend skillfully added plastic elements to her radio's button so that she can listen to music without asking for help.

Institutions are often blamed for their rigid routines. But from the resident's viewpoint, there is some blessing in routine. If tea and cake are served every day at four o'clock, it means that there is something nice to look forward to. It also means that there is no need to negotiate or ask for favors if something will be given anyhow.

Some of the more influential residents succeed in incorporating their special wishes and desires into the nursing aide's daily routine. Debra, an 86-year-old woman who has been in this ward since its opening, is well known for her achievements in that respect. She receives two glasses of warm water with lemon juice at every meal without even asking or reminding. She is also the first one to be taken to the shower every day.

If a newly admitted resident or an inquisitive researcher dares question this arrangement, he or she always gets the same answer: "Because this is how it has always been." The example of Debra illustrates successful management, where a resident's establishment of a routine makes repeated negotiation unnecessary.

The strategy of strengthening relationships with helpers involves coalition formation and reinforcing staff. Although the former strategy extracts a great deal of influential energy, the coalition formation strategy is the more widespread mode of coping. The relationships between the residents and staff were not found to be unidimensional between "inmates" and "care providers" but rather of a multidimensional nature. Coalition formation is based on common country of origin, common foreign language, previous acquaintances, shared interests, and exchange of goods and information as well as personal likes and dislikes.

Residents reinforce the staff by using negative or positive reinforcement. They threaten to report a nursing aide to the head nurse, complain or praise individuals during family visits. They ignore or show personal interest in the nursing aides' family lives. They can withhold or give small presents. In fact, the residents and their families have an active role in shaping their social atmosphere. The webbing of personal relationships between residents and staff gives a better assurance that help will be delivered when needed.

Another coping strategy in avoiding dependency is to be able to lower aspirations to match diminished capabilities. Most of the residents use this strategy to different degrees. The process of lowering aspirations could best be illustrated by the following example.

Natan, a religious old man who has a wife and five children, shared his feelings with me on Passover Eve. "I prefer to stay here," he said. "Certainly, I miss the Passover ceremony I used to conduct at home, but I get tired very easily now. I cannot use the toilet at home. On my last visit at home I was too excited. I got an awful asthma attack. They did not know what to do. I spoiled their holiday, and I was sick myself for two weeks. They all invited me to come, you know, they begged me to come. No, I'd rather stay here. Yes, now it is better for me to be here."

Conclusion

It is not easy for a person to be old, sick, and disabled or to reside in an institutional setting. Just coping with simple daily activities demands a great deal of strength, persistence, patience, and ingenuity. It also demands being able to deal with the awareness of one's decreased capabilities, regression, and despair.

During the data collection period I went through a unique and enriching experience that made me realize the tremendous strengths embodied in these people. For me, in a paradoxical way, staying with the disabled aged was not a lesson of weakness and pity, but a lesson of courage and admiration for these people and many of their care givers.

The purpose of this chapter was to describe the active role disabled aged have in shaping their lives in an institutional environment. This, however, does not deny the existence of hopelessness or passivity in some of the people, some of the time. The intention of this chapter was to emphasize that ignoring the dynamic role of the aged is not only an underestimation of old people, but is also an inaccurate perception of reality.

On one of my last visits to the ward, Shmuel asked me if I had already chosen a name for my research. I asked him if he could recommend a title that would best represent their present lives. Shmuel concentrated for a moment and said, "Call it 'The Land Without God.' "

In a reality abandoned by God, people learn to rely on themselves. Nurses are by no means substitutes for God, however, nurses should be aware of the tremendous influence that every word, gesture, or action has on our clients, for better or for worse. We cannot bring God to their land, but we can make it a better world in which to live. We can bring relief to their physical discomfort. We can communicate warmth, caring, and respect. We can help them pass time in a meaningful way and create small joys. It is on the basis of old people's strengths and not only on their weaknesses that we have to plan our nursing interventions.

Notes

1. Goldfarb, A. I. Institutional care of the aged, in Busse, E. W., & Pfeiffer, E. (eds.): *Behavior and Adaptation in Late Life,* ed. 2. Boston, Little, Brown, 1977, pp. 264-292.

2. Estes, C. L. *The Aging Enterprise.* San Francisco: Jossey-Bass, 1979.

3. Manard, B. B., Kart, C. S., & Van Gils, D. W. *Old Age Institutions.* Toronto: Lexington, 1975.

4. Kastenbaum, R., & Candy, S. The four percent fallacy: A methodological and empirical critique of extended care facility program statistics. *Aging and Human Development* 1973; 4:15-21.

5. Palmore, E. Total chance of institutionalization among the aged. *The Gerontologist* 1976; 16:504-507.

6. Chang, B. L. Generalized expectancy, situational perception and morale among institutionalized aged. *Nurs. Res.* 1978; 24:316-324.

7. Schwirian, P. M. Life satisfaction among nursing home residents. *Geriatric Nursing* 1982; 2:111-114.

8. Poul, J. M., & Fuller, S. S. Perceived choice, social integration and dimensions of morals of residents in home for the aged. *Res. Nurs. Health* 1980; 3:147-157.

9. Glaser, B. G. *Theoretical Sensitivity.* Mill Valley, CA: Sociology Press, 1978.

10. Douglas, J. D. (ed.) *Introduction to the Sociologies of Everyday Life.* Boston: Allyn & Bacon, 1980, pp. 2-3.

11. Lieberman, M. A., Prock, V. N., & Tobin, S. S. Psychological effects of institutionalization. *J. Gerontol* 1968; 23(3):343-353.

12. Lieberman, M. Institutionalization of the aged: Effects on behavior. *J. Gerontol* 1969; 24(3):330-340.

13. Oberleder, M. Emotional breakdown in elderly people. *Hosp. Community Psychiatry* 1969; 20(7): 191-196.

14. Bennett, R. The meaning of institutional life. *The Gerontologist* 1963; 3(3):117-125.

15. Curry, T., & Ratliff, B. W. The effects of nursing home size and resident isolation and life satisfaction. *The Gerontologist* 1973; 13(3): 296-298.

16. Kayser, & Jones, J. S. *Old, Alone and Neglected.* Berkeley: University of California Press, 1981.

17. Gubrium, J. F. *Living and Dying at Murray Manor.* New York, St. Martin's, 1975.

18. Tobin, S. S., & Lieberman, M. A. *Last Home for the Aged.* San Francisco: Jossey-Bass, 1976.

19. Beckett, S. *En Attendant Godot.* Les Editions de Minuit Traduit par Mouli Melzer, 1952.

14

On Being Sane in Insane Places

D. L. ROSENHAN

Abstract: Rosenhan describes the methods of participant-observation from the perspective of the health care consumer. As can be seen, role taking in regard to the patient role is not particularly difficult. Although this article is highly entertaining, several points must be kept in mind. First, the patient's perspective of the health care delivery system is not necessarily complimentary. Second, psychiatry, unlike other fields of medicine, frequently accepts the patient's valuation of himself as ill until further determination of disease process can be made. Third, health professionals interact with the label patient and not with patients as individuals. Last, as a research method, participant observation is not believed to be an objective or scientific research method, as can be seen from the furor raised by this article. (See *Science,* April 27, 1973)

If sanity and insanity exist, how shall we know them?

The question is neither capricious nor itself insane. However much we may be personally convinced that we can tell the normal from the abnormal, the evidence is simply not compelling. It is commonplace, for example, to read about murder trials wherein eminent psychiatrists for the defense are contradicted by equally eminent psychiatrists for the prosecution on the matter of the defendant's sanity. More generally, there are a great deal of conflicting data on the reliability, utility, and

---

AUTHOR'S NOTE: This chapter originally apperared in Rosenhan, D. L. (1973, January 19). On being sane in insane places. *Science, 179*, 250-258.

meaning of such terms as "sanity," "insanity," "mental illness," and "schizophrenia".[1] Finally, as early as 1934, Benedict suggested that normality and abnormality are not universal.[2] What is viewed as normal in one culture may be seen as quite aberrant in another. Thus, notions of normality and abnormality may not be quite as accurate as people believe they are.

To raise questions regarding normality and abnormality is in no way to question the fact that some behaviors are deviant or odd. Murder is deviant. So, too, are hallucinations. Nor does raising such questions deny the existence of the personal anguish that is often associated with "mental illness." Anxiety and depression exist. Psychological suffering exists. But normality and abnormality, sanity and insanity, and the diagnoses that flow from them may be less substantive than many believe them to be.

At its heart, the question of whether the sane can be distinguished from the insane (and whether degrees of insanity can be distinguished from each other) is a simple matter: do the salient characteristics that lead to diagnoses reside in the patients themselves or in the environments and contexts in which observers find them? From Bleuler, through Kretchmer, through the formulators of the recently revised *Diagnostic and Statistical Manual* of the American Psychiatric Association, the belief has been strong that patients present symptoms, that those symptoms can be categorized, and, implicitly, that the sane are distinguishable from the insane. More recently, however, this belief has been questioned. Based in part on theoretical and anthropological considerations, but also on philosophical, legal, and therapeutic ones, the view has grown that psychological categorization of mental illness is useless at best and downright harmful, misleading, and pejorative at worst. Psychiatric diagnoses, in this view, are in the minds of the observers and are not valid summaries of characteristics displayed by the observed.[3-5]

Gains can be made in deciding which of these is more nearly accurate by getting normal people (that is, people who do not have, and have never suffered, symptoms of serious psychiatric disorders) admitted to psychiatric hospitals and then determining whether they were discovered to be sane and, if so, how. If the sanity of such pseudopatients were always detected, there would be prima facie evidence that a sane individual can be distinguished from the insane context in which he is found. Normality (and presumably abnormality) is distinct enough that it can be recognized wherever it occurs, for it is carried within the person. If, on the other hand, the sanity of the pseudopatients were never discovered, serious difficulties would arise for those who support traditional modes of psychiatric diagnosis. Given that the hospital staff was not incompetent, that the pseudopatient had been behaving as sanely as he had been outside of the hospital, and that it had never been previously suggested that he belonged in a psychiatric hospital, such an unlikely outcome would support the view that psychiatric diagnosis betrays little about the patient but much about the environment in which an observer finds him.

This chapter describes such an experiment. Eight sane people gained secret admission to 12 different hospitals.[6] Their diagnostic experiences constitute the data of the first part of this article; the remainder is devoted to a description of their experiences in psychiatric institutions. Too few psychiatrists and psychologists, even those who have worked in such hospitals, know what the experience is like. They rarely talk about it with former patients, perhaps because they distrust information coming from the previously insane. Those who have worked in psychiatric hospitals are likely to have adapted so thoroughly to the settings that they are insensitive to the impact of that experience. And while there have been occasional reports of researchers who submitted themselves to psychiatric hospitalization,[7] these researchers have commonly remained in the hospitals for short periods of time, often with the knowledge of the hospital staff. It is difficult to know the extent to which they were treated like patients or like research colleagues. Nevertheless, their reports about the inside of the psychiatric hospitals have been valuable. This chapter extends those efforts.

Pseudopatients and Their Settings

The eight pseudopatients were a varied group. One was a psychology graduate student in his 20s. The remaining seven were older and "established." Among them were three psychologists, a pediatrician, a psychiatrist, a painter, and a housewife. Three pseudopatients were women, five were men. All of them employed pseudonyms, lest their alleged diagnoses embarrass them later. Those who were in mental health professions alleged another occupation in order to avoid the special attention that might be accorded by staff, as a matter of courtesy or caution, to ailing colleagues.[8] With the exception of myself (I was the first pseudopatient and my presence was known to the hospital administrator and chief psychologist and, so far as I can tell, to them alone), the presence of pseudopatients and the nature of the research program was not known to the hospital staffs.[9]

The settings were similarly varied. In order to generalize the findings, admission into a variety of hospitals was sought. The 12 hospitals in the sample were located in five different states on the East and West coasts. Some were old and shabby, some were quite new. Some were research-oriented, others not. Some had good staff-patient ratios, others were quite understaffed. Only one was a strictly private hospital. All of the others were supported by state or federal funds or, in one instance, by university funds.

After calling the hospital for an appointment, the pseudopatient arrived at the admission office complaining that he had been hearing voices. Asked what the voices said, he replied that they were often unclear, but as far as he could tell they said "empty," "hollow," and "thud." The voices were unfamiliar and were of the same sex as the pseudopatient. The choice of these symptoms was occasioned by their apparent similarity to existential symptoms. Such symptoms are alleged to arise from painful concerns about the perceived meaninglessness of one's life. It is as if the hallucinating person were saying, "My life is empty and hollow." The choice of these symptoms was also determined by the *absence* of a single report of existential psychoses in the literature.

Beyond alleging the symptoms and falsifying name, vocation, and employment, no further alterations of person, history, or circumstances were made. The significant events of the pseudopatient's life history were presented as they had actually occurred. Relationships with parents and siblings, with spouse and children, with people at work and in school, consistent with the aforementioned exceptions, were described as they were or had been. Frustrations and upsets were described along with joys and satisfactions. These facts were important to remember. If anything, they strongly biased the subsequent results in favor of detecting sanity, since none of their histories or current behaviors were seriously pathological in any way.

Immediately upon admission to the psychiatric ward, the pseudopatient ceased simulating *any* symptom of abnormality. In some cases, there was a brief period of mild nervousness and anxiety, since none of the pseudopatients really believed that they would be admitted so easily. Indeed, their shared fear was that they would be immediately exposed as frauds and greatly embarrassed. Moreover, many of them had never visited a psychiatric ward; even those who had, nevertheless had some genuine fears about what might happen to them. Their nervousness, then, was quite appropriate to the novelty of the hospital setting, and it abated rapidly.

Apart from that short-lived nervousness, the pseudopatient behaved on the ward as he "normally" behaved. The pseudopatient spoke to patients and staff as he might ordinarily. Because there is uncommonly little to do on a psychiatric ward, he attempted to engage others in conversation. When asked by staff how he was feeling, he indicated that he was fine, that he no longer experienced symptoms. He responded to instructions from attendants, to calls for medication (which was not swallowed), and to dining-hall instructions. Beyond such activities as were available to him on the admissions ward, he spent his time writing down his observations about the ward, its patients, and the staff. Initially these notes were written "secretly," but as it soon became clear that no one much cared, they were subsequently written on standard tablets of paper in such public places as the dayroom. No secret was made of these activities.

The pseudopatient, very much as a true psychiatric patient, entered a hospital with no foreknowledge of when he would be discharged. Each was told he would have to get out by his own devices, essentially by convincing the staff that he was sane. The psychological stresses associated with hospitalization were considerable, and all but one of the pseudopatients desired to be discharged almost immediately after being admitted. They were, therefore, motivated not only to behave sanely, but to be paragons of cooperation. That their behavior was in no way disruptive is confirmed by nursing reports, which have been obtained on most of the patients. These reports uniformly indicate that the patients were "friendly," "cooperative," and "exhibited no abnormal indications."

The Normal Are Not Detectably Sane

Despite their public "show" of sanity, the pseudopatients were never detected. Admitted, except in one case, with a diagnosis of schizophrenia,[10] each was discharged with a diagnosis of schizophrenia "in remission." The label "in remission" should in no way be dismissed as a formality, for at no time during any hospitalization had any question been raised about any pseudopatient's simulation. Nor are there any indications in the hospital records that the pseudopatient's status was suspect. Rather, the evidence is strong that, once labeled schizophrenic, the pseudopatient was stuck with that label. If the pseudopatient was to be discharged, he must naturally be "in remission"; but he was not sane, nor, in the institutions' view, had he ever been sane.

The uniform failure to recognize sanity cannot be attributed to the quality of the hospitals, for, although there were considerable variations among them, several are considered excellent. Nor can it be alleged that there was simply not enough time to observe the pseudopatients. Length of hospitalization ranged from 7 to 52 days, with an average of 19 days. The pseudopatients were not, in fact, carefully observed, but this failure clearly speaks more to traditions within psychiatric hospitals than to lack of opportunity.

Finally, it cannot be said that the failure to recognize the pseudopatients' sanity was due to the fact that they were not behaving sanely. While there was clearly some tension present in all of them, their daily visitors could detect no serious behavioral consequences—nor, indeed, could other patients. It was quite common for the patients to "detect" the pseudopatients' sanity. During the first three hospitalizations, when accurate counts were kept, 35 of a total of 118 patients on the admissions ward voiced their suspicions, some vigorously. "You're a journalist, or a professor [referring to the continual note-taking]. You're checking up on the hospital." While most of the patients were reassured by the pseudopatient's insistence that he had been sick before he came in but was fine now, some continued to believe that the pseudopatient was sane throughout his hospitalization.[11] The fact that the patients often recognized normality when staff did not raises important questions.

Failure to detect sanity during the course of hospitalization may be due to the fact that physicians operate with a strong bias toward what statisticians call the type 2 error (see Note 5). This is to say that physicians are more inclined to call a healthy person sick (a false positive, type 2) than a sick person healthy (a false negative, type 1). The reasons for this are not hard to find: it is clearly more dangerous to misdiagnose illness than health. Better to err on the side of caution, to suspect illness even among the healthy.

But what holds for medicine does not hold equally well for psychiatry. Medical illnesses, while unfortunate, are not commonly pejorative. Psychiatric diagnoses, on the contrary, carry with them personal, legal, and social stigmas.[12] It was therefore important to see whether the tendency toward diagnosing the sane insane could be reversed. The following experiment was arranged at a research and teaching hospital whose staff had heard these findings but doubted that such an error could occur in their hospital. The staff was informed that at some during the following 3 months, one or more pseudopatients would attempt to be admitted into the psychiatric hospital. Each staff member was asked to rate each patient who presented himself at admissions or on the ward according to the likelihood that the patient was a pseudopatient. A 10-point scale was used, with a 1 and 2 reflecting high confidence that the patient was a pseudopatient.

Judgments were obtained on 193 patients who were admitted for psychiatric treatment. All staff who had had sustained contact with or primary responsibility for the patient—attendants, nurses, psychiatrists, physicians, and psychologists—were asked to make judgments. Forty-one patients were alleged, with high confidence, to be pseudopatients by at least one member of the staff. Twenty-three were considered suspect by at least one psychiatrist. Nineteen were suspected by one psychiatrist *and* one other staff member. Actually, no genuine pseudopatient (at least from my group) presented himself during this time period.

The experiment is instructive. It indicates that the tendency to designate some people as insane can be reversed when the stakes (in this case, prestige and diagnostic acumen) are high. But what can be said of the 19 people who were suspected of being "sane" by one psychiatrist and another staff member? Were these people truly "sane," or was it rather the case that in the course of avoiding the type 2 error the staff tended to make more errors of the first sort—calling the crazy "sane"? There is no way of knowing. But one thing is certain: any diagnostic process that lends itself so readily to massive errors of this sort cannot be a very reliable one.

The Stickiness of Psychodiagnostic Labels

Beyond the tendency to call the healthy sick—a tendency that accounts better for diagnostic behavior on admission than it does for such behavior after a lengthy period of exposure—the data speak to the massive role of labeling in psychiatric assessment. Having once been labeled schizophrenic, there is nothing the pseudopatient can do to overcome the tag. The tag profoundly colors others' perceptions of him and his behavior.

From one viewpoint, these data are hardly surprising, for it has long been known that elements are given meaning by the context in which they occur. Gestalt psychology made this point vigorously, and Asch[13] demonstrated that there are "central" personality traits (such as "warm" versus "cold") which are so powerful that they markedly color the meaning of other information in forming an impression of a given personality.[14] "Insane," "schizophrenic," "manic-depressive," and "crazy" are probably among the most powerful of such central traits. Once a person is designated abnormal, all of his other behaviors and characteristics are colored by that label. Indeed, that label is so powerful that many of the pseudopatients' normal behaviors were overlooked entirely or profoundly misinterpreted. Some examples may clarify this issue.

Earlier I indicated that there were no changes in the pseudopatients' personal history and current status beyond those of name, employment, and where necessary, vocation. Otherwise, a veridical description of personal history and circumstances was offered. Those circumstances were not psychotic. How were they made consonant with the diagnosis of psychosis? Or were those diagnoses modified in such a way as to bring them into accord with the circumstances of the pseudopatient's life, as described by him?

As far as I can determine, diagnoses were in no way affected by the relative health of the circumstances of a pseudopatient's life. Rather, the reverse occurred: the perception of his or her circumstances was shaped entirely by the diagnosis. A clear example of such translation is found in the case of a pseudopatient who had had a close relationship with his mother but was rather remote from his father during his early childhood. During adolescence and beyond, however, his father became a close friend, while his relationship with his mother cooled. His present relationship with his wife was characteristically close and warm. Apart from occasional angry exchanges, friction was minimal. The children had rarely been spanked. Surely there is nothing especially pathological about such a history. Indeed, many readers may see a similar pattern in their own experiences, with no markedly deleterious consequences. Observe, however, how such a history was translated in the psychopathological context, this from the case summary prepared after the patient was discharged.

> This white 39-year-old male . . . manifests a long history of considerable ambivalence in close relationships, which begins in early childhood. A warm relationship with his mother cools during his adolescence. A distant relationship to his father is described as becoming very intense. Affective stability is absent. His attempts to control emotionality with his wife and

> children are punctuated by angry outbursts and, in the case of the children, spankings. And while he says that he has several good friends, one senses considerable ambivalence embedded in those relationships also. . . .

The facts of the case were unintentionally distorted by the staff to achieve consistency with a popular theory of the dynamics of a schizophrenic reaction.[15] Nothing of an ambivalent nature had been described in relations with parents, spouse, or friends. To the extent that ambivalence could be inferred, it was probably not greater than is found in all human relationships. It is true the pseudopatient's relationships with his parents changed overtime, but in the ordinary context that would hardly be remarkable—indeed, it might very well be expected. Clearly, the meaning ascribed to his verbalizations (that is, ambivalence, affective instability) was determined by the diagnosis: schizophrenia. An entirely different meaning would have been ascribed if it were known that the man was "normal."

All pseudopatients took extensive notes publicly. Under ordinary circumstances, such behavior would have raised questions in the minds of observers, as, in fact, it did among patients. Indeed, it seemed so certain that the notes would elicit suspicion that elaborate precautions were taken to remove them from the ward each day. But the precautions proved needless. The closest any staff member came to questioning these notes occurred when one pseudopatient asked his physician what kind of medication he was receiving and began to write down the response. "You needn't write it," he was told gently. "If you have trouble remembering, just ask me again."

If no questions were asked of the pseudopatients, how was their writing interpreted? Nursing records for three patients indicate that the writing was seen as an aspect of their pathological behavior. "Patient engages in writing behavior" was the daily nursing comment on one of the pseudopatients who was never questioned about his writing. Given that the patient is in the hospital, he must be psychologically disturbed. And given that he is disturbed, continuous writing must be a behavioral manifestation of that disturbance, perhaps a subset of the compulsive behaviors that are sometimes correlated with schizophrenia.

One tacit characteristic of psychiatric diagnosis is that it locates the sources of aberration within the individual and only rarely within the complex of stimuli that surrounds him. Consequently, behaviors that are stimulated by the environment are commonly misattributed to the patient's disorder. For example, one kindly nurse found a pseudopatient pacing the long hospital corridors. "Nervous, Mr. X?" she asked. "No, bored," he said.

The notes kept by pseudopatients are full of patient behaviors that were misinterpreted by well-intentioned staff. Often enough, a patient would go "berserk" because he had, wittingly or unwittingly, been mistreated by, say, an attendant. A nurse coming upon the scene would rarely inquire even cursorily into the environmental stimuli of the patient's behavior. Rather, she assumed that his upset derived from his pathology, not from his present interactions with other staff members. Occasionally, the staff might assume that the patient's family (especially when they had recently visited) or other patients had stimulated the outburst. But never were the staff found to assume that one of themselves or the structure of the hospital had anything to do with a patient's behavior. One psychiatrist pointed to a group of patients who were sitting outside the cafeteria entrance half an hour before lunchtime. To a group of young residents he indicated that such behavior was characteristic of the oral-acquisitive nature of the syndrome. It seemed not to occur to him that there were very few things to anticipate in a psychiatric hospital besides eating.

A psychiatric label has a life and an influence of its own. Once the impression has been formed that the patient is schizophrenic, the expectation is that he will continue to be schizophrenic. When a sufficient amount of time has passed, during which the patient has done nothing bizarre, he is considered to be in remission and available for discharge. But the label endures beyond discharge, with the unconfirmed expectation that he will behave as a schizophrenic again. Such labels, conferred by mental health professionals, are as influential on the patient as they are on his relatives and friends, and it should not surprise anyone that the diagnosis acts on all of them as a self-fulfilling prophecy. Eventually, the patient himself accepts the diagnosis, with all of its surplus meanings and expectations, and behaves accordingly (see Note 5).

The inferences to be made from these matters are quite simple. Much as Zigler and Phillips have demonstrated that there is enormous overlap in the symptoms presented by patients who have been variously diagnosed,[16] so there is enormous overlap in the behaviors of the sane and the insane. The sane are not "sane" all of the time. We lose our tempers "for no good reason." We are occasionally depressed or anxious, again for no good reason. And we may find it difficult to get along with one or another person—again for no reason that we can specify. Similarly, the insane are not always insane. Indeed, it was the impression of the pseudopatients while living with them that they were sane for long periods of time—that the bizarre behaviors upon which their diagnoses were allegedly predicated constituted only a small fraction of their total behavior. If it makes no sense to label ourselves permanently depressed on the basis of an occasional depression, then it takes better evidence than is presently available to label all patients insane or schizophrenic on the basis of bizarre behaviors or cognitions. It seems more useful, as Mischel[17] has pointed out, to limit our discussions to *behaviors,* the stimuli that provoke them, and their correlates.

It is not known why powerful impressions of personality traits, such as "crazy" or "insane," arise. Conceivably, when the origins of and stimuli that give rise to a behavior are remote or unknown, or when the behavior strikes us as immutable, trait labels regarding the *behaver* arise. When, on the other hand, the origins and stimuli are known and available, discourse is limited to the behavior itself. Thus, I may hallucinate because I am sleeping, or I may hallucinate because I have ingested a peculiar drug. These are termed sleep-induced hallucinations, or dreams, and drug-induced hallucinations, respectively. But when the stimuli to my hallucinations are unknown, that is called craziness, or schizophrenia—as if that inference were somehow as illuminating as the others.

The Experience of Psychiatric Hospitalization

The term "mental illness" is of recent origin. It was coined by people who were humane in their inclinations and who wanted very much to raise the station of (and the public's sympathies toward) the psychologically disturbed from that of witches and "crazies" to one that was akin to the physically ill. And they were at least partially successful, for the treatment of the mentally ill *has* improved considerably over the years. But while treatment has improved, it is doubtful that people really regard the mentally ill in the same way that they view the physically ill. A broken leg is something one recovers from, but mental illness allegedly endures forever.[18] A broken leg does not threaten the observer, but a crazy schizophrenic? There is by now a host of evidence that attitudes toward the mentally ill are characterized by fear, hostility, aloofness, suspicion, and dread.[19] The mentally ill are society's lepers.

That such attitudes infect the general population is perhaps not surprising, only upsetting. But that they affect the professionals—attendants, nurses, physicians, psychologists, and social workers—who treat and deal with the mentally ill is more disconcerting, both because such attitudes are self-evidently pernicious and because they are unwitting. Most mental health professionals would insist that they are sympathetic toward the mentally ill, that they are neither avoidant nor hostile. But it is more likely that an exquisite ambivalence characterizes their relations with psychiatric patients, such that their avowed impulses are only part of their entire attitude. Negative attitudes are there too and can easily be detected. Such attitudes should not surprise us. They are the natural offspring of the labels patients wear and the places in which they are found.

Consider the structure of the typical psychiatric hospital. Staff and patients are strictly segregated. Staff have their own living space, including their dining facilities, bathrooms, and assembly places. The glassed quarters that contain the professional staff, which the pseudopatients came to call "the cage," sit out on every dayroom. The staff emerge primarily for caretaking purposes—to give medication, to conduct a therapy or group meeting, to instruct or reprimand a patient. Otherwise, staff keep to themselves, almost as if the disorder that afflicts their charges is somehow catching.

So much is a patient-staff segregation the rule that, for four public hospitals in which an attempt was made to measure the degree to which staff and patients mingle, it was necessary to use "time out of the staff cage" as the operational measure. While it was not the case that all time spent out of the cage was spent mingling with patients (attendants, for example, would occasionally emerge to watch television in the dayroom), it was the only way in which one could gather reliable data on time for measuring.

The average amount of time spent by attendants outside of the cage was 11.3 percent (range, 3 to 52 percent). This figure does not represent only time spent mingling with patients, but also includes time spent on such chores as folding laundry, supervising patients while they shave, directing ward cleanup, and sending patients to off-ward activities. It was the relatively rare attendant who spent time talking with patients or playing games with them. It proved impossible to obtain a "percent mingling time" for nurses, since the amount of time they spent out of the cage was too brief. Rather, we counted instances of emergence from the cage. On the average, daytime nurses emerged from the cage 11.5 times per shift, including instances when they left the ward entirely (range, 4 to 39 times). Late afternoon and night nurses were even less available, emerging on the average 9.4 times per shift (range, 4 to 41 times). Data on early morning nurses, who arrived usually after midnight and departed at 8 a.m., are not available because patients were asleep during most of this period.

Physicians, especially psychiatrists, were even less available. They were rarely seen on the wards. Quite commonly, they would be seen only when they arrived and departed, with the remaining time being spent in their offices or in the cage. On the average, physicians emerged on the ward 6.7 times per day (range, 1 to 17 times). It proved difficult to make an accurate estimate in this regard, since physicians often maintained hours that allowed them to come and go at different times.

The hierarchical organization of the psychiatric hospital has been commented on before,[20] but the latent meaning of that kind of organization is worth noting again. Those with the most power have least to do with patients, and those with the least power are most involved with them. Recall, however, that the acquisition of role-appropriate behaviors occurs mainly through the observation of others, with the most powerful having the most influence. Consequently, it is understandable that attendants not only spend more time with patients than do any other members of the staff—that is required by their station in the hierarchy—but also, insofar as they learn from their superiors' behavior, spend as little time with patients as they can. Attendants are seen mainly in the cage, which is where the models, the action, and the power are.

I turn now to a different set of studies, these dealing with staff response to patient-initiated contact. It has long been known that the amount of time a person spends with you can be an index of your significance to him. If he initiates and maintains eye contact, there is reason to believe that he is considering your requests and needs. If he pauses to chat or actually stops and talks, there is added reason to infer that he is individuating you. In four hospitals, the pseudopatient approached the staff member with a request which took the following form: "Pardon me, Mr. [or Dr. or Mrs.] X, could you tell me when I will be eligible for grounds privileges?" (or " . . . when I will be presented at the staff meeting?" or " . . . when I am likely to be discharged?"). While the content of the question varied according to the appropriateness of the target and the pseudopatient's (apparent) current needs the form was always a courteous and relevant request for information. Care was taken never to approach a particular member of the staff more than once a day, lest the staff member become suspicious or irritated. In examining these data, remember that the behavior of the pseudopatients was neither bizarre nor disruptive. One could indeed engage in good conversation with them.

The data for these experiments are shown in Table 14.1, separately for physicians (column 1) and for nurses and attendants (column 2). Minor differences between these four institutions were overwhelmed by the degree to which staff avoided continuing contacts that patients had initiated. By far, their most common response consisted of either a brief response to the question, offered while they were "on the move" and with head averted, or no response at all.

The encounter frequently took the following bizarre form: (pseudopatient) "Pardon me, Dr. X. Could you tell me when I am eligible for grounds privileges?" (physician) "Good morning, Dave. How are you today?" (Moves off without waiting for a response.)

It is instructive to compare these data with data recently obtained at Stanford University. It has been alleged that large and eminent universities are characterized by faculty who are so busy that they have no time for students. For this comparison, a young lady approached individual faculty members who seemed to be walking purposefully to some meeting or teaching engagement and asked them the following six questions.

1. "Pardon me, could you direct me to Encina Hall?" (at the medical school: ". . . to the Clinical Research Center?").
2. "Do you know where Fish Annex is?" (there is no Fish Annex at Stanford).
3. "Do you teach here?"
4. "How does one apply for admission to the college?" (at the medical school: ". . . to the medical school?").
5. "Is it difficult to get in?"
6. "Is there financial aid?"

Without exception, as can be seen in Table 14.1 (column 3), all of the questions were answered. No matter how rushed they were, all respondents not only maintained eye contact, but stopped to talk. Indeed, many of the respondents went out of their way to direct or take the questioner to the office she was seeking, to try to locate "Fish Annex," or to discuss with her the possibilities of being admitted to the university.

Similar data, also shown in Table 14.1 (columns 4, 5, and 6), were obtained in the hospital. Here too, the young lady came prepared with

TABLE 14.1 Self-Initiated Contact by Pseudopatients With Psychiatrists and Nurses and Attendants, Compared to Contact With Other Groups

	Psychiatric Hospitals		*University Campus (Nonmedical)*	*University Medical Center*		
				Physicians		
Contact	*(1) Psychiatrists*	*(2) Nurses and Attendents*	*(3) Faculty*	*(4) "Looking for a Psychiatrist"*	*(5) "Looking for an Internist"*	*(6) No Additional Comment*
Responses						
Moves on, head averted (%)	71	88	0	0	0	0
Makes eye contact (%)	23	10	0	11	0	0
Pauses and chats (%)	2	2	0	11	0	10
Stops and talks (%)	4	0.5	100	78	100	90
Mean number of questions answered (out of 6)	*	*	6	3.8	4.8	4.5
Respondents (No.)	13	47	14	18	15	10
Attempts (No.)	185	1283	14	18	15	10

* Not applicable.

six questions. After the first question, however, she remarked to 18 of her respondents (column 4), "I'm looking for a psychiatrist," and to 15 others (column 5), "I'm looking for an internist." Ten other respondents received no inserted comment (column 6). The general degree of cooperative responses is considerably higher for these university groups than it was for pseudopatients in psychiatric hospitals. Even so, differences are apparent within the medical school setting. Once having indicated that she was looking for a psychiatrist, the degree of cooperation elicited was less than when she sought an internist.

Powerlessness and Depersonalization

Eye contact and verbal contact reflect concern and individuation; their absence, avoidance and depersonalization. The data I have presented do not do justice to the rich daily encounters that grew up around matters of depersonalization and avoidance. I have records of patients who were beaten by staff for the sin of having initiated verbal contact. During my own experience, for example, one patient was beaten in the presence of other patients for having approached an attendant and told him, "I like you." Occasionally, punishment meted out to patients for misdemeanors seemed so excessive that it could not be justified by the most radical interpretations of psychiatric canon. Nevertheless, they appeared to go unquestioned. Tempers were often short. A patient who had not heard a call for medication would be roundly excoriated, and the morning attendants would often wake patients with, "Come on, you m——f——s, out of bed!"

Neither anecdotal nor "hard" data can convey the overwhelming sense of powerlessness which invades the individual as he is continually exposed to the depersonalization of the psychiatric hospital. It hardly matters *which* psychiatric hospital—the excellent public ones and the very plush private hospital were better than the rural and shabby ones in this regard, but again, the features that psychiatric hospitals had in common overwhelmed by far their apparent differences.

Powerlessness was evident everywhere. The patient is deprived of many of his legal rights by dint of his psychiatric commitment.[21] He is shorn of credibility by virtue of his psychiatric label. His freedom of movement is restricted. He cannot initiate contact with the staff, but may only respond to such overtures as they make. Personal privacy is minimal. Patient quarters and possessions can be entered and examined by any staff member, for whatever reason. His personal history and anguish are available to any staff member (often including the "grey lady" and "candy striper" volunteer) who chooses to read his folder, regardless of their therapeutic relationship to him. His personal hygiene and waste evacuation are often monitored. The water closets may have no doors.

At times, depersonalization reached such proportions that pseudopatients had the sense that they were invisible, or at least unworthy of account. Upon being admitted, I and other pseudopatients took the initial physical examinations in a semipublic room, where staff members went about their own business as if we were not there.

On the ward, attendants delivered verbal and occasionally serious physical abuse to patients in the presence of other observing patients, some of whom (the pseudopatients) were writing it all down. Abusive behavior, on the other hand, terminated quite abruptly when other staff members were known to be coming. Staff are credible witnesses. Patients are not.

A nurse unbuttoned her uniform to adjust her brassiere in the presence of an entire ward of viewing men. One did not have the sense that she was being seductive. Rather, she didn't notice us. A group of staff persons might point to a patient in the dayroom and discuss him animatedly, as if he were not there.

One illuminating instance of depersonalization and invisibility occurred with regard to medications. All told, the pseudopatients were administered nearly 2,100 pills, including Elavil, Stelazine, Compazine, and Thorazine, to name but a few. (That such a variety of medications should have been administered to patients presenting identical symptoms is itself worthy of note.) Only two were swallowed. The rest were either pocketed or deposited in the toilet. The pseudopatients were not alone in this. Although I have no precise records on how many patients rejected their medications, the pseudopatients frequently found the medications of other patients in the toilet before they deposited their own. As long as they were cooperative, their behavior and the pseudopatients' own in this matter, as in other important matters, went unnoticed throughout.

Reactions to such depersonalization among pseudopatients were intense. Although they had come to the hospital as participant observers and were fully aware that they did not "belong," they nevertheless found themselves caught up in and fighting the process of depersonalization. Some examples: a graduate student in psychology asked his wife to bring his textbooks to the hospital so he could "catch up on his homework"—this despite the elaborate precautions taken to conceal his professional association. The same student, who had trained for quite some time to get into the hospital, and who had looked forward to the experience, "remembered" some drag races that he had wanted to see on the weekend and insisted that he be discharged by that time. Another pseudopatient attempted a romance with a nurse. Subsequently, he informed the staff that he was applying for admission to graduate school in psychology and was very likely to be admitted, since a graduate professor was one of his regular hospital visitors. The same person began to engage in psychotherapy with other patients—all of this as a way of becoming a person in an impersonal environment.

The Sources of Depersonalization

What are the origins of depersonalization? I have already mentioned two. First are attitudes held by all of us toward the mentally ill—including those who treat them—attitudes characterized by fear, distrust, and horrible expectations on the one hand, and benevolent intentions on the other. Our ambivalence leads, in this instance as in others, to avoidance.

Second, and not entirely separate, the hierarchical structure of the psychiatric hospital facilitates depersonalization. Those who are at the top have least to do with patients, and their behavior inspires the rest of the staff. Average daily contact with psychiatrists, psychologists, residents, and physicians combined ranged from 3.9 to 25.1 minutes, with an overall mean of 6.8 (six pseudopatients over a total of 129 days of hospitalization). Included in this average are time spent in the admissions interview, ward meetings in the presence of a senior staff member, group and individual psychotherapy contacts, case presentation conferences, and discharge meetings. Clearly, patients do not spend much time in interpersonal contact with doctoral staff. And doctoral staff serve as models for nurses and attendants.

There are probably other sources. Psychiatric installations are presently in serious financial straits. Staff shortages are pervasive, staff time at a premium. Something has to give, and that something is patient contact. Yet, while financial stresses are realities, too much can be made of them. I have the impression that the psychological forces that result in depersonalization are much stronger than the fiscal ones and that the addition of more staff would not correspondingly improve patient care in this regard. The incidence of staff meetings and the enormous amount of record-keeping on patients, for example, have not been as substantially reduced as has patient contact. Priorities exist, even during hard times. Patient contact is not a significant priority in the traditional psychiatric hospital, and fiscal pressures do not account for this. Avoidance and depersonalization may.

Heavy reliance upon psychotropic medication tacitly contributes to depersonalization by convincing staff that treatment is indeed being conducted and that further patient contact may not be necessary. Even here, however, caution needs to be exercised in understanding the role of psychotropic drugs. If patients were powerful rather than powerless, if they were viewed as interesting individuals rather than diagnostic entities, if they were socially significant rather than social lepers, if their anguish truly and wholly compelled our sympathies and concerns, would we not *seek* contact with them, despite the availability of medications? Perhaps for the pleasure of it all?

The Consequences of Labeling and Depersonalization

Whenever the ratio of what is known to what needs to be known approaches zero, we tend to invent "knowledge" and assume that we understand more than we actually do. We seem unable to acknowledge that we simply don't know. The needs for diagnosis and remediation of behavioral and emotional problems are enormous. But rather than acknowledge that we are just embarking on understanding, we continue to label patients "schizophrenic," "manic-depressive," and "insane" as if in those words we had captured the essence of understanding. The facts of the matter are that we have known for a long time that diagnoses are often not useful or reliable, but we have nevertheless continued to use them. We now know that we cannot distinguish insanity from sanity. It is depressing to consider how that information will be used.

Not merely depressing, but frightening. How many people, one wonders, are sane but not recognized as such in our psychiatric institutions? How many have been needlessly stripped of their privileges of citizenship, from the right to vote and drive to that of handling their own accounts? How many have feigned insanity in order to avoid the criminal consequences of their behavior, and, conversely, how many would rather stand trial than live interminably in a psychiatric hospital—but are wrongly thought to be mentally ill? How many have been stigmatized by well-intentioned, but nevertheless erroneous, diagnoses? On the last point, recall again that a "type 2 error" in psychiatric diagnosis does not have the same consequences it does in medical diagnosis. A diagnosis of cancer that has been found to be in error is cause for celebration. But psychiatric diagnoses are rarely found to be in error. The label sticks, a mark of inadequacy forever.

Finally, how many patients might be "sane" outside the psychiatric hospital but seem insane in it—not because craziness resides in them, as it were, but because they are responding to a bizarre setting, one that may be unique to institutions which harbor nether people? Goffman (see Note 4) calls the process of socialization to such institutions "mortification"—an apt metaphor that includes the processes of depersonalization that have been described here. And while it is impossible to know whether the pseudopatients' responses to these processes are characteristic of all inmates—they were, after all, not real patients—it is difficult to believe that these processes of socialization to a psychiatric hospital provide useful attitudes or habits of response for living in the "real world."

Summary and Conclusions

It is clear that we cannot distinguish the sane from the insane in psychiatric hospitals. The hospital itself imposes a special environment in which the meanings of behavior can easily be misunderstood. The consequences to patients hospitalized in such an environment—the powerlessness, depersonalization, segregation, mortification, and self-labeling—seem undoubtedly countertherapeutic.

I do not, even now, understand this problem well enough to perceive solutions. But two matters seem to have some promise. The first concerns the proliferation of community mental health facilities, of crisis intervention centers, of the human potential movement, and of behavior therapies that, for all of their own problems, tend to avoid psychiatric labels, to focus on specific problems and behaviors, and to retain the individual in a relatively nonpejorative environment. Clearly, to the extent that we refrain from sending the distressed to insane places, our impressions of them are less likely to be distorted. (The risk of distorted perceptions, it seems to me, is always present, since we are much more sensitive to an individual's behaviors and verbalizations than we are to the subtle contextual stimuli that often promote them. At issue here is a matter of magnitude. And, as I have shown, the magnitude of distortion is exceedingly high in the extreme context that is a psychiatric hospital.)

The second matter that might prove promising speaks to the need to increase the sensitivity of mental health workers and researchers to the

Catch 22 position of psychiatric patients. Simply reading materials in this area will be of help to some such workers and researchers. For others, directly experiencing the impact of psychiatric hospitalization will be of enormous use. Clearly, further research into the social psychology of such total institutions will both facilitate treatment and deepen understanding.

I and the other pseudopatients in the psychiatric setting had distinctly negative reactions. We do not pretend to describe the subjective experiences of true patients. Theirs may be different from ours, particularly with the passage of time and the necessary process of adaptation to one's environment. But we can and do speak to the relatively more objective indices of treatment within the hospital. It could be a mistake, and a very unfortunate one, to consider that what happened to us derived from malice or stupidity on the part of the staff. Quite the contrary, our overwhelming impression of them was of people who really cared, who were committed and who were uncommonly intelligent. Where they failed, as they sometimes did painfully, it would be more accurate to attribute those failures to the environment in which they, too, found themselves than to personal callousness. Their perceptions and behavior were controlled by the situation rather than being motivated by a malicious disposition. In a more benign environment, one that was less attached to global diagnosis, their behaviors and judgments might have been more benign and effective.

Notes

1. P. Ash, *J. Abnorm. Soc. Psychol.* 44, 272 (1949); A. T. Beck, *Amer. J. Psychiat.* 119, 210 (1962); A. T. Boisen, *Psychiatry* 2, 233 (1938); N. Kreitman, *J. Ment. Sci.* 107, 876 (1961); N. Kreitman, P. Sainsbury, J. Morrisey, J. Towers, J. Scrivener, *ibid.*, p. 887; H. O. Schmitt and C. P. Fonda, *J. Abnorm. Soc. Psychol.* 52, 262 (1956); W. Seeman, *J. Nerv. Ment. Dis.* 118, 541 (1953). For an analysis of these artifacts and summaries of the disputes, see J. Zubin, *Annu. Rev. Psychol.* 18, 373 (1967); L. Phillips and J. G. Draguns, *ibid.* 22, 447 (1971).

2. R. Benedict, *J. Gen. Psychol.* 10, 59 (1934).

3. See in this regard H. Becker, *Outsiders: Studies in the Sociology of Deviance* (Free Press, New York, 1963); B. M. Braginsky, D. D. Braginsky, K. Ring, *Methods of Madness: The Mental Hospital as a Last Resort* (Holt, Rinehart & Winston, New York, 1969); G. M. Crocetti and P. V. Lemkau, *Amer. Sociol. Rev.* 30, 577 (1965); E. Goffman, *Behavior in Public Places* (Free Press, New York, 1964); R. D. Laing, *The Divided Self: A Study of Sanity and Madness* (Quadrangle, Chicago, 1960); D. L. Phillips, *Amer. Sociol. Rev.* 28, 963 (1963); T. R. Sarbin, *Psychol. Today* 6, 18 (1972); E. Schur, *Amer. J. Sociol.* 75, 309 (1969); T. Szasz, *Law, Liberty and Psychiatry* (Macmillan, New York, 1963);

The Myth of Mental Illness: Foundations of a Theory of Mental Illness (Hoeber-Haper, New York, 1963). For a critique of some of these views, see W. R. Grove, *Amer. Sociol. Rev.* 35, 873 (1970).

4. E. Goffman, *Asylums* (Doubleday, Garden City, NY, 1961).

5. T. J. Scheff, *Being Mentally Ill: A Sociological Theory* (Aldine, Chicago, 1966).

6. Data from a ninth pseudopatient are not incorporated in this report because, although his sanity went undetected, he falsified aspects of his personal history, including his marital status and parental relationships. His experimental behaviors therefore were not identical to those of the other pseudopatients.

7. A. Barry, *Bellevue Is a State of Mind* (Harcourt Brace Jovanovich, New York, 1971); I. Belknap, *Human Problems of a State Mental Hospital* (McGraw-Hill, New York, 1956); W. Caudill, F. C. Redlich, H. R. Gilmore, E. B. Brody, *Amer. J. Orthopsychiat.* 22, 314 (1952); A. R. Goldman, R. H. Bohr, T. A. Steinberg, *Prof. Psychol.* 1, 427 (1970); unauthored, *Roche Report* 1 (No. 13), 8 (1971).

8. Beyond the personal difficulties that the pseudopatient is likely to experience in the hospital, there are legal and social ones that, combined, require considerable attention before entry. For example, once admitted to a psychiatric institution, it is difficult, if not impossible, to be discharged on short notice, state law to the contrary notwithstanding. I was not sensitive to these difficulties at the outset of the project, nor to the personal and situational emergencies that can arise, but later a writ of habeas corpus was prepared for each of the entering pseudopatients and an attorney was kept "on call" during every hospitalization. I am grateful to John Kaplan and Robert Bartels for legal advice and assistance in these matters.

9. However distasteful such concealment is, it was a necessary first step to examining these questions. Without concealment, there would have been no way to know how valid these experiences were; nor was there any way of knowing whether whatever detections occurred were a tribute to the diagnostic acumen of the staff or to the hospital's rumor network. Obviously, since my concerns are general ones that cut across individual hospitals and staffs, I have respected their anonymity and have eliminated clues that might lead to their identification.

10. Interestingly, of the 12 admissions, 11 were diagnosed as schizophrenic and one, with the identical symptomatology, as manic-depressive psychosis. This diagnosis has a more favorable prognosis, and it was given by the only private hospital in our sample. On the relations between social class and psychiatric diagnosis, see A. deB. Hollingshead and F. C. Redlich, *Social Class and Mental Illness: A Community Study* (Wiley, New York, 1958).

11. It is possible, of course, that patients have quite broad latitudes in diagnosis and therefore are inclined to call many people sane, even those whose behavior is patently aberrant. However, although we have no hard data on this matter, it was our distinct impression that this was not the case. In many instances, patients not only singled us out for attention, but came to imitate our behaviors and styles.

12. J. Cumming and E. Cumming, *Community Ment. Health* 1, 135 (1965); A. Farina and K. Ring, *J. Abnorm. Psychol.* 70, 47 (1965); H. E. Freeman and O. G. Simmons, *The Mental Patient Comes Home* (Wiley, New York, 1963); W. J. Johannsen, *Ment. Hygiene* 53, 218 (1969); A. S. Linsky, *Soc. Psychiat.* 5, 166 (1970).

13. S. E. Asch, *J. Abnorm. Soc. Psychol.* 41, 258 (1946); *Social Psychology* (Prentice-Hall, New York, 1952).

14. See also I. N. Mensch and J. Wishner, *J. Personality* 16, 188 (1947); J. Wishner, *Psychol. Rev.* 67, 96 (1960); J. S. Bruner and R. Tagiuri, in *Handbook of Social Psychology,* G. Lindzey, Ed. (Addison-Wesley, Cambridge, Mass., 1954), vol. 2, pp. 634-654; J. S. Bruner, D. Shapiro, R. Tagiuri and L. Petrullo, Eds. (Stanford Univ. Press, Stanford, CA, 1958), pp. 277-288.

15. For an example of a similar self-fulfilling prophecy, in this instance dealing with the "central" trait of intelligence, see R. Rosenthal and L. Jacobson, *Pygmalion in the Classroom* (Holt, Rinehart & Winston, New York, 1968).

16. E. Zigler and L. Phillips, *J. Abnorm. Soc. Psychol.* 63, 69 (1961). See also R. K. Freudenberg and J. P. Robertson, *A.M.A. Arch. Neurol. Psychiatr.* 76, 14 (1956).

17. W. Mischel, *Personality and Assessment* (Wiley, New York, 1968).

18. The most recent and unfortunate instance of this tenet is that of Senator Thomas Eagleton.

19. T. R. Sarbin and J. C. Mancuso, *J. Clin. Consult. Psychol.* 35, 159 (1970); T. R. Sarbin, *ibid.* 31, 447 (1967); J. C. Nunnally, Jr., *Popular Conceptions of Mental Health* (Holt, Rinehart & Winston, New York, 1961).

20. A. H. Stanton and M. S. Schwartz, *The Mental Hospital: A Study of Institutional Participation in Psychiatric Illness and Treatment* (Basic, New York, 1954).

21. D. B. Wexler and S. E. Scoville, *Ariz. Law Rev.* 13, 1 (1971).

22. I thank W. Mischel, E. Orne, and M. S. Rosenhan for comments on an earlier draft of this manuscript.

V

Ethnoscience

Ethnoscience is a type of ethnography designed to get at the structure or cognitive domain of the world view of the informants. The assumption is that all knowledge is ordered and may be acquired or understood using interviews, observations, and interview techniques, such as asking comparative questions, card sorts, and sentence frames to elicit the unique features and structure of the underlying semantic domains (see Werner & Schoepfle, 1987). As with ethnography, the context is usually provided by description as it is in Spradley's (1970) classical work, *You Owe Yourself a Drunk,* in which the context was provided by letters from his primary informant, Bill.

Ethnoscience data are not only presented descriptively but are also presented as taxonomies or trees to illustrate the relationships or interconnections of each domain, segregate and subsegregate. Because ethnoscience seeks to identify relationships among characteristics of things, it is best used to describe familiar concrete concepts rather than abstract concepts, such as affective phenomena. Classical ethnoscience articles have described kinship patterns, types of firewood or snow, or disease categories.

Chapter 15 is derived from Spradley's 1970 skid row study. "Beating the Drunk Charge" describes the categories that may be used to beat a drunk charge and Spradley includes a table illustrating the conditions that influence the tramps in selecting a particular method. He then describes the cultural values that appeared to underlie the penalties for public drunkenness and identifies from these three implicit cultural rules that determine the severity of the punishment.

In the second chapter illustrating the method of ethnoscience, "The Structure and Function of Gift Giving in the Patient-Nurse Relationship" (Chapter 16), I obtained data from nurses about the things that patients gave them and the meaning or the circumstances and the stories surrounding these gifts. The nurse informants then sorted these gifts into groups, describing the characteristics of each category of gifts. I used a taxonomy to illustrate the interrelationships among the types of gifts given to nurses.

Again, as with ethnography, the underlying meanings of the gifts are not always clear even to the nurses themselves. However, the methods of ethnoscience facilitated the identification of the underlying structure. Categories of gifts ranged from acts of retaliation for poor care, or manipulation to ensure care, to serendipitous rewards, or planned expressions of gratitude for excellent care. Gifts were seen as a way of "giving back" to the staff and reflected the patients' perception of quality of care. Gifts were used to balance the nurse-patient relationship by reciprocating for care given, and they reflected the standard of care. They were intended to remove obligations and equalize relationships. As such, gifts are important yet often ignored components of a nurse-patient relationship.

Examine both chapters, and discuss how the results are lifted from a level of description to some level of abstraction. How does this process influence generalizability? How should the limits of generalizability be determined?

References

Spradley, J. (1970). *You owe yourself a drunk: An ethnography of urban nomads*. Boston: Little, Brown and Co.

Werner, O., & Schoepfle, G. M. (1987). *Systematic fieldwork. Volume 2: Ethnographic analysis and data management*. Newbury Park, CA: Sage Publications.

15

Beating the Drunk Charge

JAMES P. SPRADLEY

Abstract: In the urban American court used in the following study, nearly 12,000 men are charged each year with public drunkenness. While many post bail and go free, most of the poor appear in court and place themselves at the mercy of the judge. They are not entirely destitute, however, and have an elaborate set of strategies for "beating the drunk charge." James Spradley analyzes these strategies, shows their differential effectiveness, and demonstrates how they reflect certain values of American culture.

It could be Miami, New York, Chicago, Minneapolis, Denver, Los Angeles, Seattle, or any other American city. The criminal court may be in the basement of a massive public building constructed at the turn of the century, or high above the city in a modern skyscraper. The judges who hear the never-ending list of cases may be veterans of the bench or men whose memories of law school are fresh and clear. But one scene does not change. Each weekday morning a group of unshaven men file into court with crestfallen faces, wrinkled clothing, and bloodshot eyes. They stand before the prosecuting attorney and hear him say, "You have been charged with public drunkenness, how do you plead?"

AUTHOR'S NOTE: Those interested in the meaning of various terms not explained here should consult this ethnographic study. This chapter originally appeared in Spradley, J. P. (1984). Beating the drunk charge. In J. P. Spradley and D. W. McCurdy (Eds.), *Conformity and conflict: Readings in cultural anthropology*. Glenview, IL: HarperCollins.

The most staggering problem of law and order in America today is public drunkenness. In 1968 the F.B.I. reported that one and a half million arrests for this crime made up nearly one third of all arrests. This means that every twenty seconds another person is arrested and charged with being drunk in public. During 1967, in Seattle, Washington, 51% of all arrests and 65% of all cases that appeared in the criminal court were for intoxication. In that same year the chief of police stated, "As a public official I have no choice. Whether alcoholism is a disease or not would not affect my official position. Drunkenness is a crime. So we must enforce the law by arresting people. We know in the Police Department that probably right at this moment there are more than two hundred men in the city jail serving sentences for drunkenness who have never posed any threat to the community in any fashion at all."

Who are these men that are repeatedly arrested for drunkenness? Who are the ones who spend much of their lives in jail for their public behavior? The first task in this study was to discover how these men identified themselves. This was necessary because the police, courts, social scientists, and most citizens see them as criminals, homeless men, derelicts, and bums who have lost the ability to organize their behavior in the pursuit of goals. The word these men used to identify their subcultural membership was the term *tramp*. There were several different kinds of tramps recognized by informants; for example, a "mission stiff" is a tramp who frequents the skid-road missions, while a "rubber tramp" travels about in his own car. This category system constitutes one of the major social identity domains in the subculture.

Tramps have other ways to conceptualize their identity when they "make the bucket," or are incarcerated. As an inmate in jail one is either a *drunk,* a *trusty,* a *lockup,* a *kickout,* or a *rabbit.* In the particular jail studied there are over sixty different kinds of trusties. This fact led some tramps to believe they were arrested to provide cheap labor for the police department. In their capacity as trusties, nearly 125 men provide janitorial service for the city hall, outlying police precincts, and the jail. They assist in the preparation of food, maintain the firing range, care for police vehicles, and do numerous other tasks. Most men soon learn that doing time on a drunk charge is not a desirable occupation, so they use many strategies to escape the confines of the jail or to reduce the length of their sentence. When a man is arrested he is placed in the drunk tank where he awaits his arraignment in court. Those sentenced to do time will spend it in close association with other tramps. If a man is not experienced in the ways of this culture, he will learn them while he is in jail, for it is a veritable storehouse of invaluable information for those who are repeatedly arrested for public intoxication. He will learn to think of himself as a tramp and to survive on the street by employing more than a dozen "ways of making it." More important, as he discovers that the jailhouse has a revolving door for drunks, he will do his best to "beat the drunk charge." The casual observer in court may find the arraignment and sentencing of drunk cases to be a cut-and-dried process. From the perspective of these men, however, it is more like a game of skill and chance being played by the tramp and law-enforcement agencies. In this chapter we shall examine the rules of this game, the strategies employed by tramps, and the underlying American cultural values that make it intelligible to the outsider.

Plans for Beating the Drunk Charge

Every culture contains one type of shared knowledge called *plans*. These are related to the achievement of goals. A plan is a set of rules that specifies a goal, conditions under which the goal will be chosen, techniques for the attainment of the goal, and conditions under which a particular technique will be used to attain the goal. The methods of ethnoscience are designed to map culturally shared systems of knowledge, and were used in this study to discover the plans tramps employ in their relationship to law-enforcement agencies.

The goal: Maximize freedom—minimize incarceration. There are many goals that tramps pursue. Most aims are referred to in a specific manner, such as "making a flop," "making a jug," "getting a dime," or "bailing out." Freedom is a general objective that includes such specific goals as rabbiting from jail, concealing one's identity, making a pay-off to a bull, leaving town, avoiding the police, and beating a drunk charge. Men do not always select one of these goals in order to maximize freedom—they sometimes even choose paths leading to *incarceration*. In a sample of a hundred men, 10 percent reported they had gone to jail and asked to be locked up in order to stop drinking. At other times a tramp will go to jail on his own to request a place to sleep or something to eat. Such cases are rare, and most tramps abhor imprisonment because they have learned a life style of mobility and the restrictions in the bucket lead to intense frustration. A testimonial to the fact that men do not seek imprisonment, as some outsiders believe, is the large number of strategies this culture has for avoiding incarceration. Almost every experience in the tramp world is defined, in part, by noting the degree of risk it entails for being jailed.

Techniques for the attainment of the goal. Because of the public nature of their life style, sooner or later most of these men end up in jail. Their specific objective at that time is to "beat the drunk charge." If successful, this could mean freedom in a few hours or at least a sentence of shorter duration than they would otherwise have received. The techniques for reaching this goal were discovered during interviews in which informants were asked: "Are there different ways to beat a drunk charge?" They responded with many specific instances in which they had taken action to beat the charge. These were classified as follows:

1. Bail out.
2. Bond out.
3. Request a continuance.
4. Have a good record.
5. Use an alias.
6. Plead guilty.
7. Hire a defense attorney.
8. Plead not guilty.
9. Submit a writ of habeas corpus.
10. Make a statement:
    a. Talk of family ties.
    b. Talk of present job.
    c. Talk of intent to work.
    d. Tell of extenuating circumstances.
    e. Offer to leave town.
11. Request the treatment center (alcoholic).

Each of these techniques labels a *category* of many different acts that are considered equivalent. For example, a man may bail out by using money he had with him when arrested, by borrowing from another man in jail, by contacting an employer who loans or gives him the money, and so on. There are several ways to "have a good record": a man must stay out of jail for at least six months for his record to begin to affect the length of his jail sentence. In order to do this a man may travel, quit drinking, stay off skid road, or go to an alcoholism treatment center for a long stay. Each kind of statement includes specific instances, varying from one man to another and from one time to the next. This category system is extremely important to tramps. Once they have learned these techniques, they practice them until their skill increases. Judges may consider an old-time tramp as a "con artist," but in this culture he is a man with expertise in carrying out these culturally shared techniques.

Conditions influencing selection. When a man is arrested he must process a great deal of information before he makes a decision to employ one or more of these techniques. He must assess his own resources, the probabilities of success, the risk of doing more time, etc. He needs to know the sentencing practices of the judge, the population of the jail, and the weather conditions. The most important factors that influence his decision are shown in Table 15.1.

American Cultural Values

Every society is based upon shared values—conceptions of the desirable in human experience. They are the basis for rewards and punishments. It is not surprising to most Americans that our culture, like most others, has rules about the undesirability of certain behavior *in public*. We have outlawed nudity, begging, drinking, elimination of wastes, and intoxication in public places. We are offended by many other acts—if they occur in public. Tramps are booked for public intoxication, but they are often arrested because they urinate, sleep, or drink in some public place. Poverty has made it impossible for them to conceal their behavior behind the walls of a home. The extent of these restrictions upon *public* acts are in contrast to many non-Western societies where there is a wider range of acceptable public behavior. Because public drunkenness, which covers a multitude of other public sins, involves more arrests each year than any other crime, we may conclude that *privacy* is an important value in our culture.

Above the judge's bench in the criminal court where this study took place, there is a large wooden plaque inscribed "Equal Justice for All Under the Law." Given the laws prohibiting public behavior of various kinds, we might still expect that the punishment for violation would be distributed *equally*. Thus, if two men with the same criminal record are found guilty of the same crime, they should receive the same punishment. If two men are found drunk in public for the first time, it would be unfair to fine one a few dollars and require the other to pay several

TABLE 15.1 Conditions Influencing Selection of a Way to Beat a Drunk Charge

Strategy	*Risk of outcome?*	*Risk offending bulls?*	*Risk getting more time?*	*Risk doing dead time?*	*Money needed?*
Bail out	No	No	No	No	$20
Bond out	No	No	No	No	$20+
Request a continuance	Yes	Yes	No	Yes	Yes
Have a good record	No	No	No	No	No
Use an alias	Yes	Yes	Yes	No	No
Plead guilty	Yes	No	No	No	No
Hire a defense attorney	Yes	Yes	No	Yes	Yes
Plead not guilty	Yes	Yes	Yes	Yes	No
Submit a writ of habeas corpus	Yes	Yes	Yes	Yes	No
Make a statement	Yes	No	Yes	No	No
Request a treatment center	Yes	Yes	Yes	Yes	No

hundred dollars. Upon examining the penalties given for public drunkenness, we discover a rather startling fact: *the less a man conforms to other American values, the more severe his punishment*—not because he violates other laws, but because he does not conform to the values of *materialism, moralism,* and *work.* These values are the basis for a set of implicit "punishment rules." Although they are unwritten, those who administer justice in our society have learned to punish the drunk offender on the basis of these rules.

Rule 1: When guilty of public drunkenness, a man deserves greater punishment if he is poor. In every society, when individuals violate legal norms they are punished. Physical torture, public humiliation, incarceration, and banishment from the society are some of the forms this punishment takes. It is not surprising that in our society, with its emphasis upon the value of material goods, violators are punished by making them give up some form of property. An individual may be fined after he has been convicted of public drunkenness. Most offenders pay money in the form of a "bail" prior to conviction. A few hours after being arrested, most men are able to be released from jail in a sober condition. They are still innocent before the law and an arraignment is scheduled at which time they may plead guilty or not guilty. If they enter the later plea, they must appear in court at another time for a trial. In order to insure that a man returns for his arraignment he is asked to deposit bail money with the court, which will be returned to him when he is sentenced or acquitted. In most courts a man may choose to ignore the arraignment and thereby "forfeit" his bail. It is still within the power of the court to issue a warrant for his arrest in this case and compel him to appear in court, but this is seldom done. Instead, much like bail for a traffic violation, forfeiture of the drunk bail is considered as a just recompense to society for appearing drunk in public.

When arrested, tramps are eager to post bail since it means an immediate release from jail. They do not need to wait for the arraignment which may not occur for several days. The bail is $20 and is almost always forfeited. This system of punishment treats offenders equally—*unless a man does not have $20.*

Those who are caught in the grip of poverty are usually convicted, and their punishment is "doing time" instead of "paying money." In America, the rich have money, the poor have time. It might be possible to punish men equitably using these two different commodities but such is not the case. If a man is poor he must be unwilling to expend his energies in the pursuit of materialism, and therefore his punishment should be more severe than that given to those with money. How does this occur? Each time a man is arrested his bail is always twenty dollars, but if he is indigent, his sentences become longer with each conviction. A man can be arrested hundreds of times and bail out for only twenty dollars, but not if he is poor. Consider the case of one man who was arrested in Seattle over one hundred times during a twenty-one-year period. On many arrests he bailed out, but for about seventy convictions he was sentenced to jail, and gradually his sentences grew to the maximum of six months for a single arrest. During this period he was sentenced to nearly fourteen years in jail—a punishment he could have avoided for only a hundred dollars for each of those years. This man was given a life sentence on the installment plan, not for being drunk but for being poor. There are many cases where a rich man and a poor man are arrested and booked for drunkenness on the same night. The rich man is released in a few hours because he had twenty dollars. The poor man is released in a few months because he did not have twenty dollars. One way then to beat a drunk charge is to bail out. If you do not have money, it is still possible to use this strategy by bonding out or asking for a continuance. A bond requires some collateral or assurance that the twenty dollars *plus* a fee to the bondsman will be paid. A continuance enables you to wait a few more days before being sentenced, and during that time, it may be possible to get money from a friend or an employer. Whether he can use these ways to beat a drunk charge or not, the tramp who is repeatedly arrested soon learns he is being punished because he does not conform to the value of materialism.

Rule 2: When guilty of public drunkenness, a man deserves greater punishment if he has a bad reputation. Most cultures have a moralistic quality that often leads to stereotyping and generalizing about the quality of a man's character. In our society once a person has been convicted of a crime, he is viewed by others with suspicion. He may never violate legal norms again, but for all practical purposes he is morally reprehensible. Since judges increase the length of a man's sentence with each arrest, he must engage in behavior designed to give him a "good record" if he is to beat the drunk charge. One way to do this is by traveling. For example, if a man stayed out of jail in Seattle for six months, subsequent convictions would begin again with short sentences; thus, when arrested several times, he often decided it would be better if he went to another town. When his arrest record began to grow in this new place, he would move on; after a period of time he would return to Seattle. Men learn to calculate the number of "days hanging" for each city where they are arrested, and their mobility is determined by the magnitude of the next sentence. Some men use an alias when arrested in an attempt to obscure the fact that they have a long record. If this ploy is successful, a man who, because of his record, deserves a sentence of six months, may only be given two or three days. Another way to beat a drunk charge is to volunteer to go to an alcoholism treatment center. A man may not believe that he is an alcoholic or even that he has a "drinking problem," but if he will agree with society's judgment—that his long record of arrests shows he is morally debased—and ask to be helped, his incarceration will be reduced. But not all men are candidates for treatment. Those with the worst records are rejected and must do their time in jail. A man with a bad reputation thus will be given a more severe punishment for the same crime than one with a good reputation.

Rule 3: When guilty of public drunkenness, a man deserves greater punishment if he does not have a steady job. American culture places great value on work as an end in itself. Resistance to hippies and welfare programs alike is based, in part, on the value of work. Tramps know that judges punish more severely those who do not have steady employment. If a man cannot beat a drunk charge in some other way, he will make a statement telling the judge that he will find a job, return to a former job, or provide evidence that he is currently employed in a respectable occupation. Tramps often earn a living by "junking" to find things to sell, "spot jobbing," or "panhandling" (begging on the street)—but all these "occupations" are not admired in our society and cannot be used as evidence that one is conforming to the value of work. When a man appears in court with evidence that he is working, the judge will often suspend or shorten his sentence.

Tramps who have been unable to beat the drunk charge before being sentenced may capitalize on this value in another way. One man reported that he had written a letter to himself while in jail. The letter appeared to have been written by an employer in another city offering the man a steady job. The inmate asked another man who was being released from jail to carry the letter to that city and mail it from there. When it arrived, he used it to convince the judge that he should receive an early release in order to accept steady employment. Another inmate, when released from jail, went personally to the judge and pretended to be a contractor; he told him that a man who had worked for him was in jail and he would employ him if he were released. The judge complied with the request, and the two tramps left town together—proud of their achievement, surer than ever that one of the best ways to beat a drunk charge was to understand the value of work in American culture.

The values our culture places upon privacy, materialism, moralism, and work are not the only ones affecting the lives of tramps. These are men who live in a society that holds no place for them. Their life style is offensive to most Americans, and for this reason they are arrested, jailed, and punished by standards that do not apply to the rest of society. In response to these practices they have learned a culture with well-developed plans for survival. They have adopted a nomadic style of life—moving from one urban center to another to maximize their freedom. In spite of their efforts, sooner or later, most tramps find themselves arrested, and it is then that the techniques for beating a drunk charge will be found most useful.

16

The Structure and Function of Gift Giving in the Patient-Nurse Relationship[1]

JANICE M. MORSE

> She must make no demands upon her patients for reciprocation, for acknowledgement or even perception of her services; since the best service a nurse can give *is* that the patient shall scarcely be aware of any—shall perceive her presence only perceiving that he has *no* wants.
>
> —*Florence Nightingale (ca. 1899/1981, p. 12)*

In the late 1800s, Florence Nightingale included the above statement in her admonishments of "what a nurse must be," listing as the third virtue that a nurse must be "honest, not accepting the most trifling fee or bribe from patients or friends" (p. 12). Overall, the rule continues today, with the policies of most institutions including regulations instructing nurses not to accept gifts from patients. Yet despite the efforts of administration to halt the practice, it is widespread and exceedingly common for patients to give gifts to individual members of the nursing staff or to the staff as a whole (Morse, 1989).

Elsewhere (Morse, 1989), I argued that the practice of reciprocity continues, as it is a necessary part of the therapeutic process. As nurses

AUTHOR'S NOTE: This chapter originally appeared in Morse, J. M. (1991). The structure and function of gift giving in the patient-nurse relationship. *Western Journal of Nursing Research, 13*, 5, 597-615.

work for the hospital, the act of *giving* care to the patient creates an imbalance, a feeling of indebtedness in the patient toward the nurse. Unless the patient has the opportunity to reciprocate, the patient may continue in a passive and dependent role. Inhibiting acts of reciprocation may, therefore, work against therapeutic goals, unless the patient is able to transform the gift by "going out" and giving to others, thereby passing on the gift.

Despite the fact that gift giving in the patient-nurse relationship has not been investigated, several authors have implied that accepting gifts places the nurse in an untenable position. For example, Clark (1971) stated that the patient in the psychiatric ward "buys extra attention" through manipulative acts of gift giving, thus obligating the nurse to the patient. Citing Pepleau, Clark states that the act of giving may be "an expression of the patient's illness," which the nurse reinforces when the gift is accepted. The resulting "loss of power" leads to a "problematic" nurse-patient relationship. Alternatively, refusing the gift without "exploring the meaning of the gift" may cause anxiety when the gift is refused.

This position, however, is limited. Gifts from the care receiver to the caregiver occur in all cultures. They continue to be given despite the method of payment for the care (i.e., direct or indirect) and despite regulations prohibiting the custom. Furthermore, clinical experience illustrates that forbidding the practice and insisting that nurses refuse and return gifts is harmful to the caregiving relationship. The practice must be examined and understood in context so that reasonable and acceptable guidelines may be developed if necessary.

Method

This study, examining gift giving in the patient-nurse relationship, was conducted in a northern Canadian city. A nominated sample of 44 nurses who were interested in being interviewed were contacted by eight research assistants. The sampling began with the research assistants seeking informants (n = 32) from eight clinical areas with which they were not familiar: psychiatry, medical-surgical, long-term care, home care/community, intensive care, pediatrics, maternity, and palliative care. Later in the study, purposeful sampling was used to interview an additional 12 nurses who had either been patients and were interviewed from the patients' perspective or who were nurse administrators or nurses from special care areas, such as the operating room and the organ donor and transplant program. Twelve informants were interviewed once, 26 were interviewed twice, and 6 were interviewed three times, for a total of 82 interviews. Demographic information on the informants is shown in Table 16.1.

Ethnoscience (Spradley, 1979) was used to elicit the information pertaining to the patterns and purpose of gift giving. In this technique, the first interviews are usually unstructured. Participants are asked to reflect on gifts they have received from patients and to "tell the story" concerning these patients. Interviewers were asked to obtain information on what kinds of gifts were given, who gave the gifts, when the gifts were given, and why they were chosen. Were the gifts given to the nurses personally, or were they given to the staff as a whole? What kinds of "speeches" were made by patients when they gave gifts? Were the patients who gave gifts different from those who did not? If so, why? Had these nurses ever refused a gift? If so, how and why was the gift refused, and what were the consequences? What was the administration's attitude toward gift giving?

Content analysis of the descriptive data provided a context for data obtained from a card sort administered during the second interview. For this procedure, the interviewer selected gifts that were given to the participant and wrote one gift on each card, preparing approximately 40 cards in triplicate. The participant was then given one set of cards and, for the triadic card sort, was asked to sort them into three piles, thinking aloud while sorting. The participant was then asked to name each pile, give the characteristics of each pile, and discuss how each pile differed from the other. Next, a diadic card sort was conducted in which the participant sorted the second set of cards into two piles. Finally, the q-sort was conducted with the third set of cards; here, the participants sorted the cards into as many piles as they wished, again naming and comparing the characteristics of each pile. Data from these procedures were then used to create a taxonomy displaying the characteristics of gifts according to communalities (Field & Morse, 1985; Spradley, 1979).

Results

Nurses considered gifts presented by the patient as a *symbol of the patient-nurse relationship*. The gifts had varying degrees of importance, were carefully assessed, and were never considered trifling. The timing of the gift and the patient's underlying intent were of utmost

Table 16.1 Demographic Characteristics of Participants ($N = 44$)

Characteristic	*n*	%
Highest level of education		
Diploma	19	43.2
Baccalaureate	20	45.5
Master's	4	9.0
Doctorate	1	2.4
Years of work experience		
1-5 years	5	11.4
5-10 years	7	15.9
11-15 years	11	25.0
16-20 years	4	9.1
>21 years	10	22.7
Missing	7	15.9

significance to the nurse, while the nature and the value of the gift were usually considered of less importance.

Gifts were given to the unit for all nurses to share or were given to individual nurses as a personal acknowledgment of that nurse's contribution to the patient's care. If the gift was an individual one, it was because that particular nurse's care was perceived to have "made a difference" at a critical point in time or was seen to have "gone an extra mile" for the patient, for which the patient felt particularly indebted. Occasionally, some patients, not wishing to single out the care of any one nurse as "special," attempted to thank all nurses on the unit as individuals by, for example, carving rosary beads for all the nurses or giving all a box of chocolates or a movie pass and writing each nurse's name on their gifts.

Overall, nurses reported feeling frustrated and in a quandary when presented with a gift. Early in their nursing education, they were taught not to accept gifts from patients, although some nurses reported that they were unsure why gifts should not be accepted. On the other hand, nurses felt that refusing the patient's gift was unacceptably rude behavior, cruel to the patient, and an action that would destroy their relationship. Consequently, nurses usually accepted the gifts graciously, concealing the fact from their co-workers and supervisors or sharing the gift with all the staff, often concealing this from the patient.

Refusing a gift invariably resulted in the gift being persuasively offered again and again. Explanations such as "Nurses are *not* permitted to accept gifts" were met with scorn and considered circumventable by patients. Attempts to deflect the gift by persuading the patient to give the gift to the unit as a whole or to the hospital were also met with dismay by the patient: "But I meant that gift for *you*!" One nurse said,

> If you go ahead and refuse a gift from someone you have known for a period of time and become attached to, it's like rejecting them. . . . I wouldn't want to do that, so I guess I'd accept it and take the flak if someone found out about it, rather than hurt this person by refusing it. . . . I always try to refuse money—I say we don't need it, we get paid for this kind of thing. But often times, they get very insistent. At that point, I say, "What I'll do is give you a receipt. The agency needs the money." Often times, they will be happy with that—at least they feel their gift has been accepted. But sometimes they feel quite upset and insist that the money was for you: "No, no, it is for you. It's not for them. Go home and buy something for your kids." And I say, "No, no, I can't take money." And I write a receipt and leave the receipt with that person. [In one particular case,] I don't think I left him feeling very good. I had refused the gift, really [that] is what it was. He had wanted to give me a personal gift, and I wouldn't accept it. So you feel like you've rejected them. I think that is how I would think they would feel, too.

Paradoxically, these incidents when gifts are received legitimately, yet illicitly, are never forgotten, as both the guilt of the transaction and the generosity of the gesture remain with the nurse:

> A little old lady I got to know—she came in several times. She gave me half a crown—that's a quarter—all wrapped up in tissue paper, and she insisted that I take this because she liked me and "blah, blah, blah." I took it. I didn't know it was half a crown until I opened it later. But I felt it would have offended her if I had not taken it. I never told anybody because I was scared of the consequences. Rather than get an old lady into, you know, have somebody go and lecture her that she shouldn't do it, I felt in my heart that she wanted to give me this. And I haven't told anybody before.

When nursing administration did interfere and insist that the gift be returned, the result was embarrassing for all concerned. A nurse reported an incident when nursing administration insisted that an expensive watch be returned to the patient:

> He [the patient] was very mortified that other individuals who had no say in this relationship would come in and tell him that he had no right to give so much away.

> He was very upset. We were upset because we were placed between a rock and a hard place. We had the family and another agency that had contracted our service (and can terminate it) tell us that the nurse had to give the watch back.

In some Canadian hospitals, there is a policy that cash gifts received by the wards must be forwarded to the hospital's fund-raising foundation; these gifts would often be used for targeted purposes, such as the purchase of equipment for diagnostic or treatment purposes or for medical research. Such policies annoyed nursing staff, who felt they "deserved" the gift and, as professionals, should have control over gifts they had "earned" without being accountable to other departments. In addition, this policy was disconcerting to the donors, who felt their nurses were being "shortchanged." One patient, who presented cash for the purchase of a VCR for a unit, even made a special trip back to the unit to make sure the nurses had eventually received their VCR. A nurse stated, "We were supposed to have the money as a travel fund for nurses, but one day, when I had been here about 2 years, I suddenly realized that the money wasn't coming back."

When examining the nature and purpose of patients' gifts, the dilemma for the administrators is obvious because a gift may, on the surface, appear ambiguous, yet only the recipient and the receiver can be aware of its meaning. Furthermore, the recipient may conceivably be unaware of the full intent underlying a gift or the future ramifications of accepting the gift, such as becoming indebted to a patient. For example, chocolates may be given as an act of reciprocation or as a bribe. Only the donor and the recipient can recognize the difference. Furthermore, the presentation of a gift to one nurse is frequently perceived to be inappropriate by administration, who consider the care of the patient to be the responsibility of the nursing team. Nursing care is designed (even when primary care is used) to be interchangeable. When the primary nurse is off duty, the quality of the patients' care should remain unchanged, although this assumption denies the significance of the nurse-patient relationship in the planning and implementing of care and devalues the psychosocial aspects of care. Nevertheless, administrators and some nurses feel that others might resent one nurse being recognized above others, and they feel it might damage the morale of the unit if individual gifts are received.

In this study, nurses perceived gifts as falling into five categories: gifts to reciprocate for the care given; gifts intended to manipulate or

Gifts in the Patient-Nurse Relationship				
As beneficiary				Donations to the hospital foundation
				Equipment for the hospital
Serendipidous	Rewards			Spiritual—'Doing good'
				Clinical outcomes (pts condition improves)
				Personal growth (insight about self)
				Social ('click' with pt)
	Perks			Flowers —left behind by patient
As a perceived obligation	As presents			Seasonal—Christmas, Easter, Valentines Day
		To personally acknowledge nurse		Marriage, birthday, birth of a child
				Career, exams, promotion, graduation
	As custom			Ward norm
				Pts cultural norm
To manipulate	To coerce	To change Pt-Nse relationship		Invitations to dinner, proposals
				Overtures to become a 'part of the family'
				Suggestive gifts—Lingerie, perfume
		To obtain privilege		gift given—later followed by request
		As advocate		Beg, complain, explain, reiterate, moan
	To ensure care			Bribes—$$
				Chocolates (individual—on locker)
		To reinforce continuance of care	Direct	Chocolates/sweets (individual—on locker)
				Tips, gifts of cash
				Cajole, false compliments
			Indirect	Thanks, smiles, praise and waves
				For unit (all staff share)
				For nurse's kids
To reciprocate	As atonement	From family		Food—donuts, cakes, cookies and chocolates
		From patient		Gifts from hospital canteen
				Verbal apology, note, card
				Gifts made in OT
	Of gratitude	At the end of'the relationship	Connected nse-pt relationship	Cpmplete trust
				Significant personal gifts
			Normal nse-pt relationship	Flowers, chocolates
				Thanks, cards, letters
		In midst of relationship	Celebrate milestones	Party food—Cake, pizza
			Appreciation	Something admired by nurse
				Something made by patient
			Nurturance	Give sympathy, withhold requests
				Chocolates
	Retaliation	Nse controlled clinical relationship		Withhold gifts, thanks
				Letters of Complaint, Sabotage
		Incompetence		Sue

Figure 16.1. Types of Gifts in the Patient-Nurse Relationship.

to change the quality of care yet to be given or to change the relationship between the nurse and the patient; gifts given as a perceived obligation by the patient; serendipitous gifts or perks and rewards received because of the nature of nursing or by chance; and, finally, gifts given to the institution by a patient as a benefactor recognizing excellence in care received. A taxonomy delineating these types of gifts is shown in Figure 16.1.

GIFTS TO RECIPROCATE

Things that patients "give back" for the care given fall into three classes: retaliative acts for substandard or incompetent care, gifts as atonement for "putting things right" for behaving badly, or gifts of gratitude for the nurse or nurses who gave excellent care.

Retaliative Acts

The ultimate retaliative act of a patient for incompetence is the right to sue a nurse. This is an act of "giving back," a means of legally obtaining equitable compensation for suffering or injustices that occurred in the course of receiving nursing care. However, relatively few patients use lawsuits as a means of "getting even" with the nursing staff. Hospitalized patients may sabotage attempts for care. For example, one patient (who was also a nurse) was so disgusted, angry, and ashamed of the standards of nursing and medical care given to herself and her roommates that she persuaded the patient in the next bed to sign herself out rather than be readmitted for a tubal ligation. In this case, due to an error, operating room time had not been scheduled for this patient to have a tubal ligation performed during the scheduled laporotomy:

> After the physician came in, I heard the locker door slam, slam slam, bang, and she just got dressed and flew out and never looked at me and never said a word and about an hour later I knew . . . I knew that she had signed herself out because she couldn't have the two surgeries done. . . . But the student flew after her and talked to her and the patient said to explain to me what had happened.

More commonly, patients refuse to comply with treatments and become "difficult patients." They complain about the care, lose control, and voice complaints to their physician or to administration. Following discharge, they write letters of complaint to the hospital administration, ombudsman, or hospital board. On discharge, they withhold thanks and leave the unit without saying goodbye to the staff:

> I felt so poorly toward everybody that I couldn't even—the only person I thanked was the nursing student—the nurses I wanted nothing to do with. And yet I can remember working on units in which the patients—all the patients—would be appreciative of the ward clerk, everybody. The ward clerk was useless. Everybody was useless.

Gifts of Atonement

Gifts of atonement may come either from the patient's family or directly from the patient. Sometimes, gifts are given in the form of an apology, for example, the Alzheimer's patient's family may bring a homemade cake to the ward, saying "We know Mother is difficult to care for." The food that is given in these instances is for the *staff* to share on their coffee breaks and is not to be shared with the patients. When patients themselves are seeking atonement, the gift may be something made for the nurse at occupational therapy or purchased at the gift shop. One nurse on the pediatric floor told the following story:

> I had a little girl with cancer this past while, and this was way past Valentine's. And she had some construction paper and she cut it out in the shape of a heart. This little girl happened to be in a lot of pain, but she was a sweet little 5-year-old girl. But she took this heart and handed it to me very brusquely and said: "Here, happy Valentine's." And I knew, like—it was from the heart. She really wanted to give me something to make me feel that she wasn't that bad.

In community nursing, the gift may be homemade jam, garden produce, or things made or acquired by the patient's own skill. A northern community nurse reported that

> one day an old Inuit man and his wife came in and they were standing in my kitchen. I don't recall what his problem was, but I happened to look down and all of a sudden there was urine coming out, like over his pant leg and off his mukluk and streaming across the kitchen floor. And there was this big puddle of urine, and I said nothing. He made sure that he didn't step in it when he left, so he obviously knew that he had done it. About a week later, there was a knock on the door and he had a great huge fish. Frozen fish. It would have been about 15 pounds. And he just handed me

> this fish and smiled and left. . . . He obviously had an incontinence problem.

However, sometimes the nurses are still upset with the patient's behavior, and when this occurs, the gift to "put things right" feels more like a "payoff":

> The last gift I remember getting—I think it was to pay a debt. It was in the intensive care nursery. This baby had been born, I think, at 30 weeks, and the mother was a pain. She would panic way long after she should have. She was immature . . . and she had her husband buy brass camels [for all the nurses]—the physician got a gold camel to hang on a chain—and it really seems like a payoff now.

These gifts are important for the restoration of the patient's self-esteem, and they should be accepted. They are also most significant to the nurse who considers these gifts as coming directly "from the heart" and are particularly appreciated when the patients are perceived to have planned and worked at making the gift themselves. Gifts of atonement may also be a card, a letter, or a verbal apology. Although they are significant to the nurse, and appreciated, they are not considered essential, and the behavior, perceived by the patient to be so problematic, is usually viewed by the nurse within the context of the illness or pain and often considered "normal." Anticipating feelings of shame, nurses frequently try to diminish or prevent these feelings by normalizing the behaviors or putting them into perspective. For example, one nurse who worked in the delivery room explained that

> they [the mothers] always surprise themselves when they hear themselves screaming and yelling and groaning. The noises that they make when they are pushing embarrass them. So I do reassurance stuff, like "It makes a lot more sense to do this than all the shrieking that goes on at the hockey game." Some noises are just more appropriate for certain places—so "What the heck," I say. "You don't look half as silly as those guys jumping up and down and screaming 'cause someone put a little black thing in the net, you know."

Gifts of Gratitude

Reciprocal gifts of gratitude are the most significant gifts to nurses. These may be given either in the course of the relationship or at the end of the relationship. During the relationship, the patient may give a gift to empathize with the nurse or to "nurture the nurturer." Patients may give sympathy ("You must be tired, you were late off last night"), withhold requests for assistance, thereby attempting to make things "easier for the nurse," or preface each essential request with "I hate to bother you, but . . . ." Patients try to make the work easier for the nurse, especially when the unit is busy, by helping and doing all they can for themselves. "Having" a student gave the patients a feeling of being able to reciprocate:

> She wanted to know so much, and she was friendly, and she wanted to know how I felt, my reaction to the situation, how I felt about the surgery, and she did come and visit us at home and want to know how we were coping. . . . At that point, I was helping her.

Gifts of appreciation may be given spontaneously, as when something is admired by the nurse. For instance, a home care nurse said,

> One client I have has this horrendously messy, messy house, and she's a hoarder and she's the kind of woman who goes to the sales for the sake of sales. And buys stuff that she doesn't need. And I was helping her with a bath one day and there was this thing on the side of the bath that I thought was the soap dish. It was a polar bear lying on its back with little holes in its stomach. So I put the soap in there. And she says, "Oh, well, that's not really the soap dish, dear! That's a pomander for your fridge. You put baking soda in it. . . . I have a number of those around. Do you like that?" I said, "Yeah, it's kind of cute." Next time I came, she said, "Here's one of those polar bears for you!"

Other gifts may be less spontaneous, with the patient making extensive plans to prepare a special surprise for the nurse:

> I had a lady in her late 60s with a very strange illness. . . . But she was an avid knitter. We had been talking at one point about my interest in camping: My only dislike of camping is that when it gets rainy I can't sleep because my feet are cold. So, she knit me a pair of bed slippers that covered me from my toes to my knees. [laughter] I was unaware that she was doing it. She only worked on them on my days off, so I didn't see what she was doing. She went to a lot of effort to make it a surprise for me.

Other gifts were highly symbolic. An emergency room nurse described one: "There was a little wicker basket full of those rainbow-colored Life-savers [candies], and I thought it was so appropriate . . . [when] I read the card: Thank you to the lifesavers. I never would have made it without you!"

With longer hospital stays, gifts may be given to celebrate milestones. For instance, a patient may purchase pizza or a cake and hold an impromptu party when having made a significant step toward a particular treatment goal. The type of food purchased for such a celebration differs from food given to nurses at other times. This food is purchased to *celebrate*; it is party food, which the patients and the nurses share together.

Gifts of gratitude given at the end of the relationship are symbols of a relationship, and the type of nurse-patient relationship is reflected in the significance of the gift. If the relationship has been one in which the patient's needs were not great and were met (the pain relieved, the bed pan brought promptly, and so forth), the nurse (or nurses) will be given chocolates, flowers, perhaps a plant for the unit, or sent a complimentary letter or card. The gift is seen as a "nice gesture" but not special. Occasionally, the patient will want to celebrate an event, such as the birth of their child:

> I remember this lady—she had twins, and she was in quite a while—she promised us a bottle of champagne. I don't know how to pronounce it—it's quite expensive. So, the night she had her babies, we drank it. We each had 30 ccs. In a med cup, too!

If, on the other hand, the patient and the nurse had a close, involved relationship, or if the patient perceived that they "had been through a lot together," or that the nurse's care was critical for the patient's recovery and that the nurse was there when needed, the gift is highly significant to both the nurse and the patient; neither ever forgets. As one nurse said, "It doesn't matter what they give me—it could be an old onion—it is the look in their eyes." Nurses kept cards and letters and gifts given by patients for decades, remembering patients in detailed and loving ways, reminiscing with laughter and tears. Nurses said that it was these gifts that make nursing worthwhile; these gifts "keep them there at the bedside."

GIFTS TO MANIPULATE

Gifts intended to manipulate the nurse occur only in relationships where trust is lacking. These gifts are to ensure, either directly or indirectly, the continuance of care. They are also used to coerce the nurse into serving as a patient advocate, to obtain a privilege, or to change the nurse-patient relationship. The ironical aspect to these gifts is that nurses, by and large, are aware of the covert or hidden agenda behind the gift and do not hesitate to confront the patient and refuse it. These gifts are considered inappropriate or even insulting by nurses and have the paradoxical effect of increasing (rather than decreasing) the distance between the nurse and the patient.

The most common gift to ensure care is the cash bribe. The cash is offered to the nurse at the beginning of the relationship, sometimes by a relative: "Here, take good care of Dad tonight." Many nurses realize that bribery may be appropriate and even necessary in some cultures. Thus if the patient is from another ethnic group, the nurse will take time to explain that such gifts are not expected, not acceptable, and not permitted in this culture. Nurses stated that they were extremely uncomfortable when offered a bribe, as it implied that they would not take "good care" of a patient without it or that they gave preferential care to some patients.

Tips were considered differently. Tips, by definition, were offered after the service was rendered or at the time of discharge. For example, a nurse reported being offered $5.00 when taking a discharged patient down to his car. Such a gift made her feel unprofessional.

Manipulative gifts to ensure the continuance of care and to reinforce caring may be a personal gift offered directly to the nurse or indirectly to the whole unit or to the nurse "to buy something for her children." A very common direct reinforcer for care was the chocolate or sweets that some patients kept in their lockers or in their drawer. When the nurse came into the room to check on the patients or to answer the call bell, the nurse was invited to "have a sweetie." These patients also offered the nurses money: "Here, buy yourself some coffee."

More common, however, was the gift offered in the form of copious thanks for small tasks performed. From the nurses' perspective, these patients exaggerated the worth of the smallest task, claiming that the nurses were "The best!": "*Oh thank you*! That feels wonderful! You do that so *well*!" or "The nurses at [another hospital or another unit] don't do backrubs like that! No such service there!" These patients also praised the nurses loudly to other patients and relatives, usually when the nurses themselves were in earshot: "The nurses here are so good." These strategies of "buttering up" the nurses were considered by the nurses to be insincere, false endearments, and manipulative. A patient who was also a nurse observed: "They'd say: 'What a nice girl' or 'What a pretty girl' when the nurses could hear, and I didn't think they were nice or pretty!" The patients apparently considered it important to befriend the nurses, to keep on their good side. These behaviors were particularly evident in the long-term care areas, where residents made considerable effort to smile and wave at the nurses as they passed and to befriend the staff.

The degree of the patients' dependency on the staff and the powerlessness of the patients to do as they chose as free individuals was evident when strategies to coerce the staff were examined. When giving false praise was ineffective or when something of importance was needed, the patients resorted to cajoling ("Come *onnnn*!") or teasing the nurses to get their own way. The camaraderie, initiated often by the patients, implied an intimate relationship based on good humor between the nurses and the patients, yet one that had a real and earnest goal. If a request was underlying the teasing, the requests were "for real."

Some patients made requests of staff, and when these requests were denied or an answer was not forthcoming, they then resorted to begging, complaining, or reiterating their requests. Other patients subtly presented the nurse with a small gift and followed this with a request a short time later or assumed that they were now due a privilege. For example, in long-term care,

> it's a "come on" gift. Like I'll buy you something for the staff tonight, and the next minute, where is so-and-so? "Oh my—I just saw him call a taxi." So then you have to run and say, "Oh, where are you going?" So, you give him back his money, and "No, the staff all have their lunches here tonight."

Finally, gifts were offered to nurses when families or a male patient admired the nurse to the extent that they wished to extend the relationship to a more personal level. Relatives would invite nurses to their home for dinner, or male patients would give distinctly personal gifts, such as lingerie or silk stockings. Nurses were clear that they politely refused the overtures to become a part of the family, usually learning the hard way. It was a matter of "not crossing the line" between a personal and a professional relationship. As one home care nurse explained in response to the researcher's question as to what constituted the line between personal and professional:

> It's really hard to put your finger on it. . . . You would be caring, but you wouldn't carry caring beyond what you were in the house for. From my own experience—I did dressing for a lovely widower. I feel now I crossed the line because I stayed for coffee. Because I had lunch with him a few times. Because I gave him my home address—he ended up on my doorstep one night just for a visit. Those went beyond the professional and become uncomfortable to me as a nurse. He did not look at me as a nurse anymore. He looked at me as a granddaughter. . . . Both parties have to recognize the limits of the relationship, and that sounds really one-sided—that I'm allowed to enter his house, but he's not allowed to enter mine. He needed a granddaughter. I needed a patient.

GIFTS AS A PERCEIVED OBLIGATION

Nurses reported that often gifts were given because the patient felt it was the correct thing to do. Frequently, these patients were from a cultural group that gave gifts to caregivers on discharge or at the termination of the relationship. Often, these gifts were ethnically correct and were accepted and remembered by staff. For example, following a Chinese custom, a nurse was given a red envelope with gold characters on it. Inside the envelope was a 10-cent piece.

Occasionally, nurses reported that gift giving at discharge was common, and cards and flowers were prominently displayed around the nursing station. As these gifts were in full view of all patients, nurses felt that other patients felt obligated to also give a gift on discharge. As this norm was established, even the type of gift given was predictable, so that nurses learned to rate the value of the gift by the type and number of chocolates given. Black Magic® chocolates were not considered special, but some patients made an effort to get special ones: "When I was discharged, I gave the nurses chocolates because I thought it was expected—but I purposefully bought 'run of the mill' ordinary chocolates because their care was nothing special." One nurse recalled "one lady—on her way home from the hospital, she got her husband to stop at the specialty chocolate shop and sent him back to give them to us. Oh, what chocolates! Melted in your mouth."

SERENDIPITOUS GIFTS

Serendipitous gifts fell into two categories: perks and rewards. Perks were gifts that were not intended for a particular nurse nor "given" with a particular meaning; rather, they were such things as flowers that were left behind by the patient because the patient had too many to carry home or the flowers were "almost finished." The nurses found such things useful or nice:

> Sometimes, because they've got so much stuff, they'll leave them at the desk for us, and they'll say, "Well, you guys can have these, or if some other kid wants them, they can have these, or give these to some kid that needs them."

On the other hand, the serendipitous gifts that were significant were considered the rewards of nursing. These gifts were intangible and "accidental," as they were not intended as a gift by the patients; rather, they were an integral part of nursing that the nurse found rewarding and personally satisfying. These gifts included meeting and enjoying special patients with whom the nurse had a particular relationship and never forgot:

> I'll always remember this—H_____ was a German nurse who died of multiple myeloma. And she had an amazing spirit. She's just a wonderful woman . . . and there she was bedridden at the end of her illness. One day, I said, "Well, H____, you got any advice for somebody like me? I mean, when you look back on your life, what would you say to somebody like me?" She said, "A____, if I had known what I know now, I would never have cleaned my house every day as much as I did." And I said, "That's what I wanted to hear." She says, "Take this wisdom from a dying woman." She says, "Don't clean your house so much!" [Laughter] And I've taken that to heart! [Laughter] [The researcher asks, "Do you think of her when you leave it dirty?"] I do! When I leave it dirty, I say, thank you, H____, that was good advice! [Laughter]

These patients gave the nurses inner strength and courage to continue nursing; they teased and put humor into their lives, gave nurses special insights about themselves, and "made them better people" for having known these patients: "And so, when I got gifts and recognition of that from them, it made me feel very good and made me feel like nursing's a wonderful job. And it made me really value it."

Nurses are supposed to get their *real* satisfaction from nursing as a career. Not too many decades ago, this "reward in heaven" phenomenon supposedly compensated for salary. Nursing is still considered by some as a profession which "born" nurses are supposed to "love." A born nurse loves people and enjoys helping them get better and comforting them in their time of need:

> One thing I've always found in labor and delivery, if you've worked hard with them, both the woman and her husband, and they're pushing or they have to blow because there's still some cervix there, but they look at you and they listen to you. And at the end of it, they're holding their baby, and they're exhausted and sweaty and their husbands are there and they're just glowing. And they turn and look at you full in the eyes, and say, "Thank you, W____!" That is worth everything!

Nurses found great satisfaction in assisting patients and seeing results from their efforts, saying that these factors "kept them in nursing": "It is the people that I have met in the capacity of a nurse and the skills that I have as a nurse and what has kept me motivated is what people have given me in return."

BENEFICIARY GIFTS

Donations of cash were solicited openly by hospitals, and nurses reported that most hospitals had foundations that overtly solicited gifts. Frequently, gifts were given because of the excellent nursing care received; however, these gifts were usually given as a memorial in the name of the patient who died rather than to recognize the service of one particular nurse. Nurses in this study reported that gifts given to the hospital were too far removed to have any special significance for them.

THE MEANING/SIGNIFICANCE OF THE GIFTS

The five categories of gifts discussed (gifts of reciprocation, manipulation, obligation, serendipitous gifts, and donations) all served different purposes to both the patient and the nurse and had different meanings. Donations were the least significant to the nursing staff. The aim of the hospital as an organization was to maximize donations to the institution. Thus patients were usually given an envelope on admission for their contribution to *caring*. The fund-raising efforts of the hospital foundations were visible in every hospital, with goals for the annual contributions in large hospitals often into the six figures. This fund-raising, unfortunately, often redirected the donations that were normally made to nurses on the units. Despite the fact that many of these donations were made to the institutions because of the excellence in nursing, nurses felt they had little control over these gifts and that they more directly benefited the medical staff. As such, donations were meaningless to nurses and had no personal significance. Even if these gifts were targeted for the unit, the delay in returning the gift to the unit meant that many nurses who knew the patient were no longer on that unit to appreciate the gift.

Serendipitous perks and obligatory gifts and presents were considered "nice" but not special for nursing staff. Such giving occurs in any work setting with supportive employees and is not unique to nursing. Serendipitous *rewards* were important, however, and the part of nursing as a career that nurses felt was very satisfying.

Nurses reported it was most satisfying to receive reciprocal gifts of atonement and gratitude from patients with whom they had a profound and involved professional relationship; these patients were convinced that the illness experience would have been less pleasant and would have resulted in a different outcome if that nurse had not "been there for them, at that time." The relationship may have been short in duration (but one characterized by intense need for the patient), or it may have extended over a longer period of time and been based on absolute trust by the patient, or the relationship may have been one in which the nurse put the patient's interests first and was prepared to serve as an advocate to buffer, break, and bend rules for the patient's well-being. The relationship was one which both the patient and the nurse will "never forget," and the gift, at the end of the relationship, served as a symbol of the relationship, a reminder of the worth of the nursing care.

Discussion

Gift giving is a complex phenomenon, and gifts are given for many reasons. While the manipulative category of gifts are those that should not be accepted, gifts of gratitude and gifts of obligation should be accepted: the former is an essential part of the patient's recovery process, and the latter is a normative courtesy. The wise nurse knows the difference, and it should not be necessary for administration to interfere with this process of exchange. Administration's fear that patients are vulnerable and will be exploited by nurses appears to be unwarranted. Although such an occurrence is possible, it is as rare as other abuses of the system (e.g., petty theft or drug abuse) and should be treated accordingly. If nurses are to behave as professionals, then, first and foremost, administration must treat their own staff as such. The abhorrence that nurse administrators have for gift giving is apparently an outmoded attitude, perhaps enforced by a perception of a lost opportunity to build a fund to be used for their own purposes under the auspices of common good. However, such a policy runs the risk of offending patients and may actually result in lost "revenue," as patients who have been prevented from compensating those they feel it is their due to repay will not feel generously toward the institution that blocked the compensatory act.

This research supports the anecdotal observations of Geach (1971) that the process of gift giving reflects the underlying nurse-patient relationship. Whether direct or indirect, manipulative gifts to ensure the continuance of care suggest that the patient is dissatisfied with the care relationship, perhaps lacks trust, or is afraid. Rather than exploring the patient's reason for the gift (as suggested by Pepleau, cited in Clark, 1971), the nurse should regard the bribe as a symptom of an inadequate relationship with the patient, explore the underlying reasons, and alter the nature of care accordingly, for example, by increasing surveillance or providing reassurance. Coercive gifts suggest unmet needs that should be acknowledged. Frequently, families invite the nurse to sit with them during a funeral. The decision to accept or reject such gifts should be the privilege of the nurse, and made according to the relationship she had with the patient and has with the family, irrespective of administrative policy. Identifying manipulative behaviors from other types of gift giving is particularly difficult in some areas, such as psychiatry, where such behaviors are considered symptoms of the illness rather than resulting from the caregiving context per se. Consequently, psychiatric nurses learn to always maintain an objective perspective of gift giving. Inexperienced nurses in these areas may need counseling to avoid "getting suckered."

Reciprocal gifts of retaliation are formalized as a part of the legal system in the case of incompetent care that results in harm to the patient. Minor infractions or the lack of patient confidence in the care will be manifest in patients' "getting back" at nurses, using sabotage or noncompliance. Responsibility for these behaviors should be considered by staff before attributing noncompliance to other factors, such as conflicting theories of disease causation, explanatory models, and treatment modalities (see, e.g., Kleinman, Eisenberg, & Good, 1978).

Acceptance of gifts of atonement is essential for the patient to restore self-esteem and to reestablish an active relationship with the caregiver. The timing and nature of these gifts are essential; nurses must feel they are sincere and that the gift rectifies a legitimate misendeavor. Nurses felt that repetitive apologies for "normal" sick behavior are unnecessary and absurd.

Acceptance of gifts of gratitude is also important for the patient's therapeutic process. Attempts to interrupt these gifts, to replace them with less valuable gifts, such as a card or a letter, or to redirect them to a hospital fund do not satisfy the patient's need to reciprocate. The act of reciprocation must balance the perceived debt and compensate the individual to whom the debt is owed. Albeit nurses are employees of the hospital and although the hospital may take credit in general reputation for the excellence of its care, it is the individual nurse who must receive the credit.

This aspect is significant. Although nursing is organized to provide individualized care to the patient, establishment of the nurse's identity is discouraged. Present staffing arrangements are organized so that nurses are interchangeable: If one nurse goes on break or off duty, the nurse replacement should provide care of equal quality and quantity, following the same care plans. Yet such a practice denies that individual nurses establish relationships with patients and that patients may have preferences for particular nurses. The practice assumes that all nurses provide identical and similar standards of care. Perhaps this is why "punishment" of nurses who provide substandard care is tolerated, and, on the other hand, why administration is reluctant to accept the recognition of excellence in care, particularly when this acknowledgment comes from a patient to one particular nurse in the form of a gift. However, this notion must be investigated further.

Despite the importance of trust, commitment, and involvement in the patient-nurse relationship to therapeutic goals, there is relatively little research in this area; consequently, future research must explore the nature of the developing patient-nurse relationship. Meanwhile, as the gift is the *symbol* of this relationship, the taboos regarding gift giving must be removed and the nature and circumstance of the gift recognized as an opportunity for the nurse to change the approach to care or to accept the reward graciously.

Note

1. This research could not have been completed without the assistance of nurses who, on their own time, "told their stories." J. Bottorff, B. Cameron, P. Donahue, J. Greenhalgh, J. Johnson, B. Lorencz, K. Olson, C. Park, and S. Wilson served as research assistants for

this project, and their contribution is gratefully acknowledged. The research was supported by the Alberta Foundation for Nursing Research and by an MRC/NHRDP Research Scholar Award.

References

Clark, J. (1971). The patient's gift. In S. F. Burd & M. A. Marshall (Eds.), *Some clinical approaches to psychiatric nursing* (pp. 90-95). London: Collier-Macmillan.

Field, P. A., & Morse, J. M. (1985). *Nursing research: The application of qualitative approaches.* London: Croom Helm.

Geach, B. (1971). Gifts and their significance. *American Journal of Nursing*, 71, 266-270.

Kleinman, A., Eisenberg, L., & Good, B. (1978). Culture, illness and care: Clinical lessons from anthropologic and cross-cultural research. *Annals of Internal Medicine, 88*, 251-258.

Morse, J. M. (1989). Gift-giving in the patient-nurse relationship: Reciprocity for care? *Canadian Journal of Nursing Research, 21*, 33-46.

Nightingale, F. (1981). Training of nurse and nursing the sick [Microfiche]. Ann Arbor, MI: University Microfilms International [Adelaide Nutting Historical Collection]. (Reprinted from Dr. Quain [Ed.], *The dictionary of medicine*, ca. 1899, London: Spottiswoode.)

Spradley, J. P. (1979). *The ethnographic interview.* New York: Holt, Rinehart & Winston.

VI

Grounded Theory

Grounded theory, developed in sociology, has a theoretical basis of symbolic interactionism. Symbolic interactionists suggest that individuals order their world by engaging in processes of negotiation and renegotiation; by making reflexive use of symbols, and by interpreting and eliciting meanings in situations, rather than simply by reacting. Individuals respond and create meaning in situations, and this meaning is shared. Grounded theory, therefore, provides a means for eliciting these meanings and for describing the psychological and social processes that have been developed to assist people make sense of their world.

As with ethnography and ethnoscience, grounded theory relies primarily on unstructured interviews, observations, and other sources of data. As reality is considered to be fluid and constantly created and modified, the method is process oriented. Therefore, rather than producing a description focusing on cultural beliefs and values (as with ethnography) or the cognitive structure of the world view (as with ethnoscience), grounded theory allows for change over time, for the description of stages and phases within an experience.

In the first example (Chapter 17), "Becoming Ordinary: Leaving the Psychiatric Hospital", Lorencz interviewed inpatients with schizophrenia who were expected to be discharged in the near future. As the "revolving door" patterns of readmissions were of concern, she wanted to understand the hopes and expectations of these patients and their perceptions of factors leading to admission and readmission. This study is impressive, because of the difficulty in interviewing these patients when competing with multiple realities and multiple voices of the mentally ill patient. Nevertheless, Lorencz was able to obtain these data and construct a meaningful theory that explains the process of "becoming ordinary".

When examining the experiential aspects of nursing mothers learning to express their breasts, Morse and Bottorff noticed an extraordinary phenomena: Some of the mothers were able to express successfully and others were not able to express at all (Chapter 18). This phenomena did not appear to be related in any way to the mothers' "success" with nursing their infants. Grounded theory was the ideal method for developing explanatory models from these data.

The third example (Chapter 19) is a part of the study in gift-giving in the patient-nurse relationship. (The structure of gift-giving was described in Chapter 16.) In this example, I used grounded theory to reveal the process of negotiation that was inherent in the patient-nurse relationship when either the nurse or the patient wanted to change the relationship. It also permitted me to identify four types of nurse-patient relationships and allow me to develop a model to illustrate the movement between levels.

Do you think models developed using grounded theory should be tested? If so, how? If not, why not?

17

Becoming Ordinary: Leaving the Psychiatric Hospital

BEVERLEY J. LORENCZ

Schizophrenia has been referred to as the "cancer of psychiatry" (Green, 1984). Only 50% of those diagnosed with schizophrenia are expected to achieve either a complete or good recovery (Bland, 1984). Whereas at one time schizophrenics were institutionalized on a long-term basis, they are now encouraged to live in the community. Research has revealed, however, that the majority of schizophrenics require repeated hospitalizations (Bland, Parker, & Orn, 1976, 1978; Cottman & Mezey, 1976). The repeated admissions of schizophrenics is known as "the revolving door syndrome."

The past decade has witnessed the development of several community programs for schizophrenics; however, the persistently high admission rates attest to the failure of these programs. Although much research has been published about discharged schizophrenics the researchers have examined the problem from the perspective of the care provider. In order to plan and implement effective community-based treatment an understanding of the schizophrenics' experiences must be gained. Schizophrenics in the community are "free-agents" and the programs planned must meet their needs and address their concerns, not just the concerns of health professionals. Therefore, a study was conducted to

AUTHOR'S NOTE: This research was supported in part by grants from the Alberta Association of Registered Nurses and the Alberta Foundation for Nursing Research. This chapter originally appeared in Lorencz, B. J. (1988). Becoming ordinary: Leaving the psychiatric hospital. In Morse, J. M., & Johnson, J. L. (Eds), *The illness experience: Dimensions of suffering* (pp. 140-200). Newbury Park, CA: Sage.

examine the perceptions of predischarge chronic schizophrenics who have experienced at least two years of illness.[1]

Preadmission Experiences: Being a Failure

Individuals do not become psychiatric inpatients solely due to the existence of mental hospitals. Although psychiatric admissions may coincide with the application of the label *mentally ill,* numerous factors interact before culminating in these admissions. One factor is the patient's prehospitalization functioning. The informants in this study consistently characterized their preadmission functioning as inadequate. Their perceptions of their failure to function in the community combined with the assigned meaning of their admission to the hospital produced the context for the occurrence of the process of *becoming ordinary*. This chapter begins with a review of the informants' preadmission experiences and the meanings they assigned to their hospital admissions.

The informants in this study divided their preadmission experiences into two periods of time: the extended past and the preadmission past. The pivotal point which demarcates these periods of time from each other is the participants' first contact with mental health care (please note that "I" stands for Informant and "R" stands for Researcher):

I: Then I had a lot of freedom. And then all of the sudden, wham, I'm stuck up in a hospital, and I was changed. I was—I didn't—I didn't give a damn for awhile, eh? And then, and then, it got harder, even harder. And then the doctors got at me, and that's where I'm at. The doctors are talking about me, eh? What they think I am, and what they think, feel I want, and what I—what I do, and what I think, and stuff like that.

R: What ways is the atmosphere "not peaceful"?

I: I don't know. Until I went home, I used to hang around with some really good friends, and I found that really relaxing and peaceful. And then I went home and, ah, I ran into this mental health stuff. And I can't say I've had a peaceful moment since.

R: You haven't had a peaceful moment since you've been involved with mental health people?

I: That's right.

R: What's been happening?

I: Uh, I get deeper and deeper into quicksand, I guess.

R: You feel you're deeper in quicksand?

I: Yeah, there's no way out.

R: I don't understand. There's no way out of . . .

I: Out of mental health.

The themes underlying the two periods of time that constitute the past are different. The extended past is best characterized as "the good old days." Conversely, the participants' preadmission past is an extended period of *not making it* in the community culminating in the informants' present admission. The preadmission past, which includes previous hospitalizations, ranges from approximately three to fifteen years, and the preadmission past is contingent upon the past psychiatric history of the informant.

THE EXTENDED PAST

Events recalled from the extended past are characteristically experiences that illustrate successful management in the community. The informants primarily recalled two types of experiences: previous interpersonal relationships and occupational experiences:

> Uh huh, someone to come home to. When I worked on the rigs, I was living common-law. I'd come home after work, there'd be a bacon and tomato sandwich there and a beer. The little boy, he'd be jumping and rolling around, giggling, and squealing, and cooing. [pause] And, ah, it made me feel like a man. [pause] Made me feel real good. Like you'd come home after sweating and working your muscles real hard, getting screamed at by some ratty driller.
>
> I had a heck of a time on the first couple of rigs I was working on. Finally, I hit one I liked. That was, ah, a step up sub. I got offered a drilling job on one of them, at one time. That's how come I like them.

Although recalled events might have occurred in the distant past, the informants often spoke about them as though they had occurred recently. For example, one informant's interviews were dominated by his recollections of his experiences as a laborer. He frequently spoke as if these events had occurred in the recent past. Clarification revealed that these events had occurred more than ten years prior to the interview:

I: Actually, it was tough with that rig. But then I had my cement forms in mind. I had worked for, eh, eighteen months on a drilling rig straight. Seven hours, no, well, it would be seven days a week for eighteen months. And I just wanted to get away.

R: You'd get pretty tired?

I: Yeah, I was pretty sick of drilling rigs.

R: Was that two years ago when you quit?

I: No, that was, ah, back when I was about twenty-three years old.

Two further points can be made about the data gained from the informants in this study. First, the informants did not reminisce about childhood days with their families. They predominantly recalled experiences away from home, or, if still living at home, experiences with their school peers. Second, the informant with the longest history of previous psychiatric care made the fewest references to the extended past. In comparison to the more recent histories of the other informants (three to four years), this informant had a fifteen year history of psychiatric care and his references to the extended past were limited to relating illicit drug experiences shared with his peers:

> We had the sense not to smoke drugs, hash or marijuana, after we were on acid because we're an elite. We were, we were in [a] generation that was lost in space. We, we had things to do, and we did them.

THE PREADMISSION PAST

The preadmission past is best characterized as a long period of *not making it* in the community accompanied by feelings of discouragement, loneliness, and a sense of being overwhelmed. Some of the informants initiated compensatory behaviors to alleviate these feelings; however, these behaviors were often dysfunctional because the outcome tended to deepen their feelings of alienation and thereby compounded their sense of isolation from the greater community.

Not Making It

The informants defined *not making it* as inadequate functioning in the community: "Ah, I didn't think I'd get mentally thick—sick. I thought I'd be able to function." The yardstick generally used to measure their ability to function in the community was social norms, which the informants unquestioningly accepted as appropriate standards for self-evaluation:

I: Kind of instead of going against the grains of society, I'll go along with it.

R: Do you consider yourself going, as in the past, as going against the grains?

I: Yeah, with a name like ____, I sure do.

R: What are the grains of society, going with the grains of society? What does that mean?

I: Um, laughter, I suppose, and money, [pause] comfortably involved with endeavors.

A second informant said he had deviated from "the norm, from the righteous side of society":

R: We were talking about before you went into ____, you were doing a lot of drugs and alcohol and you flipped out. Can you kind of describe what's flipped out. What happens when you flip out?

I: Being out of the norm from the righteous side of society. [pause] When you do that, you become persecuted by yourself and the people around you.

Self-comparisons were occasionally made with others in the community whom the informants felt had achieved the social norms for functioning:

> You can always say that you're gonna make, make something out something, but it doesn't always work. That's, that's the bugger. It's different, it's strange 'cause when—my brothers and sisters are all super people. Like not super people, but they all can make something work for them and I can't. I don't know. I don't know why. It's amazing. I've been trying.

Community members (including peers) whom the informants felt did not emulate these norms were rejected as yardsticks for comparison. One informant described his previous peer group in the community as "the dregs of society" because the group members abused drugs and alcohol. Discharged psychiatric patients living in the community were also rejected as standards for comparison:

> You see, I spent some time in another group home. . . . It's not nice at all because you realize that people that are there . . . are there because of the same reason you're there.

The informants based their evaluation of not making it in the community on their retrospective appraisal of their personal well-being while residing in the community. They recalled both their level of functioning and the accompanying mental well-being.

SELF-EVALUATION OF COMMUNITY FUNCTIONING

All of the informants in this study characterized their preadmission functioning in the community as inadequate. They identified two areas of inadequate functioning: employment and intimate interpersonal relationships. Only one informant expressed satisfaction with the quality of his preadmission peer relationships. The majority of informants expressed feelings of loneliness and this lack of a sense of fellowship in the community resulted from either the absence of companionship or the presence of nonsupportive peers in the community:

R: And you find it not such a good idea being alone?

I: Nah, I miss half of the world. Sleep through half and miss another half . . . the whole world goes by.

I: My friends generally persecute me. They thought I was a joke.

R: They thought you were a joke?

I: Uh huh, they'd play my emotions that way, find a weak spot and tease me about it. It's just a subtle way of giving me strength. . . . By joking about somebody's inadequacies, you give them strength. Although you may frustrate them and put them down, but, eventually, you gain strength from the situation.

Unfortunately, the presence of peers in the community cannot be equated with the availability of emotional support. Although this informant felt his peers were helping him by rejecting his behavior, he did not identify this peer group as supportive. He complained of feeling "loneliness to the max" when he attempted to quit smoking marijuana. He also stated that being mentally ill is being frustrated: "You can't reveal your emotions properly—somebody to care about or somebody who will listen."

Employment was the second area of inadequate community functioning identified by the informants in this study. The informants in this study were young adult males in their twenties and thirties, and from their perspective, the fundamental aspect of *not making it* in the community was their failure to be self-supporting. Only one informant had been employed during the previous two years. He described his job in a convenience store as "boring" and "unfulfilling." Due to termination from his place of employment, this informant had been receiving unemployment insurance for the past year.

The informants were ambivalent about accepting supplementary sources of financial support. Although they recognized their need for this assistance, they thought social assistance was unearned income:

R: It sounds like you don't particularly like being on it [pension].

I: In some ways, it's necessary; in some ways, it's a hand out.

R: Can you tell me more about that?

I: Well, you don't ever have to worry about being fired. So the stress there is gone, so it's beneficial that way. Ah, getting something for nothing has always disturbed me, so it's negative in that way. That's my only beef about being on it.

SELF-EVALUATION OF MENTAL WELL-BEING

The predominate emotional state recalled by the informants is congruous with their perceived functioning in the community. All the informants referred to feeling overwhelmed while residing in the community. Some of them explicitly identified stress as the underlying basis for these feelings:

> I never missed a day of work, you know. And things were really piling up on me, you know, a lot of stress and stuff like that. My hair was just falling out. You should have seen that. I could go like this [running fingers through his hair]. I could go like this with my [showed researcher hand with hair between the fingers] like that, and have about ten hairs.

Other informants implicated stress in their descriptions of being overwhelmed. These informants recalled feeling "bogged down," being in a "real panic," "everything was moving kind of fast anyway, just not enough time," and "the whole world was upside down there for a little while."

The level of stress experienced by the informants was not temporarily related to their admissions; instead, they described this stress as chronic and encompassing the entire preadmission period. For example, although the preadmission past included previous psychiatric hospitalizations, the informants did not describe a transient period of reduced stress following these discharges:

R: How about the other times when you left, how did you feel then?

I: I felt good. I felt good that I was leaving, but I wasn't as certain as I am now, you know. Like I thought, I didn't think I'd come back, but you know, but, but I still had the problems. I was just on a fake medication, you know. They had me on the wrong meds, and, um, it was just a phony reality. Really, because I was walking around in a daze all day. That's 'cause I was on pretty heavy medication, you know.

A second informant spoke of his anticipated success following treatment:

> I took Assertiveness Training and I thought, "Ah, ah, I got it made, I can set myself in any direction I want" and then, it's people that get to me, eh. It's the people, it's not the—maybe it is the surroundings. I dunno.

BEING OVERWHELMED

The informants identified factors which intensified or precipitated feelings of being overwhelmed in the community. These factors are categorized into two main groups: the informants' behaviors and environmental influences. Environmental influences are further subdivided into nonintrusive and intrusive influences.

Environmental Influences

Environmental influences are those influences that the informants identified as having an external origin. Intrusive influences encompassed intrusions into the informants' cognitive sphere by either known or unknown others. One informant described intrusive experiences as "things that aren't there, but pop in there, out of thin air." Nonintrusive influences were events/conditions occurring in the informants' objective environment.

Intrusive Influences

Mental health professionals consider intrusive influences an intrapsychic phenomenon, a cardinal sign of psychosis; however, the informants in this study who experienced this phenomenon did not accept this premise:

> And, ah, I was laying on my bed and I was—I felt like I was dying. It was this patient next to me cursing me to death. And I was resentful for what he said. And, ah, I felt like my spirit was leaving my body.

This experience occurred prior to this informant's transfer from a community hospital. Another informant also experienced mental intrusion by a known other. He initially expressed disbelief at what was happening:

> Okay, okay, just listen to me, okay. That's all I ask. And, um, one day, I was, I was sitting in bed and I was thinking about ____, you know. And I, I felt really bad about it, and everything like that. And I just started crying, eh? And, um, all of sudden, all of sudden, all my thoughts were being displayed, you know. I could hear my thoughts being said. And then I asked them, I asked them through my mind. I said "How, how, how do, [are] you doing this?" and they told me "ESP." And I said "That's bullshit, I don't believe in ESP." And they said, "Some people have this special gift," you know, and it was really amazing.

Although health care professionals categorize such experiences as intrapsychic, the informants in this study believed they were externally generated. Furthermore, they continued to conceive of these experiences as interpersonal problems throughout their hospitalization. The following quote illustrates how the informants envisaged them as relationship problems rather than indicators of psychological problems:

R: So when you'd go out, what would happen?

I: I'd drink a little bit too much [laugh] and get really plastered and forget to take my meds, and then I'd get sick again and terrible.

R: What sort of things happened when you got sick again?

I: Um. I was just hearing really bad voices and, um, telling me really strange things, bizarre things. And I'd believe them, and I'd get sick, you know. They'd make me really sick.

For this informant the presence of the voices was not indicative of illness; rather, illness resulted from his relationship with the voices, that is, he believed them.

The informants' feelings of being overwhelmed were directly and indirectly magnified by intrusive experiences. The informants who experienced these phenomena described direct changes in their mental well-being, which they attributed to the effect of these experiences. One informant said he felt "stifled" during these intrusive experiences and another informant described himself as "mentally restricted":

> Um, I was restricted because I felt that there was people reading my thoughts and, um, you know, and knew what I was doing, and everything like that, you know. And that used to bother me a lot. So I couldn't really function the way I want to function, eh.

This informant also described experiencing an extended period of "total depression" while residing in the community.

All of the informants considered these intrusions a restrictive burden and as a result of these intrusions the informants had fewer personal resources available for dealing with their nonintrusive surroundings as their personal resources were used to manage the intrusive experiences. The informants' methods for managing intrusive experiences will be described later in this chapter.

Nonintrusive Influences

Nonintrusive influences are the second type of environmental factors identified by the informants in this study. Nonintrusive influences are burdensome events/conditions occurring within the informants' objective environment. The two major categories of nonintrusive influences affecting the informants' sense of mental well-being (which were examined earlier in this chapter) were the lack of paid employment and the lack of supportive interpersonal relationships in the community. Each of these influences contributed to the informants' sense of declining mental well-being in several ways.

The informants described feelings of inadequacy and failure arising from their inability to obtain long-term employment. Two of the informants attributed their failure to obtain paid employment to the lack of understanding employers in the community: "Like, I'm not lazy, and I like to work, but I just, I can't, I can't connect on a good job or [a] patient employer." As well, losing a job adversely affected the informants' confidence in their abilities to function in the community.

> I use to work in a glass factory in _____. . . . The guy knew damn well that I was sick, eh, and so he gave me the boot. The same with, um, the same with the—it sort of makes me wonder about myself. Just what—where I am, and what kind of functions I do have, you know.

The informants experienced several stressful incidents due to their lack of supportive relationships in the community. These incidents involved the rejection of the informants' behavior by significant others, for example rejection by members of community institutions (such as churches), requests by family members to seek alternative living arrangements, and, finally, rejection by peers.

The informants did not feel supported by their community. Half of the informants related incidents of perceived rejection by other community members: "Sometimes, you see, I get the strangest looks. . . . I'm not gonna worry about it. I's too bad for them." Another informant described himself as a "modern day leper":

> As soon as someone finds out you've got a disease of the mind, they right away start treating you as a second class citizen. As if they're superior 'cause they're somewhat more normal than you are.

The majority of the informants identified specific aspects or events in their social environment which contributed significantly to their feelings of being overwhelmed, for example rejection by significant others. There was one exception to this: The participant with the longest history of previous psychiatric care indiscriminately described the social community outside the hospital as threatening and punitive. This informant believed that the community was composed of powerful, malevolent others:

> If I, if I try to do something, there's always someone out there, that, that's there to outsmart me, you know. So, I gotta be careful. I gotta—I can't just give up, right?

Behavioral Influences

The informants said the misuse of drugs and alcohol intensified or precipitated feelings of being overwhelmed in the community. All of the informants described drug and alcohol related experiences. Although the majority of the informants described continuous use of these substances throughout the preadmission period, one informant said his use of alcohol was limited to the extended past. Although environmental influences such as peer group pressure were present for some informants, all of them felt they voluntarily used these substances.

The informants accounted for their use of drugs and alcohol in two ways. First, for some of the informants the use of drugs and alcohol was an expected and acceptable peer group behavior.

> In the group I was dealing with it was socially acceptable, and it made me feel good, sometimes paranoid. It would strengthen the ties between me and my friends, so I became to be dependent on them, the dope and the company. It was a socializing skill.

Second, the informant described the use of drugs and alcohol as an accessible method for reducing feelings of insecurity as well as for helping them persevere in the community. For the informants the use of these substances was a means for gaining temporary respite from life in the community:

> I like smoking hash, you know. It keeps me, it keeps me going. I don't get burnt out and stuff like that. . . . But I like smoking dope, and it's a great antidepressant.

> It's just something to get me away from where I am.

Another informant said the use of drugs and alcohol alleviated his feelings of insecurity and enhanced his sense of fellowship with his peers:

R: When you say it helped you feel good, in what sort of ways?

I: I was able to relax, it took away the frustration.

R: Frustration from . . .

I: Self-insecurities.

I: I felt more at one with people in the room. I could carry out a conversation better.

When the intended effect was not achieved the use of drugs and alcohol was detrimental to the informants; however, any adverse effects were not attributed to the use of these substances but to their misuse:

> I was drinking too much. I'd drink every day. I was, I was nearly an alcoholic by the time I got out of that place.

> I just take, I just, I overindulge. I just do too much of—I go to the bar, I drink myself crazy.

This overuse of drugs and alcohol adversely affected the respondents' mental well-being:

R: It helped you relax?

I: Right. Actually, it added stress in certain cases too. People get paranoid when they use a lot of dope.

R: Uh huh, what does it mean to "get paranoid"?

I: Oh, cold, clammy physically, and your thoughts racing mentally.

The informants also reported isolated, indirect effects of substance overuse. For example, one informant said he would forget to take his prescribed medication when inebriated and as a result of failing to comply with his drug therapy he would hear "really bad voices." Only one informant reported experiencing negative feelings associated with the use of illegal substances: "Guilt because you're breaking the law. Guilt because you're dependent upon a substance."

Unfortunately, no influences that helped the informants adjust to the community were discussed during the interviews and the informants only identified those factors that precipitated or intensified their feelings of being overwhelmed while residing in the community. For the informants in this study the preadmission period was an extended period of *not making it* in the community.

Also, the informants identified few volitional behaviors that contributed to their perception of *not making it*, and behaviors which others may identify as detrimental to community living (such as violence against others) are excluded because they were not labeled as such by the respondents.

Finally, it was noted earlier that the preadmission period ranged from three to fifteen years and this period was contingent on the informant's history of previous psychiatric care. The identified influences also fit into this extended time period. For example, one informant said he believed that being asked to seek alternative living arrangements precipitated his feelings of being overwhelmed; however, this incident had occurred at least three years prior to his present admission. Personal rejection by a significant other was identified by another informant as a major contributing factor to his sense of social isolation in the community. This rejection had also occurred at least two years prior to his present admission.

Admission to the Hospital

The meaning the informants assigned to their admission to the hospital had behavioral and social implications and involved the integration of three facets of admission to psychiatric hospitals: the level of preadmission functioning, the perceived initiator of admission, and the informant's conception of mental hospitals *per se*. For the informants, being admitted to the hospital meant they were functioning poorly in the community and that their behavior was unacceptable to the greater community.

A factor influencing the meaning assigned to admission was the informants' assessment of their preadmission functioning. The informants described themselves as *not making it* in the community during this period of time. The informants said that during the preadmission period they felt overwhelmed and frustrated. The preadmission period ended with the informant's admission to the hospital.

A second influencing factor was the informants' perception of who initiated their admission. A striking feature apparent in the data was the fact that the informants did not believe their admission was the result of their own actions. This phenomenon was apparent regardless of the informant's admission status: voluntary (i.e., signed self in for treatment) or involuntary (i.e., admission certificates):

> And then I got *called back*.

> This was why I got *sent here.*
>
> I got *committed.*
>
> *He just sent me* straight up here. [referring to family physician]
>
> *I got taken* out the room, the police came, off duty, and, ah, you see there was no evidence. And the next thing I was told [was] "You're beyond our rules, *we're shipping you* to ____." And the next thing I knew, I was in an ambulance and up here.

These quotes are from the informants who were certified at the time of admission. Only one informant in this study voluntarily admitted himself to the hospital. He also described his admission as initiated by others, in this case his father: "*He, he took me* out for a drive away from the home, and *he said to get back* to the place."

The informants' tendency to feel that their admission was initiated by others was present regardless of the events precipitating the admission:

> My doctor was sick and tired of me ODing. . . . He was fed up with me, man. He just wasn't gonna take no more of my shit. *He just sent me* straight up here. He called as soon as he found out. He called straight up here. He was very firm with me, you know.

Although this informant had attempted suicide, he still attributed his admission to the actions of his physician. Another informant was admitted following a violent attack on another patient in a city hospital. This informant also did not attribute his admission to his violent behavior; instead, he attributed it to the intervention of others.

Related to this phenomenon was the informants' failure to identify significant events that resulted in the deterioration of their feelings of well-being immediately prior to admission. Although two informants described events that precipitated their admission, they did not describe any deterioration in their sense of well-being prior to these incidents. Both informants described having problems functioning in the community prior to these incidents. For example, the informant whose suicide attempt precipitated his admission described experiencing an extended period of depression while he was living in the community:

> It's a terrible feeling living in depression, you know. It really is, um, I've, I've lived with it for years, you know. Like months on end I was living in total depression, you know.

A third factor influencing the meaning assigned to admission to the hospital was the informants' perceptions of psychiatric hospitals *per se*. The informants' impressions of psychiatric hospitals varied and depended on their previous psychiatric treatment. Informants undergoing their first admission to a provincial psychiatric treatment center became afraid when first informed of their impending admission:

I: I didn't like it, you know. I, I wondered, "Oh, no, they're sending me to _____, a crazy place," you know. Like you hear so many things about _____, and they're such negative things.

R: What sort of things did you hear?

I: Um, just, just like this is a really terrible place to come to and a lot of bad memories from the people that come here, usually come back and stuff like that. Just a lot of negative things, you know.

A second respondent said that coming into the hospital "scared the hell out of [him]":

> I'd heard all kinds of stories about _____. I was expecting thumb screws and stuff like that. . . . Quite scared. I didn't know what to expect. I was expecting ECT [electroconvulsive therapy] treatment and large needles and lobotomies and stuff like that.

The informants with histories of previous admissions did not experience this fear. They tended to regard psychiatric care centers as institutions for people who fail to *make it* in the community. One informant described the hospital as "just a warehouse to start over, I guess." A second respondent said he was admitted to hospital because he "burns out" in the community: "Somehow I can't function and I can't perform, sort of thing." He also said "it's not too bad" being admitted to the hospital.

It was indicated earlier that the meaning informants assigned to their admissions has behavioral and social components. Behaviorally, the informants' admissions objectively substantiated their perceptions of themselves as failures:

> I seen my folks, and I broke down in front of my father. I started crying, and he, he took me out for a drive away from the home. And, um, he said to get back to the place. And I said . . . "What about my position in life?" Eh? "Why aren't I such a big success like everyone else?"

Another informant said, "I'm not too proud of the place or myself being in here, I suppose. Just not interested. . . . [It is] just about the bottom."

Socially, the informants in this study felt admission to the hospital symbolized condemnation of their behavior by the greater community: "I thought I was being condemned [by] the government and I would never get out. . . . At least, that's what I thought at the time." Other informants also made reference to feeling that they were being punished by others for their behavior in the community:

> Like I didn't do anything to make it in here. . . . I didn't take anybody's life. I didn't murder anyone. I didn't steal anything. Well, I might of stole a pack of smokes or something from the corner drug store, but nothing.

Only one informant openly expressed resentment toward those he thought were responsible for his admission. He said he "was set up," and he maintained that others in the community display the same behavior that he felt contributed to his admission:

> I get into a fist fight every five or six years, it seems like, or an act of violence of some sort. [pause] And there's other people that I know on the outside that get into fist fights almost daily or bi-daily, and they never get put away.

Consequently, the informants felt that admission to a psychiatric care center represented official redress to their inability to function in the community.

The respondents' preadmission experiences combined with the meaning assigned to hospital admission resulted in the informants entering into a *becoming ordinary* process. This process occurred when the respondents saw themselves as failures in comparison to others or to accepted social norms. All of the respondents emphasized behavioral inadequacies and not psychological difficulties when discussing their preadmission past.

The informants in this study emphasized functional normalcy, not psychological wellness; consequently, "*becoming ordinary*" was used to designate this process in preference to *"becoming normal."* To some normality may imply judgment of the psychological well-being of the informant, but *"becoming ordinary"* does not imply psychological well-being.

Readiness to Return to the Community: "Anticipating Mastery"

The primary criterion for selecting informants for this study was that the informants in cooperation with their treatment team were seeking community placement. Although the informants were selected in accordance with this criterion, it is apparent from the data that the informants' expressed desire to leave the hospital may not have represented their own assessment of their readiness to return to the community. It is also apparent from the data that the meaning the informants assigned to their return to the community was different from the meaning they assigned to the act of being discharged.

All of the informants in this study wanted to leave the hospital. One informant, however, was uncertain about his readiness to reside in the community (see Figure 17.1). In contrast, the other informants anticipated making a successful transition to community living. Although they did not refer to their anticipated future adjustment solely in terms of their ability to manage community demands, these informants were *anticipating mastery* of their posthospital communities. The informants who were *anticipating mastery* were anticipating personal excellence in their pursuit of *ordinary* goals. These informants expected to meet the community's demands and become independent and self-sufficient. For the informants in this study, *anticipating mastery* meant that they could attain their personal goals by meeting the demands of their community.

INDICATORS OF "ANTICIPATING MASTERY"

The informants expressed *anticipating mastery* of posthospital communities in three ways: by anticipating a successful transition to community living, by planning concrete strategies for attaining goals in the community, and by expressing positive self-regard.

Desire	*Anticipated Functioning*	*Readiness*
#1: I wanted to get the hell out of this hospital that's what I want.	If I was, if I was, ah, to go out in the world, I'd never make it. I just can't, I just can't put it together. I just can't put enough of myself together.	Absent
#2: Ah, I just don't like spending my time in here.	I'm looking—I'm kind of excited about finding a job and earning some money to put in the bank.	Present
#3: I don't, I don't like being here, you know. I'd jump at the chance to get out of here.	Um, I see myself working, and I see myself progressing. I see myself as being single and loving every minute of it.	Present
#4: [It's been] long enough. Half a year to me anyway. That's as much as I want to spend in this place.	In a month from now, I should be on AICSH [pension], working part time, attending programs, getting back into society on an even basis, or a controlled basis rather.	Present

Figure 17.1. Comparison of Informant's Desire for Discharge and Anticipated Community Functioning.

Anticipating Successful Transition to Community Living

The informants who were *anticipating mastery* felt returning to the community was an opportunity to "start over." In spite of their preadmission failures these informants anticipated positive postdischarge experiences. For the informants in this study discharge did not precede the resumption of life in the community; instead, discharge was seen as the start to a "new life":

> It's gonna be a new experience. I'm looking forward to it, and it's gonna be wonderful.

> It's a new beginning in the sense that, um, I'm starting my life over. I'm, I'm moving out of the house, and, you know, I'm gonna be going to school and all those things.

> Just a new beginning for me anyway. . . . Oh, just starting to hoard things for the future again. Maybe buy a new car or whatever.

These informants also anticipated a successful transition to community living:

> It'll be a lot of hard work too, you know. Like, it'll definitely, you know, be its pros and cons, but I'm sure that I'll be able to adjust and fit in right.

> I feel most comfortable out in the community right now. After living in a place like that [hospital], I think I'm more than prepared to survive in the community.

> I found it hard to make a living before, but now life seems a lot simpler.

These informants also stated they were ready for discharge. One informant said, "I'm just ready to go. I can't put it into words. . . . You know when you're ready to, and I'm ready to go." Another informant reported being "ready and able to deal with myself and society."

Only one of the informants was unequivocal regarding future inpatient treatment. This informant said his problems were resolved and "this time I won't be coming back. Like this is the last time I'll be here. I know that for a fact." The other two informants were uncertain about their need for future hospitalization. This uncertainty was associated with their belief that they might experience a decline in their present state of personal well-being. "I'll never have to come back to a place like this again. If I ever got sick, I hope I don't have to come back to this place."

The fourth informant in this study did not feel his impending return to the community indicated "starting a new life." This informant believed his return to the community was a continuation of his preadmission "struggle to make it":

> It's the people that get to me, eh? It's the people, it's not the—maybe it's the surroundings. I dunno. Something's gotta hook on my line or something. Because always when I'm there . . . if I try to do something, there's always someone out there . . . that's there to outsmart me, you know. So I gotta be careful. I gotta. I can't just give up.

This informant did not anticipate a successful transition to community living; instead, he was uncertain about his readiness to reside in the community:

> Probably end up back here in another half year. Will be some tiny . . . incident at the group home. Either that or 'cause I can't find work. Somehow . . . I can't function, and I can't perform sort of thing.

This informant was also uncertain about his need for future admissions. His uncertainty, however, was associated with a lack of self-confidence about his ability to manage in the community.

The informants' ideas concerning their anticipated community environments did not account for the variance in *anticipating mastery* of these environments.

Anticipated Community Environment

The informants in this study anticipated two types of community environments: nonthreatening, hospitable environments and threatening, malevolent environments. Two informants anticipated a nonthreatening, hospital community environment, and two informants anticipated a threatening, malevolent community environment.

A Nonthreatening, Hospitable Environment

Two informants believed their discharge communities would offer both employment opportunities and emotional support from family members and friends. Although only one of these informants felt this environment would be charitable, neither of the informants thought the environment would be punitive or restrictive:

> I got a job waiting for me in ____. I got buckets of money waiting for me in, ah, ____, which is a nice town. I'm closer to the phone. . . . I'm never broke either. I can always phone up service rigs and go to work for them. Um . . . they make about the same. Like, ah, you can work about maybe ten days for a service rig and make a month's pay.

> It just goes . . . to say, you know, all you have to do is hold out your hand, you know. If you're in need, that's all you have to do is hold out your hand,

> and it's given to you. It's a great song, you know. This is a great country. . . . It's a great country, you know. Everything is set up for me, you know. There's, you know, I don't have to be a genius to, you know, survive and nothing like that.

A Threatening, Malevolent Environment

Two informants thought their anticipated community would be threatening and malevolent. They described this environment as containing anonymous, punitive others. One of these informants described the world as "painful" and anticipated requiring daily deprogramming "from all the nasty people" in the community:

> I suppose that's the hardest thing that happens to a person during the day, out in society is slander and common assault. . . . [Common assault] is double talking a person when he's having another conversation, [two conversations going on at once] one malicious and one benign.

> Somebody that's—what's the word I'm looking for—is, ah, up to date on my problems. Is able to counsel me at the daybreak and the day end. [pause] That's about it. Somebody to deprogram me at the end of the day. . . . Well, every day somebody gives you certain information, derogatory or positive or whatever. And you just gotta sort the good from the bad and have a good night.

Although this informant said supportive friends were present in his community, he also spoke of being "damned" by the "righteous people. The ones that feel too self-righteous. There's a difference between righteous and self-righteous."

The second informant who anticipated a threatening, malevolent community environment did not identify any sources of emotional support within his discharge community. He felt the world was oppressive and immoral:

> You know, like . . . if the world doesn't settle down, like there will be bugs and everything else. People will be putting bugs in people's brains. And it's all a Chinese factor, right? Like the Chinese are out to kill, eh? I don't know why, but they're out to frighten the world, its population and to seduction. It's . . . very terminal. It's . . . you have to be careful or you can get caught in that. Who knows. . . . It's very sin. . . . It's a . . . big sin. It's

> a large sin, and I don't like it—being part of it. . . . I mean there's . . . a lot of young in the world . . . that are really strong. And, um, and, ah, their power tripping ways take them wherever they wanna go. They power trip at the face of the person.

The first indicator of *anticipating mastery* was anticipating a successful transition to community living. The informants who thought they were ready to return to the community characterized their return as starting over. In contrast, the one informant who did not believe he was ready to return to the community did not see entry into the community as an opportunity to reestablish himself in the community. In fact he did not think his forthcoming discharge would have much impact on his present life course.

PLANNING CONCRETE STRATEGIES FOR ATTAINING GOALS IN THE COMMUNITY

The second indicator of *anticipating mastery* was planning concrete strategies for attaining personal goals in the community. Although one informant defined his impending return to the community differently, his long-term aspirations were similar to those expressed by the other informants.

Aspirations

All of the informants wanted to achieve a sense of personal achievement in the community. Prior to their admissions they occupied marginal, dependent community roles. At predischarge they expressed a desire to become productive, self-supporting community members:

> It's my turn . . . to give back to society. . . . I've taken so much, why not return it? I've lived my life in sin, and I'm not afraid to admit it. It's about time I did something good for the world.

> I'll do it. I have lots of time yet, but, you know, but I wanna start producing and making some constructive progressions in life.

> I wanna work. I wanna get back. I wanna work in the work force. I wanna work for a living, earn a living.

The majority of the informants preferred manual labor employment; only one informant aspired to become a professional. This informant, however, planned to finance his education by working in restaurants. The places of employment preferred by the other informants included "managing a greenhouse," being "a carpenter," and working in a "warehouse." Although they did not consider their past employment histories in the community, the informants did not believe their employment aspirations were unrealistic ambitions considering their age and gender.

Three of the informants also wished to establish long-term relationships with members of the opposite sex. They felt these relationships would contribute to their sense of fulfillment in the community:

> Because I want a lasting relationship. I've seen how happy some married couples are. I've seen my brother and his girlfriend. They're married common-law. But, ah, a long-standing relationship means security for me.

> I want a nice wife, and, you know, a happy little family, you know, to raise. And, you know, be my own and that. That seems great. That's what it's all about.

These informants stated, however, that financial self-sufficiency was necessary before they could make commitments to others. The informant who felt his return to the community was a continuation of his "struggle to make it" did not seem to anticipate interpersonal relationships within the community:

> Full time job, a steady girlfriend, some leisure activities. I think that would make for a healthy lifestyle . . . um, just the everyday things.

> I'm gonna make a promise to myself that I'm gonna get out of that group home in ____, and get an apartment. And earn a . . . wage and eventually, eventually get back on my own and eventually earn my own keep, you know.

> Just going to school and getting a good education so I can get a good job, and so, you know, I can eventually get a girlfriend and settle down and have a family, you know. Work to live. . . . So that's what I want out of life. That's what I'm working towards. Yeah, I'll get it someday.

The informants' long-term aspiration was to become *ordinary*. In his last interview one of the informants confirmed that his aspiration was to become *ordinary*:

I: To be as ordinary as possible. [pause] Like mother wanted me to go into law, but, ah, law and politics. I don't think I'll ever be able to do that now. I'm too scandalous.

R: As ordinary as possible. In what sort of ways?

I: As far as holding down a job. [pause] Ah, [pause] just holding a normal job, leading a normal life. Going to the movies once a week. Taking a girlfriend out for dinner. Cleaning house.

The informants did not anticipate instant fulfillment of their aspirations and as a result all of them had strategies for gaining entry into the community.

Gaining Entry to the Community

Before leaving the hospital the informants in this study recognized their need for living accommodations and for financial support in the community. Securing living accommodations was a concern for these informants as they anticipated being unable to return to previous residential arrangements. Although the informants desired independent living in the distant future, this was not an immediate posthospitalization preference. Most of the informants initially anticipated placement in alternative living arrangements (approved or group homes) within the community. One informant anticipated living with family members. The informants sought shared accommodations because they recognized their need for companionship and support in the community:

> Ah, this time I feel I'll be stronger and more capable of dealing with it, especially with living in a group home situation. I'll have support there . . . you have somebody to talk to after the day and reveal your problems to.

The informant who planned to reside with family members said that independent accommodation "seemed kind of lonely, I guess. I don't know if I could handle it."

The informants who requested referrals to alternative community placements felt they had a choice regarding these placements. For example, one informant said procurement of an alternative community placement would hasten his attending physician's decision to discharge him:

> They [alternative living arrangements] are the easiest and quickest way to get discharged. . . . Well as long as you have a place to live, you get a discharge. As long as someone is willing to take responsibility for you.

When asked about independent living accommodations, he said, "I'd probably get a place and be discharged, [but] I feel an approved home is the best situation for me right now."

This freedom of choice, however, was limited by the informants' reluctance to enter into independent living arrangements and they usually agreed to the first available placement that accepted them regardless of their assessment of the appropriateness of the placement:

> Temporary, I don't want to live there very long. If I'm there for a year, I'm . . . it's gonna be a miracle 'cause I know darn well the people of ____ don't—aren't—isn't—aren't, they're not ready for me, and I'm not ready for them.

> It's a different situation, um, it's not an easy one to do, you know. Especially like . . . I don't really like her. [laugh] To tell you the truth, to tell you the truth, I don't really like her, and I don't like the way she does things. But it's my only home for right now, so I'm just gonna, you know, do the best I can, and you know, try to, try to make it work, you know, and everything.

Both of these informants, however, intended to be discharged to these community placements.

Only one of the four informants obtained accommodation in his preferred community placement. This was the informant who planned to live with family members. The plans of the other informants failed to materialize after the community agencies rejected them as candidates for placement. Consequently, two of the three informants decided to seek independent living accommodations within their preadmission communities:

> Well, I figured the group homes weren't available to me and the approved homes weren't available for me in the ____ area. The next best thing to do was get a place of my own.

> She's been feeling a little bit sick, so she didn't really need the extra stress on her, or anything like that. So, um, she just said that she couldn't take me and that . . . I'm ready to find my own place. Like, I wanna go to school and stuff like that, you know. I don't wanna be sitting in here any longer.

At the time this study was completed, the fourth informant remained in the hospital.

The second immediate concern for the informants was the arrangement of financial support. All of the informants aspired to achieve financial independence in the distant future; however, immediate financial support was required in order for them to be discharged. This financial support was arranged by the hospital's social services department. Although the informants expressed satisfaction with the available financial support, they felt this support was temporary assistance.

Anchoring Future Aspirations

The informants wanted to be independent, productive members of their community. In addition to securing accommodation and financial support, the informants who *anticipated mastery* of their community environments formulated plans of action oriented toward attaining their goals. The informant who did not feel entry into the community was an opportunity to start over did not formulate any plans beyond attaining community placement.

The informants who felt their entry into the community constituted "starting a new life" had strategies for achieving their future goals. The intended outcome of these plans was to establish themselves in the community, culminating in the achievement of financial self-sufficiency. Because the informants felt financial self-sufficiency was necessary before they could make any romantic commitments, their primary focus was on finding employment.

These informants understood the influence of community factors on employment opportunities, and they anticipated retaining supplementary financial support until paid employment was obtained:

> I'll, I'll try to find a job. If I can't find a job, I'll live off social assistance awhile until I can go to school.

> Um, Canada Pension said that if I couldn't work they would pay me four hundred dollars a month, and I figure that's fair. If I can't work at least I won't starve or put anyone out.

Two of the informants anticipated rapid transition to productive roles in the competitive marketplace. Both of these informants initiated their plans for procuring employment in the community prior to discharge. The first informant contacted family members regarding employment opportunities in his community. The second informant, who wanted to become a nurse, planned to enroll in high school upgrading courses offered at a community college, and he obtained a college application form during a leave of absence from the hospital.

The third informant did not anticipate immediate employment in the competitive marketplace. Because he felt he needed a slower transition he sought self-satisfaction in the community through less competitive means. He was the only informant in this study who purposefully planned to attend community-based treatment programs. This informant believed such treatment programs would help him achieve self-reliance:

> I don't know if it's life skills, or whatever it's called. It'll be psychotherapy in one degree or another, and rehab in another. [To put me] in a position to be able to go back to work again. . . . In a month from now, I should be on AISCH [disability pension], working part time, attending programs, getting back into society on an even basis, or a controlled basis rather.

If unable to obtain part-time employment this informant said he might volunteer to work with the Canadian Mental Health Association as an alternative means of contributing to the community.

All of the informants anticipated contact with health care professionals in the community. Only one informant felt these professionals would help him adjust to community life. The other two informants felt that community-based professionals would only be helpful for follow-up drug therapy. Neither of these informants expressed unconditional acceptance of the continued need for drug therapy in the community.

The first of these two informants compared mental health care to quicksand:

> Well, you're not ever gonna get away from it. . . . Like, I'll have to go home, and I'll have to take medication for the rest of my life.

Although this informant reluctantly accepted his need for continued drug therapy in his interviews, he denied his need for drug therapy in his statements to a family member. The family member told the researcher that this informant had suggested he may discontinue his medications after discharge. When this relative informed him that compliance with his drug therapy was a condition of his accommodation he consented to comply with continued drug therapy. The second informant planned to seek professional assistance in undertaking a drug-free trial in the community:

> Like, when I get to ____, I'm gonna see a doctor, and I'm gonna gradually take myself off this, and see how I do, you know.

The informant who felt he was not ready to return to the community did not describe strategies for achieving his future goals. Beyond obtaining community placement, this informant was uncertain about his future plans:

> I don't know. . . . If I can't find something to do, I might have to leave it. . . . Well, I go into the group home on December the first, I guess. They promised me that, go into the group home on December the first. So I got that, but then I, I don't know how I'll manage after that.

Furthermore, this informant recognized his inability to formulate concrete plans for the future. For example, beyond his inability to obtain employment he could not identify a reason for his jobless status:

> I don't think there is. . . . I'm gonna go out and earn it. So I just don't know how to go about it. I need guidance . . . [from] people, myself, things around me.

This informant also recognized his need for further rehabilitation in the community, but his references to community-based treatment were uncertain. He did not establish either explicit time lines or anticipated behavioral outcomes he hoped to achieve by attending community-based programs:

> Well, I'd probably have to be a whole bunch of rehabilitation somewhere. And that's maybe what I'm must sort of entering into. Maybe I should take . . . that daycare program up at the hospital in ____. Well, I'm gonna have to do something in ____, so maybe that'd be a good start.

Although all the informants in this study wanted to become self-supporting community members, apart from strategies associated with gaining entry into the community one informant did not formulate concrete plans for attaining his long-term goals. This informant did not feel he was ready to return to the community and as a result he was unsure about his future plans.

EXPRESSING POSITIVE SELF-REGARD

The third indicator of *anticipating mastery* was expressing a positive self-regard. The self-references made by the informants in this study varied as much as their assessments of their readiness to return to the community. Those respondents who felt they were ready for discharge expressed positive self-regard. These informants said their present mental well-being had improved in comparison to their preadmission well-being:

> I just feel better about myself. I'm able to breathe properly. I've got a song in my heart, a whistle on my lips.

> I feel really good about myself. I like myself a lot.

Although the third informant did not make direct self-references, he described himself as feeling less "bogged down" and "discouraged": "Well, I kind of hope I'm never in this . . . get bogged down and as bad shape as when I started anyway."

In contrast, the informant who felt he was not ready to return to the community made disparaging self-references:

> I'm, I'm just a creep, you know. I'm just a creep in sheep's clothing. . . . I'm just afraid whether you'll think I'm a joke or something—as some kind of

> a last joke going on in the universe or something really stupid. . . . My mind is so small, you know. Sometimes I feel like I don't even have a mind.

This informant also described himself as "degenerating" and "pretty screwed up," and he did not identify any changes in his mental well-being since his admission to hospital:

> You know, I'm, ah, I'm pretty screwed up, man. But later on maybe I'll get it together. But [pause] it's still the same. I'm, I'm a human being, right? . . . I just hate the thoughts going [on] in my head.

Moreover, he consistently said that his mental well-being had deteriorated since his first contact with mental health professionals:

> I started to do stupid things at home so my father figured I needed help, and I probably did. But I don't know what kind of help it was. It didn't seem to help too much. . . . When I went there the first time, it never [worked] so . . . look at where I am now. I'm worse off than I was when I went in there. I would have been better off just to stay the hell away! . . . But I, I don't think I'll ever be the same as I was when I was growing up. I don't know how it happened. I just got involved. I got the first series of treatment, and then, and then I just never recovered, you know.

The variance in the informants' self-regard was also reflected in their feelings of self-confidence. One informant described self-confidence as:

> being able to walk into a place with my head up. Being able to sit down and be pleasant and bright; order a meal without any hassles within myself.

The informants who felt they were ready to return to the community expressed self-confidence:

> Oh, I admit I have problems, it's just that I've learned how to deal with them.

> I've got the brains and stamina enough to, um, take advantage of this and make something out of my life.

The informant who believed he was not ready to return to the community described his present abilities as inadequate: "It's only manual dexterity and skills . . . that if I had more accomplishment and more know how, I wouldn't be in trouble." In addition, this informant continued to express feelings of being overwhelmed:

> Somethings, somethings make it—somethings will start me up and then shut me down, eh, in this hospital. It's very unreal. Sometimes I feel better than others, and then automatically I'll switch back to a bad mood.

He also characterized himself as "decentered":

> I don't have any problem, you see. I don't happen to have a center of gravity there, that's all. I go tumbling down the hill all the time.

This informant's lack of self-autonomy precluded feelings of self-confidence.

The informants in this study who felt they were ready for discharge expressed feelings of positive self-regard and self-reliance. In contrast, the informant who did not believe he was ready to return to the community was self-depreciating and he continued to describe himself as being overwhelmed.

GAINING CONTROL OF INTRUSIVE EXPERIENCES

Two informants described gaining control of the effects of intrusive experiences on their behaviors. As a result, they experienced unique changes in their well-being. Also, disagreements with hospital professionals regarding their readiness for discharge based on the presence of these experiences resulted in these informants assuming a more assertive stance when seeking discharge.

The particular control behaviors initiated by these two informants were derived from their perception of the nature of the intrusive experiences. The informants did not absolutely accept the professionals' contention that these experiences were intrapsychic phenomena:

> It's true, let me tell you. As God is my witness. I believe it's because I . . . hear voices, and I know for sure that it's true because they can read my thoughts. Like I have someone right now even reading my thoughts.

The other informant said what he hears is "real":

I: I figure I don't hallucinate it half as much as what I hear.

R: Yeah, you've told me that before—what you hear is real.

I: Generally. I'll grant some of what I hear . . . is garbled, is misinterpreted by me. But if I misinterpret something, I generally ask the question "Why" or "What" or "Did you say that."

The failure of psychotropic drugs to eradicate these experiences was interpreted by these informants as substantiating their contention that these experiences were objectively real:

R: And that's when they tried you on that new drug?

I: Yeah, yeah, but it didn't work, you know. I mean, if there's a transmitter in your room, I mean, no matter I was on 900 milligrams of chlorpromazine a day, and I was still hearing voices. So that must tell you something. I could be on 1800 milligrams of chlorpromazine a day, and I could still hear voices if they're there. Lately, they haven't been there.

R: But if they're there, they're there.

I: They're there, they're there. No drug's gonna—I know what I hear. I know what I see.

The second informant also had similar beliefs:

> With this medication, the super drugs they put me on, and the heavy doses they put me on, I shouldn't hallucinate. . . . Actually, I didn't tell them that. I—the thought just came to me. I'm gonna use it the next time they tell me I'm hallucinating. Usually, I just kept my mouth shut and grin and bear it.

These informants attempted to identify the external sources of these auditory stimuli. One of them maintained that his proclaimed source is indisputable:

> She believed that I hear voices, but she didn't believe there was a transmitter in my room, you know. And, of course, there is, you know. It might not be inside my room, but it's, it's just outside my room possibly, you know. And I hear these voices. That's it.

The second informant was not as certain about the source of these experiences. He said some of his auditory stimuli *may be* hallucinations.

He defined hallucinations as "hearing things that aren't there." Distinguishing between objectively-based auditory stimuli and hallucinations, however, was difficult for this informant. An experience was classified as a hallucination only after all possible sources of environmental causation were eliminated:

> As in where I am, where I am in relation to the room. What I'm picking up could be conversations down the hall. It's echoing, or it could be something coming through the air vent that's shares with, like the nursing offices. There's an air vent that comes down, and I can sometimes hearing them talking in there. . . . Then if I can't, if I can't analyze it scientifically and decide, if I can't give it a feasible reason where it's coming from, then I decide it's a hallucination.

Nevertheless, this informant accounted for the intrusive experiences by referring to a broad range of potential environmental sources:

> Well, lately it's been—I've been called a child abuser, a faggot. . . . Staff do it to stress me out and see if I can take it or not. Patients do it just to be downright nasty. They want some sort of power over each other. . . . It's like a pecking order in a hen house. . . . Oh, [pause] one of the games like "Wear my face" or [pause] something like that or stuff like that. . . . If you look at somebody and they don't like the way you look at them, they'll say, "Wear my face." . . . It means you're supposed to hallucinate and think that you're wearing their face. This is a reminder that you are not supposed to look them in the eye. . . . Yeah, it's hypnosis is all it is. Suggestion and feeling suggestions, and—I don't know. Half of the hallucinations I ever got in my life are due to hypnosis.

When this informant was not experiencing or discussing probable intrusive experiences he was able to relate to these experiences as if they were hallucinations:

I: If I have an overload of information, I hallucinate. Uh, [pause] that's about it, and when that happens, I get frustrated and angry, and I get paranoid. . . . I kept hearing other conversations and figured they were talking about me.

R: During that, do you realize what's going on?

I: I do now.

When this informant was experiencing these sensations during the interviews or was discussing probable intrusive experiences, however, he related to them as if they were objectively real experiences. For example, he was frequently distracted during the interviews. He would occasionally turn his head aside and mutter profanities. He attributed the cause of his distraction to environmental stimuli such as voices in a passing car.

Regardless of the attributed source of these experiences both of these informants described gaining some control over the behavioral effects of the experiences. The methods they used to gain control may be classified as proactive and reactive behaviors. Proactive behaviors were behaviors initiated by the informants in order to affect the quality/quantity of the incoming stimuli. In contrast, the intent of reactive behaviors was to modify the informants' response to the incoming stimuli.

Proactive Strategies

Modification of the quality and/or the quantity of incoming auditory stimuli was achieved by enacting behaviors designed to alter one of two aspects of the intrusive experience. The first type of proactive behaviors were behaviors directed toward the perceived source of the stimuli. One informant described confronting the perceived source in order to suppress further intrusions:

> I was taking my meds, minding my own business, and another guy was talking while I was distracted. And then all of the sudden he starts calling me "Faggot! You fairy! Everybody hates you!" and this and that and started walking away. And I yelled out his name, right, very loudly. And he turned around and says "Ah, you faggot, fairy! You coward!" I blew up, just went into a rage. . . . I jumped him. I pushed him down actually.

Proactive behaviors directed toward the perceived source of the auditory stimuli were not necessarily aggressive behaviors. The second informant described using his "voices" as mediators in order to bargain with the perceived source of the intrusive experiences:

I: I'm still trying to get them to tell me that she'll have coffee with me, but I can't convince them. [laugh]

R: You can't convince them yet?

I: No, I try, try everything, I'm telling you, I do.

As well as attempting to contact the perceived source through his "voices," this informant also endeavored to establish contact through associates of the perceived source living in the community:

> And she just wrote me a letter back and just told me everything was okay, you know. Everything was—"Hey, you never did that much to our family." And, you know, "We forgive you for anything that you might of done." And all that, so, you know, everything is okay.

It should be noted that the content of these informants' intrusive experiences were markedly different. The "voices" of the first informant were punitive, while the "voices" of the second participant were positive and nonthreatening.

The second type of proactive behaviors involved deflecting incoming stimuli by directing attention away from the intrusive "voices." These behaviors were implemented by the informant who heard punitive "voices." Redirection strategies included concentrating on conversations with others and concentrating on bodily movements:

> I was a little stressed out in the restaurant tonight. You were there, and you were talking to me, so I didn't feel too bad. . . . So I just kept listening to my mouth chewing and listening to you, and I felt okay.

Reactive Strategies

The intent of reactive behaviors was to alter personal responses to auditory stimuli. Reactive behaviors consisted of both passive and active behaviors. Both informants described passively ignoring auditory stimuli:

> I don't let certain things bother me anymore. By certain things I mean just small problems that arose in day-to-day life living in an institution. . . . Ah, I would say people stealing things spiritually [pause] or giving things spiritually. Things that can't be seen . . . because I feel that as long as I'm breathing and thinking that I don't have to worry about spiritual things anymore. And it's—if they're there, they're there. And if they're not, they're gone.

> I know that they're lies. I know that they're lies. They're not, they're not truth. They lie, so I just don't believe them. . . . I just don't believe everything I hear these days. I use to believe in everything I was told, eh?

The informant who heard punitive "voices" described implementing active-reactive behaviors. These were purposeful behaviors designed to reduce this informant's feelings of anger and tension:

> I sigh and relax. Make yourself be nonviolent. Make yourself be as calm as possible. . . . Then it's a fantasy, and then I resolve that and say, "That was a fantasy, and I'm not going to listen to it anymore, and it's not there" and go on to something different. . . . With me it goes away. Sometimes it takes a little work. Sometimes I have to go take a bath or a long walk or just go to sleep and forget about it.

This informant felt the psychotropic medications were an adjunct to his reactive strategies:

> It's, ah, a matter of overabundance of stimulus or stimuli—I hallucinate. Where with the neuroleptic drugs, the tranquilizers, or neuroleptic would be a major tranquilizer, I don't freak out about it anymore. It comes and passes. . . . I feel sedated but not restrained. [pause] Uh, the violence in me is restrained, but the rest, the freedom of thought isn't.

Although he said the medications alleviated his feelings of depression, the informant who described his present intrusive experiences as nonthreatening did not think medications affected those experiences or his immediate reaction to them:

> Now I feel, I feel lots better. This flupenthixol is a miracle drug. It is! It is! Who ever invented it, I'd like to write them a letter and tell them "Thank you for helping me." I really would because it's, it's so good that I feel, I feel so much better. It's—it had an antidepressant effect on ya and, um, it's so much better.

Gaining control over the effects of these experiences contributed to these informants' improved sense of well-being. Prior to gaining this control these informants characterized the intrusions as repressive. In order to protect their well-being they reacted either through acting out or withdrawing. Gaining control of these experiences reduced their repressive effects allowing them to direct their attention to other aspects of their environment.

The informants' predischarge descriptions of the effects of intrusive experiences on their personal well-being were antipodal to those recollected during the preadmission period. One of the informants recalled being "preoccupied" and "mentally restricted" as a consequence of these experiences. At predischarge he described himself as emancipated from these effects:

> You know, they don't, they don't interfere with my, you know, they don't preoccupy me too much, you know. They don't interfere with my daily routines and stuff like that. . . . I can go out and do the things that I want to now. And before, I was basically restricted mentally, you know.

The other informant recalled being "distracted" and "frustrated" by these experiences. He described himself as being in a "cold rage." During the predischarge period he said this rage had dissipated: "I'm much more calm, my head is clearer. . . . I don't feel the inner turmoil that I use to." He also stated he was less distracted: "I'm able to read and write again. I'm able to listen to television and radio again."

These two informants rejected the professionals' contentions that their experiences were intrapsychic phenomena and they also rejected the idea that these experiences implied mental illness. They felt their experiences were unique because they or the source of the intrusions possessed exceptional characteristics. For example, during one interview one of the informants asked the interviewer if she heard a voice call him "murderer." He said her failure to hear this voice was due to her less "acute" hearing. The second informant said his experiences were unique because the source had an exceptional ability: "She hired a person that has this special gift to read my mind." Basically, these two informants felt they were psychologically ordinary people who had extraordinary experiences.

The Hospital Experience: Being in a "Boot Camp"

One informant said being in hospital is analogous to being in an army "boot camp." He based his comparison on the similarities between the structures and the functions of these organizations. In much the same way as a boot camp, the hospital segregates patients from the pedestrian community, is a temporary situation designed to prepare patients for community living, is a residential facility established and managed by service providers for service recipients, is a receptacle for "conscripted" service recipients, and is an institution in which interpersonal relationships are based on "expert authoritarianism":

> It's like entering boot camp in the army. . . . It's an exercise in discipline for yourself, the staff, from the staff. You have to be good. . . . When you are able to accept discipline from somebody that's in a position to give it to you and have discipline for yourself, take care of yourself, that's when you're ready to leave.

Although the other informants in this study did not make this analogy, their interviews confirmed the appropriateness of this comparison.

BEING IN A BOOT CAMP

Segregating Patients From the Pedestrian Community

The informants in this study perceived the hospital as an institution detached from the community. They described their admission in terms of being "sent away" from their preadmission communities:

> He just sent me straight up here.

> We're shipping you to ____.

In contrast, leaving the hospital was referred to as "reentering" the community:

> It's a reentry into society.

> It'll mean I'm finally accepted back into society.

Furthermore, the informants felt the hospital was detached from its surrounding community: "Well, you're a few miles from any civilization. It's extremely quiet outside." Excursions into the neighboring town were referred to as going "up to town" or "going into the town."

Leaves of absence from the hospital were sanctioned excursions into the pedestrian community. The informants characterized these leaves as trials to evaluate their readiness to return to the community:

> It's just that I'm feeling more adapted to it as each LOA [leave of absence] confirms.

> Ready and able to deal with myself and society.

> I was—I wasn't making no trouble at my approved home, you know. I was being in on time and going to sleep and not getting up quite when I was supposed to, but that can be worked on.

Leaves of absence were planned, temporary reintegrations into the community, although excursions into the town adjacent to the hospital were seen as recreation because they were privileges granted by the hospital's professionals:

> A couple of weeks ago I got full privileges. . . . I'm able to go to town and come back when I please. I can walk into town whenever I want to. I don't have to check in during the day. I just have to be here for meal times and med times.

Despite being outside of the geographical boundaries of the institution the informants with town privileges continued to see themselves as appendages of the hospital community.

Preparing Patients for Community Living

The belief that psychiatric hospitals are institutions for the treatment of people unable to function in the community persisted throughout the interviews in this study. During a termination interview one informant said that psychiatric care centers are for:

> people that are emotionally sick or have psychological problems or physiological problems. That means they just can't cope with society on a day-to-day level.

All of the informants felt their hospitalizations were temporary and they anticipated returning to the community in the future: "At least there's a beginning and an end to ____, anyway." According to these informants the primary function of the hospital was to resolve their personal problems and help them return to community living:

> It's, you see, it's an establishment for putting you back on your own again.

> The facility's good, you know. I'd suggest it to anyone that is having problems coping with life, and you know, you know, just to get their problems set up.

The informants in this study felt that guardianship issues should not be the primary concern of the hospital staff:

> Perhaps it's not so much of a dodge as people covering their back, covering their back door. Making sure when I go home I'm not a time bomb and go out and get physical. Go out and start trouble, eh?

When the informants felt guardian concerns were taking precedence over perceived treatment needs, they became angry and frustrated:

> I find it's an insult. I don't go around generally attacking people, verbally or mentally, or verbally or physically, rather.

A Residential Facility Managed by Service Providers

Recipients of psychiatric care live in a milieu created by others. Admission to a psychiatric hospital compels the individual to relinquish previous life-styles and adapt to communal institutional living and the institution's standards of expected conduct; however, the characteristics of the institutional milieu vary within the hospital. The hospital is partitioned into nursing units, each with a designated patient population. The milieu of these units varies markedly and it is contingent on the type of service provided by the unit. All of the informants in this study began their stay in the hospital on admission units and later they were transferred to rehabilitation units.

Admission Units

All of the informants had a negative view of the admission unit. They said their experience on this unit was similar to being incarcerated, that is, being "locked up":

> I didn't like it at all when I was on ____, you know. It was . . . terrible, you know. Just . . . the feeling of being locked up is just an awful feeling, you know. I can never stand being in jail or anything like that, you know. Like, I wouldn't do anything to go to jail or anything like that, you know. But I

don't know. . . . It was a terrible feeling. I can't even explain it, you know. I just, it's just . . . terrible, you know, being locked up like that. Like, like you're locked up in a cage, eh? You can't go nowhere. You can't do anything. Sure they have pool tables, and they have ping-pong tables, and they have juice, and they have people around to talk to, and stuff like that, but still, it's not a good feeling to be locked up in a place like that.

The informants also said that the service providers on the admission unit were authoritative:

The staff can be extremely domineering on the admission wards. It's their . . . exerting their authority. And you come to know, and come to grips with the reality of being in an institution where there are certain rules that must be followed.

They lock you out of bed, and go along there, and hustle you in a group all the time.

The informants also felt they were overmedicated and received impersonal care on the admission unit:

It's a very heavy sedate ward. They sedate you like crazy on the ward, and then they send you to another ward from there if you're not able to leave. Well, usually the stay is quite long, eh? So you get fed up to the point where you're kicking or hitting someone, and they send, they fire you into another part of the hospital.

One informant said he could not recall his feelings regarding his transfer to a rehabilitation unit:

I was pretty knocked out and wacked out, severely medicated, and I was very confused. . . . I was just being handled like a crate.

Rehabilitation Units

The informants had both positive and negative opinions about the rehabilitation unit, and the quality of their evaluation depended on their standard of comparison. The informants were positive about the rehabilitation unit when they compared it to the admission units:

> Well, on ____, like that's a pretty open ward. There's a lot of freedom there. There isn't much freedom on—when I first came in here.

> The same thing only not as intense. They're more of your buddies here. Once you get better, it's sort of like, ah, after shock.

> I came over to ____, and it was even better, eh? You know, open ward. I can come and go as I please, you know. I don't have to check in at any time, you know. I can just go whenever I want to, you know, and that was great.

When the informants compared the rehabilitation unit with their previous life-style, however, they said these units were similar to "jails." Although the informants did not feel locked up, which was their main impression of the admission units, they felt the rehabilitation unit was similar to jail because it involved group living and the regulation of their behavior by others:

> I have to eat meals with a lot of people. I have to sleep in my own cubicle with other people around. I have to sit in the same room with a lot of other people. [pause] If I fist fight, I'm in trouble. [pause] If I blow my cool, I get medication . . . and I have people exerting an authority over me. I'm used to being independent and living on my own.

> Just whereas your freedoms are confined to a certain area. You have to be in at a certain time. Um, your meals are all cooked for you. You go down, stand in line like you would in jail, you know, and get your food and, you know, eat and then go back up to the ward. Take you meds, hang out for awhile, you know, make a call once in awhile, have visitors once in awhile.

> Um, just um, 'cause you're, you're restricted to a ward. You gotta be in at a certain time. Um, you have to get up in the mornings and go to work, you know. . . . I've never been to jail so I can't—I'm just saying it as a fact that, um, that it seem like to me, it's, it's a lot like what jail would be like.

A Receptacle for "Conscripted" Service Recipients

The informants in this study attributed their admission to the interventions of other people, and not one informant described his admission as self-initiated. As a result they felt the hospital community was composed of two broad groups of people: "insiders" and "outsiders." From the informants' perspective, service recipients are the insiders and service providers are the outsiders of the institution. Insiders are totally immersed in the institutional milieu; whereas outsiders, in addition to creating the milieu, are detached from it:

> The way they give their treatment . . . it's based on real society. [pause]. . . . On being on the outside. How an outside person would deal with you. After all, they are from the outside. Living, working on the inside. We have to live it, but they work it.

Once they were admitted to the hospital the informants became members of the insider group; however, this mandatory group assignment was not favored by the informants as none of them wanted to be associated with the insider group:

> You have to come back [from leaves of absence (LOAs)] and sit around with sick people again and listen to them cry and whine. You know, I suppose, I suppose, I suppose it's to evoke some compassion in a person, but to live with it, day in and day out, gets kind of tiring.

> What am I doing here? You know, there's all these sick people around me and, you know, I'm totally sane, you know. There's nothing wrong with me. How am I supposed to feel?

Another informant told the researcher that the other study participants were "crackpots." Usually, when the informants did make references to peer relationships with other patients, they described these patients as not "sick."

The informants in this study wanted to be associated with the outsider group, and because they felt the members of the nursing staff were exemplars of this group the informants aspired to emulate their qualities: "Something like the people here in this hospital. Like the . . . nurses and stuff. You know what I mean." One informant said his desire to become a nurse was a result of his experiences with the hospital's nurses:

> I just met a lot of nice nurses and stuff like that, and I like the job that they do and everything like that. That's what I'd like to be doing myself, eh?

A third informant explicitly rejected affiliation with the insider group. He described the nursing professionals as his "peers":

> Talking to the staff is, because they're educated. I've got a certain amount of education myself. . . . To me, they're my peers unless, unless the patients have been to school and studied. It's just not the same.

An Institution in Which Relationships Are Based on "Expert Authoritarianism"

Expert authoritarianism refers to relationships that are characterized by obedience to experts and this term describes four recurring themes in the data associated with the relationship between the hospital's professionals and the informants: institutional privileges and community resources were accessed through the professionals; the decision to "promote" patients was the prerogative of experts; experts' assessments of readiness for "promotion" were valued by the informants; and the informants complied with aspects of their treatment they considered nontherapeutic.

Institutional Privileges and Community Resources

At admission the hospital's professionals imposed constraints on the informants' freedom of movement. Personal liberties were incrementally regained as professionals granted the informants privileges, which were described as having three levels. The first level, "close watch," required that the informant be accompanied by staff members when leaving the unit. When limited privileges were granted the informant was "allowed to go out for a few hours at a time, not up to town, but to stay on the hospital's grounds." Acquisition of full privileges allowed the informants to leave the hospital's grounds; however, they were required to return to their units for meals and medications. One informant who had full privileges described himself as a "trusty": "Well, now that I'm a trusty, it's not too bad."

Community resources were also accessed through professionals. The type of formal community assistance sought by informants in this study depended on their personal resources in the community. For example, in order to leave the hospital supplementary financial support was required by all the informants. This financial support was arranged by the hospital's social services department and the informants said they had no difficulties accessing this support:

> I kept on him [social worker] by asking him about getting out and making arrangements to get my AISCH [pension] reinstated and things like that. So he went down with me a week ago Thursday, a week ago today, and we got the ball rolling for paper work on my AISCH.

The second type of formal community assistance sought by the informants was alternative community placements. Three of the informants required these placements because they were unable to return to their previous living accommodations. In order for these informants to obtain these placements two groups of experts had to approve the informants' candidacy: hospital professionals and community placement operators.

The hospital's professionals referred the informants to community placements. As previously indicated, the informants had a choice regarding placement in alternative living arrangements; however, access to the hospital's social workers was limited because of these professionals' caseloads:

> We tried various placement programs, and seeing as the social worker is dealing with thirty to sixty other people at the same time, I have to wait my turn.

Once the informant was approved for community placement the operators of these community residences assessed the informant's suitability for placement. Although the hospital's professionals assessed the informants' readiness for placement, frequently the community placement professionals did not concur with their assessments. Two of the informants were rejected as placement candidates; the third informant was conditionally accepted. One informant who was rejected was advised by the community placement operators to reapply for placement in one month:

> They said come back in a month. We're not turning you down permanently. We just feel that you are not ready yet, and we want you to come back in a month and reapply.

The operators of another community residence imposed conditions on the informant before they would accept him:

> I, ah, I'm happy to go there, but I wasn't, I didn't want to go on their arrangements. They wanted me to come there in a matter of three or four [four LOAs] and at the first of December move in.

The Decision to Promote Patients
Was the Prerogative of Experts

The informants' discharge from the hospital depended on their attending physicians; consequently, the act of discharge was an action performed by others:

> Actually if they said a few days and that was a week ago, it should have been a couple of days ago. . . . I don't think they're in any rush to let me go.

> Just the fact that she [physician] wouldn't, you know, she wouldn't let me go, or nothing like that, you know. She wouldn't, she was being obstinate with me and stuff like that. Especially after I saw that other doctor, um, you know. She . . . really wanted me to stick around for awhile.

> Every time I say within two to three weeks, it ends up being a month later. So . . . I believe them when they come up to me one day and say, "____, pack your bags. We're going to ____."

> It's like the donkey and the carrot. Holding the discharge in front of my nose, and then, the last minute snatching it away.

All of the informants in this study were voluntary patients, and they were aware of their legal right to leave the hospital:

> And now that I got the voluntary status, I know that I have the choice to leave. I can leave.

> Of course, I could, I could leave right now. I could just pack my things and say, "I'm going." There's nothing they could do about it.

Although limited personal resources prohibited the informants from discharging themselves against medical advice, even when alternative community resources were obtained, they still sought a professional discharge. The informants' desire for a professional promotion was related to their perception of the professionals' area of expertise.

Experts' Assessment of Readiness for Promotion

The hospital's experts evaluated the informants' mental well-being and formed authoritative judgments regarding their readiness to return to the community:

> Well, the doctor, Dr. ____, didn't believe me. She . . . believed that I was still too sick to go out into the community.

> They've decided that I'm more coherent in my speech. I'm not deluded, or I have very few delusions. Things that aren't gonna make me incompatible with the people around me or on the outside.

Also, it was important to the informants who assessed themselves ready to return to the community to obtain professional approval:

> By going through, going through the ropes, to use a cliché, I feel more comfortable having the approval of somebody professional saying, "Yes ____, you're ready to leave."

For these informants, professional consent to leave the hospital represented professional confirmation of their sanity:

> It will mean that I am certifiably sane . . . and I can say to somebody, if somebody says to me, "Ah, you're crazy," I can say, "No, I'm not. I've got a piece of paper to prove it."

> Well, that's a good feeling [to get discharged]. At least you know you're half sane anyway. . . . Well, [pause], you never know. There could be something wrong, like you watch on TV all the time.

The informant who felt he was not ready to return to the community was uncertain about the meaning of being discharged from hospital.

When asked what discharge meant to him, he said, "I don't know. I'm not around any of my relatives."

Participants Were Compliant With Treatment They Considered Nontherapeutic

The informants said they complied with all aspects of their hospital care, regardless of the perceived therapeutic value of specific interventions. They complied with therapies they considered nontherapeutic because of their subordinate position within the organization and the accompanying dependency on the benevolence of experts:

> They told me, they told me the shots that were being taken. So I just . . . agreed with that and went peacefully, you know. I wasn't gonna put up too much of a fight, you know. . . . I could have, you know. I could have really raised hell, you know, around here, but there's no use in it, you know. There's no satisfaction out of it, you know. I don't get nothing out of it for raising hell, so I'll . . . just do what they tell me to do, you know. For once in my life, I'll listen to somebody, you know, rather than doing my own thing, you know. Yeah. . . . Ah, it would get me nowhere. It would just upset things, you know. Screw up the whole system and, you know, it's . . . not worth it.

One informant said he attended structured therapy sessions he perceived as nontherapeutic because "if I wanna get a place in the group home or approved home, I have to go through this course." Two of the informants felt their vocational programs had no therapeutic value, and compliance with authoritative directives accounted for their attendance:

> They send you to OT [occupational therapy] for one hour a day, you know, and you're suppose to work and stuff like that, you know. But I just . . . find little use in it, you know. I . . . don't like it. Maybe I'm a rebel. I don't know, but I don't like it one bit.

Only one informant felt his vocational program had any therapeutic value. He did not, however, believe these programs helped him develop work skills; instead, he felt they provided an environment for testing his ability to manage stressful situations:

> When I started working in the snack bar, I felt more competent about being around more other people, and being—putting myself in a social situation

> where the noise level and the conversation level was quite high—the potential for getting strained.

Although the informants in this study disliked institutional living, their overall evaluation of their hospital experience was not negative. The informants who had previous admissions to the institution were neutral about their hospital experience: "Oh well, it's not too bad [to be here]. I can think of worse places." Although one informant said his hospitalization had not helped him recover his mental well-being, he felt his treatment was exemplary:

> I can't . . . see any better way than doing it than the way they are doing it. Just exactly the way they are doing it. 'Cause they're coming as close as I think they'll ever come to problem solving. As far as I am concerned.

The two informants who experienced their first admission to the hospital evaluated their overall experience positively. In comparison to the treatment they received in community hospitals, both of these informants said the professionals were "caring," and the hospital offered the "best" treatment in Alberta:

> If you're sick and you need treatment, it's probably the best in Alberta or in western Canada. I'd say Alberta for sure seeing as I've been in a few hospitals around. If you want treatment, it's good for a certain amount of time.

From the informants' perspective, the primary function of the hospital was to ameliorate personal problems that hinder their functioning in the community; therefore, discharge was sought when the informants felt they were ready to return to the community or when they thought the treatment provided in the hospital was not helping them return to the community.

Pathways to Discharge: "Getting Out"

The informants in this study felt that discharge from the hospital was granted by the experts and they described three patterns of discharge behaviors: marking time, taking charge, and breaking out. The particular pattern of behavior demonstrated by the informants was contingent on two factors: self-assessment of readiness to return to the community

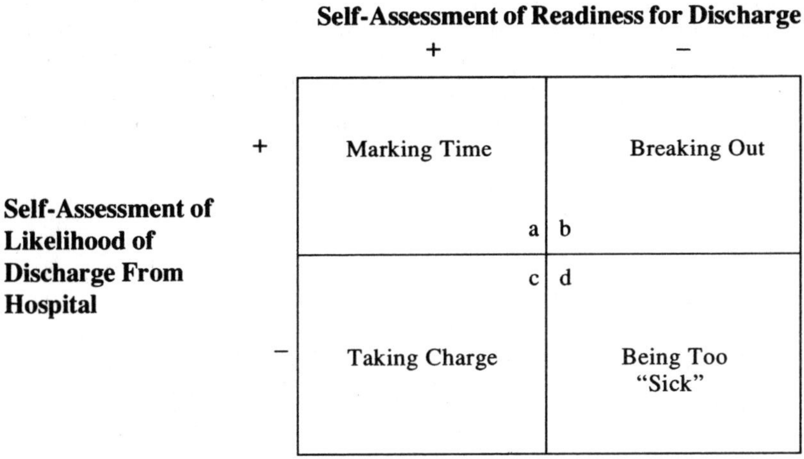

Self-Assessment of Readiness for Discharge
+
–
+
–
Self-Assessment of Likelihood of Discharge From Hospital
Marking Time
Breaking Out
Taking Charge
Being Too "Sick"
a
b
c
d

Figure 17.2. Pathways to Discharge: Patterns of Predischarge Behavior.

and self-assessment of the likelihood of being discharged. Figure 17.2 illustrates the interaction between these conditions. Each of the four cells in the diagram describes constellations of behaviors displayed by the informants in this study. As the conditions determining the behavioral pattern vary, there is an accompanying change in the "getting out" behavior. If there is variation in the conditions affecting his discharge, one informant can be classified as fitting into more than one cell.

MARKING TIME

For the informants in this study, marking time meant enduring continued hospitalization: "I'll . . . make the best of it. I'll just do my thing, and just wait. I'm just doing time right now." This pattern of behavior was present when the informants felt they were ready to return to the community and when they felt there was a good chance of being discharged. The informants attributed marking time to the lack of available alternatives in the community, and they characterized their predischarge behavior as "doing time."

Attributing Inpatient Status to a Lack of Available Alternatives

The informants who were marking time felt they were ready to return to the community, and they said their continued inpatient status was a result of their lack of personal resources necessary for community living:

> I feel like, you know, I don't have any other place to go right now, so you know, it's . . . peaches and cream as far as I'm concerned, you know, for . . . the time being.

> Ah, [pause] I'm in a hurry if they got some money that I can live on. . . . I don't have anything to live on unless they are going to give me a pension.

Characterizing Predischarge Behavior as "Doing Time"

When the informants exhibited marking time behavior they felt their continued hospitalization was nontherapeutic because they had regained their mental well-being. From this perspective the informants considered the hospital a temporary accommodation until they could obtain a community placement:

> I feel it in my soul, you know. I don't need to stay here any longer. I'm just bumming off the government right now, you know, waiting so. . . . It's a joke. It's a total joke. I . . . there's nothing more that they can do for me, you know. Like, I'm just doing time, that's all I'm doing.

> I'm just waiting for placement.

Also, the informants felt bored and frustrated waiting for community placement:

> I've been waiting for almost two months, I'd say. So . . . it gets rather impatient, you know. I get bored to tears sometimes here, you know. But I just try to look for things to do and go down to the snack bar and have coffee and stuff like that when I can. And see girls and socialize a bit, and that's about it.

> I've been waiting for placement for the last two and a half months. . . . It's frustrating. It's like waiting for a big pay-off in a lottery.

BREAKING OUT

The informants said breaking out of hospital was returning prematurely to the community: "I wanted to get the hell out of this hospital. That's what I want." This pattern of "getting out" behavior occurred when the informants felt they were not ready to return to the community and had a good chance of getting discharged. Although this situation seems improbable, the informants did discuss this behavioral pattern. The breaking out behavior occurred when the informants felt their treatment was futile, and when this happened they had an impulsive desire to leave the hospital.

Characterizing Continued Inpatient Status as Futile in Terms of Expected Outcome

The informants who manifested breaking out behaviors felt that they were not ready to return to the community and that their treatment was not helping them recover their mental well-being:

> I have to get hold of my folks and tell them that I'm coming up that way and then head, maybe head west. Because, um . . . I can't seem to get it together here.

> I get very terrified as you can notice. Unless that's what basically I am. I'm just terrified of this place. . . . I'm terrified of what it can do to me and where it can take me. . . . Um, the fact that it's . . . gonna take me nowhere.

Impulsively Proposing to Leave the Hospital

The informants who had an impulsive desire to leave the hospital said their present hospital stay was nontherapeutic. The rationale for this judgment was their perception that their treatment was not improving their mental well-being; therefore, the primary reason for seeking discharge was to get away from the hospital. These informants impulsively proposed leaving the hospital without considering their expected proficiency in managing in the community or the availability of placement:

> The more I think about it, the more I think I should just pack up and leave right now.
>
> Yeah, we should take off tonight, and just go there for awhile.
>
> I have to get a hold of my folks and tell that I'm coming up that way and then head, maybe head west.

TAKING CHARGE

When the informants displayed taking charge behavior, they were demonstrating their readiness to leave hospital:

> When I first got turn[ed] down for the group home, and then it became a real battle. . . . Well, I had to prove myself that I was ready to be discharged. And, ah, [pause] that's about it. I just had to prove that I was ready, capable of surviving on my own.

This pattern of "getting out" behavior was evident when the informants assessed themselves ready for discharge and felt there was little chance of being discharged. The informants attributed taking charge behavior to the professionals' unwillingness to authorize their discharge, and they characterized this behavior as convincing professionals of their readiness to be discharged.

Attributing Present Inpatient Status to Professionals' Unwillingness to Authorize Discharge

The informants who exhibited taking charge behavior felt they were ready to return to the community. They attributed their present hospitalization to the professionals' refusal to discharge them:

> I felt that they were just playing games and trying to keep me in here as long as possible. . . . I think they are just grasping at straws to keep me in here.
>
> I felt pissed off because she's [physician] looking at me as if I'm sick and I have a psychiatric problem, and I don't. I'm totally sane. . . . I swear to God on my mother's grave. I'm totally sane. There's nothing wrong with me, not a thing. There's no reason why I should stay here any longer.

Characterizing Behavior as "Convincing" Professionals of Readiness for Discharge

The basis for the difference between the informants' and the professionals' assessments of the informants' readiness for discharge centered on disagreement regarding the criteria for assessment. The informants felt that their readiness to leave the hospital should be evaluated on the basis of continued evidence of the behaviors that precipitated their admissions, regardless of the presence or absence of other abnormal symptoms:

> I'm not gonna OD, that's, it's not the point of the voices. It's the point of, of me ODing all the time and taking too many drugs, and stuff like that. And I'm not gonna do that no more because I feel good. There's no reason why.

> Ah, probably on my admission file, there's some strange things about my sexual nature and . . . what I was hearing at the time. [pause] I was hypnotized. . . . They're holding it against me.

Because the informants believed the major problem behaviors had been eradicated, they felt they were ready for discharge.

In order to institute behaviors intended to convince professionals of their readiness for discharge, the informants identified behaviors they thought the professionals used as criteria for assessing readiness for discharge. They then initiated these behaviors with the intention of convincing professionals of their readiness for discharge. The informants who exhibited taking charge behaviors were also those informants who described intrusive experiences.

The first of these informants felt that the professionals' criteria for his readiness to be discharged was his demonstrated ability to control his anger: "I think it was anger control—is the main thing that they are concerned about." His anger was associated with the threatening and punitive intrusive experiences which he attributed to others in his immediate environment. Although this informant did not think his reaction to these intrusions was inappropriate, he described purposefully controlling this reaction in order to prove his readiness to be discharged:

> In my case, I have to play a kitten and take shit and abuse from everybody. . . . In my case, that's like taking away the wings off an airplane. . . . In the—in the fact that I don't use it for aggression, I use it for self-defense.

> I was quiet and kept to myself—didn't lash out in anger at anybody. At least when I did, I made peace afterwards, which is exactly what I did today. He still thinks he's got one up on me, but I'm laughing inside at him anyway. It's a children's game.

The second informant believed that his attending physician wanted his "voices stopped" prior to his discharge: "They wanted to get those stopped." He initiated behaviors to convince his physician this had occurred:

> By just talking to him patiently and, um, telling him that, um, I wasn't hearing voices anymore. So I . . . told a little white lie, but I don't . . . need to be in hospital any longer. . . . Well . . . I just told them that just because they're asking me about my voices and, you know, I . . . don't hear them all the time anymore, you know. Um . . . just once in awhile I hear them, and they don't preoccupy me, so there's no problem there, you know.

Although the behaviors described by these informants were different, the intended effect was the same, that is, to convince the professionals of their readiness to be discharged.

Both of these informants avoided situations in which they would have to address the source of their psychological experiences:

> And she [physician] wouldn't believe me that there's a transmitter in my room, so I just refused to talk to her after awhile, you know.

When the second informant was told by professionals he was hallucinating, he said, "I just kept my mouth shut and grin and bear it." Following the physicians' authorization for their discharge, both of these informants said their attending physicians were on their side:

> I feel great now that Dr. ____ has realized I'm no longer a danger to myself or society. So she's on my side now.

> He's [physician] . . . basically looked at it in my . . . eyes and seen that I'm ready to go, so . . . I think he's carrying through with it, eh?

The fourth cell in figure 17.2 (Cell *d*) consists of patients who do not assess themselves as ready for discharge and do not consider it likely that they will be discharged. They were considered too sick, and they were excluded from the study. Ideally, during the course of recovery, patients move from Cell *d* to Cell *a* prior to leaving the hospital; however, the informants in this study moved from Cell *a* to Cell *c* when disagreements emerged between them and the hospital professionals regarding their readiness to leave the hospital. These disagreements were precipitated by rejection of candidacy for placement in alternative living accommodations.

To the informants in this study, being in the hospital was comparable to being in an army boot camp. In addition to organizational and structural similarities the primary function of both institutions is to prepare its service recipients for roles autonomous from institutional roles. The informants in this study sought discharge from the hospital when they assessed themselves ready to return to the community or when they felt their hospital treatment was not helping them return to the community. When the informants wished to attain a discharge from the hospital they displayed three types of getting out behaviors: marking time, breaking out, and taking charge.

Conclusion

All of the informants recalled pleasant experiences from their extended past. Moreover, they described this past as discontinuous from their preadmission past, which began with their first contact with formal mental health care. The preadmission past is an extended period of *not making it* in the community, culminating with their present admissions.

The actual and anticipated life experiences of the informants are schematically presented in Figure 17.3. The first row of circles represents the life experiences of the informants who assessed themselves ready to return to the community. These informants were *anticipating mastery* of their community environments and characterized their immediate future as "new beginnings." Their life experiences, therefore, can be depicted as progressing linearly.

The second set of circles (Figure 17.3) represents the life experiences of the informant who did not assess himself ready to return to the community. This informant characterized his immediate future as a continuation of the preadmission "struggle to make it," and he predicted the need for future hospitalizations. Because he anticipated eventual

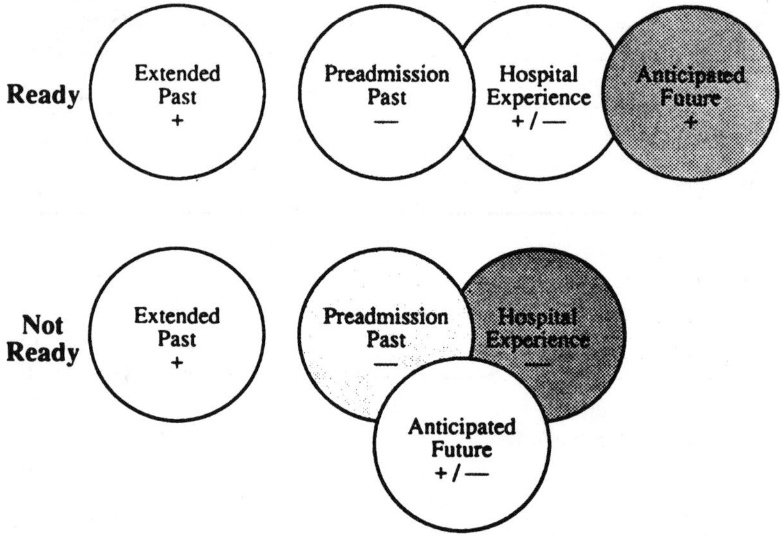

Figure 17.3. Actual and Anticipated Life Experiences of Informants.

acquisition of productive community roles, the circle representing his anticipated future is not obliterated by circles representing present hospital and preadmission experiences.

BECOMING ORDINARY

The core explanatory variable of the results was *becoming ordinary*. A process labeled *becoming ordinary* outwardly appeared to be paradoxical. Adults are not generally viewed as striving for ordinariness; rather, adults usually move toward outstanding life careers. When viewed from the informants' frame of reference, however, this concept lost much of its paradoxical impact. The informants' frame of reference was their preadmission experiences and all of them described themselves as failures during this extended time period because they were *not making it* in the community. Their admission to a hospital removed them from overwhelming community environments.

At predischarge all of the informants aspired to become self-supporting and independent; however, they did not all anticipate immediate progress toward *becoming ordinary*. The predischarge informants who were

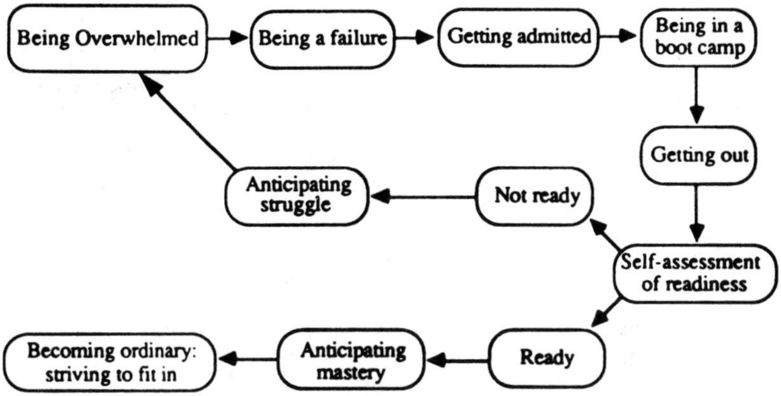

Figure 17.4. Flow Chart Depicting the Process of "Becoming Ordinary".

anticipating mastery of their communities were also anticipating immediate acquisition of productive community roles. From their perspective, they were *becoming ordinary*. The informant who was anticipating continuation of his preadmission struggle to *make it* in the community was not anticipating immediate progress toward *becoming ordinary*. Self-assessment of unreadiness to return to the community was accompanied by anticipated inability to manage in the community and the prediction of the need for future hospitalizations. Figure 17.4 schematically represents the process of *becoming ordinary*.

The concept *becoming ordinary* embodied the informants' perceptions of their anticipated future as well as their past experience and subsequently it was superordinate to all other concepts. To recapitulate, informants who characterized themselves as past failures in the community were anticipating assuming *ordinary* roles in the community. The informants in this study felt that *becoming ordinary* meant becoming normal, productive community members.

Note

1. The sample consisted of four males in their twenties and thirties, three of whom had been diagnosed with paranoid schizophrenia (the fourth participant was diagnosed with residual schizophrenia). All of the informants had lengthy histories of mental illness ranging from 3 to 15 years, were hospitalized at the time of the study, and were awaiting discharge. Only one of the informants had admitted himself to the psychiatric care facility

voluntarily. Each informant was interviewed a total of four to six times. Individuals with schizophrenia typically display less complex ideas, exhibit frequent speech errors, and tend to repeat themselves. For these reasons, the interview techniques typically used by grounded theorists were modified by the researcher to include frequent verbal probing and direct leading questions. All of the probes and direct questions, however, were grounded in previously obtained data.

References

Bland, R. C. (1984). Long term mental illness in Canada: An epidemiological perspective on schizophrenia and affective disorders. *Canadian Journal of Psychiatry, 29,* 242-246.

Bland, R. C., Parker, J. H., & Orn, H. (1976). Prognosis in schizophrenia: A ten-year follow-up of first admissions. *Archives of General Psychiatry, 33,* 949-954.

Bland, R. C., Parker, J. H., & Orn, H. (1978). Prognosis in schizophrenia: Prognostic predictors and outcome. *Archives of General Psychiatry, 35,* 72-77.

Cottman, S. B., & Mezey, A. G. (1976). Community care and the prognosis of schizophrenia. *Acta Psychiatrica Scandinavica, 53,* 95-104.

Green, R. S. (1984). Why schizophrenic patients should be told their diagnosis. *Hospital and Community Psychiatry, 35*(1), 76-77.

18

The Emotional Experience of Breast Expression

JANICE M. MORSE
JOAN L. BOTTORFF

Abstract: Observation of 61 successful lactating mothers showed that while some mothers were able to express their breasts easily, other could not. Open-ended, interactive interviews on the process and problems of expressing were conducted. Data analysis, using grounded theory methods, revealed that expressing had a different meaning to the two groups of mothers. Those mothers who perceived expressing as mechanical and messy experienced feelings of embarrassment and awkwardness; These feelings interfered with let-down when expressing, and mothers became total breastfeeders or used mixed feeding without expressing. Mothers who expressed their breasts easily had a relaxed attitude toward expressing; The milk obtained increased their confidence in nursing. The knowledge that their infant was receiving breastmilk even in their absence was considered to be the "door to freedom."

> . . . The information that is made available is so scientific . . . you forget the emotion that is involved with something like this.
>
> *Subject 61, Interview 9*

AUTHORS' NOTE: This research was supported by the Alberta Foundation of Nursing Research, the University Research Awards Committee, University of Alberta, Edmonton, and in part by the National Health Research and Development Program through a National Health Research Scholar Award to Janice Morse. We would like to acknowledge the assistance of Karen Williams and Jeannette Boman with interviewing, Carolynne Tonn for transcription, and Robert Morse for designing a computer program for qualitative analysis. This chapter originally appeared in Morse, J. M., & Bottorff, J. L. (1988). The emotional experience of breast expression. *Journal of Nurse-Midwifery, 33*(4), 165-170. Reprinted with permission.

Teaching mothers about expressing their breasts is a routine part of prenatal education, and most women are shown how to express their breasts prior to discharge from hospital. However, despite the common use of such a technique, there is a remarkable absence of literature about expressing. The few articles that have been located addressed the mechanics of breast expression[1-3] or evaluated the various types of manual or mechanical breast pumps.[4-7] Other articles addressed such aspects as the nutritional value of expressed breast milk,[8] the methods of collection and storage for milk banks,[9,10] or the benefits of feeding expressed breast milk to premature or sick infants.[11,12]

These articles are largely prescriptive. Although mothers in the clinical setting have reported ambivalent or strongly negative feelings about expressing, frustration and pain at not being successful at expressing, or appeared complacent and confident with the ease of expressing and the freedom that it brings, affective reports on the experience of expressing could not be located. The purpose of this research is to examine the responses of mothers about expressing and their attitudes toward, and their methods of managing, breast expression.

Methods

SAMPLE AND DATA COLLECTION

This research is part of a larger longitudinal study investigating the experience of breastfeeding mothers who return to work. Monthly telephone interviews with 61 breastfeeding mothers were conducted, commencing within the first two months of the infant's birth. A prenatal interview was included for eight mothers. The ages of mothers participating in the study ranged from 19-45 years (mean, 29.8 *SD* 4.02). Twenty six of the mothers were primiparas. All 35 multipara mothers had previously breastfed. Their total breastfeeding experience ranged from 0.5-40 months (mean, 9.5 months). Those in the sample were highly educated. Only 5% of the sample had not completed high school, while over 60% had completed undergraduate degrees or diplomas and 10% had completed post-graduate degrees.

Data related to expressing were collected during telephone interviews using open-ended questions. The following questions guided this section of the interviews: What are the experiences of mothers who express? What feelings and attitudes are evoked by expressing? How do mothers learn to express? All interviews were tape-recorded and transcribed.

DATA ANALYSIS

Using the grounded theory approach, the researcher collects and analyzes data simultaneously in an attempt to discover the dominant processes with a particular experience. The understanding that emerges from the research is, therefore, an outcome of the interaction that occurs between the researcher and the phenomenon under study.

In this project, the first major task undertaken was that of coding categories. Several strategies used were: asking questions of researchers or of the data (e.g., What is going on here? What is significant?), the data were read line by line and paragraph by paragraph to identify specific incidents or facts (e.g., "I never thought it [expressing] was the greatest fun thing you could ever think of. . . . but it's something that you really should be doing in certain circumstances"), and sorting first level codes into categories that represent concepts or abstractions of the data.[13,14] For example, the above attitude, in addition to others, yielded three categories: tolerating the objectionable, loosening the ties, and proving the milk is there.

Results

The results were sorted into four major categories, and from these categories a model illustrating the inability of some mothers to express and a model illustrating the process of successful expressing were developed. The categories were acquiring the skill, justifying one's choice, tolerating the objectionable, and expressing successfully.

ACQUIRING THE SKILL

"Try it and hope to God!"

Much to the surprise of new mothers, the ability to express was not automatic, reflexive nor easy. Mothers expected to be able to express milk like "turning on a tap", to be able to will the milk to come down and flow, and were astonished and disappointed when this did not occur. As one mother stated:

> Any time you talk to anybody who expresses milk they'll never say, "Oh, it hurts like crazy" or "Oh, you're going to feel funny doing it." They just

say that they do it and it's great and that's it. So when you fail at it you feel like: " . . . I don't know how to do this. I'll never learn or something must be wrong with me." (Ss 55 Int 15)

In spite of the fact that many mothers had been shown how to express or had read about expressing in lay literature, they found the information was little help when actually attempting to do it themselves. Instead, mothers found that it was necessary to learn through trial and error in a relaxed situation. For example, experimenting in the bathtub was more likely to be successful than following technical directives.

I learned how to express by hand. One of those days that I was engorged, I was sitting in the bathtub. . . . and I thought, well, I don't have my pump here and I hate doing that pump. I just hate it. So I thought I don't want to be uncomfortable and the solution was right there, so I just started expressing . . . , its sort of like milking a cow, I guess . . . We're kind of cut off from our bodies. . . . people frown on . . . experimenting that way. But I think that's really the key because it's probably different for every woman. And you just have to fiddle around a bit. (Ss 73 Int 29)

When learning to express by hand, mothers explained that it was necessary to learn where to place one's fingers in order to feel the ducts, how to stimulate let-down, how much pressure to apply, and how to obtain a rhythm of stroking that would enable milk to flow in a steady stream. When using a breast pump, the control of pressure was important. Initially, before the milk came down, a gentle low pressure should be used to stimulate the breast, and then pressure increased when the milk starts to flow.

Mothers stressed that instructions for one mother did not necessarily work for all. The ways that mothers used their hands to milk the ducts was highly individualized, and some suggested that the location of the ducts appeared different for each woman. Other mothers suggested that the ease of expressing was related to the strength of the let-down and whether or not the breasts leaked. Expressing was considered something to "get used to" and that was learned by doing. Successful expressing took time, patience and practice.

Once you get the hang of it and get the pumping action, it seems to flow easier. . . . I needed the practice. The first time I thought, "Oh no, this isn't easy at all." . . . My girlfriend said she needed practice too, so she told me to keep it up and try it again and again. She said, "By about the fourth or

> fifth time you'll get the hang of it." It does become easier cause you get used to it. . . . (Ss 12 Int 5)

It is interesting to note that although mothers felt comfortable enough to ask experienced friends about expressing, most tried to learn on their own in a private situation behind closed doors. Nevertheless, the descriptions by friends were reported to be more useful than the descriptions and illustrations in breastfeeding books. However, many mothers experienced pain and/or bruising of the nipples by attempting to express and were angry that they had not been told that might happen. Further, they were afraid that the pain was an indication they were expressing incorrectly and damaging their breasts.

In general, husbands were not involved in this part of the breastfeeding process, although a few husbands were permitted to observe and assist with interpreting the instruction manuals. Expressing was considered a more private activity than nursing the infant. Some mothers were reluctant to express in front of others, even their own small children.

> I was uncomfortable—I found I would lock myself in the bathroom or in the bedroom when my son was around, or my husband. . . . It was a very private thing, but not a private thing I was comfortable with even by myself. (Ss 84 Int 12)

> The other day we had company and I wanted to watch the show they were watching. So I sat up in the kitchen, pumping, with a blanket over me. "Oh gross!" I said. "Don't turn around." . . . I felt gross. . . . The pumping doesn't, but pumping with people there! You know nursing with people there doesn't bug me at all. (Ss 68 Int 14)

One mother told of an experience where she was forced to express in the corner of a crowded washroom. Whereas the younger women were openly curious as to what she was doing, the older women were unsympathetic, condemning, shocked, and disgusted at her openness.

Mothers fell into four categories according to the amount of practice they engaged in and the amount of information they sought as shown in Figure 18.1. The first were those who followed directions prescriptively and practiced conscientiously (cell a). Other mothers used the information to attempt to express (cell b). If this was successful, then they continued expressing; if not, they stopped. Mothers who repeatedly practiced (cell c) and reported that "the books do not seem to make any sense," thought that one could only learn to express by doing. These mothers were sometimes successful. In the last cell (cell d) were those mothers who neither practiced nor used information and would try it once and give up. Note that mothers in both cells, b and d try to express to see what will happen. The difference is in their use of instructional manuals.

JUSTIFYING ONE'S CHOICE

Given that expressing was such a difficult and sometimes painful activity, we asked mothers why they expressed. Three of the reasons were maternally motivated: breast engorgement resulting in pain and unwanted leaking, the leaking of one breast while nursing on the other, and the need for reassurance that milk was actually there.

Other reasons were for the benefit of the infant, that is, to remove contaminated milk, to provide breast milk during occasional absences of the mother, to stimulate production in the event of inadequate milk supply, to teach the infant how to suck an artificial nipple, or to avoid giving formula to the baby.

The last reasons, to involve the father in the feeding process and to provide an alternate method of feeding the infant during unexpected absences, were for the benefit of both parents. The method of expression and whether the milk was saved or discarded were different depending on the reasons for expressing.

Maternal reasons for not expressing related to lack of time due to other children to care for or lack of breaks at work, the ease of giving formula, lack of privacy and facilities, and feeling that expressing was an impossible, unnatural and mechanical task. For some expressing was unnecessary as they did not feel breast discomfort or leaking. Reasons that affected the infant were that expressing was considered to be "stealing from the baby" or was unnecessary as it did not harm the infant to take a bottle of formula.

ATTITUDES TOWARD EXPRESSING

Tolerating the Objectionable

Although mothers enjoyed nursing their infants, many mothers described expressing as a "necessary evil". It was considered "a drag to sit down and pump", and mothers felt they were "a slave to the pump". Mothers reported that it consumed energy, was a mechanical task

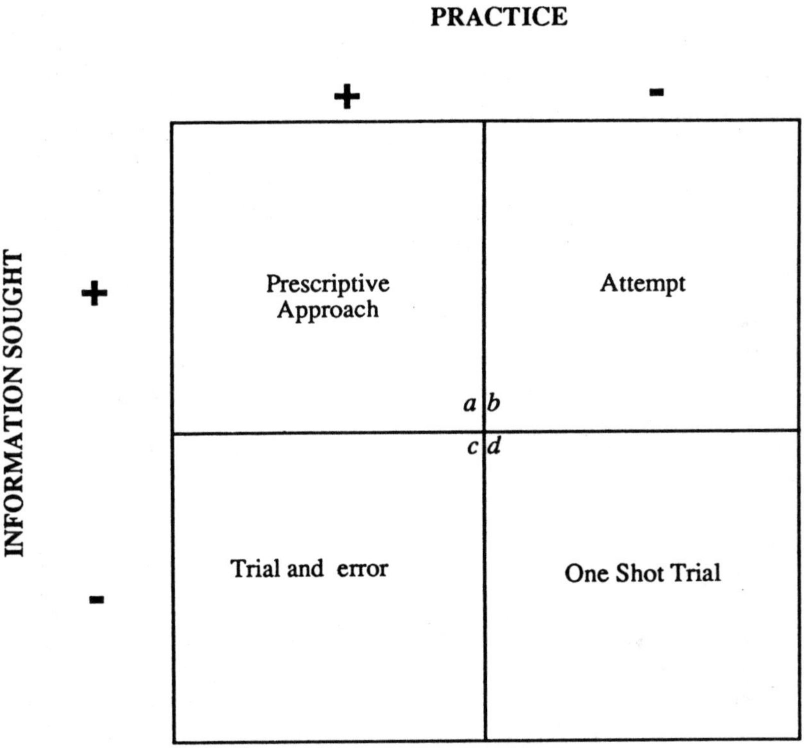

Figure 18.1. The Approaches to Learning to Express.

without pleasure and made breastfeeding three times as long. Nevertheless, they continued to express their breasts, reporting that it was something that had to be done.

Many mothers strongly expressed embarrassment and discomfort in expressing. They stated that it made them feel "like a cow".

> An uncle of mine had a dairy farm. That's what I feel like, I feel like a cow, on one of those . . . electric pumps on the farm and I sit there and laugh myself silly if I'm doing this. And I also think . . . that it's terribly unerotic too. (Ss 69 Int 2)

> I think there's a real pleasure involved in actually feeding the baby. Cause he's there and . . . you're holding him and it's obviously nursing, I mean

> you can see it nursing . . . But, expressing milk is just mechanical. You know, it makes me feel like I'm a cow. (Ss 73 Int 21)

This feeling of embarrassment was relieved somewhat with humor and gentle teasing. One mother reported that her husband was present while she first attempted to express:

> When I was first shown how to use the breast pump in the hospital, my husband was visiting. The nurse brought this machine in and pulled the curtain around. He was really laughing and he just said "Say moo!" . . . [laughter] . . . (Ss 3 Int 3)

The third aspect of this category was anger in one's inability to express adequate amounts of milk. Mothers said, "I know it's there but it won't come out." The frustration of repeatedly trying to express milk frequently resulted in bruised and painful breasts.

Loosening the ties. Despite these objectionable aspects, some mothers continued to practice expressing. The major perceived advantage was the freedom that expressing provided. Mothers could leave their infants with the knowledge that the infant would not be screaming.

> By expressing the milk, I could be late for a feeding, I could be absent at a feeding. I could work. My basic diet didn't change. If I could express, I didn't have to go through breast engorgement. . . . It was just a door to freedom. (Ss 61 Int 22)

As the infant received breast milk rather than formula, mothers were not afraid that the infant would become ill or allergic, and this countered the guilt they felt being absent. Thus, mothers who expressed did not feel as tied down and it appeared to be a trade-off between the inconvenience of expressing and the convenience of breastfeeding.

Proving the milk is there. Those mothers who could express appeared calmer and more confident than those who could not. Mothers used the measure of expressed milk as an indicator of the success of lactation.

> I like to be able to do it. I feel it really increases my confidence with nursing her to be able to express it, to have it on hand, to know I'm doing it right. . . . If I can't express it, I probably don't have enough for her either. It's

> like, you know, you have lots if you have leftovers at supper. If everything is cleaned up, you are sure you didn't cook enough. (Ss 61 Int 5)

Some mothers also indicated that their ability to express was satisfying in itself. Achieving the goal of learning to express increased their self-esteem as a mother.

> That pump is really quite comfortable . . . now that I have the proper hang of it anyway. I wouldn't use it daily, but every now and then. At least I feel good I can do something, that she'll take when I'm gone. I don't have to worry about it. (Ss 12 Int 10)

On the other hand, those who could not express considered themselves somewhat less than "good" mothers as they were forced to leave the infant formula in their absence or constantly be available to nurse the infant. The lack of evidence of breast milk also endorsed the mother's fears that they might not indeed have enough breast milk.

THE PROCESS OF FAILURE

Synthesizing the information of mothers who were unable to express revealed an interesting process (see Figure 18.2). The mother's feelings that expressing was sticky, messy, painful, ugly and mechanical led to feelings of self-disgust about the animal-like methods of removing the milk, akin to milking the cow. This feeling resulted in mothers resorting to hiding in the toilet and other private places, while expressing. The stress led to mothers being tense, awkward, and "reduced to tears" when expressing, so that the let-down reflex was also suppressed. The inability to express fed a sense of inadequacy, as mothers now had "concrete proof" that their milk supply was inadequate. Mothers in this group responded in two ways: the first was to become a total breastfeeder, available at all times to the infant, and the second was to mix feed the infant, combining formula with breastfeeding and letting the breasts adjust if feedings were missed.

THE PROCESS OF SUCCESS

In contrast, mothers who expressed easily were confident and relaxed. Because they felt comfortable with themselves and with the idea of expressing, they practiced and expressed quantities of milk quickly.

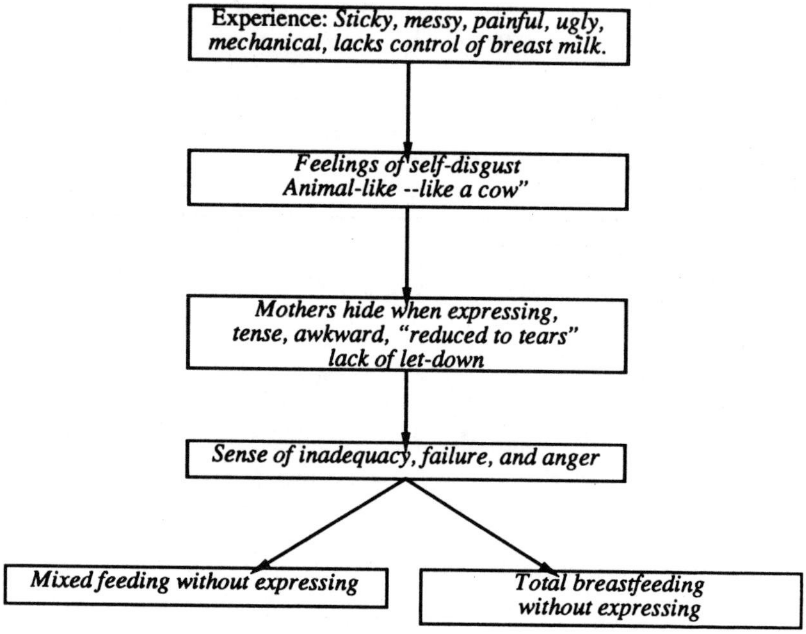

Figure 18.2. The Process of Failure to Express.

These mothers were less concerned about the quantity of milk expressed and frequently pooled small amounts until enough for a feed was obtained. This success increased mothers' self-confidence and facilitated their ability to express.

When comparing and contrasting the qualities of mothers with either a positive or negative attitude toward expressing with their ability to express, four types of breastfeeding mothers were identified. First, mothers with both positive attitudes toward expressing and the ability to express were confident and capable. For them, expressing was an essential part of breastfeeding bringing additional rewards and gratifications.

Some mothers had the ability to express, but resented the activity. They continued to express despite time constraints and other barriers. For example, even though some mothers "hated the pump" or were uncomfortable with the whole notion of expressing their breasts, they continued to do so. The pain of engorgement or the fact that their infants

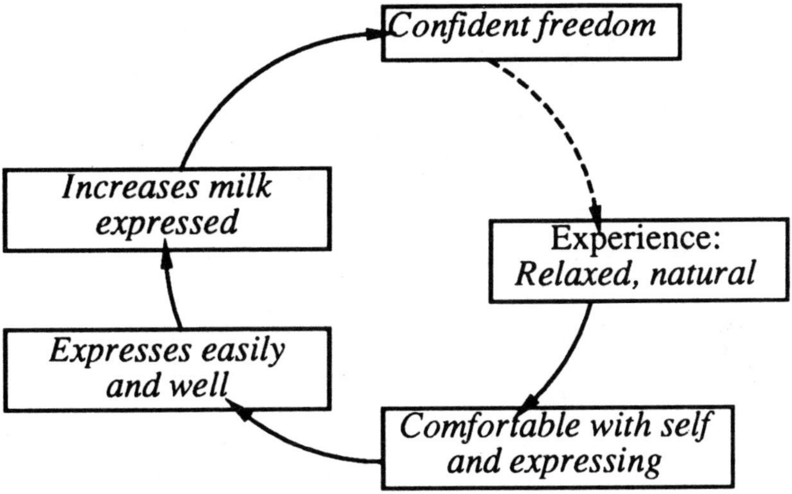

Figure 18.3. The Process of Successful Expression.

refused formula and would only accept breast milk while they were away provided little choice.

The experience of expressing heightened feelings of inadequacy for the third group of mothers who were unable to express, but perceived it as an important aspect of breastfeeding. To overcome the accompanying feelings of guilt, these mothers resorted to being totally accessible to the infant for nursing at all times.

The last group of mothers rationalized their inability to express milk by espousing the practicality and accepting the introduction of mixed feeding as "no risk" to infant health. Because these mothers had no desire to express, the ability to express was inconsequential and they did not feel guilty about giving their infant formula when they were away from their infants. During these short absences, they just allowed their breasts to adjust to the decreased demand for milk. In this way, mothers in this group who were away from their infants on a regular basis established a pattern of feeding described elsewhere[15,16] as minimal or part-time breastfeeding.

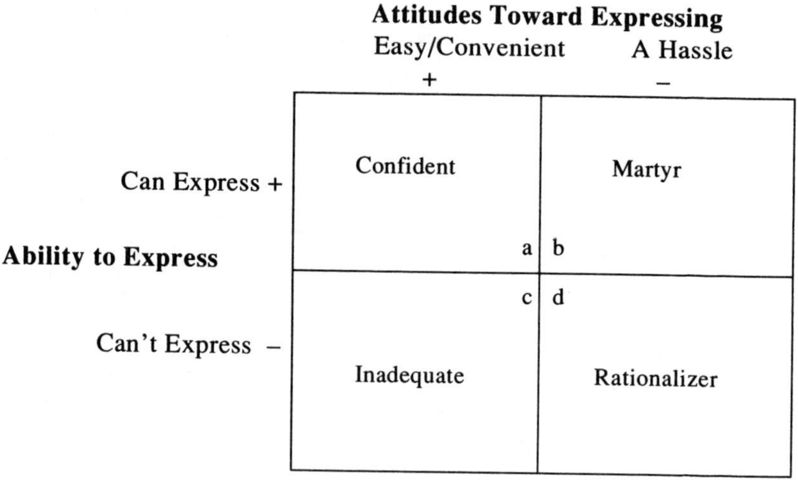

Figure 18.4. Attitudes Toward Expressing and the Ability to Express.

Discussion

IMPLICATIONS FOR PRACTICE

The models explicating success and failure with expressing have important implications for pre- and postnatal programs. If a negative attitude toward expressing is a part of a mother's value system prior to learning to express, then expecting her to express will increase feelings of self-disgust and set the mother up for an increased sense of inadequacy and failure. On the other hand, if a mother has a positive attitude toward expressing and has the potential to express, the teaching of expressing provides the mother "with the door to freedom". Further research is needed to test these models and to determine if teaching should be targeted to the latter group.

Understanding the complex feelings toward expressing and the experiential nature of learning to express has important implications for the way that expressing is taught. It would be helpful for mothers to have information available that was less prescriptive and included a discussion on feelings about expressing. We suggest that teaching encourage exploratory private practice and that the use of humor by the instructor will assist in reducing the embarrassment. Discussion of feelings associated with touching one's own breasts and the advantages of breast pumps for those who are uncomfortable with doing so, should also be included.

SUGGESTIONS FOR FURTHER RESEARCH

The first task in subsequent research is the development of a Likert scale to measure attitudes toward expressing. Items may be derived from the qualitative data, and once this scale has been validated and reliability established, the models of success and failure could be tested. A series of studies exploring the relationships between ability to express and attitudes toward expressing could be conducted. In addition, other variables, such as the mother's inability to let-down, could be correlated with attitudes so that the phenomenon of some mother's inability to express could be understood. The relationship between attitudes toward expressing and attitudes toward other aspects of sexuality and perceptions of body image could also be explored. Further research will be necessary to determine if such variables as age and parity are related to ability to express.

Notes

1. Behrman, R., Vaughan, V.: *Nelson Textbook of Pediatrics*, 12 ed. Philadelphia, W. B. Saunders, 1983.

2. Clements, C. J.: Expression of breast milk. *Midwives Chron* 9:234-237, 1982.

3. Neifert, M. R.: Infant problems in breast-feeding, in Neville, M. C., Neifert, M. R. (Ed.), *Lactation, Physiology, Nutrition and Breast-feeding*. New York, Plenum Press, pp 303-332, 1983.

4. Johnson, C. A.: An evaluation of breast pumps currently available on the American market. *Clin Pediatr* 22(1): 40-45 1983.

5. Boutte, C. A., Garza, C., Fraley, J. K., Stuff, J. E., O'Brian-Smith, E.: Comparison of hand- and electric-operated breast pumps. *Hum Nutr Appl Nutr* 39A:426-430, 1985.

6. Tibbetts, E., Cadwell, K.: Selecting the right breast pump. MCN 5:262-264, 1980.

7. Wennergren M., Wiqvist N., Wennergren G.: Manual breast pumps promote successful breast feeding. Acta Obstet Gynecol Scand 64:673-675, 1985.

8. Spencer, S. A., Hull, D.: Fat content of expressed breast milk: a case for quality control. *Br Med* J 282:99-100, 1982.

9. Tyson, J. E., Edwards, W. H., Rosenfeld, A. M., Beer, A. E.: Collection methods and contamination of bank milk. *Arch Dis Child* 57:396-398, 1982.

10. Garza, C., Johnson, C. A., Harrist, R., Nichols, B. L.: Effects of methods of collection and storage on nutrients in human milk. *Early Hum Dev* 6:295-303, 1982.

11. Stewart, D., Gaiser, C.: Supporting lactation when mothers and infants are separated. A clinical guideline for perinatal nurses. *Nurs Clin North Am* 13(1):47-61, 1978.

12. Choi, M. W.: Breast milk for infants who can't breast-feed. *Am J Nurs* 78: 852-855, 1978.

13. Hutchinson, S.: Chemically dependent nurses: The trajectory toward self-annihilation. *Nurs Res* 35:196-201.

14. Glaser, B. G.: *Theoretical Sensitivity*. Mill Valley, CA., The Sociology Press, 1978.

15. Morse, J. M., Harrison, M. J., Prowse, M.: Minimal breastfeeding. *J of Obstet Gynecol Neonatal Nurs* 15(4):333-338, 1987.

16. Morse, J. M., Harrison, M. J.: Patterns of mixed feeding. *Midwifery*, 4(1):19-23, 1988.

19

Negotiating Commitment and Involvement in the Nurse-Patient Relationship

JANICE M. MORSE

The relationship that is established between the nurse and the patient is the result of interplay or covert negotiations until a mutually satisfying relationship is reached. Depending on the duration of the contact between the nurse and the patient, the needs of the patient, the commitment of the nurse and the patient's willingness to trust the nurse, one of four types of mutual relationship will emerge: a clinical relationship, a therapeutic relationship, a connected relationship or an over-involved relationship. If the nurse is unwilling or unable to be committed to the patient, a unilateral relationship will develop, with the patient continuing to use manipulative or coercive behaviors, attempting to increase the nursing involvement in the relationship. If the patient is unwilling to trust the nurse and accept his or her illness situation, she or he will manifest "difficult" behaviors, be withdrawn or elope. The changing

AUTHOR'S NOTE: This research could not be completed without the assistance of the participants who agreed to be interviewed in their own time. J. Bottorff, M.Ed., M.N.; B. Cameron, M.N.; P. Donahue, B.Sc.N.; J. Greenhaulgh, M.N.; J. Jonson, M.N.; B. Lorencz, M.N.; K. Olson, M.Sc.; C. Park, M.Ed.; and S. Wilson, M.Ed., M.N. all served as research assistants for this project and their contribution is gratefully acknowledged. This research was supported by the Alberta Foundation for Nursing Research and by an MRC/NHRDP Research Scholar Award. This chapter originally appeared in Morse, J. M. (1991). Negotiating commitment and involvement in the nurse-patient relationship. *Journal of Advanced Nursing, 16,* 453-468. Reprinted with permission of Blackwell Scientific Publication, Ltd.

nature of the relationship, and the conditions and consequences of each type of relationship are discussed.

Introduction

Despite the vast amount of literature on care in the nurse-patient relationship, and the routine and compulsory course in all undergraduate programs on communication skills, information about the development and types of nurse-patient relationship is sparse. Most of the literature focuses on descriptions of techniques for responding therapeutically or non-therapeutically, examples of patient management (e.g., Magnan 1989) or discussions about the "problem" patient (such as the difficult, confused or violent patient) (see English & Morse 1988). Although there is some literature on the establishment and development of the nurse-patient relationship, an explanatory model for the development of various types of nurse-patient relationships has not thus far been developed.

Research in this area is important. Although included under the umbrella of the humanistic perspective, presently the content of communication courses is taught to student nurses in a static stimulus-response mode. For instance, students are taught how to respond to angry patients, fearful patients, defensive patients, and so forth, yet there is no theory about the process of the developing relationship available to students. Although there is some content about how students should introduce themselves and how to prepare the patient for the termination of the relationship, these instructions do not imbue the nurse with an in-depth notion of the meaning and significance of the relationship.

RESEARCH PROJECT

This research project addresses this area and describes the development of the nurse-patient relationship and the patient-nurse relationship and presents an explanatory model for describing the various types of relationship that occur. This project began as a study of gift-giving as a response to care in the patient-nurse relationship. During data analysis, it became clear that the gift was merely a *symbol* of the type of relationship developed; therefore, it was necessary to extend the theoretical sampling to obtain data on the development and types of nurse-patient relationship and on the parallel patient-nurse relationships.

Method

The study was conducted in a northern Canadian city. The sampling began with eight research assistants seeking participants from eight clinical areas with which the interviewers were not familiar. The areas were: psychiatry, medical-surgical, long-term care, home care/community, intensive care, pediatrics, maternity and palliative care. Later in the study, purposeful sampling was used to interview nurses who had also been patients and who were interviewed from the patients' perspective, nurse administrators, and nurses from special care areas, such as the operating room and the organ donor and transplant program. Twelve nurses were interviewed once, 26 were interviewed twice and six were interviewed three times, to give a total of 86 interviews. In addition, the emerging theory was validated with 59 secondary informants and clarified in the light of their perceptive questions.

Demographic characteristics of primary informants were as follows: 19 (43.2%) had a diploma in nursing, 20 (45.5%) a baccalaureate, four (9.0%) a masters and one (2.3%) a doctoral degree. The age of informants ranged from 25 to 65 years with a mean of 44.4 years. Eleven (25%) informants were single, 27 (61.4%) were married, four (9.0%) were divorced and two (4.6%) were widowed. The sample contained one male nurse.

The tape-recorded interviews were transcribed onto a microcomputer. Content analysis was conducted using a Macintosh® IIcx computer and Microsoftword® software (Morse 1991). By opening multiple windows simultaneously, the investigator was able to read the interview file in one window, use italics or bold text to emphasize significant phases or paragraphs, and insert comments or notes directly into the file. (This method of analysis was brought to my attention by Katharyn A. May, personal communication, 1989.) Significant segments of the interview were then copied and sorted into their respective category/file, which remained as an open window on the screen. Each segment copied was identified with a code indicating the interviewer, the subject's number, the interview number, and the page number on the original interview document. This method of analysis had the advantage of manual methods of sorting in that each category could be reviewed instantly without conducting a time-consuming and costly search, and it allowed the researcher to retain highlighted text and inserted notes (even during reprinting or further sorting), while at the same time utilizing the efficiency of computer sorting. Page breaks were inserted between each segment of text so that the printed pages could be easily handled if further resorting was necessary.

DATA ANALYSIS

Data were analysed using the techniques of grounded theory. The process of the nurses' and patients' experiences over the course of the relationship was identified and the characteristics of each type of relationship, including the causes or external or internal factors and circumstances pertaining to the interaction, were elicited. The core variable, "negotiating the relationship," was identified. In order to add insights into the types of relationship evident, an explanatory typology (2 × 2) was constructed by comparing the effects of the presence or absence of characteristics. The evolving model was then presented to the primary and secondary informants for verification, and modified according to their perceptive questions, comments, or suggestions.

Results

TYPES OF RELATIONSHIPS

The relationship between the nurse and the patient may be either mutual or unilateral, according to the outcome of covert interactive negotiations or implicit interplay between the two persons. Mutual relationships are of four broad types and depend upon certain circumstances (such as the length of time the nurse and the patient have together), the needs and desires of the nurse and the patient, and personality factors. The relationship proceeds from first contact, when the relationship is a more superficial clinical one, to the type that the nurse and the patient implicitly agree upon.

In unilateral relationships, there is asynchrony between the nurse and the patient, with one person unwilling or unable to develop the relationship to the level desired by the other. For example, if the nurse is not committed to the patient as a person or is "burnt out" and does not have the emotional energy to invest in the relationship, or if the patient desires a less clinical relationship, then the patient might resort to coercive or manipulative behaviors to try to entice the nurse to become more involved. On the other hand, if the patient is "difficult" and resents his or her illness, the hospitalization and/or the nurse, a committed nurse will persevere, waiting until the patient changes the undesirable behavior or until the nurse learns to tolerate the patient's idiosyncrasies. If the patient is psychotic or unconscious, then the relationship will remain at the clinical level. It is important to note that these relationships have little to do with technical competence. Competence is inherent in the definition and role of a nurse and is perceived as present by patients.

MUTUAL RELATIONSHIPS

The four main types of mutual relationship in ascending order of involvement and intensity are the clinical relationship, the therapeutic nurse-patient relationship, the connected relationship and the over-involved relationship. Each of these relationships and their characteristics, listed in Figure 19.1, will be described.

Clinical Relationships

Clinical relationships often occur when the patient is being treated for a minor concern. The contact between the nurse and the patient is relatively brief: the nurse makes the assessment and applies the treatment, and the patient is satisfied with the care provided. The patient has no expectations of the nurse beyond the care requested and received, and the nurse meets those needs quickly and efficiently as a professional. The interaction between the nurse and the patient is superficial, courteous, and by rote: "How are you today? Nice day out". If the patient is an in-patient, then he or she is usually a short-term patient that makes few demands and is generally satisfied with the care. As there is little personal emotional involvement, nurses rarely remember these patients, and the patients often may not remember which nurse gave them care or recall the nurse's name.

Therapeutic Nurse-Patient Relationships

Most of the nurse-patient relationships are in the therapeutic category, and it is the relationship that is considered "ideal" by administrators and educators. This relationship is usually of short duration, the patient's needs are not great, care is given quickly and effectively, and the investigations or treatments given do not involve anything serious or life threatening.

Characteristics	Types of relationship			
	Clinical	Therapeutic	Connected	Over-involved
Time	Short/transitory	Short/average	Lengthy	Long-term
Interaction	Perfunctory/rote	Professional	Intensive/close	Intensive/intimate
Patient's needs	Minor Treatment-oriented	Needs met Minor–moderate	Extensive/crisis 'Goes the extra mile'	Enormous needs
Patient's trust	Nurse's competence	Nurse's competence Tests trustworthiness	Nurse's competence and confides Consults on treatment decisions	Complete: 'puts their life in the nurse's hands'
Nurse's perspective of the patient; patient's perspective of own role	Only in patient role	First: in patient role Second: as a person	First: as a person Second: in patient role	Only as a person
Nursing commitment	Professional commitment	Professional commitment Patient's concerns secondary	Patient's concerns primary Treatment concerns secondary	Committed to patient only as a person Treatment goals discarded

Figure 19.1. Types and Characteristics of Nurse-Patient Relationships.

In the therapeutic nurse-patient relationship, the nurse views the patient first within the patient role and second as a person with a life "outside" (Figure 19.1). The patient expects to be treated as a patient, and may have a reasonable support system comprised of family or friends who meet most of their psychosocial needs. Any of the patient's psychosocial needs that must be met by the nurse are usually routine, such as the "normal" fears that accompany surgery and anaesthesia. Early in the relationship, the patient may test the waters; for example, using the call bell for a minor request to see if the nurse will actually answer it. These preliminary trials are necessary if the patients are to develop a feeling of security and confidence that the nurse will watch over them until they are again able to take care of themselves.

Connected Relationships

With a connected relationship, while maintaining a professional perspective, the nurse views the patient first as a person and second as a patient (Figure 19.1). The patient and the nurse have either been together long enough for the relationship to have evolved beyond a clinical and a therapeutic relationship or the process is accelerated because of the patient's extreme need. In this relationship, the patient chooses to trust the nurse ("they give you their complete trust") and the nurse chooses to enter the relationship and to meet the patient's needs. The nurse will bend and break "rules" for the patient. For example, a palliative care nurse, providing home care, described how she would surreptitiously eat a patient's porridge for him each morning: "Then he would smile at me and wink, 'Oh, thank you . . . She [his wife] will have such a good day now believing that I ate this porridge.' "

These nurses will serve as a patient advocate, interceding on behalf of a patient with family or medical staff, and will buffer or protect patients from some of the more unpleasant aspects of care. The patient will consult this particular nurse about recommendations for changes in treatment modalities. In this relationship, the patient believes that the nurse has "gone an extra mile", respects the nurse's judgment and feels grateful; the nurse believes that her care has made a difference to the patient. The following is an example of a connected relationship initiated:

> There was a woman who was also a nurse—she had no family. The ex-husband—they weren't divorced then—knew she was in labor, but didn't show up. She had an anacephalic. We tried to induce her. It took a

> long long time and, well, the baby lived. The baby was alive when it was born. And she ended up having a Caesarean but, well, they decided they wouldn't do anything—usually we don't have to do anything with these babies—they go to ICU and die there, but [this time] they had decided to let it die [here]. She was in intensive care just because it was quiet, and I thought "How am I going to deal with this?" So I asked her what I could do for her to help her be with this baby while it expired, and she asked me if she could have a rocking chair—she just wanted to get out of bed and rock it till it died. I went to the NICU and got her a chair and helped her out, because she had just had a section 2 hours before that. And she was in the chair. I strapped her in and made her comfortable, and then, in about an hour, the baby died. And so she and I bathed it together and we wrapped it and cried a lot together . . . I'll never forget her. . . . But I think she appreciated the humanness. The fact that I could cry with her or that it would upset me as much as it upset her . . . She had no one. I remember staying a couple of hours late with her so she wouldn't have to meet anyone else. And when I left, we hugged one another. And that was meaningful—a hug.

This account reveals many of the characteristics of a connected relationship. In this case, there was not enough time for the nurse and the patient to get to know each other before the relationship developed to the intensity of a connected relationship: the patient was in crisis, and the nurse, recognizing her need, made a commitment to help her. The nurse bent and broke rules for her patient: she borrowed a rocking chair for her from another department, and she helped her out of bed only two hours after the Caesarian section with epidural. She "went the extra mile", staying with her after work "so she would not have to meet anyone new". In this case, the patient was so grateful that she donated an IVAC machine to the hospital, with the nurse's name engraved on a brass plaque and an inscription that read "To . . ., for her humanness and caring". Although the relationship did not continue following the patient's discharge, neither the nurse nor the patient will forget their relationship.

Over-Involved Relationships

An over-involved relationship occurs when the patient has extraordinary needs and the nurse chooses to meet those needs, or when the patient and the nurse have spent an extensive length of time together and mutually respect, trust and care for each other (Figure 19.1). The nurse is committed to the patient as a person, and this overrides the nurse's commitment to the treatment regime, the physician, the institution and its need, and her nursing responsibilities toward other patients. She is a complete confidant of the patient and is treated as a member of the patient's family. The relationship continues beyond work hours, and if the patient is discharged, or the nurse is transferred to another institution, the nurse remains a key figure and advocate for the patient. Thus, the nurse views the patient as a person, the patient relinquishes the patient role, and the nurse relinquishes the impersonal professional relationship. The following account is an example of an over-involved relationship

> I had a friend who became very involved with a patient dying of leukaemia, and the patient actually ended up in remission and seemed OK, and they became very very close friends. Then she was readmitted and was very very ill and basically given a week to live—she turned up on the unit at 5 o'clock and was told that there was nothing that they could do. She said, "I want to go home", and so my friend, her nurse, just walked off the ward with this patient to take care of her, to take her home to die. In some ways, the nurse just walked off the ward. I mean she was totally saying goodbye to a lot of things here, and leaving people in the lurch to a certain degree, although she tried to check it out with people [before she left].
>
> The patient died at home—3 days later. [The nurse] cared for her night and day until she died—and came back very depressed and burned out. I think, in my mind, that's what the hospital was afraid of—she was in no shape to do her work. [Were there any ramifications?] . . . No—she was quite senior. But there were undercurrents, such as, "See what happens . . ." and "She should have known better than to get so involved . . ." After a few months, she left.

In this case, the relationship between the nurse and the patient developed beyond a professional relationship to a very close personal relationship. When the crisis of recurrence arose and the nurse realized how sick her "friend" was and that she wished to die at home, she realized that this wish was probably not possible unless she went with her to care for her. One indicator of over-involvement is that the nurse becomes territorial about providing care: the nurse thinks that she is the only one who can give proper and appropriate care to the patient. Thus, there is a loss of objectivity which destroys the "team" approach to nursing care. As the nurse in the above account valued her commitment to her patient above her commitment to the other patients, her co-workers or the institution, she seriously "broke rules" and walked away from her job.

From the institution's perspective, her judgment "was clouded", and her action was one that could be censured by firing. From her co-workers' perspective, she left them short staffed. But from her friend's and her friend's family's perspective, she was considered a heroine. Although her ability to give care on her return to work was impaired, the loss of employment did not occur immediately, and when it did, it was the nurse's and not the institution's decision. The real cost of such a relationship to the nurse was the emotional cost associated with the death of her friend. Any pretense of a professional relationship was abandoned, and she mourned her friend in the weeks following and found her job too emotionally stressful to continue.

NEGOTIATING THE RELATIONSHIP

Any of these relationships (i.e., clinical, therapeutic, connected or over-involved) may be the end point of negotiations or an interplay between the patient and the nurse. The intensity of the negotiation depends upon the patient's perception of the seriousness of the situation and his or her feeling of vulnerability and dependence. As stated, if the patient's needs are considered minor and the contact with the nurse is brief, then there may be virtually no process of negotiation at all. Technical competence is assumed, and as the patient presented him/herself for technical care and received such care, they are satisfied with the clinical relationship.

On the other hand, the more threatening the situation, the greater the patient's dependence on the nurse. Relinquishing oneself to the patient role requires more than blind faith in the nurse's technical competence; the patient trusts the educational, licensing, hiring and supervisory system to ensure that a nurse knows how to satisfactorily perform a task. Patients also realize that there are various kinds of nurses, such as "angels", "bossy" or "careless" types, and as they recognize their own safety depends on the investment the nurse has in caring for them, they carefully assess the nurse that has been assigned to them.

The Patient's Assessment of the Nurse

The first aspect that is evaluated by the patient is whether the nurse is a "good person" or not (Table 19.1). They invariably ask the nurse personal questions guised as social conversation: "Are you from around here?" "Are you married?" and "Do you have children?" These questions help them to place the nurse in a social context. They decide whether the nurse is "nice" and whether they can "get along" together.

They observe the nurse to see if she is dependable. "Do things happen as she said they would?" "Will she check up on me without my asking?" "Does she come if I ring the bell?"

Next, patients determine whether the nurse is a "good nurse" or not. Patients ask: "Do you like nursing?" "Have you been a nurse long?" "Where did you go to nursing school?" They ask other patients for references ("Is she good?"), feeling that a nurse who "loves" her job and is respected by other patients should be able to care for them. Patients observe and listen while their nurse gives care to other patients, and they note whether she is kindly, patient and sympathetic toward other patients. When the nurse gives care to them, if her touch is confident, gentle, experienced and does not hurt, they relax. She has "good hands". Finally, patients test the nurse's trustworthiness. They give the nurse a small confidence, a minor secret, to see if she keeps the confidence or shares it with others. If the nurse behaves appropriately, then the patient is willing to trust and place themselves in her care.

Next, patients make overtures toward the nurse so that the nurse will willingly become involved in their care. These overtures consist of calling the nurse by her name, acting in a friendly way and waving to the nurse as she passes by. They joke, tease and praise the nurse to build camaraderie, and they may give gifts to the nurse, and keep chocolates or candies on their locker to share with her. They try to "be no trouble" and not to "make waves" or to complain. They try not to ring the bell and not to make requests, and if something is absolutely necessary they try to hold such requests until the nurse comes into the room. A patient who was also a nurse said:

> I'm always conscious of not being difficult. . . . I would do things for myself rather than ask for something. . . . I would never ring the bell. I never rang the bell. I would wait until someone came into the room for the other person or whatever, and then I'd say, "Excuse me". But I'd never ring.

As these patients had not yet learned to trust the nurse, they would give gifts in an attempt to change the nurse-patient relationship by increasing the investment of the nurse in their care. These gifts were manipulative gifts, such as leaving chocolates on the locker to entice the nurse to come into the room, giving gifts for the nurse's children, and occasionally offering cash bribes (which invariably had the unfortunate

TABLE 19.1 Strategies Used by the Nurse and the Patient for Increasing Involvement in the Nurse-Patient Relationship

Strategies	
Nurse	*Patient*
Demonstrating commitment	Determining if the nurse is a "good person"
notes personality "click"	seeks nurse self-disclosure
responds to patient as a person	evaluates "likability"
closes personal physical distance	tests for dependability
establishes common ground	Determines if nurse is a "good nurse"
gives patient time	looks for indicators of kindness and empathy
anticipates needs	obtains references from other patients
	does she like nursing?
	does she "know what she is doing"?
	does she have "good hands"?
	tests: can she keep "something to herself"?
Perseverance	Making overtures
get to know the patient's family	being a "good patient"
	being friendly, joking
	gives gifts
Connecting	Deciding to trust
Becoming involved	Relinquishing vigilance
becomes a patient advocate	
bends rules, breaks rules	
buffers	

effect of widening the distance between the nurse and the patient). A patient's family would often help the patients "get on the good side of the nurse" by bringing in home-made biscuits or cakes for the staff.

The Nurse's Assessment of the Patient

While the patient is assessing the nurse, the nurse is assessing the patient to determine if she or he should enter or facilitate a connected relationship (Figure 19.1). This assessment is different from the nursing assessment; the nurse evaluates the patient's personal needs and support system, assesses the patient as a person, and consciously chooses whether or not to make an emotional investment in the patient, or whether to just do her job. The nurse will look for a personality "click" and determine if she can work with the patient. Patients with special needs and patients who "touch" or appeal to the nurse are more likely to enter a connected relationship.

> I remember having a young single girl from an outport in Newfoundland. And she was 16 and decided to have this baby and I don't know. My heart just bled for her because she was on welfare and she was trying to make a go of it. She was going to go to night school and try to get off welfare.

Next, the nurse responds to the patient as a person, sharing some personal information about herself and trying to establish a common ground with the patient in an attempt to entice the patient to become more involved:

> I would actually consciously look for common ground; shared or common issues, whether that be the number of kids, I like chocolate, you're into football, you know—something. With the motorbiker, who really liked fishing, my love of nature was the bond. About the only bond we had. . . . The Dutch family who travelled back to Europe, I could talk about being raised in Denmark and how I liked Dutch cookies or something. I would work on developing common ground; sometimes it was easy, sometimes it took a bit of creativity. I would facilitate them knowing me; they didn't have to struggle to get to know me.

The nurse closes personal distance with the patient when she speaks, by perhaps sitting at the same level or on the bed, and making eye contact. The nurse uses humor, trying to reduce the stress of the experience. A midwife explained:

> I use humor a lot. I just sat on one of those little foot stools down in front of the toilet and we had a monitor over here and her hubby's there and we spent an hour on the toilet. And sort of joked about this. I said, "I bet in your fantasies about birth you didn't think you would be sitting on the toilet with me while I had my coffee and all that!"

The nurse gives the patient time, trying to connect. If the patient is unwilling to accept the nurse, the nurse demonstrates her willingness by persevering, by continuing to provide care no matter how difficult or rude the patient continues to be: "You don't barge in and take charge. You allow them to invite you in, and you make yourself want to be invited in; you facilitate that connection".

The decision to enter a connected relationship with a patient is usually a conscious and deliberate decision. One nurse described this connecting as follows:

> One old guy—I've known him on and off for years—he's been coming into emergency . . . and I like him. I really, really like him. One day he was just rolled into emergency and I was walking down the hall and I stopped the ambulance stretcher and spoke to him. And that was the day I think that we really decided we were friends. . . . He's an old drunk is what he is. . . . Why him? I don't know. I think I made a conscious decision I liked him.

When the patient feels that the relationship with the nurse is secured, she or he trusts the nurse to make the right decisions about care, relinquishes vigilance and relaxes. The relatives also relax and feel they can go home and rest.

> We were in a four-bedded unit, and I got to see her interact with the other children, and she was very efficient, very delightful and very good with the parents. . . . And I felt so comfortable, and I guess my daughter did too because that very first night before surgery she said to me, "Mom, I don't want to sleep here tonight. I'd like you to go home". She [my daughter] says, "I feel good". And I thought, "Oh, oh, bless you, because I'd love to go home because there's nothing like my own bed." But I felt very good with that nurse on. She was excellent!

Unilateral Relationships

Involvement denotes mutual endeavor: one person cannot decide simply to form a connected relationship with another. Relationships that are not characterized by mutual commitment never reach this level and may be considered "out of step" or unilateral. The nurse may continue her commitment to the patient, yet the patient may prevent the development of an involved relationship, or vice versa. For instance, if the patient is unconscious or in a psychotic state and is unable to participate in the relationship, mutual involvement is not possible. The patient may appear so undesirable that the nurse does not want to enter into a close relationship, or the nurse may be "burnt out" and unwilling to invest emotional energy in the relationship. On the other hand, a student, new to the clinical area, cannot have an impersonal relationship with the patient for the student has not learned to depersonalize the patient's experience or, in Gadow's (1989) terms, to become "disembodied from the patient". Consequently, the new student finds it difficult to inflict pain by giving an injection or performing other necessary procedures. Nurses who worked in the operating room used this strategy of depersonalization, including the transformation, not only of a person into a patient, but of a patient into a "case". It is interesting to note that operating-room nurses are now reversing this process and changing the case back into a patient by making preoperative visits and providing support when the patient arrives in the operating room.

Additionally, because of the nature of psychiatric illnesses, nurses working with psychiatric patients who lack trust are wary and afraid of "being suckered". Ironically, because these nurses are afraid of entering a connected relationship with a patient, they find it difficult to trust patients.

> Sometimes when a depressed patient smiles and says thank you, it's harder for that person to have made a smile than someone who's feeling well.
>
> Now, I don't want them to be depressed, but I want to have an accurate picture of where they're at. And I don't want to get things muddled by wondering "Are they doing this for me? What have I done to create this kind of situation where the patient's doing things so that I feel better?" You know? I suppose, on the other hand, it could be that maybe the patient genuinely wants to say thanks for all the trouble you're taking. You know, "Thanks for being here." Well, I'm not giving you a definite answer here, but I guess I'm seeing both possibilities.

From the patient's perspective, trust and acceptance of his or her situation, that is, the hospitalization and the illness experience, are the significant factors. If the patient both trusts the nurse and recognizes the illness and the necessity for hospitalization, then the patient is grateful (cell *a,* Figure 19.2). If the patient trusts the nurse but does not accept the ramifications of the illness, then the patient will attempt to coerce the nurse into assisting him or her, as an ally or advocate, to negotiate with the physician, to arrange for a transfer, and so forth (cell *b,* Figure 19.2). If the patient does not trust the nurse but accepts his or her illness and need for treatment, then he or she will enter a manipulative relationship, attempting to ensure nursing care. Unfortunately, many of the strategies used by patients in coercive or manipulative relationships to ensure nursing care, such as giving gifts or bribes, cajoling, nagging, demanding and begging, have the opposite effect and actually increase nurse-patient distance. Patients in the last cell (cell *d*) do not accept the nurse or their illness and hospitalization. They may be labeled "difficult" patients and withdraw or elope. The withdrawal may be due to the illness experience itself. For example, a midwife reported that some maternity patients are so mortified at their sickness behavior or their loss of control that they are too ashamed to relate to the caregiver:

> Some women will go on and on, and you absolutely can't reassure them. There's not a word or a way that does it. I've tried everything. I imagine they're afraid of being rejected . . . or [think] I may not want to be around them—I don't know. They will go on and on until you want to say, "Look, shut up! It happens all the time!" And there's such a difference. Some people can barf in your pocket and poop in your shoes and not feel sorry or let it bother them one minute. And another one will just go on and on and on because she cried or something.

Figure 19.2 is not a static model and patients may move between cells as circumstances change. For instance, if a nurse perseveres with helping a difficult patient and this patient has insight about his illness and decides to trust the nurse, she or he will move from cell *d* to cell *a*. A manipulative patient may move from cell *c* to cell *a*, again by learning to trust; similarly, a coercive patient may move from cell *b* to cell *a* by gaining insight about his or her condition. Unfortunately, patients may also move in the opposite direction; for example, from cell *a* to cell *c* if the patient perceives the nurse to be incompetent, or across to cell *d* if the patient feels well and diagnostic tests are inconclusive.

CHANGING THE NATURE OF THE RELATIONSHIP

Both the nurse and the patient have control over factors that will increase and decrease the rate and level of the developing relationship. The strategies nurses use to increase involvement were discussed previously; strategies that decrease or inhibit a relationship from developing assist both the nurse and the patient to maintain control (Table 19.2).

One such strategy used by nurses is deliberately depersonalizing the patient. Nurses will refer to the patient by medical diagnosis or bed number ("That lady in bed 6") and, when addressing the patient, they will always use a formal form of address, even with younger adults. Patients complain that these nurses are cool and brisk and have no eye

Patient's Attitude to Illness/Hospitalization

Patient's Attitude Toward the Nurse	Accept +	Reject −
Accept +	Grateful a	b Coercive
Reject −	c Manipulative	d Withdrawn Difficult Elope

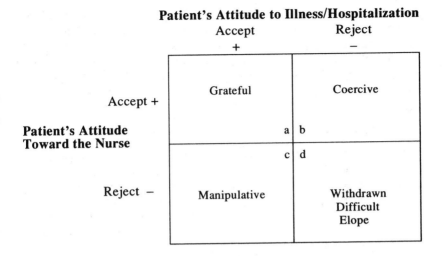

Figure 19.2. Types of Relationships According to Patient's Attitude Toward the Nurse and Illness Situation.

contact with you, even though everything is done for them physically. Alternatively, if these nurses lack commitment to their work, they are described as being very lackadaisical and just being there for the pay check. Their work is just a job to them. Patients say that these nurses are not interested in them, do not take time to talk and have an attitude which says "you're just taking up my time".

> They never warmed up and I didn't either. I didn't make demands and I wasn't rude to them, but I didn't get to know them the way I did the other nurses. They didn't chit chat. If they had to make my bed, it was done in a very very quick, perfunctory manner.

Of another patient who had a miscarriage, the patient in the next bed reported:

> And they didn't talk to her at all about how she felt. You know, it was all matter of fact. "Here you go." "Put this on." Whatever. "Sign this consent," and then all that waiting. And no one really came in and talked to her. . . . It was in and out in no time.

TABLE 19.2 Strategies Used by the Nurse and the Patient for Inhibiting or Decreasing Involvement in the Nurse-Patient Relationship

Strategies	
Nurse	*Patient*
Depersonalizes the patient uses formal terms of address refers to patient by bed number and/or medical diagnosis refuses to chat does not make eye contact	Prevents the nurse from "knowing" him or her does not share information about self focuses interactions on symptoms and treatment fidgets if conversations get "personal" does not make eye contact
Maintain an efficient attitude gives the patient the impression of busyness does not counsel: focuses on the physical acts of care does not provide information: keeps the patient "in the dark"	
Does not trust the patient suspects ulterior motives	Does not trust the nurse becomes demanding, coercive and/or manipulative

These nurses also withheld information or did not give patients satisfactory responses. A mother, whose infant had cardiac catheterization, said:

> "What's wrong with her leg?" All I could focus on was her leg! . . . But it worried me and all I got told was, "Don't worry." "But," I said, "what's wrong with it?" And if they could have just given me an explanation of why it was blue, I think I might have felt better. . . . I wanted more information.

Patients also had strategies for keeping the nurse at a distance. Nurses reported that patients would do this by avoiding eye contact, by looking into space, and by fidgeting when the nurse spoke to them. They would share less, and talk less about themselves and keep the conversation focused on professional concerns.

> They would just keep focusing on the patient's symptoms. . . . "I just want to talk about the pain, the nausea."

Although many negotiating factors are within the control of the nurse and the patient, other factors that may inhibit the relationship are outside their control. The first such external factor is the nurses' obligation to respect the family's wish to withhold information from the patient, and this withholding is invariably recognized by the patient and interferes with the development of trust between the nurse and the patient.

> I think sometimes we have to be diplomatic. Once I had a cancer patient who had not been told [of his diagnosis] at the family's request, and this gentleman wasn't dumb, and he obviously knew something was very wrong and he cornered me one night point blank with, "Do I have cancer?" and my reaction was, where's the hole, I've got to fall in it. I said, "Well, you had tests". And he said, "Yes, but I can't get an answer." So I said, "Well, can I go out and check your chart?" and he said, "Only if you promise to come back". I went out, thought for a minute, and then I phoned the family and told them he had really put me on the spot. "He obviously knows, I think, and at this point he had to be told." So the family very reluctantly said, "Yes, perhaps you should tell him." I said, "Perhaps it would be a good idea if you came in to visit him—he's going to need your support" and so on. And that was how I handled that one. I did go back and tell him and stayed with him until his family came in.

A second external factor of major concern is the issue of multiple caregivers. Thus far, the necessity for a nurse-patient relationship and how one nurse establishes a relationship with one patient has been described. Yet, in reality, nurses are considered by administrators to be interchangeable. Even in settings that utilize primary care, when one nurse is responsible for establishing a care plan, other nurses must be fully aware of that nurse's patient and his or her needs, so that when one nurse is relieved for coffee or goes off duty another nurse will be able to care for the patient without compromising the quality of care. In reality, this concept is nonsense. In the caring relationship, caregivers are not interchangeable: counseling centers do not operate on a "take a number" basis but have some consistency with caregivers. Nursing is the only caregiving profession that subscribes to the notion that the identity of the caregiver is insignificant. Indeed, if a patient prefers one nurse over another, this fact is not considered as a mark of excellence but as a nuisance by the remaining staff, and both the nurse and the patient suffer:

> My special patient was K., and she was 18 months [old], had lung disease, and had spent most of her life in hospital—she was so desperately ill. And I used to be in the ward 2 days a week, and [during that time I] carried her around on my hip. She was a typical hospital kid—full of smiles but attached to no one. And her mother used to get in as often as she could, but she had other kids at home. And K. used to look for me.
>
> Then one day I came in and there was this note pinned on her back "Please do not pick me up." "What is this?" I said. And they said it was because she was being spoiled. "Spoiled, my foot!" She needed to be hugged and loved, but they couldn't see it. . . . I suppose they had to pay for it, because I was only in 2 days a week and she would look for me and, I guess, "play up" in between times. And her mother had eight parking tickets.

Furthermore, the charting or reporting of information that the patient considers confidential, but which must be shared because the information is necessary for the providing of care, is used by other caregivers when interacting with the patient. Such violations are the norm and seriously undermine the patient's trust in the system. If it is imperative that the information be shared, then the relieving nurses should use this information as a clue to spend additional time with the patient, instead of just "taking over" where the previous nurse left off. Alternatively, an appropriate referral should be negotiated with the patient. Specialization is the third factor outside the control of the individual nurse that interrupts the establishment of a connected relationship. The specialization that interrupts these relationships may occur from within the nursing profession. Speaking as an instructor, a nurse explained how she and a student cared for a laboring woman all night. Eventually, it was decided that a Caesarian section was necessary and, at that time, the husband was only permitted to watch through the operating room window. When the infant was delivered, it was obvious that something was wrong, and the infant had a high meningomyelocele. The student and the instructor comforted and cried with the father. But as this "case" was now a "problem", the clinical specialist interrupted, and took over managing the parents to the exclusion of the student and her instructor. The result was that the student was not able to resolve her grief with the parents and shortly afterwards she left nursing. The instructor reported: "and that was in 1973, and I'm still angry!"

Equally disruptive and destructive is the interruption of the relationship from specialists outside nursing who may intercede blindly, uninvited, in a situation.

> There was a little baby born with cystic hydroma that affected the whole of the respiratory system. There were growths all the way down—they hadn't known there was something wrong before the baby was born, and the family—the parents were Jehovah's Witnesses—said, "No heroics." You know, nothing unusual, but it had been done anyway. The baby got intubated, put on a respirator, brought to the [medical center]. And then, in order to do treatment, they apprehended the child. And then they did this exploratory surgery, only to decide that the baby couldn't be treated, couldn't be saved. And then they decided to extubate it and let it die.
>
> And, of course, they expected the baby to die within a few minutes. And it doesn't. And I sit in the rocking chair with it, and it keeps breathing and breathing and breathing and wheezing and wheezing and wheezing. And then the father arrives and he's a German fellow. And I went into this little room with him and he was angry. He was so angry! He was just beside himself. He was angry and he wouldn't let his wife come to be with this baby. So I'm sitting there holding this baby who's "Hii-hu, hi-hu" wheezing away. You don't know when any breath is going to be its last breath, and all this man can talk about is how angry he is and how during the war it was so-and-so and I thought that was over and I left the country so I had freedom and there is no freedom here. And he goes on and on. So I listen and listen and finally I start to get more directive with it and I said: "You know, your son's dying." Like, "Do you want to . . ." I don't remember the words, but I got him to hold the baby. He just started to touch him— and somebody came into the room! A social worker. Like he just crossed the bridge to relate to this kid and this woman walked in. And, you know, I could have just died. And then, he went back to the "H-gmgm!" Because he had to go through it all again and tell her how angry he was. But we got there for just—just a fraction of a second, you know.

The fourth factor that prevents the establishment of a connected relationship is the lack of time to spend with the patient. Frequently, there is not enough time in one shift to allow the patient to assess the nurse, and then the nurse may be off for several days, and the patient is then discharged, transferred, had surgery and is much sicker, or the nurse may be assigned to other patients. This gap in the continuity of care is such an important factor that nurses, when explaining how they developed relationships with patients, always mentioned how much time they had together with the patient.

> I had her for 4 days in hospital. She happened to time me right. We developed a really strong, solid relationship. . . . We had put in time together, and we knew each other. I was almost at the level of friendship, except I would still be her nurse and still helping her.

CONTROLLING THE LEVEL OF INVOLVEMENT

Given the factors that increase or decrease the level of involvement and the type of relationship, how then does a nurse determine whether or not to get involved or what level of involvement is optimal for her or for the patient? It was clear when comparing interviews with nurses from different care settings that involvement was necessary in some care settings, for example, in palliative care and in long-term care, and more difficult to establish in acute-care settings, such as the intensive care or the emergency room.

> With long-term care patients I think you automatically become involved. You see them every day and they get to know you and you get to know them as people. . . . I think the patients almost live vicariously through the staff. They would say, "Did you have a nice holiday?" "Did your girl graduate?" and they would want to see the pictures, and it is rather a nice relationship.

Experienced nurses reported the harm of over-involved relationships as the risk of destructiveness. Nurses who were over-involved couldn't "be objective", and their "judgment became impaired", particularly their clinical judgment. Furthermore, the emotional pain when the relationship ended, especially if the patient died, interfered with the nurse's ability to do her work: "They are crying, and, goodness knows, you can't work when you are crying!" Wise nurses, experienced nurses, learned painfully, by trial and error, how to find the right level of involvement in a relationship.

> I don't have a need to take over or to live their life for them. . . . I think you have to be able to let go. You have to be able to say here's where my life ends and the person's begins.

Discussion

In this paper, a model for understanding the relationships that are mutually negotiated between the nurse and the patients is described.

Insights into unilateral relationships, in which either the nurse or the patient are dissatisfied with the relationship and attempt to change it, are also presented. Of the four mutual relationships, the first three are considered satisfactory, while the fourth, over-involvement, is usually considered dysfunctional.

Although it is a concern of both administrators and nurses outside the relationship, the over-involved relationship has not been previously well described in the nursing literature. Benner and Wrubel (1989) describe a nurse who enters an involved relationship as an "omnipotent rescuer" and they imply that the behavior is attributed to dysfunctional early childhood development in an alcoholic family or one with mental illness and state that these nurses may also be "avoiding intimacy in relationships outside of nursing". As most nurses in this study had been over-involved with a patient at some point in their career—and had learned from this experience—there was little support for this notion, and the inference is probably based on incorrect theoretical assumptions. The characteristics of over-involvement may be better defined, incorporating Hoff's (1989) definition of intimacy, as the development of an intimate relationship between the nurse and the patient. There is "affection, reciprocity, mutual trust, and a willingness to stand by each other in distress without expectation of reward". In an over-involved relationship, decisions are based upon the desires of the individual patient rather than on what is best for the family, other patients, staff or institution, and the patient's personal goals take precedence over treatment goals.

Some of the strategies described in this paper have been described previously by other authors. Patient conformity has been described by Lorber (1975), and Robinson and Thorne (1984) note that families of patients attempted to establish an alliance with caregivers by using such strategies as "giving gifts, using jokes to put the health care provider at ease, and inquiring into the health care professional's personal health". Drew (1986) interviewed patient's perceptions of their interactions with caregivers, in particular "distressing" and "nurturing" encounters, and identified distancing behaviors, which she labeled "exclusion", and caring behaviors, labeled "confirmation". The characteristics of exclusion behaviors resembled the strategies used by nurses in this study to prevent involvement and the confirming behaviors resemble those that nurses used to increase involvement. However, Drew's (1986) model lacks information about the reciprocal behavior of the patient, and it does not consider the development of relationships over time.

Surprisingly, the concept of trust has not been extensively examined in the nurse-patient relationship, and it is sometimes even omitted from the index of communication texts (for example, see Adler, Rosenfeld, & Rosenfeld 1986). Meize-Grochowski (1984) analyzes the concept, defining trust as "an attitude bound in time and space in which one *relies with confidence* on someone or something. Trust is further characterized by its fragility" (emphasis added). However, although she notes that trust may be destroyed or built within relationships, she does not refer to the two types of patient trust identified in this study: the immediate trust in the nurse's technical competence, followed by the development of interpersonal psychosocial trust. Thorne and Robinson (1988) view trust as a linear model that changes from the initial naive trust in the health care professional's competence and is destroyed and rebuilt or reconstructed as "guarded alliance" in one of four patterns: trust of certain individuals, trust in the patterns or behavioral norms of health professionals, a general distrust, or an intimate relationship with "carefully selected individuals". These authors note the reciprocal nature of trust as health care professionals regard the patient as a reliable and competent informer and one capable of participating in decisions and treatment regimes.

As this work is directed at health care professionals in general and does not delineate the nurse-patient role, it is evident that further work on the concept is needed, particularly into factors that interfere with the development of trust in the nurse-patient relationship and in the different patient care areas. In this study, it was clear that one strategy that some psychiatric nurses used for maintaining distance between themselves and the patient was not trusting the patient, by always being vigilant, and by suspecting the patient of having an ulterior motive when they engage in behaviors designed to connect with the nurse. This is ironic for this lack of trust from the caregiver could conceivably increase the patient's pathology and paranoia. Maintaining a therapeutic relationship in psychiatry appears to be one of the most difficult aspects of caring for patients in this speciality.

PATIENT'S CONFIDENCES

Some legitimate nursing behaviors work to destroy the development of trust in the nurse-patient relationship, proving a cause for concern.

One of these behaviors, the practice of reporting on all patient confidences considered pertinent to the patient's care without first getting the patient's permission, is most harmful. The nurse's dilemma has been noted previously (Thomas 1978) and the recommendation that the nurse obtain the patient's permission to report the information should be followed more carefully.

From the patient's perspective, the clinical relationship means that nurses are invisible and interchangeable, rather like an excellent waiter, unnoticed and in the background, as long as one's needs are met. This invisibility and interchangeability of nursing may be attributed in part to work patterns, such as shift rotation and days off when working 12-hour shifts, which shorten the length of contact between any one patient and a nurse. Thus, work patterns and assignments interfere with the development of nurse-patient relationships, forcing patients to establish relationships afresh with sequential replacement staff. Even when it is possible to provide continuous care, this is often not done, and nurses are assigned from one side of the ward to another. Although the principles of primary nursing care are excellent, unless the primary nurse is regularly assigned to the same patients, the concept breaks down. Further, the notion that caregiving breaks down with multiple caregivers is not new (see Mayeroff 1971, Van Hooft 1987). Nurses need to re-examine carefully their practice from a humanistic, rather than a legalistic, administrative perspective, and change those things that they can control. Further, the patient-nurse relationship has rarely been examined, yet this "reverse" perspective reveals clues to many previously described maladaptive behaviors. The consistency of caregivers may be an important variable that would reduce patient confusion, anger and other difficult behaviors.

Another unique aspect of this study is the description of strategies used to increase involvement, especially the strategy of the nurse sharing personal information about herself. This strategy is not taught in communication texts; rather, it is advised against. However, as students new to the clinical area have difficulty in viewing patients in the patient role, perhaps this strategy should be taught in advanced classes, after the student has learned to converse in the professional role and has gained competency in most nursing procedures.

Van Hooft (1987) notes that commitment consists of both "actions and attitudes" and by examining the motivations for commitment, priorities become evident. Data from this study reveal that commitment to the patient as a patient or as a person was an important factor in determining the kind of relationship that developed. The lack of development of significant nurse-patient relationships means that nurses do not "get involved" with patients. Patients are denied an advocate, and nursing, as a profession, is impotent. Watson (1988) and Gadow (1989) advocate a type of nurse-patient relationship that has characteristics of connectedness and involvement. They argue that a lack of involvement depersonalizes patients, denies their dignity as humans and reduces them to objects. Interestingly, neither Watson nor Gadow write on the concept of over-involvement with patients.

COMMITMENT

Examination of this concept in nursing is important. From this study it appears that "commitment" may be a more appropriate term to use than "caring" in the nurse-patient relationship. In the emotional sense, caring has connotations of "fondness" or "love", neither of which may be present (or desirable) in a professional relationship. Further, commitment fits the emerging model of patient-nurse relationships and commitment may be applied to other aspects of the nurse's role and evident in nursing behavior. Theoretically, if the nurse is committed to treatment goals, to the cure or to the physician, enforcement of these objectives may take priority over humanistic goals. To implement these goals, the nurse may unwittingly violate human rights by obtaining orders for restraints or by forcibly administering treatments, and she may also be more likely to work in the "high tech" treatment settings, such as the intensive care unit. Should the nurse be committed to herself rather than to the patient, she may do only what is necessary for the patient, and perhaps be less likely to invest in connected relationships with patients, preferring clinical relationships. Significantly, a wise nurse is committed to all of these goals and can balance priorities, for the good of the patient, for the good of the profession and for the good of herself.

References

Adler, R. B., Rosenfeld, L. B. & Rosenfeld, N. T. (1986) *Interplay: The Process of Interpersonal Communication*. CBS College Publications, Rinehart & Winson, New York.

Benner, P. & Wrubel, J. (1989) *The Primacy of Caring: Stress and Coping in Health and Illness*. Addison Wesley, Menlo Park, California.

Drew, N. (1986) Exclusion and confirmation: A phenomenology of patients experiences with caregivers. *Image: Journal of Nursing Scholarship 18*(2), 39-43.

English, J. & Morse, J. M. (1988) The "difficult" elderly patient: Adjustment or maladjustment? *International Journal of Nursing Studies 25*(1), 23-29.

Gadow, S. (1989) Clinical subjectivity: Advocacy with silent patients. *Nursing Clinics of North America 24*(2), 535-541.

Hoff, L. A. (1989) *People in Crisis: Understanding and Helping* 3rd edn. Addison Wesley, Menlo Park, California.

Lorber, J. (1975) Good patients and problem patients: Conformity and deviance in a general hospital. *Journal of Health and Social Behavior 16*(2), 213-225.

Magnan, M. A. (1989) Listening with care. *American Journal of Nursing 89*, 219-221.

Mayeroff, M. (1971) *On Caring*. Harper & Row, San Francisco.

Meize-Grochowski, R. (1984) An analysis of the concept of trust. *Journal of Advanced Nursing 9*, 563-572.

Morse, J. M. (1991) Using the Macintosh® computer for textual data analysis. *Qualitative Health Research 1*(1), 117-122.

Robinson, C. A. & Thorne, S. (1984) Strengthening family "interference". *Journal of Advanced Nursing 9*, 597-602.

Thomas, M. (1978) Trust in the nurse-patient relationship. In *Behavioral Concepts and the Nursing Intervention* 2nd edn (Carlson, C. ed.). J. B. Lippincott, Philadelphia, pp. 164-170.

Thorne, S. E. & Robinson, C. A. (1988) Reciprocal trust in health care relationships. *Journal of Advanced Nursing 13*, 782-789.

Watson, J. (1988) *Nursing: Human Science and Human Care: A Theory of Nursing*. National League for Nursing, New York.

Van Hooft, S. (1987) Caring and professional commitment. *The Australian Journal of Advanced Nursing 4*(4), 29-38.

VII

The Semistructured Questionnaire

The semistructured questionnaire is used when the researcher is familiar with the boundaries, the domain, and the components of a phenomena but is unable to anticipate all the possible responses to a particular question and cannot structure the answers. The researcher, therefore, can create questions with reasonable confidence and create questionnaires with certainty that they are comprehensive and valid and that nothing significant is omitted. Thus the semistructured questionnaire consists of questions that can be answered freely. If, while listening to an answer, the researcher discovers information that is new or interesting, she or he then has the freedom and opportunity to obtain additional information, to probe and to discuss any of the answers. Thus, rather than giving the participants the "freedom to tell their stories" as they desire, the researcher has some control over the direction of interviews, while participants have control over the information provided.

In Chapter 20, "Social Coercion for Weaning," Morse and Harrison were interested in successful breastfeeding and the duration of breastfeeding. Inherent in the duration of breastfeeding is the notion that sooner or later infants will be weaned. To collect information on the process and rationale for weaning, they interviewed 60 women every month following the birth of their infants for 12 months.

The structure of the semistructured interview ensures that all informants are asked the same questions in more or less the same order. This allows interview data from one participant to be compared with the responses of others. When content analysis is performed on the responses, the responses may be numerically coded and nonparametric statistics may even be used to identify patterns and relationships in the data. In this article, we compared the reasons for weaning obtained from all mothers over time and, consistent with previous information, we noted that weaning occurred most often at specific points in time. However, the unique information we identified in this study was that significant others facilitated the weaning process when the infant was considered "old enough" to be weaned. The process of "social coercion" to facilitate weaning and the severance of this breastfeeding stage of the mother-infant relationship was initiated by support persons in different roles at different times.

The use of larger samples for studies using semistructured interviews compensates for the smaller amount of interview data obtained from each participant. The larger sample size also provides some compensation for the lesser amount of care that is taken in selecting good informants. Although attrition of the sample is a concern when 60 participants are used, if informants do not have all the characteristics of good informants (that is, they are articulate, reflective and willing to be interviewed) that is less of a concern than it is an ethnographic study that has only 10 primary informants.

Again, consider the generalizability of this study. In your opinion should this study be replicated? If so, discuss the methods that could be used.

20

Social Coercion for Weaning

JANICE M. MORSE
MARGARET J. HARRISON

Abstract: Research investigating the duration of breastfeeding is generally based on the assumption that if lactation is established, then the mother will breastfeed successfully. Longitudinal, qualitative research suggests, however, that it is the attitude of others toward the breastfeeding mother that determines the duration of breastfeeding. When the infant is a newborn, breastfeeding is encouraged. As the infant develops, the support of others toward the nursing mother is withdrawn and the mother is encouraged to wean. Further, the doula not only facilitates breastfeeding, but also, when the infant is perceived to be "old enough," facilitates weaning.

In current breastfeeding research, there is an assumption that the method of infant feeding and the duration of breastfeeding are decided by the mother. Based on this assumption, the following premises give direction to most breastfeeding research and educational programs. First, when given adequate information on the advantages of breastfeeding (and the disadvantages of not breastfeeding), the mother will make a rational choice for the method that will be most advantageous for her infant (i.e., breastfeeding). Second, once lactation is established, the mother will continue nursing. Therefore, conditions in the immediate postpartum

AUTHORS' NOTE: This work was funded by the University of Alberta and in part by an NHRDP Research Scholar Award to Dr. J. Morse. This chapter originally appeared in Morse, J. M., & Harrison, M. J. (1987). Social coercion for weaning. *Journal of Nurse-Midwifery, 32*(4), 205-210. Reprinted with permission.

period are made to facilitate breastfeeding. Efforts are made to maximize maternal-infant attachment, to minimize breast complications, and to provide a supportive environment to ease the breastfeeding process and the establishment of lactation.[1] Finally, so that lactation will succeed, care is taken to ensure that the infant's interest and ability to suckle is maximized. Supplements that may interfere with the infant's appetite are not given, and the infant is breastfed "on demand."[2,3] Inherent in this paradigm is the notion that if breastfeeding is initially a positive experience, then mothers will continue to successfully breastfeed. "Success" is usually measured by the medical profession in *time*, which is often defined as maintaining breastfeeding for at least 3 months and ideally for 6 months.[4]

Research investigating the duration of breastfeeding is consistent with this general paradigm. For instance, most research examining the rapid attrition in breastfeeding rates have focused on the perinatal period, statistically correlating factors from this period with the duration of breastfeeding.[5] We are not denying the importance of these factors for the *initiation* of breastfeeding. Instead, we argue that events in the perinatal period may have a very weak association with the maintenance of breastfeeding for 3, 6, 9, 12 months or longer. We suggest that the nursing experience is a dynamic, open relationship occurring within a social context, and it is the attitude of *others* toward breastfeeding that modifies the mother's choice of how the infant is fed, where the infant is fed, and for how long breastfeeding is maintained. In this chapter, we will critique present research on the duration of breastfeeding, discuss the development of a theory of *social coercion for weaning*, and suggest further research to test this theory.

Importance of the Problem

In spite of the health advantages of breastfeeding for the mother and the infant, many mothers choose not to breastfeed. Extensive educational programs on the benefits of breastfeeding have been only partially successful, with the number of mothers breastfeeding their infants increasing over the past 15 years to 62%.[6,7] However, there is a rapid decline in the percentage of women breastfeeding after discharge from hospital. By the fourth month postpartum, only 44% and by the sixth month 31% of mothers continue to breastfeed.[7] The current recommendation by the American Pediatric Association[8] is that breastfeeding be continued for 6 months. The rapid decline in breastfeeding rates is of sufficient concern that in the Public Health Services objectives for the United States in 1980, 1 of 17 nutritional objectives listed was to increase the incidence of breastfeeding to 75% by 1990.[6,9,10]

Current Research

Researchers have sought to delineate factors that correlate with the duration of breastfeeding so the characteristics of the "successful" breastfeeding mother may be understood and the variables that inhibit or facilitate breastfeeding may be identified. The variables can be placed within three separate timeframes: the prenatal period, the time of birth, and the immediate postpartum period.

PRENATAL VARIABLES

Several studies have shown that the successful breastfeeding mother has a higher level of education[11-15] and socioeconomic status.[12-14] She is married,[13] older,[11-16] and less likely to smoke[17,18] than her bottle feeding counterpart. These successful feeding mothers also attend prenatal classes,[12,17,19,20] have previously breastfed,[12] and demonstrate the desire or motivation to breastfeed.[11,13,14] They also have more friends that breastfeed and perceive their husbands to be supportive.[11,13,15,16,21]

BIRTH VARIABLES

The mother most likely to succeed at breastfeeding has a normal, singleton birth, a healthy baby,[22,23] an opportunity to nurse the infant shortly after delivery,[1,24,25] and forms an immediate attachment with the infant.[26] Indicators for a less successful breastfeeding experience are a long and difficult labor, an aesthesia, a cesarean birth,[27] and an infant who is preterm, exhausted by labor or is handicapped.[18,27]

POSTNATAL VARIABLES

The majority of the research on successful breastfeeding has focused on the immediate postnatal period. Many authors suggest that breastfeeding will be more successful if the infant is rooming-in with the mother, fed on demand,[20,27] and supplements are withheld.[1,28] Nursing staff should be supportive and knowledgeable about breastfeeding.[1,13,28,29] The mother will benefit from a doula, perhaps her husband or her mother.[30,31] Breast complications, such as cracked nipples or engorged breasts, will be avoided.[32] Because supplements will have been withheld, the infant will be eager to nurse.[32]

In the hospital, educational programs on the benefits and methods of breastfeeding are correlated with an increased duration of breastfeeding.[33] The provision of mothers with formula samples and/or exposure to advertisements for formula are associated with a decreased duration of breastfeeding.[34,35]

Research in the subsequent postnatal period is relatively sparse. One of the most frequent reasons given for weaning is "insufficient milk,"[13,14,36] but it is unclear in many studies what this term actually means to mothers. This phrase could be used to describe a crying or fussing infant, perceived to be hungry by the mother, as well as a physiological decrease in milk supply.[18,36,37] The early introduction of solid foods is associated with a decrease in lactation and early weaning.[38] Finally, "convenience"[18] or "returning to work"[39] is frequently given as a reason for weaning, although studies do not consistently agree on this factor.[37,40]

Critique on Current Research

A major problem in the research literature is the predominance of retrospective, cross-sectional surveys based on subject recall over a considerable period of time.[41,42] Researchers using these methods have confused causality with associated events[43,44] by seeking statistical correlations between past events and subsequent breastfeeding outcomes that are separated by a period of several weeks or months. Researchers have disregarded the effects of history[45] in a period of rapid and significant role change within the family. Furthermore, many of the researchers have applied univariate statistical methods to a complex, multivariate situation. Such techniques frequently give spurious correlations,[46] and this fact alone may account for some of the discrepant results in the literature. In making a plea for longitudinal studies, Simmopoulus and Grave (1984)[41] note:

> In general, demographic variables are easier to incorporate into questionnaires and easier to administer, explain, test and score than psychosocial, and especially, attitudinal variables. Yet the latter are probably closer to true causal determinants of choice in infant feeding practices than demographic variables.

For the past two decades, most of the research has been deductive. Variables identified in the literature or from previous research have been tested repeatedly in different settings and with different populations. Because many of the researchers have no practical experience for addressing the problem, the underlying assumptions have rarely been examined or challenged. It is time to question the present paradigm and, using inductive methods, develop alternate explanations on the duration of breastfeeding.

Social Coercion for Weaning

In 1983, we conducted a longitudinal study of 30 breastfeeding mothers.[47] We were investigating *minimal breastfeeding* (i.e., the management of lactation when mothers breastfeed once or twice a day, without expressing). As current advice to nursing mothers is that the breasts must be expressed if she cannot nurse, we were interested to know how long and for what reasons mothers minimally breastfed. A longitudinal study was planned to determine the rational for minimal breastfeeding and how mothers learn about this style of breastfeeding. A convenience sample of mothers who were nursing once or twice a day was obtained by advertising in the public health immunization clinics. The demographic characteristics of the sample follow. Mothers ranged in age from 21 to 31 years (mean age, 28.5 years). All mothers were upper-middle class and well educated: 25 mothers (i.e., 83%) were educated beyond high school, 4 completed high school, and 1 did not complete high school. All but two mothers were married. Twelve mothers had breastfed previously (nine had breastfed once, two had breastfed twice, and one mother had breastfed three times), and 18 mothers had not breastfed previously. The number of people residing in each household, including the infant, ranged from 2 (i.e., mother-infant dyads) to 7 (one family), with most families (n = 16) consisting of 3 members.

The partners' (n = 28) ages ranged from 24 to 42 years (mean age, 31.1 years). Twenty (i.e., 71%) were educated beyond high school, 7 completed high school, and 1 did not complete high school. The infants in the study consisted of 15 males and 15 females. Birth weights ranged from 3.09 to 9 lb (mean weight, 7.83 lb).

Semistructured, taperecorded telephone interviews were conducted with these mothers each month until the infant was weaned, or for 12 months. Altogether, 88 interviews were conducted, transcribed and analyzed. It is important to note that this was a select sample: all mothers were, by present criteria, successful at breastfeeding, having continued to breastfeed at least 6 months. Approximately one-third of the sample were employed outside the home, one-third were weaning their infants slowly, and one-third were comfort nursing older infants. Data used in this discussion were derived from one part of the questionnaire related to the support for breastfeeding: who the mothers perceived as the most supportive and as least supportive of their breastfeeding, and of mothers' perceived attitudes of others, including their physician, nurses, family, friends and acquaintances, toward their breastfeeding.[48]

Unexpectedly, mothers' responses to these questions varied over time. Responses of each mother about their husband or "doula," parents and parents-in-law, physician and nurse, and friends and colleagues in the workplace were sorted into three general categories: supportive/encouraging, noncommittal/silent, or discouraging. These responses were then placed on a time-line according to the infant's age.

Definite trends were immediately apparent. All mothers, without exception, reported in the immediate postpartum period that "everyone was supportive of breastfeeding." However, when the infant was about 6 to 8 months of age, mothers reported that their friends became silent and "didn't say anything" about breastfeeding. Later, when the infant was 9 to 10 months of age, mothers reported that their friends began to make comments such as "Are you still nursing?" These comments resulted in a behavior change for the nursing couple. Mothers withdrew from those friends who were most negative and sought friendship from mothers who were also "still nursing," or they actively sought contacts in the La Leche League. Mothers who continued to nurse avoided listening to those who were negative and told them to "mind their own business." They deliberately kept secret the information that they were "still nursing" so that others could not comment. Mothers no longer nursed in public nor permitted the child to try to nurse in public, and they developed a special word (one that no one else would understand) to refer to nursing. If the child asked to nurse, he/she would be told to wait until they got home. One mother reported:

> People are making negative comments—for example in the baby room at church. They say, "He's getting too old! It's bad for your health" I start feeling guilty and anxious.

When these infants were approximately 10 months of age, the mother's parents and parents-in-law (who were previously supportive) became silent about the breastfeeding and withdrew support. Then, as the infant approached 12 months, the mother or mother-in-law would suggest that continuing breastfeeding was "draining her (the mother's) body," and perhaps if the child were weaned, he could stay overnight with them. Thus, the grandparents actively encouraged weaning:

> My mother and mother-in-law feel I should quit at 12 months. They were quite vocal about this! My mother-in-law feels I will get cancer from the prolonged tugging at the breast.

Comments from the grandparents would also be directed at the toddler: "They tell her she's too big for that, now." If the mother chose to continue breastfeeding, this fact was withheld by the mother from her parents and parents-in-law. One mother who continued to breastfeed finally weaned because her parents-in-law were coming to visit for the Christmas holidays; the continued breastfeeding could no longer be concealed with houseguests present.

This study, consistent with other North American studies,[21,30,31] showed the main source of support (i.e., the doula) was the husband. Early in the study, mothers all reported that their husbands were most supportive and felt that "breast was best." However, when the infant was approximately 12 months of age, mothers reported that their husbands became quiet about their breastfeeding: "He doesn't say anything." Mothers described their husbands' embarrassment if, for example, the infant pulled at the mother's blouse in public in an attempt to get at the breast. If the mother continued to breastfeed, the husband would consistently try to coerce his wife into weaning by making comments such as: "What's a big boy like that doing there!" After the husband withdrew his support, all mothers weaned within a few weeks, with the exception of one mother who continued to nurse without telling her husband.

Importantly, mothers who continued to nurse their infants beyond the social norm did so in secret:

> Now that she's older I don't talk about it—except to moms who have also breastfed.

Sometimes, however, breastfeeding could not be concealed, and this resulted in awkward situations for the mother:

> My neighbor was really shocked that I'm still nursing. We were grocery shopping yesterday and it was around Kelley's usual nap time and he began to fuss and started pulling at my blouse. My neighbor just looked at me and said, Are you still nursing him? It was so obvious that I couldn't say no! (Infant 16 months)

> I feel pressured sometimes. We always have to sit in the front of the church; we're always late. When we're at church for an hour and a half, that's all that Carl can think of because he's sitting there and he's on my lap and so he's pulling and arching his back. I give him to my husband and I feel a little uncomfortable! . . . I nursed him in the front row when he was younger, but not now! (Infant 16 months)

From these data, it is apparent that the duration of breastfeeding is influenced by social and cultural norms and not solely determined by the mother. The course of breastfeeding is a dynamic process, and although the variables examined by other researchers may be associated with the duration of breastfeeding, social support for the nursing mother is perhaps the most significant variable. The changing attitudes of others over time are shown in Figure 20.1.

Raphael[30] and others[21,31] have suggested that lactation cannot be established without a doula; we suggest that the role of the doula is also to facilitate weaning and to assist with severance when, as determined by the cultural norm, the infant is "old enough to wean." Variations in the cultural or subcultural norms about when the infant is "old enough to wean" may explain the significant differences in the duration of breastfeeding that researchers have found correlated with variables such as socioeconomic class, ethnicity, and educational levels. Furthermore, through research examining patterns of weaning, indications of when the infant is "old enough to wean" may be obtained and thus provide insights into the social norms. Developmental milestones, such as when the infant begins to sit, to develop teeth, to talk or to walk, were used by mothers in this study as indicators that weaning should occur.

Suggestions for Further Research

In this study, all mothers were atypical in that they were successfully breastfeeding, and some of the mothers, those practicing prolonged

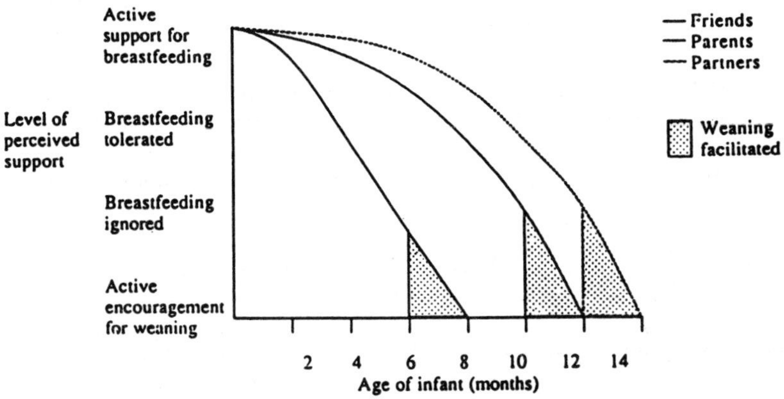

Figure 20.1. Response of Others Toward the Breast-Feeding Couple by Age of the Infant.

breastfeeding (i.e., over 12 months), may be considered extraordinary. Thus, the ages of the infants in each of the stages of coercion must be regarded as preliminary indicators only. Further research on larger, representative samples must be conducted to obtain a clearer description of cultural and social norms. It is possible that, in a population that predominantly bottle feeds their infants, the social and cultural forces against breastfeeding are so strong that breastfeeding is socially prohibited. In populations where mothers wean their infants very quickly (i.e., almost as soon as the mother is discharged from hospital), the stages we have described may occur much earlier.

To test the relationship between the attitudes of the larger society on infant feeding and the duration of breastfeeding, a large randomized survey of the city is planned. A representative sample of residents of all ages will be shown pictures of infants at various developmental stages and asked how these infants should be fed. If there is a correlation between the identified social norms for the duration of breastfeeding and the mothers' actual weaning patterns, then some additional confirmation for the theory of social coercion will be obtained.

It is interesting to observe the amount of advice that a new mother receives. Advice on infant care is provided to mothers even by strangers who would not dare to censor or to advise the mother on any other topic. Somehow, with infants, everyone is an expert. It would be interesting to examine why others dissuade the mother from breastfeeding "too long" and why the coercion to wean is an emotive social issue.

Conclusion

As stated, the present thrust of research on the duration of breastfeeding focuses on the mother. It is assumed that breastfeeding is a mother's "choice," and the responsible choice for good mothering is to breastfeed. Current trends in health education are targeted at the mother so that she will make the right choice. To quote Dr. Everett Koop (1984), United States Surgeon General: "*Persuading* more women to breastfeed their infants is a major U.S. public health goal."[10](italics added).

Considering our research, we are suggesting that it is naive to focus entirely on mothers and to attribute the lack of breastfeeding or premature weaning as a problem caused by irresponsible women not choosing "the best" for their infant. Our research suggests that if a lack of breastfeeding is a "problem," then it is a general problem of all citizens. Breastfeeding does not occur in isolation, either apart from the family context or separate from the community at large. As such, health education programs must be aimed at all sectors of the population: to grandparents and schoolchildren, to the married and the unmarried, to males as well as to females. Furthermore, at present, we doubt if women really have a *freedom of choice* regarding infant feeding methods. In some postnatal units, mothers are coerced into breastfeeding, and this may, in part, explain the very rapid change to bottle feeding[13] after discharge. Health professionals may give mothers mixed messages regarding infant feeding,[29,49] verbally supporting breastfeeding but, at the same time, giving very clear nonverbal messages to bottle feed[28,35] with supplements[23] or advising bottle feeding when minor difficulties arise.[28] Social coercion for weaning, the mourning for the loss that mothers sometimes feel when weaning occurs, and the phenomenon of closet nursing[50] suggest that the method and duration of infant feeding is not mother's choice but a response to cultural norms.

Notes

1. Winikoff B, Laukaran V H, Myer V H, et al: Dynamics of infant feeding: Mothers, professional and the institutional context in a large urban hospital. Pediatrics 77:357-365, 1986.

2. Auerbach K G: The role of the nurse in support of breastfeeding. J Adv Nurs, 4:263-285, 1979.

3. Houston M J: Indicators of successful breastfeeding, in Houston MJ (ed): Maternal and Infant Care. London, Churchill-Livingstone, pp 26-48, 1984.

4. Harrison M J, Morse J M, Prowse M: Successful breastfeeding: The mother's dilemma. J Adv Nurs 10:261-269, 1985.

5. Quant S: Biological and behavioural predictions of exclusive breastfeeding duration. Med Anthropol. 9(2): 139-151, 1985.

6. Koop C E, Brannon M E: Breast feeding—The community norm. Report of a workshop. Public Health Rep. 99(6):550-557, 1984.

7. McNally E, Hendricks S, Horowits I: A look at breastfeeding trends in Canada (1963-1982). Can J Public Health 76:101-107, 1985.

8. American Academy of Pediatrics: Policy statement based on task force report: The promotion of breastfeeding. Pediatrics 69:654, 1982.

9. Arango J O: Promoting breast feeding: A national perspective. Public Health Rep 99(6):559-564, 1984.

10. Smith S J: Surgeon general urges more moms to breast-feed babies. Times-Union, Rochester, NY, June 13, 1984.

11. Bloom K, Goldbloom R B, Robinson S C, et al: Breast versus formula feeding. Acta Paediatr Scand 300 (Suppl):3-25, 1982.

12. Clark L L, Beal V A: Prevalence and duration of breast-feeding in Manitoba. Can Med Assoc J 126:1173-1175, 1982.

13. Sacks S H, Brada M, Hill A M, et al: To breast feed or not to breast feed. Practitioner 216:183-191, 1976.

14. Sjolin S, Hofvander Y, Hillervik C: Factors related to the early termination of breastfeeding: A retrospective study in Sweden. Acta Paediatr Scand 66:505-511, 1977.

15. Switzky L T, Vietze P, Switzky H N: Attitudinal and demographic predictors of breast-feeding and bottle-feeding behavior by mothers of six-week-old infants. Psychol Rep 45:3-14, 1979.

16. Beske E J, Garvis M S: Important factors in breast-feeding success. MCN 7: 174-179, 1982.

17. Florack E, Obermann-de Boer G, Van Kampen-Donker M, et al: Breastfeeding, bottle-feeding and related factors. Acta Paediatr Scand 73:789795, 1984.

18. Goodine L A, Fried P A: Infant feeding practices: Pre- and postnatal factors affecting choice of method and the duration of breastfeeding. Can J Public Health 75:439-443, 1984.

19. Gulick E E: Informational correlates of successful breast-feeding. The American Journal of Maternal Child-Nursing 7:370-375, 1982.

20. Winikoff B, Baer E C: The obstetrician's opportunity: Translating "breast is best" from theory to practice. Am J Obstet Gynecol 138:105-115, 1980.

21. Baranowski T, Bee D E, Rassin D K, et al: Social support, social influence, ethnicity and the breast-feeding decision. Soc Sci Med 17(21):1599-1611, 1983.

22. Beyer L R: When should one discourage breast-feeding. Pediatrics 67: 300-302, 1981.

23. Ellis D J, Hewat RJ: Factors related to breastfeeding duration. Can Fam Physician 30:1479-1484, 1984.

24. de Chateau P, Holmberg H, Jakobsson K, et al: A study of factors promoting and inhibiting lactation. Developmental Medicine and Child Neurology 19:575-584, 1977.

25. Salariya E M, Easton P M, Cater J I: Duration of breast-feeding after early initiation and frequent feeding. Lancet ii:1141-1142, 1978.

26. Carlsson S G, Larsson K, Schaller J: Early mother-child contact and nursing. Reprod Nutr Dev 20:881-889, 1980.

27. Reames E S: Opinions of physicians and hospitals on early infant feeding practices. J Am Diet Assoc 85(1):79-80, 1985.

28. Verronen P, Visakorpi J K, Lammi A, et al: Promotion of breast feeding: Effect on neonates of change of feeding routine at a maternity unit. Acta Paediatr Scand 69:279-282, 1980.

29. Ellis D J, Hewat R J: Do we support breast-feeding mothers? Midwives Chronicle 97(1153):45-47, 1984.

30. Raphael D: The tender gift. Englewood Cliffs, Prentice-Hall, 1973.

31. Jelliffe D B, Jelliffe EFP: Doulas, confidence, and the science of lactation. J Pediatr 84(3):462-464, 1974.

32. Loughlin H H, Clapp-Channing N E, Gehlbach S H, et al: Early termination of breast-feeding: identifying those at risk. Pediatrics 75(3):508-513, 1985.

33. Grassley J, Davis K: Common concerns of mothers who breast-feed. The American Journal of Maternal Child-Nursing 3:347-351, 1978.

34. Bergevin Y, Dougherty C, Kramer MS: Do infant formula samples shorten the duration of breast-feeding? Lancet i:1148-1151, 1983.

35. Reiff M I, Essock-Vitale S M: Hospital influences on early infant-feeding practices. Pediatrics 76(6):872-878, 1985.

36. Gussler J, Briesemeister L H: The insufficient milk syndrome: A biocultural explanation. Med Anthropol 4(2):3-24, 1980.

37. Gunn T R: The incidence of breast feeding and reasons for weaning. NZ Med J 97:360-363, 1984.

38. Sloper K, McKean L, Baum J D: Factors influencing breast feeding. Arch Dis Child 50:165-170, 1975.

39. Ekwo E E, Dusdieker L, Booth B, et al: Psychosocial factors influencing the duration of breastfeeding by primigravidas. Acta Paediatr Scand 73:241-247, 1984.

40. Van Esterik P, Greiner T: Breastfeeding and women's work: Constraints and opportunities. Stud Fam Plann 12(4):184-197, 1981.

41. Simopoulos A P, Grave G D: Factors associated with the choice and duration of infant-feeding practice. Pediatrics 74(Suppl):603-613, 1984.

42. Winikoff B: Issues in the design of breastfeeding research. Stud Fam Plann 12(4):177-184, 1981.

43. Popper K R: The logic of scientific discovery. New York, Harper & Row, pp 88-89, 1968.

44. Puterman Z M: The concept of the causal connection. Uppsala, Uppsala Universitet, p 25, 1977.

45. Campbell D T, Stanley JC: Experimental and quasi-experimental design for research. Chicago. Rand McNally College Publ Co., 1963.

46. Bhattacharyya G K, Johnson R A: Statistical Methods and Concepts. New York, John Wiley & Sons, 1977.

47. Morse J M, Harrison M J, Prowse, M: Minimal Breastfeeding, J Obstet Gynecol Neonatal Nurs 15(4):333-338, 1986.

48. Morse J M, Harrison M J, Williams K M: What determines the duration of breastfeeding? in Michaelson K (ed): Anthropology of Childbirth in America. S. Hadley, Mass., Bergin & Garvey, in press.

49. Ellis D J, Hewat R J: Do nurses help or hinder others who breastfeed? J Adv Nurs 8:281-288, 1983.

50. Avery J L: Closet nursing: A symptom of intolerance and a forerunner of social change? Journal of Keeping Abreast 2:212-226, 1977.

About the Editor

Janice M. Morse is Professor, School of Nursing, College of Health and Human Development, The Pennsylvania State University. She has published extensively on qualitative research, coauthored or edited several books on qualitative health research methods, including *Qualitative Nursing Research: A Contemporary Dialogue*, and with Joy Johnson, *The Illness Experience: Dimensions of Suffering*. She has taught qualitative methods at the University of Alberta, Memorial University, and the University of Miami. She is currently the editor of *Qualitative Health Research*, a quarterly published by Sage.